Eclipse Rich Client Platform
Second Edition

D1082101

Eclipse Rich Client Platform
Second Edition

Jeff McAffer

Jean-Michel Lemieux

Chris Aniszczyk

✦✦Addison-Wesley

Upper Saddle River, NJ • Boston • Indianapolis • San Francisco
New York • Toronto • Montreal • London • Munich • Paris • Madrid
Capetown • Sydney • Tokyo • Singapore • Mexico City

Many of the designations used by manufacturers and sellers to distinguish their products are claimed as trademarks. Where those designations appear in this book, and the publisher was aware of a trademark claim, the designations have been printed with initial capital letters or in all capitals.

The authors and publisher have taken care in the preparation of this book, but make no expressed or implied warranty of any kind and assume no responsibility for errors or omissions. No liability is assumed for incidental or consequential damages in connection with or arising out of the use of the information or programs contained herein.

The publisher offers excellent discounts on this book when ordered in quantity for bulk purchases or special sales, which may include electronic versions and/or custom covers and content particular to your business, training goals, marketing focus, and branding interests. For more information, please contact:

U.S. Corporate and Government Sales
(800) 382-3419
corpsales@pearsontechgroup.com

For sales outside the United States please contact:

International Sales
international@pearson.com

Visit us on the Web: informit.com/aw

Library of Congress Cataloging-in-Publication Data
McAffer, Jeff.
 Eclipse Rich Client Platform / Jeff McAffer, Jean-Michel Lemieux, Chris Aniszczyk.—2nd ed.
     p.   cm.
 Includes index.
 ISBN 0-321-60378-8 (pbk. : alk. paper)
1. Computer software—Development. 2. Java (Computer program language)
3.Application software—Development. I. Lemieux, Jean-Michel. II. Aniszczyk,
Chris. III. Title.
 QA76.76.D47M383 2010
 005.13'3—dc22   2010006689

ISBN-13: 978-0-321-60378-4
ISBN-10:   0-321-60378-8
Text printed in the United States on recycled paper at RR Donnelley in Crawfordsville, Indiana.
First printing, May 2010

Contents

Foreword

In my foreword to the first edition of this book, I wrote that the Eclipse Rich Client Platform (RCP) is a lot like the enormous rockets that carry NASA's robots into space: powerful, sophisticated, essential, but ultimately just the launch vehicle that propels our creations safely to their destinations. Four years later, the RCP continues to serve as the launch vehicle for the tools that my team develops to control a broad variety of spacecraft and robots that drive, fly, float, and move in ways that defy categorization. It provides us with a firm foundation for component-based development, a flexible framework for rich user interfaces, and countless other capabilities that surround and support the small nugget of software that my team actually develops.

My team is extremely proud of our small nugget of code and what it accomplishes at NASA, but when our missions succeed, I think we all celebrate with an acute awareness that a space exploration project of interplanetary scale demands the combined success of hundreds and sometimes thousands of experts inside and outside NASA who specialize in everything from designing cruise trajectories to the art of neatly routing cables through the limbs of a robot (and trust me, it is an art—I've seen those people work). Sure, it probably took only a few people to strap a gunpowder-filled tube to the side of an arrow to make the first rocket more than a thousand years ago, but it's only through an enormous feat of simultaneous specialization and cooperation that we could hope to achieve something as complex as landing and operating a rover on Mars.

This remarkable combination of specialization and cooperation can be found in many other fields. A few handymen can get together and build a shed, but a skyscraper requires the combined effort of architects, carpenters, plumbers, electricians, masons, and hundreds of other specialists with only basic knowledge of each other's disciplines. Modern construction, just like modern space exploration, is simply too ambitious and complex to accomplish any other way.

I think modern software applications are more like deep space robotic explorers than rocket-propelled arrows and more like skyscrapers than sheds. Complex application development demands specialization and cooperation, and I think that is the fundamental reason for the existence and sustained success of the Eclipse RCP. Behind the platform described in this book is a worldwide community of experts—specialists in everything from provisioning to user assistance who have cooperated for years in their own mission to create a free, extensible framework that can be used to build almost any kind of application. If you decide to use this framework, you'll soon discover that you've joined an even larger community of people who are also building applications on the Eclipse RCP—an entirely different breed of specialists. You might be surprised to discover valuable vendors, customers, and collaborators among them. We certainly did.

My team has attended every EclipseCon (the largest yearly gathering of Eclipse developers and users) since 2005, and I've consistently been amazed by the diversity of applications that people are building on top of the RCP. I've seen RCP applications for controlling nuclear reactors, scheduling trains, trading stocks, designing data centers, managing inventory, fighting terrorism, analyzing proteins, monitoring fishing boats, sharing files, and editing every programming language that I've ever heard of. After a couple of EclipseCon conferences, we even came across another space agency building mission control applications on top of the RCP. (You can imagine we had plenty to talk about!) But what's more surprising than the diversity of RCP applications is everything that our applications have in common. For example, APC uses the same graphical editor framework to arrange server racks in their data center design program that my team uses to manipulate Mars images in our rover operations program. My team built our spacecraft command editor with the same basic components used in most of the Eclipse programming tools. These commonalities allow us to combine our resources, learn from each other, and ultimately deliver better products to our customers.

Some of your colleagues may think it's risky to base your application on software developed by such a far-flung group. It might be tempting to think that it would be easier and safer to just build it all yourselves. But would it be safe to have NASA's programmers build rocket engines or to ask a skyscraper's plumber to pour the foundation? Not only is it impossible for your team to specialize in every aspect of rich application development, but merely trying to do so is a distraction that could endanger your whole project. For example, let's say you have a team of three people who need to build an application during the next year, and one of the features it needs is a way to perform long-running tasks and keep the user aware of progress. Sure, your team could develop that from scratch, but I asked members of the Eclipse platform team and they estimated that they spent nearly three work years building the Jobs API, a robust and flexible framework for this purpose. The Eclipse RCP can save you from spending your project's budget on things that aren't even your specialty.

My specialty is developing tools that operate robots and spacecraft. Your specialty might be developing tools for anything from health care to clean energy. The authors of this book, however, are specialists in making it easier for you and me to write our tools and, in the end, spend more time focusing on our specialties. If you decide to join the community building on top of the RCP, I look forward to learning how you've used these tools to support your work at a future EclipseCon. You might even discover ways to contribute your specialty to the improvement of the RCP itself.

—Jeff Norris
  Supervisor, Planning Software Systems Group
  Jet Propulsion Laboratory
  California Institute of Technology

Preface

In many ways this book is one of the design documents for the Eclipse Rich Client Platform (RCP). The first edition was originally written during the Eclipse 3.1 development cycle by members of the development team. Its chapters were sometimes written before the related function was even implemented. The second edition was written during the Eclipse 3.5 development cycle.

The exercise of explaining how things work forced upon us the realities of using the mechanisms and concepts that make up the Eclipse RCP. This was not always pleasant. It did, however, give us a unique opportunity to correct the course of the Eclipse RCP.

Whenever we came across something that was hard to explain or complicated to use, we were able to step back and consider changing Eclipse to make things easier. Often we could, and often we (or, more accurately, the Eclipse Platform team as a whole) did. It is somewhat hard to convey the joyful feeling of deleting a complicated, detailed ten-page set of instructions or explanation and replacing it with just a paragraph detailing a new wizard or facility.

On other occasions we gained key insights that helped us produce a clearer, simpler description of a function. Fixing bugs discovered during this process provided welcome distractions as we were writing, coding, learning, and trying to have real lives all at the same time.

We learned an incredible amount about Eclipse as an RCP and trust that you will, too.

About This Book

This book guides you, the would-be RCP developer, through all stages of developing and delivering an example RCP application called Hyperbola, an instant messaging chat client.

We develop Hyperbola from a blank workspace into a full-featured, branded RCP application. The choice of the instant messaging domain allowed us to plausibly touch a wide range of RCP issues, from building pluggable and dynamically extensible systems to using third-party code libraries to packaging applications for a variety of environments. We cover scenarios ranging from PDAs to kiosks, to stand-alone desktops, to full integration with the Eclipse IDE. This book enables you to do the same with your applications.

Roughly speaking, the book is split in two. The first half, Parts I and II, sets the scene for RCP and presents a tutorial-style guide to building an RCP application. The tutorial incrementally builds Hyperbola into a functioning, branded chat client complete with Help, Update, and other advanced capabilities. The tutorial is written somewhat informally to evoke the feeling that we are there with you, working through the examples and problems. We share some of the pitfalls and mishaps that we experienced while developing the application and writing the tutorial.

The second half of the book looks at what it takes to "make it real." It's one thing to write a prototype and quite another to ship a product. We don't leave you hanging at the prototype stage; Parts III and IV are composed of chapters that dive into the details required to finish the job—namely, the refining and refactoring of the first prototype, customizing the user interface, and building and delivering products to your customers. This part is written as more of a reference, but it still includes a liberal sprinkling of step-by-step examples and code samples. The goal is to cover most of the major stumbling blocks reported in the community and seen in our own development of professional products.

A final part, Part V, is pure reference. It covers the essential aspects of OSGi, the base execution framework for Eclipse, and touches on various functions available in the Eclipse Platform but not covered earlier in the book.

Since one book could not possibly cover everything about Eclipse, and there are many existing books that cover Eclipse and plug-in development, we focus on the areas directly related to RCP functionality, API, and development.

Audience

This book is targeted at several groups of Java developers. Some Java programming experience is assumed and no attempt is made to introduce Java concepts or syntax.

For developers new to the Eclipse RCP, there is information about the origins of the platform, how to get started with the Eclipse IDE, and how to write your first RCP application. Prior experience with Eclipse is helpful but not necessary.

For developers experienced with creating Eclipse plug-ins, the book covers aspects of plug-in development that are unique to RCP development. For example, not only are there special hooks for RCP applications, but RCP applications have additional characteristics such as branding, plug-in building as part of a release engineering process, deployment, and installation, to name a few.

For experienced Eclipse RCP developers, this book covers new RCP features and functions in Eclipse 3.5 as well as the new tooling that makes designing, coding, and packaging RCP applications easier than ever before.

Sample Code

Reading this book can be a very hands-on experience. There are ample opportunities for following along and doing the steps yourself as well as writing your own code. The samples that accompany the book include code for each chapter and can be obtained from the book's Web site: *http://eclipsercp.org*. Instructions for managing these samples are given in Chapter 3, "Tutorial Introduction," and as needed in the text. In particular, the following resources are included:

- ○ A README.HTML file with installation and use instructions
- ○ Eclipse 3.5.2 SDK
- ○ Eclipse 3.5.2 RCP SDK
- ○ Eclipse 3.5.2 RCP delta pack
- ○ Code samples for each chapter as needed
- ○ A prebuilt, complete version of Hyperbola

Conventions

The following formatting conventions are used throughout the book:

Bold—used for UI elements such as menu paths (e.g., **File > New > Project**) and wizard and editor elements

Italics—used for emphasis and to highlight terminology

Lucida—Used for Java code, property names, file paths, bundle IDs, and the like that are embedded in the text

Lucida Bold—Used to highlight important lines in code samples

Notes and sidebars are used often to highlight information that readers may find interesting or helpful in using or understanding the function being described in the main text. We tried to achieve an effect similar to that of an informal pair-programming experience where you sit down with somebody and get impromptu tips and tricks here and there.

Acknowledgments

It is impossible to write a book such as this without the cooperation and help of a vast number of people. In our case, virtually the entire Eclipse Platform team contributed directly to the end result, through conversations, help with code and concepts, bug fixes, or just general support.

Beyond the book, the Eclipse RCP itself would be a mere shadow of what it is without the following people: Nick Edgar, Wassim Melhem, and Pascal Rapicault. Particular thanks go to Doug Pollock, Tom Watson, Kim Horne, Stefan Xenos, Veronika Irvine, Christophe Cornu, DJ Houghton, Tod Creasey, Dorian Birsan, Mazen Faraj, Chris Goldthorpe, Paul Webster, Boris Bokowski, Konrad Kolosowski, and Darin Swanson for taking the time to explain things, talk over ideas, and generally guide us in the right direction on various topics.

We especially want to acknowledge Simon Archer's amazing reviewing skills. He reviewed the entire manuscript in great detail and provided extremely useful and timely feedback. Simon, you're the greatest. We were also fortunate to have a large number of people from the community who reviewed various chapters and provided valuable feedback. In particular, we'd like to acknowledge Chris Laffra, Pascal Rapicault, Nick Edgar, Kim Horne, Doug Pollock, Wassim Melhem, Michael Valenta, Rafael Chaves, and Darren Lafond.

Of course, no book project is possible without a publishing team. We were lucky to have Greg Doench as our editor, Elizabeth Ryan as our production contact, and Barbara Wood as our copyeditor. Thanks to the whole crew at Addison-Wesley for making this a relatively painless and quite enjoyable experience.

About the Authors

Jeff McAffer co-leads the Eclipse RCP and Equinox OSGi projects and is CTO and cofounder of EclipseSource. He is one of the architects of the Eclipse Platform and a coauthor of *OSGi and Equinox* (Addison-Wesley). He co-leads the RT PMC; is a member of the Eclipse Project PMC, the Tools Project PMC, and the Eclipse Architecture Council; and is a former member of the Eclipse Foundation Board of Directors. Jeff is currently interested in all aspects of Eclipse components, from developing and building bundles to deploying, installing, and ultimately running them. Previous lives include being a Senior Technical Staff Member at IBM; being a team lead at Object Technology International covering work in Smalltalk, distributed/parallel OO computing, expert systems, and meta-level architectures; and getting a PhD from the University of Tokyo. You can follow him on Twitter at *http://twitter.com/jeffmcaffer*.

Jean-Michel Lemieux has been a lead architect and developer on the Jazz project (jazz.net) since 1995, which has allowed him to put his RCP experience to work on a large-scale client-server application. On Jazz he is the SCM component lead. Jean-Michel has been a committer on the Eclipse Team and CVS components since their inception.

Chris Aniszczyk is the co-lead of the Eclipse Plug-in Development Environment (PDE) project and a Senior Software Engineer at EclipseSource. Chris tends to be all over the place inside the Eclipse community by committing on various Eclipse projects. He sits on the Eclipse Architecture Council, Planning Council, and the Eclipse Foundation Board of Directors. Chris's passions are modularity, community management, tooling, and anything Eclipse. He's always available to discuss open-source or Eclipse over a frosty beverage. You can read his blog at *http://aniszczyk.org* and follow him on Twitter at *http://twitter.com/caniszczyk*.

PART I

Introduction

This first part of the book introduces Eclipse as a rich client platform—the Eclipse RCP. Chapter 1 outlines the notion of "rich client platforms" and the origins of the Eclipse RCP and illustrates its use with some real-world examples. Chapter 2 gives an overview of Eclipse concepts, terminology, and architecture to ensure that all readers have a common understanding.

CHAPTER 1

Eclipse as a Rich Client Platform

The term *rich client* was coined in the early 1990s with the rush to build client applications using the likes of Visual Basic and Delphi. The dramatic increase in the number and popularity of these client applications was due in part to the desire for a "rich" user experience.

Rich clients support a high-quality end-user experience for a particular domain by providing rich native user interfaces (UIs) as well as high-speed local processing. Rich UIs support native desktop metaphors such as drag and drop, system clipboard, navigation, and customization. When done well, a rich client is almost transparent between end users and their work—fostering focus on the work and not the system. The term *rich client* was used to differentiate such clients from terminal client applications, or *simple clients*, which they replaced.

The rise of client technology was accompanied by improvements in development environments. WYSIWYG UI designers made building rich client applications easy and fun. These development tools allowed client programmers to reuse common building blocks to reduce development time.

Early rich client platforms (RCPs) were used to glue the client's business logic to the operating system (OS). They eliminated many of the menial programming tasks required to create UIs and access databases. The middleware provided frameworks and infrastructure so developers could spend more time programming domain logic rather than reinventing the wheel.

End users were happy with the resultant rich client applications, as they were functional and easy to use. Information technology (IT) managers, however, found many hidden costs. Deploying and upgrading clients is a manual task, and users often tweaked their installs, moved files, or installed other clients that overrode shared libraries.

Then along came the Internet and Web-based applications, or *thin clients*. Thin clients promised to solve many of the deployment and management problems related to rich clients. Since applications were on servers, updates were made centrally. User machines required only a Web browser. This dramatically reduced the cost of deploying and maintaining enterprise applications at the expense of the user experience—thin clients did not provide the UI features and high-speed interactions users had come to expect.

The usability and applicability of thin clients were enhanced with the evolution of rich Internet applications, or RIAs. RIAs brought common desktop characteristics and metaphors to Web-based applications via improved UI technology. Current RIAs are built using technologies such as Adobe Flash/AIR, Google Web Toolkit (GWT), Microsoft Silverlight, and Mozilla's XULRunner.

The cost savings and deployment simplifications were popular, but the move to thin clients and RIAs was still a step back in functionality, capability, and development efficiency. Thin client applications, using the request-and-response model, require more networking capability to ensure optimal interaction performance. Typical RIA technologies lack a strong model of modularity, a setback for teams used to the power that, for example, the Eclipse modularity model brings. The Eclipse Rich Ajax Platform (RAP) is a notable exception here.

Today's users and problems continue to drive the use of rich clients from the Web to the desktop. Domains are becoming more complex, and the amount of data to visualize and manipulate is increasing, as is the need for integration with other systems. The demand for rich clients goes beyond the desire for a richer UI. Users need to be mobile, work offline, integrate their content and workflows, collaborate, and take advantage of local hardware.

The technologies outlined here at least partially address these topics but ultimately result in more and more functionality in the browser—making the thin clients not so thin and reviving many of the old thick client topics. These approaches trade the operating and window system for the browser but still leave the challenges of modularity and versioning.

But what about the deployment and maintenance problems that caused the earlier shift to thin clients in the first place? Has something changed to mitigate those issues? Yes; today an increasing number of component mechanisms, such as Eclipse, are available to rich client application developers. Componentized systems address both deployment and maintenance issues by insulating and isolating components from change. New deployment mechanisms such as Equinox p2 and enterprise management systems such as Yoxos virtually eliminate the need for personalized enterprise software management. In short, this new brand of rich clients enables the type of application integration needed for today's dynamic scenarios and provides the best of both worlds.

1.1 Eclipse

If you are new to Eclipse, you are probably wondering, "What is Eclipse?" First and foremost, Eclipse is an open-source community of people building Java-based tools and infrastructure to help you solve your problems. The most obvious output of the community is the Eclipse Java Integrated Development Environment (IDE). This world-class Java IDE regularly tops the charts in developer satisfaction and use. It's also free from *http://eclipse.org*.

Underneath the IDE is a generic tooling platform that supports a wide range of tools for languages and systems, from Java to C to Python to Web technologies to data manipulation and reporting. The Eclipse component model means that these tools can be combined and integrated as needed.

Under the tooling platform is the Eclipse RCP. This is a generic platform for running applications. The Eclipse IDE happens to be one such application. This book focuses on how you can take advantage of the Eclipse RCP to build *your* application.

1.2 The Eclipse Rich Client Platform

Why is Eclipse particularly suited to building rich client applications? To answer that question, let's look at the history of rich and thin clients and observe how the characteristics of Eclipse maintain the benefits and address the pitfalls of past approaches. Those characteristics are summarized here:

Components—Eclipse includes a robust component model. Eclipse-based systems are built by composing components known as *plug-ins*. Plug-ins are versioned and can be shared by more than one application. Multiple versions of the same plug-in can be installed side by side, and applications can be configured to run with the exact versions they need. This approach is attractive as it allows applications to evolve over time by adding and replacing components.

Middleware and infrastructure—On top of this component model is a set of frameworks and facilities that makes the job of writing client applications much easier. The Eclipse RCP is essentially the middleware function that you don't want to write because it is a means, not an end, for your domain. It includes facilities such as a flexible UI paradigm, scalable UIs, extensible applications, Help support, context-sensitive Help, network updates, error handling, and much more.

Native user experience—In contrast to what is provided by thin clients, users want a rich, comfortable, and native user experience. This includes a smooth, responsive UI that integrates into the desktop. The Eclipse Standard Widget

Toolkit (SWT) provides a graphical user interface (GUI) toolkit for Java that allows efficient and portable access to the native UI facilities of the OS.

Portability—Thin clients have the advantage of running everywhere. Eclipse provides support for heterogeneous OSs and client environments, ranging from traditional PCs, to thinner devices such as tablets and kiosks, down to mobile and embedded devices such as PDAs and smartphones. As long as you can find a Java Virtual Machine (JVM) with the J2ME Foundation libraries or greater (e.g., J2SE 6.0), you can run your client. Chapter 23, "RCP Everywhere," talks about how to use Eclipse to design clients that essentially run everywhere.

Intelligent install and update—Controlling the costs associated with deploying and maintaining rich client applications was a problem in the early days. Eclipse's component framework enables plug-ins to be deployed and updated using any number of mechanisms: HTTP, Java Web Start, repositories, simple file copying, or sophisticated enterprise management systems. Chapter 26, "The Last Mile," details the task of getting your Eclipse RCP applications to your users.

Disconnected operation—Because rich client applications run on a local machine, they can run stand-alone without a network connection. This is a major advantage over thin clients. Applications that are inherently disconnected can use local caches, replicas, and store-and-forward mechanisms to accommodate network interruptions.

Development tooling support—Developers in the first wave of rich clients enjoyed IDEs that helped them build their applications. Eclipse provides a first-class Java IDE that contains integrated tooling for developing, testing, and packaging rich client applications.

Component libraries—A component framework is not complete without a comprehensive set of components with which to build applications. The Eclipse community has produced plug-ins for building pluggable UIs, managing Help content, install and update support, text editing, consoles, product introductions, graphical editing frameworks, modeling frameworks, reporting, data manipulation, and much more. Some of these are discussed in Chapter 29, "Eclipse Ecosystem."

1.3 Eclipse RCP over the Years

The Eclipse project did not start with the intention of building an RCP. Instead, its goal was to create a platform for integrating development tools. Eclipse as an RCP started in the Eclipse 2.1 release time frame as a hacker activity. The word was out that Eclipse-based IDEs were professional, good-looking, and polished, and they performed well. A few intrepid developers further observed that the same framework that made tooling easier to write and more attractive could be used to build more generic applications.

By and large they were right, but there were many challenges. The most obvious of these were the interweaving of assumptions based on Eclipse as a tooling platform and the resultant inability to change certain elements of the environment's look and feel.

Eclipse 3.0 was a major enabling step for Eclipse as an RCP. Virtually all of the IDE-related interdependencies were eliminated, and many of the different parts of the UI were opened to customization. The groundwork for dynamic plug-in installation, removal, and updating was established with the introduction of an OSGi-based (*http://osgi.org*) runtime. These two work items amounted to a massive refactoring of the main aspects of the platform.

With these improvements, interest in RCP rose sharply and commercial applications began to emerge. IBM revamped its Lotus product suite to be based on RCP; NASA started using RCP for managing, modeling, and analyzing space missions; and RCP showed up unnoticed in applications in various domains. Today RCP is used as the basis of software platforms from banking and insurance to health care and geographical information systems.

This book's release follows closely upon the release of Eclipse 3.5 (Galileo). Eclipse 3.5 contains countless improvements, refinements, and wholesale leaps in the support of diverse application scenarios. The tooling for creating and editing product definitions is one such leap. RCP developers are now able to define the branding, content, and deployment strategies for their products using purpose-built editors and wizards.

1.4 Uses of RCP

Over the life of the Eclipse RCP, we have seen quite a number and range of applications adopting the technology. A few are noted on the RCP applications page of the Eclipse RCP Web site at *http://eclipse.org/rcp*. There are, however, too many to detail here—or there, for that matter. Rather, we highlight two uses that stand out as compelling examples of what RCP is all about: IBM Lotus Expeditor and the NASA Maestro project.

1.4.1 IBM Lotus and Eclipse RCP

The Lotus team at IBM was one of the leading innovators in the use of Eclipse for generic applications. They were looking to build the next generation of the

Lotus platform and productivity tools (e.g., e-mail, messaging, document management) for enterprises and address the following issues:

o Management costs
o Deploying coherent componentized systems
o Role-based function delivery
o Rich user experiences
o Collaboration

The Lotus team chose to build on Eclipse as a cross-platform, industrial-strength base to enable supporting applications such as messaging, document management, collaboration, and other business applications. An additional driver was that the extensible componentized Eclipse platform provides integration on-ramps for existing technologies. These requirements cannot be reasonably met with other technologies, such as the Flash and JavaScript client platforms.

The net result of this effort is the Lotus Expeditor platform, a server-managed application container that runs on the desktop. In one usage of this technology, users interact with the system through a server-based *portal*. The portal supplies various *applications* depending on the user and his or her *role*. Application implementation technology varies from portlets and JavaServer Pages (JSPs) running on the server to Eclipse RCP-based applications that are dynamically downloaded to and run on the client. The set of applications available to a user is managed by the server, as is the deployment of those applications.

The application container that runs on the client is essentially a stand-alone Eclipse RCP shell with additional middleware, security, UI, and management support. Both platform-optional components and end-user applications are incrementally provisioned by the server; that is, the server provisions Eclipse plug-ins to the client. These plug-ins are dynamically installed and run, thus giving the user access to the application. A key benefit of this model is that only the platform extensions and applications a user has permission to use are provisioned, resulting in a minimal fit-for-purpose configuration.

The container itself is highly configurable. Figure 1-1 shows a typical Expeditor configuration. On the left side is a chooser that lists the applications available to the user. This list is based on the user's role and is centrally configured. Again, some applications may run on the server, some on the desktop. Of those that run on the desktop, only the ones in use are physically installed on the desktop; the others are downloaded and installed on demand.

On the right is a set of views showing tools such as instant messaging contacts and data related to the application in the middle of the screen. In this example the application is a three-dimensional product lifecycle management tool display-

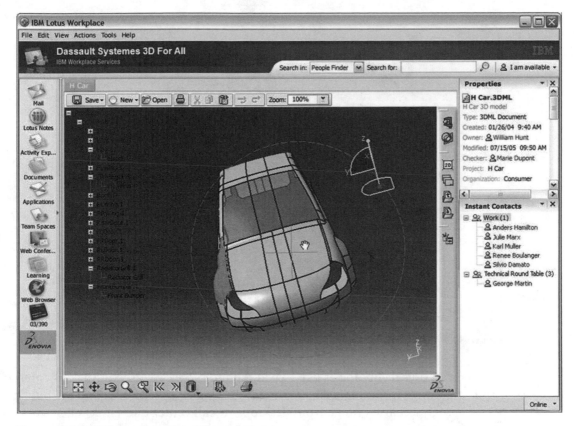

Figure 1-1   IBM Lotus Expeditor Client for Desktop

ing an automobile with its parts assembly. IBM Lotus Expeditor is completely pluggable, and the layout is highly customizable using declarative markup. A different user, in a different role, might experience a different look and feel and have access to a different set of applications. This is all configured on, and managed by, the server.

Eclipse and Expeditor proved to be a powerful platform, so in mid-2007 Lotus announced Notes V8, the Lotus Notes client within the Eclipse-based Expeditor environment, as shown in Figure 1-2. On top of that, the Lotus team revamped the Sametime V7.5 client to be based on Expeditor technology also.

Speaking of look and feel, notice that Expeditor and Notes look nothing like standard Eclipse. The Expeditor and Notes teams used the extensibility of the Eclipse RCP to create unique user interaction paradigms and models to fit their needs. They in turn expose a personality mechanism that allows consumers of Expeditor to further customize and brand the UI.

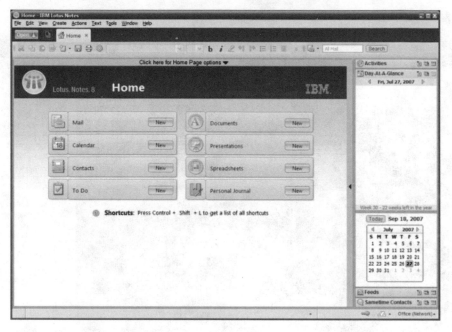

Figure 1–2   IBM Lotus Notes

Today, Lotus technologies like Expeditor and Notes are used in various enterprises that range from financial services to banking to government and the public sector. Usage scenarios range from desktops to call center and bank teller workstations to kiosks.

1.4.2 NASA and the Eclipse RCP

In the late 1990s, NASA embarked on a software project that eventually became known as Maestro. It was an ambitious project to write Java-based tools for managing remote vehicles and experiments on space missions such as the Mars Polar Lander. They started out using various Java technologies, including applets, and progressively improved the capability and usability of their applications by moving to more powerful rich client approaches. This culminated in a series of scientific analysis and planning tools used in surface missions such as *Spirit* and *Opportunity* to explore Mars.

In mid-2004, the Maestro team switched to Eclipse as their development environment and the Eclipse RCP as the base for Maestro. Figure 1-3 shows the Eclipse RCP–based Maestro manipulating some Mars rover data.

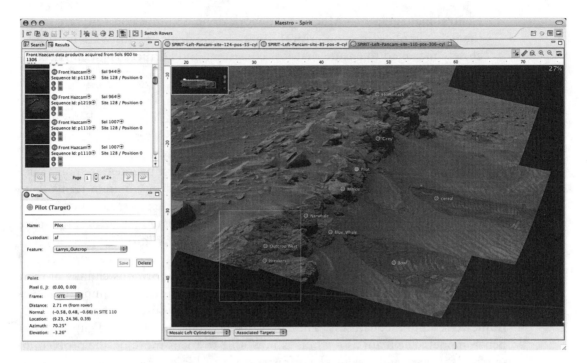

Figure 1–3   Maestro

Mission software has its unique characteristics, but by and large it is subject to the same requirements as the applications you write:

Diverse functional requirements—Any given mission involves a vast number of tools from data browsing to target acquisition to activity generation to spacecraft monitoring and reporting. These particular tools likely do not apply in your domain, but the underlying technologies (e.g., sophisticated user interaction, complex rendering, data management, reporting, etc.) and the related Eclipse plug-ins are of interest in a wide variety of scenarios.

Adaptation—The cumulative set of requirements on the system changes radically and quickly. Each mission is different, each experiment unique. In effect, each mission requires that a new suite of tools be brought together. The Eclipse component model enables the sharing and reconfiguration of functions.

Diverse user base—Mission software has a wide range of users from computer-shy domain experts to technophile engineers to members of the general public. The Eclipse frameworks simplify the creation of world-class, accessible UIs that scale to meet the needs of the user.

Central management—Much of the work done with mission software is, as the name implies, mission-critical. As such, the deployed software must be closely managed to ensure that it is consistent and correct. The Eclipse Equinox p2 update facilities ensure that the correct components are deployed.

Beyond Maestro and its use of Eclipse RCP facilities, the move to the Eclipse RCP has had a more profound impact. For example, the use of the Eclipse component model has fundamentally changed the way NASA teams build their mission systems. Components are developed independently by geographically and organizationally dispersed teams. These components must be integrated on a continuous basis. The fact that all components are defined in common terms (e.g., *plug-ins* and *features*), and their dependencies are fully expressed, brings structure and control to this process. NASA has, in effect, created a platform for space exploration mission software, and the teams are plugging into that platform.

The wealth of high-quality plug-ins available from the Eclipse project and elsewhere has allowed the NASA team to throw away enormous chunks of their existing code. For example, they had previously written their own update mechanism. Now they can use the one in Eclipse. The earlier software had its own UI frameworks and mechanisms. These have been replaced with the Eclipse Workbench model. The team as a whole is now able to focus more on the problem of mission software and less on the infrastructure and middleware inherent in writing sophisticated applications.

The use of the Eclipse RCP within NASA has spread rapidly. The team is now working toward an even more ambitious tool for the next Mars rover mission as well as numerous tools for advanced robotic systems for use on the moon and on Earth.

1.5 Summary

Eclipse is many things to many people. This book focuses on Eclipse as an RCP. As you have seen, rich client applications are making a comeback, and componentized approaches are making them even more attractive.

The Eclipse RCP addresses complex application scenarios that span the spectrum from thin to rich clients and from enterprise- and business-oriented systems to scientific and data management scenarios. The example use cases are from vastly different domains and environments, yet they illustrate Eclipse as it addresses the universal themes of

- ○ Componentization
- ○ Focus on the domain rather than the infrastructure
- ○ Adaptation to changing requirements

The goal of this book is to describe the use cases, processes, and steps for using the Eclipse RCP to similar effect and benefit while building your rich client applications quickly and effectively.

1.6 Pointers

○ The Eclipse RCP wiki (*http://wiki.eclipse.org/RCP*) is a great first stop for RCP information.

○ To see more interesting uses of RCP, including case studies, check out the RCP community site (*http://eclipse.org/community/rcp.php*).

CHAPTER 2

Eclipse RCP Concepts

The Eclipse environment is very rich, but there are just a few concepts and mechanisms that are essential to *Eclipse-ness*. In this chapter we introduce these concepts, define some terminology, and ground these concepts and terms in technical detail. The ultimate goal is to show you how Eclipse fits together, both physically and conceptually.

Even if you are familiar with Eclipse, you might want to flip through this chapter to ensure that we have a common base of understanding and terminology. Writing RCP applications is subtly different from just writing plug-ins. You have the opportunity to define more of the look and feel, the branding, and other fundamental elements of Eclipse. Understanding these fundamentals enables you to get the most out of the platform. With this understanding you can read the rest of the book and see how Eclipse fits into your world.

2.1 A Community of Plug-ins

In Chapter 1, "Eclipse as a Rich Client Platform," we described the essence of Eclipse and its role as a component framework. The basic unit of functionality in this framework is called a *plug-in* (or a *bundle* in OSGi terms), the unit of modularity in Eclipse. Everything in Eclipse is a plug-in. An RCP application is a collection of plug-ins and a *framework* on which they run. An RCP developer assembles a collection of plug-ins from the Eclipse base and elsewhere and adds in the plug-ins he or she has written. These new plug-ins include an *application* and a *product* definition along with their domain logic. In addition to understanding how Eclipse manages plug-ins, it is important to know which existing plug-ins to use and how to use them, and which plug-ins to build yourself and how to build them.

Small sets of plug-ins are easy to manage and talk about. As the pool of plug-ins in your application grows, however, grouping abstractions are needed to help hide some of the detail. The Eclipse teams define a few coarse sets of plug-ins, as shown in Figure 2-1.

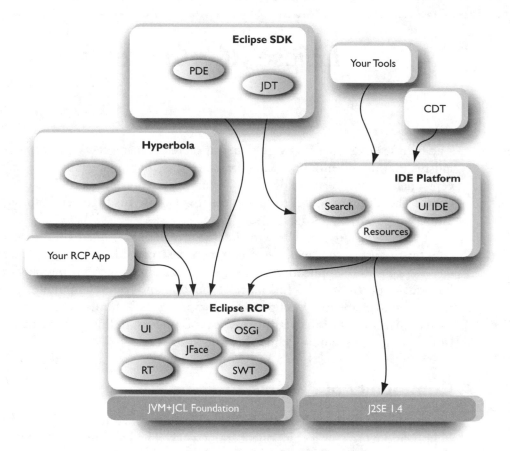

Figure 2–1   Ten-thousand-foot system architecture view

At the bottom of the figure is the Eclipse RCP as a small set of plug-ins on top of a Java Runtime Environment (JRE). The RCP on its own is much like a basic OS or the Java JRE itself—it is waiting for applications to be added.

NOTE

Don't take the boxes in Figure 2-1 too seriously. They are a guess, by the producers of the plug-ins, at groupings that are coherent to consumers of the plug-ins. The groupings are useful abstractions; but remember, for every person who wants some plug-in inside a box, there is someone else who wants it outside. That's OK. You can build your own abstractions.

Fanning upward in the figure is a collection of RCP applications—some written by you, some by others, and some by Eclipse teams. The Eclipse IDE Platform, the traditional Eclipse used as a development environment, is itself just a highly functional RCP application. As shown in Figure 2-1, the IDE Platform requires some of the plug-ins in the Eclipse RCP. Plugged into the IDE Platform is the Eclipse Software Development Kit (SDK) with its Java and plug-in tooling and hundreds of other tools written by companies and the open-source community.

This pattern continues. The general shape of the Eclipse RCP and of your products is the same—both are just sets of plug-ins that make up a coherent whole. These themes of consistency and uniformity recur throughout Eclipse.

NOTE

Notice in Figure 2-1 that the Eclipse RCP requires only Foundation Java class libraries. Foundation is a J2ME standard class set typically meant for embedded or smaller environments. See *http://java.sun.com/products/foundation* for more details. If you are careful to use only a Foundation-supported API, you can ship Eclipse-based applications on a Java Runtime that is only about 6MB rather than the 40MB J2SE 1.4 JRE.

The internal detail for the Eclipse RCP plug-in set is shown in Figure 2-2. These plug-ins form the base of your RCP applications. Here we see a set of interdependent plug-ins that provide various capabilities as noted in the callout boxes. We could have zoomed in on any of the plug-in sets in Figure 2-1 and seen the same basic uniform structure. You are in fact free to slice and dice the RCP itself or any other plug-in set to suit your needs as long as the relevant plug-in interdependencies are satisfied. In this book we focus on *RCP applications* as applications that use the full RCP plug-in set.

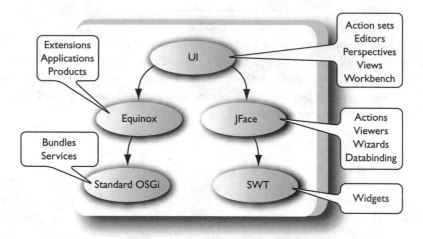

Figure 2–2   Thousand-foot RCP view

Managing the dependencies is a large part of building an Eclipse application. Plug-ins are self-describing and explicitly list the other plug-ins or functions that must be present for them to operate. The OSGi's job is to resolve these dependencies and knit the plug-ins together. It's interesting to note that these interdependencies are not there because of Eclipse but because they are implicit in the code and structure of the plug-ins. Eclipse allows you to make the dependencies explicit and thus manage them effectively.

2.2 Inside Plug-ins

Now that you've seen the 10,000- and 1,000-foot views of Eclipse, let's drop down to 100 feet and look at plug-ins, the basic building blocks of Eclipse. A plug-in is a collection of files and a manifest that describe the plug-in and its relationships to other plug-ins.

Figure 2-3 shows the layout of the `org.eclipse.ui` plug-in. The first thing to notice is that the plug-in is a Java Archive (JAR). As a JAR, it has a MANIFEST.MF. The manifest includes a description of the plug-in and its relationship to the rest of the world.

Plug-ins can contain code as well as read-only content such as images, Web pages, translated message files, documentation, and so on. For instance, the UI plug-in in Figure 2-3 has code in the `org/eclipse/ui/…` directory structure and other content in `icons/` and `about.html`.

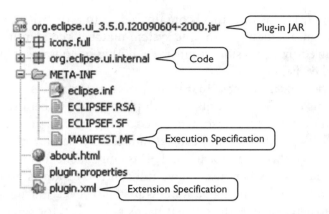

Figure 2–3   Plug-in disk layout

Notice that the plug-in also has a `plugin.xml` file. Historically, that was the home of the execution-related information now stored in the `MANIFEST.MF`. The `plugin.xml` continues to be the home of any extension and extension point declarations contributed by the plug-in.

2.3 Putting a System Together

With all these plug-ins floating around, what does an Eclipse system look like on disk? Figure 2-4 shows a typical RCP SDK install. The topmost directory is the *install location*. It includes a plug-in store, some bootstrap code, and a launcher, `eclipse.exe`, which is used to start Eclipse.

Figure 2–4   The anatomy of an Eclipse installation

The *plug-in store* (plugins directory) contains a directory or JAR file for each plug-in. By convention, the name in the file system matches the identifier of the plug-in and is followed by its version number. Each plug-in contains its files and folders as described earlier.

The *configuration location* (configuration directory) contains the configuration definition. This definition describes which plug-ins are to be installed and run. The configuration location is also available to plug-ins for storing settings and other data such as preferences and cached indexes. By default, the configuration location is part of the install location. This is convenient for standard single-user installs on machines where users have full control. Products and shared, or multiconfiguration, installs on UNIX systems may, however, put the configuration location elsewhere, such as the current user's home directory.

2.4 OSGi Framework

The Eclipse plug-in component model is based on the Equinox implementation of the OSGi framework R4.2 specification (*http://osgi.org*). You can see it at the bottom of Figure 2-5. In a nutshell, the OSGi specification forms a framework for defining, composing, and executing components or *bundles*. Think of bundles as the implementation of plug-ins. The term *plug-in* is used historically to refer to components in Eclipse and is used throughout the documentation and tooling.

There are **no fundamental or functional differences between plug-ins and bundles** in Eclipse. Both are mechanisms for grouping, delivering, and managing code. In fact, the traditional Eclipse Plugin API class is just a thin, optional layer of convenience functioning on top of OSGi bundles. To Eclipse, everything is a bundle. As such, we use the terms interchangeably and walk around chanting, "A plug-in is a bundle. A bundle is a plug-in. They are the same thing."

It is convenient to think of the OSGi framework as supplying a component model to Java; that is, think of it as a facility at the same level as the base JRE. OSGi frameworks manage bundles and their code by managing and segmenting their class loading—every bundle gets its own class loader. The classpath of a bundle is dynamically constructed based on the dependencies stated in its *manifest*. The manifest defines what a plug-in is and on what it depends. All plug-ins are self-describing.

The MANIFEST.MF shown in Figure 2-5 gives the org.eclipse.ui plug-in a *plug-in ID*, or *bundle symbolic name*, and a version. Common practice is to use Java package name conventions such as org.eclipse.ui for the identifier and [major.minor.service.qualifier] tuples for the version number. The ID and version are paired to uniquely identify the plug-in. The pairs are then used to express dependency relationships. You can see this in the Require-Bundle header of the manifest—the UI plug-in requires the Runtime, JFace, and SWT plug-ins.

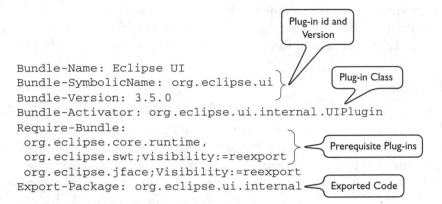

Figure 2–5 Plug-in manifest

In the context of Eclipse, OSGi's main role is to knit together the installed plug-ins, allowing them to interact and collaborate. The rigorous management of dependencies and classpaths enables tight and explicit control over bundle inter-actions and thus the creation of systems that are more flexible and more easily composed.

OSGi and Eclipse

The OSGi Alliance (*http://osgi.org*) was formed independently about the same time the Eclipse project started. Its original mission was to provide a Java component and service model for building embedded devices such as residential gateways, set-top boxes, car dashboard computers, and so on.

The RCP focus during the Eclipse 3.0 development cycle spun off the Equinox technology project (*http://eclipse.org/equinox*), which explored ways of making the Eclipse runtime more dynamic and support plug-in install and uninstall without restarting. Various existing alternatives were considered, and OSGi emerged as a standard, dynamic framework, quite similar to Eclipse. As a result, Eclipse is based on the Equinox implementation of the OSGi framework specification. Eclipse 3.5 includes a stand-alone OSGi implementation in `org.eclipse.osgi_3.5.0.jar`.

2.5 Equinox

Historically, the Eclipse Runtime included the plug-in model and various func-tional elements. As you have seen, the plug-in or bundle model has moved down to the OSGi layer. This is implemented by the Equinox project. Most of the other functionality previously supplied by the Eclipse Runtime is now also part of the Equinox project. So we distinguish between the base standard OSGi implementation and the value-added function elements of Equinox discussed in this section.

2.5.1 Applications

Like JVMs and standard Java programs, OSGi systems have to be told what to do. To run Eclipse, someone has to define an *application*. An application is very much like the `main()` method in normal Java programs. After Equinox starts, it finds and runs the specified application. Applications are defined using *extensions*. Application extensions identify a class to use as the main entry point. When you run Eclipse, you can specify an application to run. Once invoked, the application is in full control of Eclipse. When the application exits, Eclipse shuts down.

Stand-alone versus Extension Offerings

Offerings are the things that you ship to customers. We distinguish between *stand-alone* and *extension* offerings. A stand-alone offering is one that comes as a complete set of plug-ins, with its own branding and its own application entry point—end users run stand-alone offerings.

Some stand-alone offerings are closed—they are not intended to be extended. The true power of Eclipse comes from offerings that are designed to be extended by others and thus create *platforms*. The Eclipse SDK is a platform, as are the offerings described in Chapter 1.

Extension offerings are sets of plug-ins that are incomplete and destined to be added to some platform. For example, sets of tooling plug-ins such as the Eclipse Modeling Framework (EMF), Graphical Editing Framework (GEF), and C Development Tooling (CDT), which are added to the Eclipse SDK tooling platform, are extension offerings. They do not have an entry point of their own, nor do they have substantial branding.

For most of this book these distinctions are academic. When it comes to discussions of packaging, branding, and updating, the differences become apparent.

2.5.2 Products

A *product* is a level above an application. You can run Eclipse by just specifying an application, but the product branding context (e.g., splash screen and window icons) and various bits of customization (e.g., preferences and configuration files) would be missing. The notion of a product captures this diffuse information into one concept—something that users understand and run.

NOTE

Any given Eclipse installation may include many applications and many products, but only one product and application pair can be running at a time.

2.5.3 Extension Registry

OSGi provides a mechanism for defining and running separate components and a services mechanism to support inter-bundle collaboration. Equinox adds to that a mechanism for declaring relationships between plug-ins—the *extension registry*. Plug-ins can open themselves for extension or configuration by declaring an *extension point*. Such a plug-in is essentially saying, "If you give me the following information, I will do...." Other plug-ins then *contribute* the required information to the extension point in the form of *extensions*.

The canonical example of this is the UI plug-in and its actionSets extension point. Simplifying somewhat, action sets are how the UI talks about menu and toolbar entries. The Eclipse UI exposes the extension point org.eclipse.ui.actionSets and says, "Plug-ins can contribute actionSets extensions that define actions with an ID, a label, an icon, and a class that implements the interface IActionDelegate. The UI will present that label and icon to the user, and when the user clicks on the item, the UI will instantiate the given action class, cast it to IActionDelegate, and call its run() method."

Figure 2-6 shows this relationship graphically.

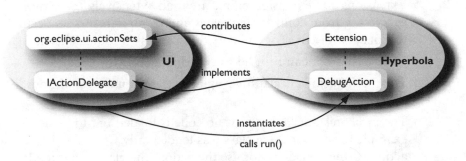

Figure 2–6 Extension contribution and use

Extension-to-extension-point relationships are defined using XML in a file called `plugin.xml`. Each participating plug-in has one of these files. In this scenario, `org.eclipse.ui`'s `plugin.xml` includes the following:

org.eclipse.ui/plugin.xml
```
<extension-point id="actionSets" name="Action Sets"/>
```

The Hyperbola plug-in, `org.eclipsercp.hyperbola`, developed later in the book, similarly contributes an extension using the markup shown in the following `plugin.xml` snippet:

org.eclipsercp.hyperbola/plugin.xml
```
<extension point="org.eclipse.ui.actionSets">
  <actionSet id="org.eclipsercp.hyperbola.debugActionSet">
    <action
        id="org.eclipsercp.hyperbola.debug"
        class="org.eclipsercp.hyperbola.DebugAction"
        icon="icons/debug.gif"
        label="Debug Chats"/>
  </actionSet>
</extension>
```

The `actionSets` extension point contract plays out as follows: The UI presents the label "Debug Chats" along with the `debug.gif` icon. When the user clicks on the action, the class `DebugAction` is instantiated and its `run()` method is called.

This seemingly simple relationship is extremely powerful. The UI has effectively opened up its implementation of the menu system, allowing other plug-ins to contribute menu items. Furthermore, the UI plug-in does not need to know about the contributions ahead of time, and no code is run to make the contributions—everything is declarative and lazy. These turn out to be key characteristics of the registry mechanism and Eclipse as a whole. Some other characteristics worth noting here are these:

○ Extensions and extension points are used extensively throughout Eclipse for everything from contributing views and menu items to connecting Help documents and discovering builders that process resource changes.

○ The mechanism can be used to contribute code or data.

○ The mechanism is declarative—plug-ins are connected without loading any of their code.

○ The mechanism is lazy in that no code is loaded until it is needed. In our example the `DebugAction` class was loaded only when the user clicked on the action. If the user does not use the action, the class is not loaded.

○ This approach scales well and enables various approaches for presenting, scoping, and filtering contributions.

2.6 Standard Widget Toolkit (SWT)

Sitting beside the OSGi and Equinox is the SWT. SWT is a low-level graphics library that provides standard UI controls such as lists, menus, fonts, and colors, that is, a library that exposes what the underlying window system has to offer. As the SWT team puts it, "SWT provides efficient, portable access to the UI facilities of the OSs on which it is implemented."

This amounts to SWT being a thin layer on top of existing windowing system facilities. SWT does not dumb down or sugarcoat the underlying window system but rather exposes it through a consistent, portable Java API. SWT is available on a wide variety of window systems and OSs. Applications that use SWT are portable among all supported platforms.

The real trick of SWT is to use native widgets as much as possible. This makes the look and feel of SWT-based applications match that of the host window system. As a result, SWT-based systems are both portable and native.

Notice that SWT does not depend on Equinox or OSGi. It is a stand-alone library that can be used outside of Eclipse or RCP.

2.7 JFace

Whereas SWT provides access to the widgets as defined by the window system, JFace adds structure and facilities for common UI notions. The UI team describes JFace as follows: "JFace is a UI toolkit with classes for handling many common UI programming tasks. JFace is window system-independent in both its API and implementation, and is designed to work with SWT without hiding it."

It includes a whole range of UI toolkit components, from image and font registries, text support, dialogs, databinding, and frameworks for preferences and wizards to progress reporting for long-running operations. These and other JFace UI structures, such as actions and viewers, form the basis of the Eclipse UI.

2.8 UI Workbench

Just as JFace adds structure to SWT, the Workbench adds presentation and coordination to JFace. To the user, the Workbench consists of some *views* and *editors* arranged in a particular layout. In particular, the Workbench

○ Provides contribution-based UI extensibility
○ Defines a powerful UI paradigm with *windows*, *perspectives*, *views*, *editors*, and *actions*

2.8.1 Contribution-Based Extensibility

Whereas JFace introduces actions, preferences, wizards, windows, and so on, the Workbench provides extension points that allow plug-ins to define such UI elements *declaratively*. For example, the wizard and preference page extension points are just thin veneers over the related JFace constructs.

More than this, however, the use of extensions to build a UI has a fundamental impact on the scalability of the UI in terms of both complexity and performance. Declarative extensions enable the description and manipulation of sets of contributions such as the action sets we discussed earlier. For example, the Workbench's *capabilities* mechanism supports progressive disclosure of functionality by filtering actions until their defining action sets are triggered. Your application may have a huge number of actions, but users see only the ones in which they are interested—the UI grows with users' needs.

Since all of these extensions are handled lazily, applications also scale better. As your UI gets richer, it includes more views, editors, and actions. Without declarative extensibility, such growth requires additional loading and execution of code. This increases code bulk and startup time, and the application does not scale. With extensions, no code is loaded before its time.

2.8.2 Perspectives, Views, and Editors

The Workbench appears to the user as a collection of windows. Within each window the Workbench allows users to organize their work in much the same way as you would organize your desk—you put similar documents in folders and stack them in piles on a desk. A *perspective* is a visual container for a set of *views* and content *editors*—everything shown to the user is in a view or an editor and is laid out by a perspective.

Users organize content in perspectives in the following ways:

- ❍ Stack editors with other editors.
- ❍ Stack views with other views.
- ❍ Detach views from the main Workbench window.
- ❍ Resize views and editors and minimize/maximize editor and view stacks.
- ❍ Create fast views that are docked on the side of the window.

A perspective supports a particular set of tasks by providing a restricted set of views and supporting action sets as well as shortcuts to relevant content creation wizards, other related views, and other related perspectives. Users can switch between perspectives, for example, to change between developing code, trading stocks, working on documents, and instant messaging. Each of these tasks may have unique layouts and content.

2.9 Summary

In Eclipse, everything is a plug-in. Even the OSGi framework and the Equinox functionality show up as plug-ins. All plug-ins interact via the extension registry and public API classes. These facilities are available to all plug-ins. There are no secret back doors or exclusive interfaces—if it can be done in the Eclipse IDE, you can do it in your application.

SWT, JFace, and the UI Workbench plug-ins combine to form a powerful UI framework that you can use to build portable, highly scalable, and customizable UIs that have the look and feel of the platform on which you are running.

In short, Eclipse is an ideal technology for building modular RCPs based on OSGi.

2.10 Pointers

○ The SWT page (*http://eclipse.org/swt*) has snippets and examples perfect for beginners.
○ The Eclipse FAQs (*http://wiki.eclipse.org/Eclipse_FAQs*) is a great resource for some common Eclipse development questions.

PART II

RCP by Example

The best way to learn about Eclipse as a rich client platform is to build a rich client application. This part of the book guides you through just that. Starting with a machine completely devoid of any Eclipse functionality, we walk through setting up Eclipse for RCP development and then creating, running, debugging, and enhancing a reasonably full-featured instant messaging client application called Hyperbola. The screen shot here shows an example of the Hyperbola chat client application you will build.

The material in Part II is presented in an informal tutorial style—assume that we are sitting with you and guiding you though Hyperbola's development. You are encouraged to follow along and do the steps described. If you would rather not follow the steps or are having difficulties, the completed code for each chapter is also available on the book's Web site (*http://eclipsercp.org*). Even though the chapters are very development-oriented, the text for each chapter is complete and can be read without following the steps or looking at the supplied code.

CHAPTER 3

Tutorial Introduction

Getting started often proves to be one of the biggest challenges. In particular, given the tutorial nature of the next dozen or so chapters, understanding the goals of the tutorial and ensuring that you have a reasonable development setup are crucial to having an enjoyable learning experience.

This chapter is designed to set the scene and show you

○ An overview of the tutorial content and evolution

○ How to set up for Eclipse RCP development

○ How to get, compare, and manage the sample code

○ Some tips for using the Eclipse IDE for exploring code

3.1 What Is Hyperbola?

Hyperbola is an instant messaging chat client developed expressly for this book. The instant messaging domain is compelling because it is simple and easy to understand. In fact, you most likely have used an instant messaging client at some point. Whether it's Google Talk, Yahoo! Messenger, AOL Instant Messenger, MSN Messenger, or Lotus Sametime, the idea is basically the same—the client connects to a server, which routes messages from one client to another.

What's so interesting about writing yet another chat client? Even though the idea is straightforward, instant messaging clients themselves are rich in challenges and feature needs. Enumerated here are a few of the challenges of putting together a full-featured chat client:

Third-party libraries—Writing a messaging library is challenging at best. Rather than writing your own, most prefer to use one crafted by experts.

Hyperbola is no different—it is based on the Smack API which uses the Extensible Messaging and Presence Protocol (XMPP) under the covers to enable messaging.

Extensibility—Simple instant messaging is quite straightforward. Hyperbola, however, is based on the Internet Engineering Task Force's (IETF's) XMPP messaging standard, which evolved out of the Jabber protocols. Remember, the X in XMPP is for "eXtensible." And it certainly is that. There are XMPP extensions for multiuser chat (MUC), file transfer, Extensible Hypertext Markup Language (XHTML) messaging, user location, and so on. This implies that a full-featured chat client must also be extensible.

Varied execution environments—Instant messaging is pervasive. People use it from their desktops, handhelds, and cell phones and integrate it with other applications. Servers and other machines use it to alert administrators. The challenge is to write a client that is useful in as many of these environments as possible.

Provisioning—Given that the domain is so extensible, the ability to update a deployed chat application's existing capabilities and add new capabilities is crucial. Updating should happen with minimal intrusion on the use of the running client.

Complex workflows—The domain is simple, but it gives rise to some interesting work and execution flows. Even simple things like logging on can be complex, and messaging is inherently asynchronous and decoupled.

Customization—Chat clients seem to be quite personal. Everyone likes to customize them. Whether you are the end user or the product designer, customizing the look and feel is becoming mandatory.

Generic—Perhaps the most compelling part of the instant messaging domain as an example is that many of the challenges just described are relatively generic—you have probably identified with at least some of these as you read the list.

Stepping back and looking at these challenges, you should notice that they are driven by the richness of the domain rather than the details of the infrastructure—that is, the Hyperbola example highlights that RCP is easy; it's the domain that is hard.

3.2 The Evolution of Hyperbola

Over the course of the tutorial chapters, we develop Hyperbola through the series of prototypes enumerated below. Each of the prototypes is set up to reach some level of application functionality and illustrate a coherent set of Eclipse RCP features and functions as well as Eclipse development environment functions. Each prototype is covered in a series of chapters, and the code added or changed in each chapter is supplied to you. You can follow along and do the steps yourself, jump around and start in the middle, just browse the code, or simply read the text.

Hello, Hyperbola (Chapter 4)—The tutorial starts off with an empty work-space and walks you through the basic elements of creating RCP applications and plug-ins, the structure and control flow of a simple Hyperbola shell, and the running and debugging of applications. By the end of this initial proto-type, Hyperbola is just a simple shell, but it runs and you know how to run it! The code for this chapter is entirely generated by templates in Eclipse.

UI sketch (Chapters 5–7)—This prototype focuses on filling out the UI of Hyperbola. The realities and details of messaging are ignored as we introduce UI concepts such as views, editors, actions, and perspectives as well as some common user features like system tray integration. The prototype finishes with a realistic-looking Hyperbola chat client prototype without the chatting function.

Branded and packaged (Chapters 8–9)—We take a break from coding and the chat domain to address the somewhat generic issues of branding and packaging. Branding Hyperbola by adding a splash screen, window images, and About information completes its look and feel. Packaging it allows you to distribute it to friends and colleagues and get their feedback. The branded and packaged Hyperbola is fully stand-alone.

Messaging (Chapters 10–12)—The main goal of this prototype is to put the "chat" in "chat client." Here we add the Smack messaging library to get real messaging capabilities. This prototype also refines Hyperbola to have key bindings, preferences, and a login dialog.

Well-rounded (Chapters 13–14)—The last prototype rounds out Hyperbola by adding Help and Update support. These are important capabilities for real-world applications. Their addition here sets the stage for the integration of further functionality. By the end of this prototype, Hyperbola is a complete XMPP-based chat client that has a number of bells and whistles, but we will still have only scratched the surface of what is possible with the Eclipse RCP.

3.3 Development Environment Installation

The first thing you need for the tutorial is a set of tools to write the code. The Eclipse SDK has a full set of Java development tooling (JDT), complete with a comprehensive Plug-in Development Environment (PDE). The code in this book has been developed and tested using the Galileo SR2 release of Eclipse (also known as Eclipse 3.5.2). You can download the release from *http://eclipse.org/downloads*.

The Eclipse downloads site contains a vast array of downloads, but the Eclipse Classic (SDK) is the most popular and should be highlighted on the site. This book details functionality that was new to Eclipse in Galileo SR2, the latest release as the book went to press. You must be using the released version of Galileo SR2 or later to follow the exercises. Be sure to get the appropriate download for your machine (OS, window system, and processor).

Once you have downloaded the file, expand it in some convenient location (say, `c:\ide` on Windows). In the examples we assume that you have extracted it to `c:\ide`.

NOTE

The Eclipse downloads do not include a JRE or Java SDK. Many systems include an acceptable JRE. If yours does not, *http://eclipse.org/downloads/moreinfo/jre.php* provides information on getting a suitable JRE.

For the work in this book, it is convenient to have a Java SDK (sometimes called a JDK), as it includes much of the Java source, convenient for debugging, and a couple of handy tools such as `jarsigner`.

Now you are set to run the IDE. Double-click on the launcher (`eclipse.exe` or `eclipse`, depending on your operating system). When Eclipse starts up, it asks for a workspace location. The workspace is the place where development artifacts such as projects and code are stored. It is typically a good idea to locate the workspace somewhere separate from the IDE install. This simplifies the management of multiple workspaces as well as changing versions of the Eclipse IDE. By default, Eclipse suggests a location in your user directory (e.g., `c:\Documents and Settings\you\workspace`). This is a fine choice.

After you select a workspace location, Eclipse continues to start and shows the welcome page. Feel free to play around with the information there. When you are ready to continue, go to the Workbench by clicking on the arrow at the top right corner.

3.4 Sample Code

As mentioned earlier, the code and resources added in each chapter are available from the book's Web site, *http://eclipsercp.org*. It turns out that managing a dozen different versions of the same plug-ins is quite complicated. Ideally, we would have just named the projects differently and allowed you to load them all at once. Unfortunately, all of the variations on that approach proved to be problematic in one way or another. In the end, we wrote a *Samples Manager* tool to help you both manage the chapter code and move from chapter to chapter.

The example code in the Samples Manager is the *final state* of Hyperbola after all steps outlined in the corresponding chapter have been completed. So, to get the starting state for Chapter N, you should load the final state for Chapter N-1 into your workspace.

To install the Samples Manager, follow these steps:

- ❍ Open the Software Updates dialog using **Help > Install New Software…**.
- ❍ On the **Available Software** page click the **Add…** button to add a new software site.
- ❍ In the dialog enter `http://eclipsercp.org`, the location of the book's software site, and click **OK**.
- ❍ Expand the tree for the RCP book site and select the Samples Manager. Pick version 2.0.0 or later to get the code for the second edition of this book.
- ❍ Click **OK** and go through the following pages of the wizard, carefully reading and accepting the licenses and warnings. After the Samples Manager is installed, a restart dialog appears. Select **Yes** to restart.

3.4.1 Moving from Chapter to Chapter

With the Samples Manager installed, there should be an **RCP Book** menu on the main menu bar. Open the tool by selecting **RCP Book > Samples Manager**. You should see a view that lists all the chapters of the book that have associated sample code. Select a chapter and click **Import** to load all related projects into the workspace. After importing a chapter, the Samples Manager highlights the chapter to remind you what is in the workspace. The tool's Help content includes the most up-to-date instructions and tips for using the tool.

3.4.2 Comparing

The Samples Manager also supports comparing the current workspace to the set of projects for a chapter. For example, if your workspace contains the projects for Chapter 5, you can see all the changes required for Chapter 6 by selecting Chapter 6 in the list and clicking **Compare**. This gives you a standard Eclipse compare editor that you can use to browse the changes or load them into the workspace.

This is extremely useful when following the tutorial steps. For example, while doing Chapter 6, you may find that something is not working or the steps are unclear. Comparing the current workspace to the Chapter 6 project tells you what is left to do or where your setup is different from the expected outcome.

Several chapters require sets of resources or large chunks of code that you are not expected to create on your own. The Samples Manager's comparison tool has a **Copy into Workspace** action, as shown in Figure 3-1, that allows you to select files and folders in the comparison and copy them into the workspace.

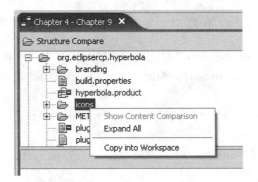

Figure 3–1   Comparing Chapter 4 to Chapter 9

To distinguish between files that are changes and those that exist only in one location, the compare editor shows a minus sign (-) if a file does not exist in the workspace but does exist in the comparison chapter. Conversely, a plus sign (+) is shown if a file exists only in the workspace.

3.5 Target Platform Setup

Before starting development, you need to set up the *target platform*. The target is the set of plug-ins on which your application is based, that is, everything except the plug-ins you are writing. The target is distinct from the bundles that happen to make up your Eclipse tooling. In our case the target will include mostly RCP bundles needed to implement Hyperbola. We can add and remove bundles in the target without affecting the tools.

TARGETING THE IDE

By default PDE uses your Eclipse IDE bundles as the target platform. This is convenient and sufficient for the initial stages of Hyperbola but will quickly become unwieldy. As such, we recommend using a distinct target platform.

PDE includes comprehensive support for defining and managing target platforms. The Samples Manager you installed also includes a predefined target suitable for the examples in this book. To get up and running quickly, you can load that target, or you can start from scratch and assemble your own target definition. We describe both workflows in the following sections.

The target should have all the supporting bundles required for these activities. Broadly speaking, you need two main things:

RCP SDK—The basic set of plug-ins upon which all RCP applications, including Hyperbola, are built.

Delta pack—Eclipse supports many different hardware and OS platforms. The binary executable and graphical libraries are platform-specific. To ease consumption, the Eclipse team has put together a *delta pack* that contains all of the parts of the basic Eclipse infrastructure that are platform-specific. This is of use to Hyperbola when exporting and building.

3.5.1 The Predefined Target

The Samples Manager comes with a handy target that includes all of the components listed above. Carry out the following steps to load the predefined target:

○ Use **RCP Book > Load Target** or open the Samples Manager and click on the **Load Target** button. This should show a progress dialog while the target contents are copied. When it completes, there will be a project called `org.eclipsercp.hyperbola.target` in the workspace.

○ Open the **Target Platform** preferences page (**Window > Preferences > Plug-in Development > Target Platform**) and look for the entry called **Hyperbola Target**. Select the check box beside that entry and click **Apply** or **OK** to use the Hyperbola target.

WARNING ABOUT THE TARGET EDITOR

Targets are defined in `.target` files. The Hyperbola target file is called `hyperbola.target` and is located in the `org.eclipsercp.hyperbola.target` project. We will talk about editing this file in the next section, but here you should be aware of a bug in the PDE tooling as of Galileo SR1 (September 2009).

When a target file is opened, the target editor attempts to *resolve* its contents. Do not click on the **Set as target platform** link in the target editor while the editor is resolving. Doing this causes a race condition that ultimately prevents the target definition from loading.

If you do this by mistake, you will see a dialog reporting a locking or synchronization error. When this happens, close the target editor and restart Eclipse. Then follow the steps above using the target preferences, or open the editor and wait for it to complete resolving before clicking the link.

Targets in the Workspace

The workflow described in this section results in part of the Hyperbola target living in a project in your workspace. In a sense this is strange—the target is all the stuff *not* in your workspace?! It turns out to be very convenient to treat the content of the target as a resource that you can put into source control and share. In the development of the book samples and our work with product teams it is quite common to have a project in the workspace and source control system to contain the content and target definition. New team members can simply check out the target. When one team member changes the target, the others need only update from the source control system.

3.5.2 Defining Target Platforms

Even if you use the predefined target from the previous section, at some point you will have to define your own. This section describes how that is done. If you are up and running with the predefined target, skip this section and treat it as a reference to come back to.

A target platform is just a list of bundles and features from various locations. Sources of content include

Directories—Specifying a directory adds to the target all bundles and features found in that directory. Directories of bundles can be acquired by downloading archives from the Web, for example, from eclipse.org.

Installations—Pointing the target at an existing Eclipse install adds all elements of the install to the target platform. This includes linked folders, drop-ins, and any other bundles and features that make up the install.

Features—Adding features is similar to adding a directory but with the added ability to select a subset of features found in the directory. All bundles indicated by the selected features are also added to the target.

Software sites—There are many software repositories around the world. Adding a software site allows you to identify a repository from which bundles and features are loaded.

The predefined Hyperbola target uses directories and software sites in its definition. Below we walk you through the steps we used to create the target platform.

In a sidebar in the previous section we talked about having targets in the workspace. We will illustrate that approach here. If you would rather not, you can put the target content wherever you like, but the target definition file still has to go somewhere in the workspace.

○ Create a simple project using **File > New > Project... > General > Project**.

○ Create a target platform definition using **File > New > Plug-in Development > Target Definition** wizard.

○ Enter a name for the target file and situate it in the new project.

○ Notice that at the bottom of the wizard there are several options for initializing your new target. Select the **Nothing** option as we are building this target from scratch. In other scenarios you may wish to prime your new target with content listed elsewhere.

○ Click **Finish** to complete the wizard and open the target editor on the new target definition, as shown in Figure 3-2.

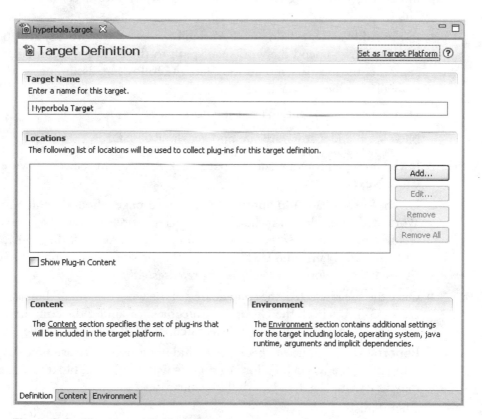

Figure 3-2 The target definition editor

In the editor you can fill in a useful name for the target definition, but the really interesting part is the **Locations** section. For the Hyperbola target we will need to add a directory for the delta pack and a software site for the RCP SDK. Let's do the delta pack first.

○ Get the delta pack by downloading it from the Eclipse project download site, *http://download.eclipse.org/eclipse.* Choose the **Latest Release** from the options given. As of this writing it is 3.5.2.

○ On the subsequent download page select **Delta Pack** on the left navigation bar. This scrolls the page to the delta pack download link. Notice that there is only one link, since by definition it is all the pieces that are platform-dependent. Select the link and save the archive to a convenient spot on your local drive.

○ When the download is complete, create a new folder called delta.pack in the target project and import the downloaded content into the folder using **File > Import... > General > Archive File**.

○ In the target editor's **Definition** page click **Add...** and select **Directory**. Click **Next**.

○ In the **Add Content** dialog click **Variables...** and select **workspace_loc** from the list. Now append the workspace path to the delta pack content. For example, the location should look like the following, assuming you called your project HyperbolaTarget:

${workspace_loc}/HyperbolaTarget/delta.pack

Next we'll add a software site and get the RCP SDK:

○ In the target editor's **Definition** page click **Add...** and select **Software Site**. Click **Next**.

○ On the subsequent **Add Software Site** wizard page, choose **Galileo** in the **Work with** drop-down. If there is a more recent release repository available, feel free to choose it. If the site you want is not listed, click the **Add...** button and enter the **Name** and URL **Location** for the site. For example, the Galileo site is at *http://download.eclipse.org/releases/galileo.*

○ Once the site is selected, the content area of the wizard should fill in as shown in Figure 3-3. Uncheck the **Group by Category** box under the content area and then type RCP in the filter area. Select **Eclipse RCP SDK** to add the RCP SDK.

○ **Important!** You must *uncheck* the **Include required software** box at the bottom left of the wizard. Failure to do this will result in a bloated target that may not work for the Hyperbola scenario.

○ Click **Finish**.

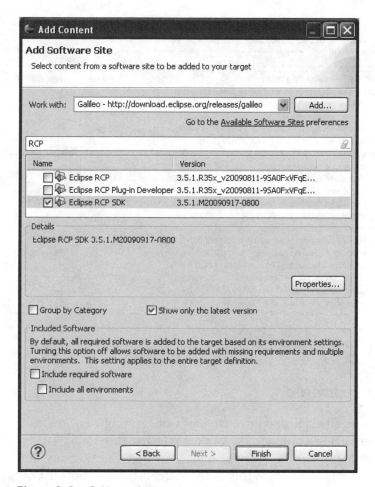

Figure 3–3 Galileo software site content

After clicking **Finish**, PDE resolves the target. This may take some time as the content is downloaded from the software site. Once the resolution is complete, take a look at the **Content** page of the target editor. You should see something similar to the editor in Figure 3-4.

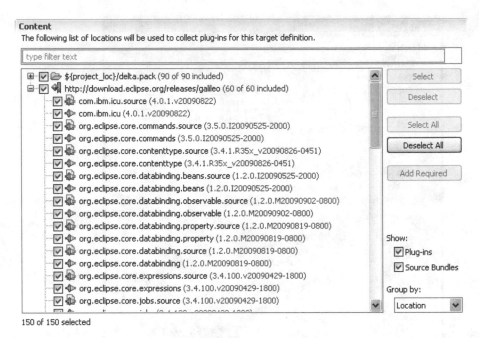

150 of 150 selected

Figure 3–4   Hyperbola target content

3.6 Learning by Example

One of the most efficient and effective ways of figuring out how to program a system is by browsing examples. We can't emphasize this enough. Eclipse itself is one huge example. It can be overwhelming, but there are various shortcuts and mechanisms you can use to help follow the code. Here is a short list of the workspace navigation operations we use on a day-to-day basis:

> **Navigate > Open Type… (Ctrl+Shift+T)**—Opens the Java type with the name you enter. Wildcards are supported. This is a fine way of discovering where a type is or if it exists.
>
> **Navigate > Open Resource… (Ctrl+Shift+R)**—Opens a resource with the name you enter. Wildcards and case-sensitive acronyms, CamelCasing, are supported. Use this to discover resources and their location.
>
> **Navigate > Quick Type Hierarchy (Ctrl+T)**—Pops up a type hierarchy rooted by the type associated with the selection in the current Java editor. For example, if the selection is on a type, a normal type hierarchy is opened. If the selection is on or in a method, all implementers of that method in the hierarchy are shown. Press **Ctrl+T** again to invert the hierarchy.

Search > References > Workspace (Ctrl+Shift+G)—Searches for references to the selected Java element (e.g., type, method, field) in the current Java editor. **Ctrl+Shift+U** does the same search but local to the current file.

Navigate > Open Declaration (F3)—Opens the declaration of the Java element selected in the current Java editor.

Navigate > Open Plug-in Artifact (Ctrl+Shift+A)—Opens the plug-in artifact with the name you enter. Wildcards are supported. This is a good way to quickly search all plug-ins within your workspace and target platform.

Ctrl-3—Presents a condensed list of commands, views, preferences, and other facilities. Simply type some words related to what you need and the list is filtered. For example, typing `targ` finds the target preference page.

Alt+Shift+F1—Presents a Plug-in Spy based on the current selection when the command is issued. The spy shows useful plug-in development-related information such as implementing class and contributing plug-ins. This is a great way to find implementation classes of views you use within Eclipse.

Since Eclipse is so decoupled, it can be hard to figure out how the various pieces interact. PDE offers various tools and mechanisms for navigating these interconnections. The **Plug-in Development** perspective (**Window > Open Perspective > Other... > Plug-in Development**) includes a Plug-ins view. From this you can easily navigate the dependencies and references. From the PDE plug-in editor you can discover the extension-to-extension-point interconnections, navigate to the classes defined in various extensions, and browse extension point documentation.

TIP

In the Plug-ins view select all plug-ins and use the **Add to Java Search** context menu entry to add all known plug-ins to the Java search scope. This is helpful because Java search looks only in projects in the workspace and their dependent projects. This means that if you open an empty workspace and try to open a type, say, using **Ctrl+Shift+T**, the dialog will be empty. By adding all plug-ins in your target platform to the search, you can more easily navigate example code and classes that you do not reference from your projects.

3.7 Summary

Once set up, Eclipse and PDE make it easy to create and run applications. The setup detailed here is robust in that you can use the IDE to work on many different workspaces, the target platform can be updated independently of the IDE or the workspaces, and the IDE itself can be updated without affecting the workspaces or the target platform.

By adding Samples Manager support, you can jump to any chapter and set up your workspace in seconds. You can also validate the tutorial steps as you go and get quick summaries of all the changes done so far and those that are left to do.

3.8 Pointers

○ The first stop if you have a question about Eclipse should be the Eclipse Community Forums at *http://eclipse.org/forums*.

CHAPTER 4

The Hyperbola Application

Where to start? The best bet is to create a simple shell that will evolve into Hyperbola. In this chapter we take you from your empty workspace to creating, running, and debugging an ultra-simple Hyperbola skeleton RCP-based application in about five minutes.

This is an introductory chapter aimed at showing you both the tooling used when developing Eclipse RCP applications and the general structure of RCP applications. In particular, the goals of this chapter are to

○ Detail the creation of a "Hello, World" Hyperbola application. All the code required for this chapter is generated by standard Eclipse templates.

○ Introduce the mechanics of creating RCP applications and manipulating code in Eclipse by creating and running a basic Hyperbola shell.

○ Walk through the code for Hyperbola and identify the major players, seeing how it all fits together.

○ Show how to use launch configurations to change the way Hyperbola runs.

○ Show how to use launch configurations to debug Hyperbola.

4.1 Hyperbola "Hello, World"

You are now set up to develop Eclipse RCP applications. Here we show you how to use the built-in wizards and tooling to create a simple skeleton for the Hyperbola chat client developed throughout the book.

The first thing you need is a plug-in project to hold your code. Go to **File > New > Project...** to start the **New Project** wizard. Choose **Plug-in Project** and click **Next**. On this page enter the project name. Since you are just starting on Hyperbola, enter `org.eclipsercp.hyperbola`. Click **Next** and you should see a page similar to Figure 4-1.

Here, enter the information about the plug-in itself—its ID, version, name, and so forth. Based on the project name, the wizard guesses reasonable initial settings for most fields. The only things to change are these:

○ Make sure to uncheck the **Generate an activator...** option; this is required only if your plug-in will do something during its start or stop lifecycle. We will use this later.

○ Select the **Yes** radio button in the **Rich Client Application** area of the page. This tells the wizard to show the RCP templates on the next page rather than the standard templates.

Figure 4–1   Defining the plug-in content

Click **Next** and the wizard moves to the RCP **Templates** page. There are templates of varying complexity. For this part of the book, pick the **Hello RCP** template to create what is probably the simplest RCP application possible, as shown in Figure 4-2.

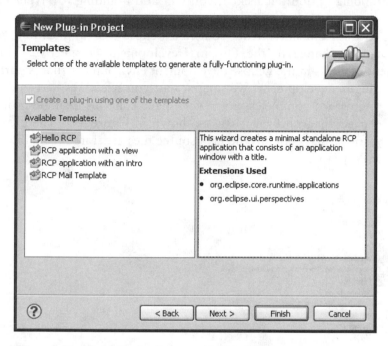

Figure 4–2 Identifying the contents of the application

Project Names and Plug-in IDs

Project names such as `org.eclipsercp.hyperbola` look a little strange at first—they look a lot like Java package names! In fact, the Eclipse community uses two conventions to manage the plug-in and project namespace. First, we use the reverse domain name convention (i.e., Java package naming) to identify plug-ins. Plug-ins are likely to end up in a pool with plug-ins from other sources, so they need to have globally unique identifiers. Using reverse domain names as plug-in ID roots is a convenient, human-readable way of managing that namespace.

Since every plug-in is developed in a project, it is a convenient convention to match project names with the IDs of the plug-ins they contain. In our example both the project and its plug-in are called `org.eclipsercp.hyperbola`. Of course, you should ensure that you own the rights to the related domain (e.g., eclipsercp.org in this case).

Both of these practices are conventions, not rules. We could have called the project Hyperbola and set the plug-in ID to `org.eclipsercp.hyperbola`, but that makes it hard to remember which project is for which plug-in.

Click **Next** to advance the wizard to the next page. Here you identify the Hyperbola application and give it a window title, perspective name, and other attributes. You should have to change only the **Application window title**. Leave the **Add branding** option unchecked; you will add branding to Hyperbola a bit later.

That's it. Click **Finish** to create your first Eclipse RCP application. You may be prompted to change to the **Plug-in Development** perspective. This is an arrangement of views in the Eclipse development environment that is particularly useful for plug-in development. We suggest that you select **Yes** here.

When the wizard completes, your workspace contains a single project with the name `org.eclipsercp.hyperbola`, as shown in Figure 4-3. The project contains an `src` folder that contains the Java source files generated from the template by the **New Project** wizard.

Figure 4–3   Hello Hyperbola project structure

If you selected **Yes** to switch to the **Plug-in Development** perspective, your new plug-in is opened in a plug-in editor. The editor provides a comprehensive view of the various parts of the plug-in definition captured in different files such as `plugin.xml`, `MANIFEST.MF`, and `build.properties`. The plug-in editor works on all of these at once—you can edit all aspects of a plug-in in one place. Figure 4-4 shows the first page of the editor.

TIP

If you close the plug-in editor and want it back, just double-click on the `plugin.xml` or `MANIFEST.MF` files, or use **Open** on the context menu for the files.

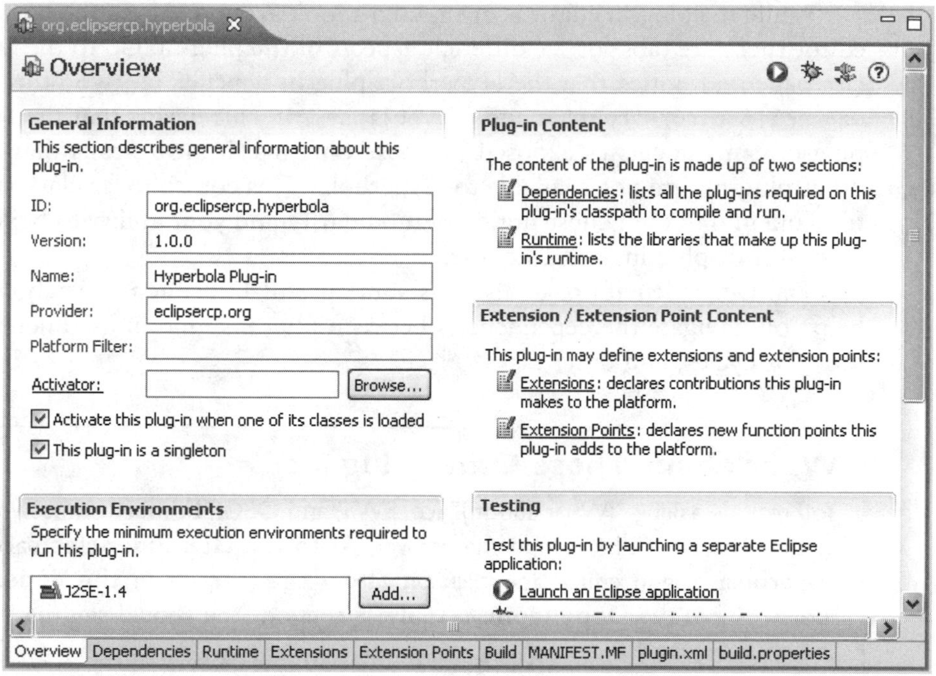

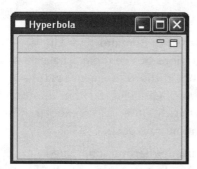

Figure 4–4 Hyperbola plug-in editor

To take Hyperbola for a spin, use the links in the **Testing** section of the **Overview** page. Click on the **Launch an Eclipse application** link and run Hyperbola. This launches Hyperbola as a separate Eclipse RCP application in its own JVM. As you can see from Figure 4-5, it doesn't do much, but it's a start.

Figure 4–5 Simple Hyperbola shell

While the plug-in editor is open, take a look around. Along the bottom of the editor there are tabs for the different aspects of the plug-in. Go to the **Dependencies** page and notice that the Hyperbola plug-in depends on two other plug-ins: `org.eclipse.core.runtime` and `org.eclipse.ui`. This means that the Hyperbola plug-in can use classes exposed by those plug-ins. It also means that classes in other plug-ins are not available to Hyperbola. This control over class visibility is fundamental to the Eclipse notion of modularity and your ability to build systems from sets of plug-ins using Eclipse.

The **Dependencies** page also has some useful **Dependency Analysis** tools to help you navigate the dependencies between plug-ins, find unused dependencies, look for cycles, and other tasks.

What about Those Other Plug-ins?

You may be asking, "What about JFace, SWT, and OSGi? I thought those were part of the RCP as well." To find the answer, go to the **Dependencies** page in the Hyperbola plug-in editor and click on **Show the plug-in in the dependency hierarchy** in the **Dependency Analysis** section. You should see the hierarchy shown in Figure 4-6.

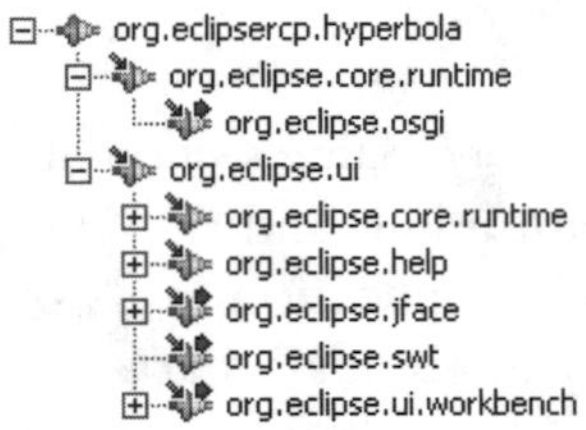

```
⊟ ⬦ org.eclipsercp.hyperbola
  ⊟ ⬦ org.eclipse.core.runtime
      └─ ⬦ org.eclipse.osgi
  ⊟ ⬦ org.eclipse.ui
      ⊞ ⬦ org.eclipse.core.runtime
      ⊞ ⬦ org.eclipse.help
      ⊞ ⬦ org.eclipse.jface
      └─ ⬦ org.eclipse.swt
      ⊞ ⬦ org.eclipse.ui.workbench
```

Figure 4–6   Hyperbola plug-in dependencies

Notice that some of the plug-ins under the Runtime and UI, for example, `org.eclipse.swt`, have little arrow decorations beside them. The arrows identify plug-ins that are *reexported* by their parents in the tree—`org.eclipse.ui` in the case of the SWT plug-in. As such, anyone depending on the UI automatically depends on the reexported SWT. Similarly, the UI reexports JFace and `org.eclipse.ui.workbench` and the Runtime reexports OSGi.

This dependency chaining mechanism is used wherever one plug-in exposes the API of another plug-in as part of its own API. For example, the UI API has classes and methods that name types found in SWT. To ensure that a plug-in requiring the UI gets a coherent dependency chain, the UI reexports SWT. Note that the UI does not reexport all of its prerequisites, just those it exposes as part of its API.

Take a look at Hyperbola's **Extensions** page next. When PDE generated the Hyperbola skeleton, it added two extensions: an application and a perspective. If you poke around in here, you can see some of the values entered earlier as well as the names of various classes that were generated by the template.

These extensions are the mechanism for linking classes into the Eclipse infrastructure. For example, Figure 4-7 shows the Hyperbola Perspective extension. Notice how it lists the new perspective class (`org.eclipsercp.hyperbola.Perspective`) and links it into the `org.eclipse.ui.perspectives` extension point.

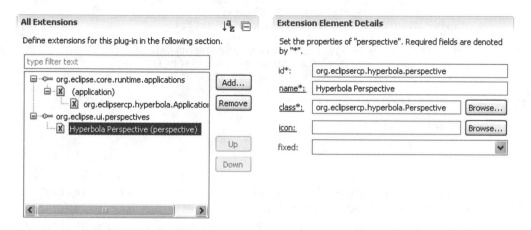

Figure 4–7   Hyperbola extensions

Take a look at the other pages in the editor if you like. If not, there will be plenty of opportunity to use them later. The next section walks through the generated code and highlights its structure. This is followed by a section on running and debugging Eclipse applications. Subsequent chapters build on this base and add more and more functionality.

4.2 Tour of the Code

Since the template did all the work of creating the code, you don't really know what it's doing. In this section we walk through the generated code and point out the interesting bits. In fact, all the generated code is included here—it's pretty small.

4.2.1 Application

The RCP SDK target you are using contains only framework libraries; you can't even run them. It's like having a JRE installed—lots of great code, but it still needs to be told what to do. In regular Java systems, this is done by writing a class that has a main() method. In Eclipse, you write an *application*. An application is the entry point to a program or product. The application is run when the Runtime starts up, and when the application exits, Eclipse shuts down.

The PDE wizard used the Hello RCP template to generate the org.eclipsercp .hyperbola.Application application below. Applications must implement IApplication and thus a run() method. Think of this as your main() method.

org.eclipsercp.hyperbola/Application
```
public class Application implements IApplication {
   public Object run(Object args) throws Exception {
     Display display = PlatformUI.createDisplay();
     try {
       int returnCode = PlatformUI.createAndRunWorkbench(
           display, new ApplicationWorkbenchAdvisor());
       if (returnCode == PlatformUI.RETURN_RESTART) {
         return IApplication.EXIT_RESTART;
       return IApplication.EXIT_OK;
     } finally {
       display.dispose();
     }
   }
}
```

The critical code is marked in bold. The application creates a Display and then starts an Eclipse Workbench by calling PlatformUI.createAndRunWorkbench(Display, WorkbenchWindowAdvisor). This opens a window and simply loops forever, handling user-generated events such as mouse clicks, key presses, and mouse moves. The event loop finally returns when the last window is closed or when it is explicitly told to exit. Before returning from the application, the created Display must be disposed to free any allocated window system resources.

NOTE

You can do just about anything you want in your application. In our example we start up a UI, but you could just as well start a server of some sort. In other words, the Eclipse RCP can also be used for nongraphical applications.

The application class must be linked into the Eclipse Runtime's *applications* extension point, as shown in Figure 4-7, thus making the Runtime aware of the application. Just as many Java JARs on a classpath may contribute classes that have a main() method, many Eclipse plug-ins in a system may contribute application extensions. In fact, one plug-in can contribute many applications. When

Eclipse is started, one and only one application is identified as *the* application to run. Again, this is directly analogous to standard Java, where you specify exactly one class to run on the command line.

4.2.2 WorkbenchAdvisor

In the application code shown in the preceding section, we glossed over the ApplicationWorkbenchAdvisor that was instantiated and passed into PlatformUI .createAndRunWorkbench(). In fact, this is the most important part of the story.

As the name implies, a WorkbenchAdvisor tells the Workbench how to behave— how to draw, what to draw, and so forth. In particular, our ApplicationWorkbenchAdvisor identifies two things:

- ○ The initial perspective to be shown
- ○ The WorkbenchWindowAdvisor to be used

```
org.eclipsercp.hyperbola/ApplicationWorkbenchAdvisor
public class ApplicationWorkbenchAdvisor extends WorkbenchAdvisor {
    private static final String PERSPECTIVE_ID =
        "org.eclipsercp.hyperbola.perspective";

    public WorkbenchWindowAdvisor createWorkbenchWindowAdvisor(
        IWorkbenchWindowConfigurer configurer) {
      return new ApplicationWorkbenchWindowAdvisor(configurer);
    }

    public String getInitialWindowPerspectiveId() {
      return PERSPECTIVE_ID;
    }
}
```

4.2.3 Perspective

The initial perspective is identified by its extension identifier, as shown at the top right of Figure 4-7. The extension gives the perspective a human-readable name and specifies a class that defines the layout of the perspective. The given class must implement the IPerspectiveFactory interface and the createInitialLayout (IPageLayout) method. The org.eclipsercp.hyperbola.Perspective perspective is a trivial implementation that simply does nothing. This perspective is added in later chapters.

```
org.eclipsercp.hyperbola/Perspective
public class Perspective implements IPerspectiveFactory {
   public void createInitialLayout(IPageLayout layout) {
   }
}
```

NOTE

As with applications, there may be many perspectives in the system. The application's WorkbenchAdvisor identifies only one of these as the initial perspective. While a WorkbenchAdvisor must define an initial perspective, that setting can be overridden using preferences. This is detailed in Chapter 16, "Perspectives, Views, and Editors."

4.2.4 WorkbenchWindowAdvisor

Every window in your application has a WorkbenchWindowAdvisor that guides the UI in rendering the window. Window advisors are consulted at various points in the lifecycle of a window (e.g., preWindowOpen() and postWindowCreate()) and have the opportunity to control the creation of the window's contents. You will visit Hyperbola's window advisor often as you update the look and feel of the application.

The ApplicationWorkbenchWindowAdvisor customizes Hyperbola windows. In the preWindowOpen() method, it sets the initial size and title of the window and hides the status line and toolbar. While we are looking at preWindowOpen(), go ahead and change the initial size of the window to make it a bit smaller than the default. Don't forget to save the file when you are done.

org.eclipsercp.hyperbola/ApplicationWorkbenchWindowAdvisor
```
public class ApplicationWorkbenchWindowAdvisor extends
    WorkbenchWindowAdvisor {

  public ApplicationWorkbenchWindowAdvisor(
      IWorkbenchWindowConfigurer configurer) {
    super(configurer);
  }

  public ActionBarAdvisor createActionBarAdvisor(
      IActionBarConfigurer configurer) {
    return new ApplicationActionBarAdvisor(configurer);
  }

  public void preWindowOpen() {
    IWorkbenchWindowConfigurer configurer = getWindowConfigurer();
    configurer.setInitialSize(new Point(400, 300));
    configurer.setShowCoolBar(false);
    configurer.setShowStatusLine(false);
    configurer.setTitle("Hyperbola");
  }
}
```

4.2.5 `ActionBarAdvisor`

`ActionBarAdvisor`s create the actions needed for a window and position them in the window. They are instantiated using `createActionBarAdvisor()` on `WorkbenchWindowAdvisor`. Since we are just starting out and have no actions, the `ActionBarAdvisor` is largely empty.

org.eclipsercp.hyperbola/ApplicationActionBarAdvisor

```
public class ApplicationActionBarAdvisor extends ActionBarAdvisor {
  public ApplicationActionBarAdvisor(IActionBarConfigurer c) {
    super(configurer);
  }

  protected void makeActions(IWorkbenchWindow window) {
  }

  protected void fillMenuBar(IMenuManager menuBar) {
  }
}
```

NOTE

The name `ActionBarAdvisor` does not do justice to this class. It actually controls what appears in the menu bar, the cool bar (also known as the toolbar), and the status line. As such, it is a focal point of customization in RCP applications.

4.2.6 Summary

That's it. You have seen all the code involved in creating the simple Hyperbola RCP application. Just to be sure you got all the steps right, use the Samples Manager detailed in Chapter 3, "Tutorial Introduction," to compare your workspace to the sample code for this chapter—they should be identical (except for possible formatting differences).

Of course the application does not do much; it doesn't even have any actions—nor does it have any branding or splash screens. Nonetheless, the example shows how the major parts of the Eclipse RCP fit together.

4.3 Running and Debugging

By this point you have set up a development environment and target platform, defined a simple Hyperbola application, and run it at least once. You have also seen how applications, perspectives, and advisors fit together to form a system. You are now ready to start putting some real functionality into Hyperbola.

Before doing that, it is worth spending a bit of time talking about how to run and debug Eclipse applications effectively. In this section we show you how to

○ Launch applications in debug mode

○ Set breakpoints and step through code

○ Manage targets, launch configurations, and control the set of plug-ins used

If you have been following along, Figure 4-8 matches your system. It shows the relationships between the IDE install you are running, the workspace in which you are developing, and the target plug-ins you are using for Hyperbola. The IDE plug-ins (bottom left) are the ones in c:\ide. They are the full Eclipse SDK. Running them starts the Eclipse IDE (top left of the diagram). Using the IDE, you work on plug-in projects that are in the workspace (center). When you decide to try running Hyperbola, PDE creates and launches a configuration that lists the relevant plug-ins from the target (bottom right) and the workspace. The result is a running Hyperbola (top right).

When the concerns are separated in this way, the IDE install can be replaced without affecting the workspace or the target. Similarly, the target plug-ins can be updated without changing the workspace or IDE. Of course, several workspaces can use the same target.

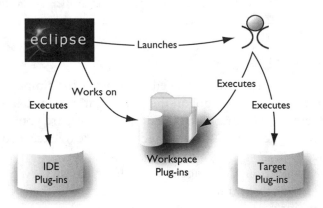

Figure 4–8   Relationships among IDE, target, and workspace

4.3.1 Debugging

Previously you ran Hyperbola using the **Launch** link in the **Testing** section on the **Overview** page of the plug-in editor. You may have noticed that there is also a

Debug link. Go ahead and click on that link now. As with launching, debugging spawns a separate JVM to run the application. The difference is that the **Debug** perspective opens and shows a list of threads in the target application. Exit the application and the threads all terminate.

The debugger is useful when things are not going as you expected. Say, for example, you are getting a `NullPointerException`. To illustrate, set up that scenario by changing `ApplicationWorkbenchWindowAdvisor.preWindowOpen()` to simulate `null` coming back from `getWindowConfigurer()`:

org.eclipsercp.hyperbola/ApplicationWorkbenchWindowAdvisor
```
IWorkbenchWindowConfigurer configurer = getWindowConfigurer();
configurer = null;
```

With the code changed, click on the normal **Launch** link in the plug-in editor. All you see is an exception reported in the console as shown next—Hyperbola does not start:

```
Unhandled event loop exception
Reason:
java.lang.NullPointerException
```

To find out more, add a breakpoint on the exception by using **Run > Add Java Exception Breakpoint...** and selecting `NullPointerException` in the type chooser.

TIP

The filter in the type chooser takes wildcards. So, to get `NullPointerException`, just open the chooser and type `null`. Keep typing until the list of choices is refined enough for you to see the type you want.

Now launch using the **Debug** link in the editor. Click **Yes** when prompted to open the **Debug** perspective. When the debugger opens, the main thread is paused at the line where the exception occurred, as shown in Figure 4-9.

The execution of the main thread has stopped in `preWindowOpen()` on the line highlighted. The debugger also contains a **Variables** view. This view shows the values of all known fields and variables for a given Java stack frame. You can navigate around the object structure by expanding the object tree along the reference paths that interest you.

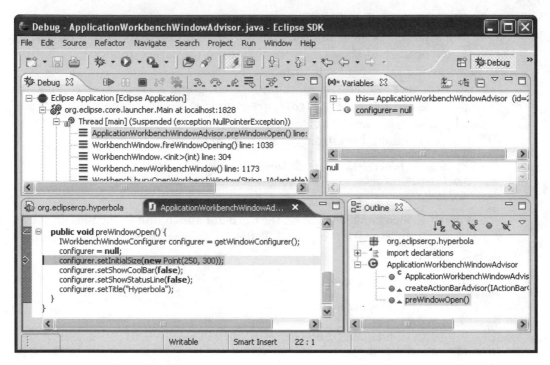

Figure 4–9   Debugging using breakpoints

TIP

Using the **Variables** view to examine object structures can be extremely informative. Note also that you can typically change the values of the variables and fields you find along the way!

Looking at the line of code and the **Variables** view, it is easy to see that the `configurer` field is `null` and to find the cause of the exception. This is the first step. Now you have to figure out why `configurer` is `null` (ignoring, of course, the fact that it is set to `null` on the previous line). One easy way to do this is to set a breakpoint on the first line of this method and then step through the code to find out how the `null` value is set.

To set a breakpoint, position the text cursor on the line you want and use **Run > Toggle Line Breakpoint**. Alternatively, you can double-click in the margin at the left of the line. Either way, a blue ball should appear at the left of the line, as shown in Figure 4-10.

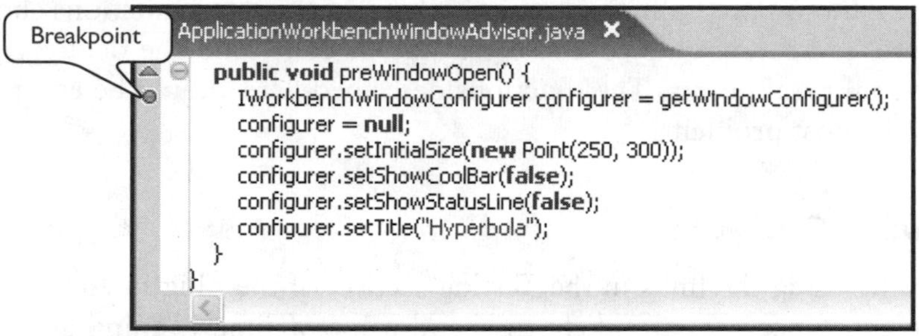

Figure 4–10 Line breakpoint

Terminate the current run using either **Run > Terminate** or by clicking on the red square button over the list of threads. Then launch again using the **Debug** link. This time execution stops at your new breakpoint. From here you can use the stepping functions described in Table 4-1 to go into `getWindowConfigurer()` and see what is going on.

Table 4–1 Debugger Stepping Functions

Image	Step Function
	Step into (**F5**)—The next method call. If you think that the problem might be near, step into. Note that Java debugging is line-oriented, so if you have multiple method calls on one line, you might have to step into several times. You can step into and then immediately step to return. You can refine this by using **Step Into Selection** (**Ctrl+F5**) in the editor's context menu.
	Step over (**F6**)—The next method call. This is useful for quickly getting around in the execution. Use step over until you start seeing things going wrong and then look in more detail.
	Step to return (**F7**)—Of the current method. As the name implies, use this function when you just want to get to the end of the method.
	Drop to frame—Drop all stack frames above the selected frame. Execution is reset to the beginning of the method in the current frame. This is useful if you've discovered a problem and want to retry the execution. Note, however, that this does not undo side effects such as writing or closing files or setting shared state.

TIP

Stepping through code is sometimes bewildering, but it can be an effective way of finding out what the system is doing and discovering API and coding patterns that are useful in your applications.

The editor's context menu has a number of other step functions such as stepping into and running up to a selected line of code, and the debugger supports conditional breakpoints. The functions described here should be enough for you to handle most problems.

4.3.2 Launch Configurations

Launching using the links in the **Testing** section of the plug-in editor is easy and convenient. Since you are likely to spend a lot of time running and debugging Hyperbola in the next chapters, here we show you some tricks to make things easier.

Whenever you click on a test link, PDE manages a *launch configuration* describing the configuration to run. You can look at this launch configuration using either **Run > Run...** or **Run > Debug...** . Either way, you get a launch configuration dialog as shown in Figure 4-11.

The **Main** tab is the most interesting at this point. It has the following parts:

❍ The **Name** of the launch configuration is currently `org.eclipsercp.hyperbola`.

❍ The **Workspace Data** section shows where the *target* Eclipse puts its *workspace* or *instance data*. Since we are running Hyperbola, there isn't any data to worry about. In general, you do not need to change this location, but you may need to know where it is. This is where Eclipse stores some preferences and plug-in-specific information. This is also where you can find the log file if something should go wrong. Look in `.metadata/.log` in the workspace location if you suspect errors are occurring.

❍ The **Program to Run** section identifies the Hyperbola application, `org.eclipsercp.hyperbola.application`, to run. Click on the drop-down arrow and take a look at the other applications known by the system.

❍ The **Java Runtime Environment** area allows you to choose a JRE to use as well as set up any command-line arguments. There are quite a number of possible command-line arguments, all of which are detailed in the online documentation. Perhaps the most interesting one for debug purposes is the `-consoleLog` program argument. This causes all log output to be echoed to the console. This helps because often messages are being logged but go unnoticed unless you check the log. When you use `-consoleLog`, these messages are somewhat more "in your face."

Now that you know about launch configurations, you can run and debug your applications directly rather than using the links on the plug-in editor's **Overview** page. As shown in Figure 4-12, the **Run** menu has a host of entries to help.

Figure 4–11   Launch configuration dialog

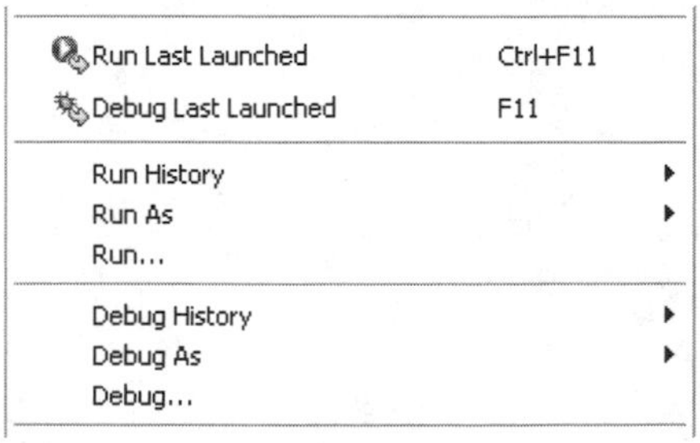

Figure 4–12   Launching entries in the **Run** menu

The context menu in the **Package Explorer** also has **Run As** and **Debug As** entries. When you pick one of these entries and specify **Eclipse Application**, it is equivalent to using the **Run** and **Debug** links in the plug-in editor. PDE finds or creates a launch configuration to match your selection and then launches it.

As you can see, there are several more tabs on the dialog. For now, these are not needed. PDE is pretty good at managing things for you in this relatively simple world. As we make Hyperbola more and more sophisticated, there will be opportunities for you to use the other tabs, in particular, the **Plug-ins** tab.

4.4 Summary

So that was easy. Once set up, Eclipse and PDE greatly simplify the creation and running of applications. Even the generated code for the application is simple. We have now covered all the major concepts, classes, tools, and techniques you need to develop the rest of Hyperbola. The rest of the book builds on this base until we have a very sophisticated, fully extensible chat client that can be deployed in a wide range of execution environments. You wouldn't think it to look at the current Hyperbola shell, but it's true. The RCP part is easy; it's your domain that is hard.

4.5 Pointers

○ The Eclipse Wiki (*http://wiki.eclipse.org/*) contains a breadth of Eclipse knowledge. Feel free to contribute once you become an expert!

○ The Eclipse Tutorial site (*http://eclipsetutorial.sourceforge.net/*) has many useful videos to get you started with Eclipse development.

CHAPTER 5

Starting the Hyperbola Prototype

At this stage you have created the skeleton for Hyperbola. You know how to run it and debug it, and you are familiar with the basic classes that are part of all RCP applications. The next few chapters focus on iteratively developing Hyperbola. This next iteration is interesting because it allows you to quickly get something running so that you can show it to your mom, your boss, or your friends. It's also a lot more fun to learn RCP while developing something concrete.

The iterative approach used to develop Hyperbola is how software is developed in most organizations. You start by creating a prototype that could be used to demo Eclipse RCP to your friends or colleagues. You iterate again and augment the prototype with real domain logic—in our case the messaging library—and start to think about packaging and branding the product. You then continue iterating, adding functionality, and managing the complexity until you have a product to ship.

Prototypes are often crude but provide an excellent way of exploring various aspects of the application to be built. In this chapter we show you how to extend the skeleton version of Hyperbola by adding the following features:

○ A primitive contacts list that shows a list of contacts and contact groups

○ A simple messaging model that is used to drive the UI components

○ Images to make the contacts list look real

For the moment we ignore the details of how to chat with someone—the focus is on getting familiar with the basics. Here we add the contacts list and its supporting model. In the next two chapters we will add the chat editor and associated actions. Figure 5-1 gives a peek at Hyperbola after that work is completed.

Figure 5–1   Hyperbola prototype

5.1 Continuing from the Shell

Chapter 4, "The Hyperbola Application," gave you a good idea of all the classes and files needed for the skeleton Hyperbola application. Let's critique the skeleton as shown in Figure 5-2 and see how we can improve it.

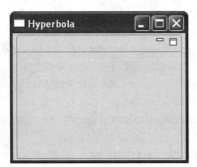

Figure 5–2   Hyperbola skeleton

○ If you resize the window, exit, and rerun Hyperbola, the window size and position are reset to their defaults.

○ The menu bar, toolbars, and status line are not shown.

○ There is no indication in the task tray that Hyperbola is running.

Let's fix the resize and position bug; we'll address the other issues in the next few chapters.

5.1.1 Saving Window Location and Size

One of the problems with the skeleton code is that when the window is resized or moved and the application rerun, the window's size and position are reset. This is annoying. The good news is that it's really easy to fix—the Workbench contains code that saves settings for open windows. It's disabled by default, as saving and restoring window state can be expensive and for some applications not even necessary.

To enable it, first override the `WorkbenchAdvisor.initialize()` method from within `ApplicationWorkbenchAdvisor`, as shown in the snippet below. A trick is to open the `ApplicationWorkbenchAdvisor` class and type `ini`, then press **Ctrl+Space**. A pop-up appears, listing the possible methods that can be overridden. Simply select the `initialize()` method to get a skeleton. This method is called by Eclipse to mark the beginning of the advisor's lifecycle. This hooks in at the earliest possible point to enable save and restore.

```
org.eclipsercp.hyperbola/ApplicationWorkbenchAdvisor
public void initialize(IWorkbenchConfigurer configurer) {
    configurer.setSaveAndRestore(true);
}
```

5.2 Adding a Contacts View

Since Hyperbola is a chat client, one of the most essential UI elements is a *contacts list* that displays your friends and their presence status (i.e., whether or not they are online).

In Eclipse, users interact with applications through *views* and *editors*. *Perspectives* are a mechanism for arranging views and editors and supporting scalable UIs. Put another way, views and editors contain the content for your application; perspectives allow those elements to be organized for users. We already have a perspective; it's just empty.

A view is added by contributing a view extension to the `org.eclipse.ui.views` extension point. Open the `org.eclipsercp.hyperbola` project's `plugin.xml` and go to the **Extensions** page. Click **Add...** and create an extension of type `org.eclipse.ui.views`. Right-click on the extension and add a view attribute using **New > view** from the context menu. When you click on the new view attribute, the **Details** pane at the right shows the default values for the view. Update the **id** and **name** fields to match those shown in Figure 5-3.

You also need a class to implement the view. Click on the **class** link to create a new class. When the **New Class** wizard appears, most of the fields, including the superclass `ViewPart`, are already filled in. All you have to do is type `ContactsView` for the class name. Click **Finish** and a skeleton view class is created and opened in an editor.

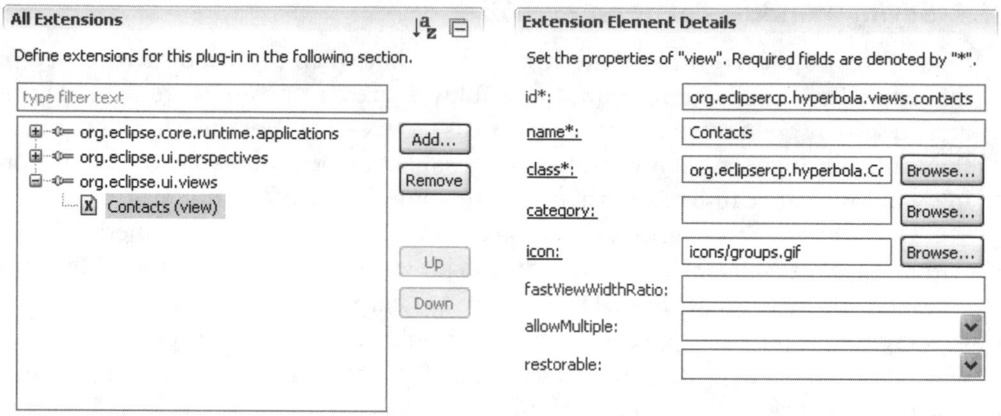

Figure 5–3   Adding `ContactsView` to Hyperbola's `plugin.xml`

TIP

You are building a view from scratch to understand how everything fits together. However, the next time you add a view, you can use the handy PDE templates. You may have noticed that the **New Extension** wizard lists the set of available templates for each extension point. There's a template for a view that creates a sample view with actions and dummy contents.

Before moving on, make a constant for the view ID. Set the value to be the same as in the extension and add it to the newly created `ContactsView` class. This will come in handy later. Save the Java file and go back to the plug-in editor. Notice that the name of the new view class is set in the **class** attribute of the extension.

```
org.eclipsercp.hyperbola/ContactsView
public class ContactsView extends ViewPart {
    public static final String ID =
        "org.eclipsercp.hyperbola.views.contacts";

    public ContactsView() {
        super();
        // TODO Auto-generated constructor stub
    }

    public void createPartControl(Composite parent) {
        // TODO Auto-generated method stub
    }
```

```
    public void setFocus() {
      // TODO Auto-generated method stub
    }
}
```

Finally, set the view's icon. View icons are optional but typically specified. You can either create your own GIF image and place it in Hyperbola's icons directory or copy the images supplied with the sample code for this chapter. Either way, fill in the **icon** field by browsing to the image or entering the location directly.

Save the plug-in and now you have created a skeleton view. The next step is to customize the perspective to include the new view and have it appear in the Hyperbola window.

5.2.1 Adding the Contacts View to a Perspective

All RCP applications must define at least one perspective; otherwise, there would be nothing to lay out the views. Think of a perspective as a set of layout hints for a window. Every IWorkbenchWindow has one page. The page owns its editor and view instances and uses the active perspective to decide its layout. The perspective details where, and whether or not, to show certain things, such as views, the editor area, and actions. Figure 5-4 provides an overview of the main parts of an IWorkbenchWindow.

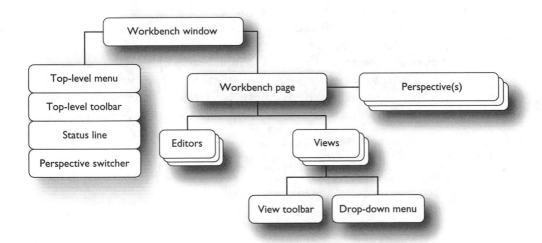

Figure 5–4   Overview of a Workbench window's parts

The initial perspective, and thus the look of Hyperbola when it is first run, is identified by `WorkbenchAdvisor.getInitialWindowPerspectiveId()`. The Hello RCP template defined the Hyperbola Perspective and contributed to the Workbench's perspective extension point, as shown in Figure 5-5. Notice that the extension defines an ID and identifies a class for the perspective.

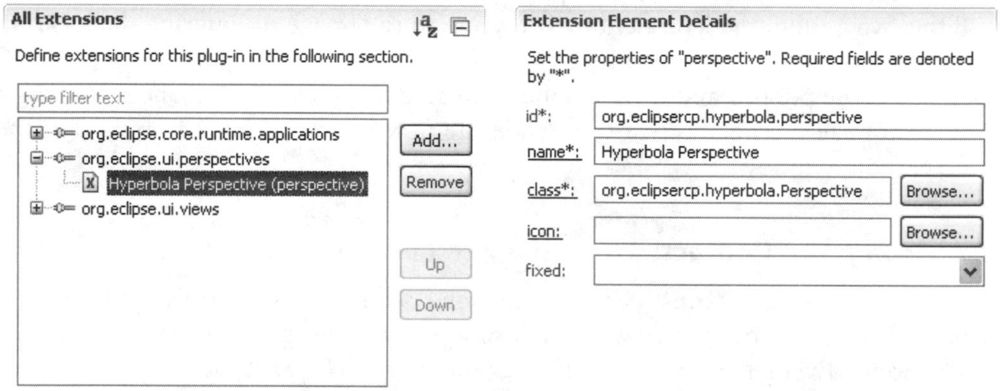

Figure 5–5   Hyperbola Perspective defined

A perspective factory provides the initial layout for a perspective. When a perspective is needed, the factory is created and passed an `IPageLayout` to which views are added. The factory is then discarded. As the user rearranges the contents of the perspective, the Workbench saves the settings on exit and restores them at startup (if so configured).

The perspective generated by the PDE template uses the default layout. This layout is just an editor area with no additional views. That's why Hyperbola is just an empty shell—the perspective is empty. Now that we have a view defined, go ahead and add the Contacts view to the Hyperbola perspective as shown here:

org.eclipsercp.hyperbola/Perspective
```
public class Perspective implements IPerspectiveFactory {
  public void createInitialLayout(IPageLayout layout) {
    layout.setEditorAreaVisible(false);
    layout.addView(ContactsView.ID, IPageLayout.LEFT,
        1.0f, layout.getEditorArea());
  }
}
```

`IPageLayout` contains several methods for defining the layout of a perspective. Everything added to a perspective is related to something else. Here the editor area is used as the base for placing the Contacts view. The Contacts view is added to the left of the editor area and is given all available space in the page by speci-fying 1.0f as the layout ratio. The ratio describes how to divide the available space between the Contacts view and its reference part, in this case, the editor area. The ratio must be between 0.0f (only the title bar is shown) and 1.0f (the view takes up the entire window area).

NOTE

Editors cannot be added to a perspective layout. Instead, you position the area in the perspective in which editors are opened. It's also possible to hide and show the editor area using IWorkbenchPage.setEditorAreaVisible(boolean).

When you run Hyperbola now, you should see the Contacts view, as shown in Figure 5-6.

Figure 5–6   Hyperbola showing the Contacts view

It looks a little strange to have a tab when there is only one view shown, and there is no reason to allow the view to be closed. Views added to a perspective using IPageLayout.addView() inherit various default behaviors that allow them to be moved, undocked, closed, minimized, and maximized. Using IPageLayout.addStandaloneView(), however, adds a *stand-alone view*. Stand-alone views hide the title area, thus preventing the view from being closed, moved, and so forth.

Make the Contacts view stand-alone by changing the code to use addStandalone-View(), as shown here. Notice that the new code is almost identical to the previ-ous except for the Boolean parameter that specifies whether the title area should be hidden. The new Hyperbola looks like Figure 5-7.

```
org.eclipsercp.hyperbola/Perspective
public class Perspective implements IPerspectiveFactory {
  public void createInitialLayout(IPageLayout layout) {
    layout.setEditorAreaVisible(false);
    layout.addView(ContactsView.ID, IPageLayout.LEFT,
        1.0f, layout.getEditorArea());
    layout.addStandaloneView(ContactsView.ID, false,
        IPageLayout.LEFT, 1.0f, layout.getEditorArea());
  }
}
```

When you rerun Hyperbola, you may be surprised. The view still shows a title. The changes you made to the perspective seem to have been ignored. Since we told the Workbench to save settings on shutdown, it saves the perspective layouts in the workspace location and on startup does not consult with the perspective factory at all. IPerspectiveFactory is needed only the first time a perspective is created.

To debug changes to a perspective factory, you must configure your launch configuration to clear the workspace area on each launch. Open the launch configuration dialog as shown in Section 4.3.2, "Launch Configurations," and check the option called **Clear workspace data before launching** and uncheck **Ask for confirmation before clearing**. Rerun Hyperbola. You should see the empty view without a title bar, as shown in Figure 5-7.

Figure 5–7   Hyperbola with the stand-alone Contacts view

5.3 The Chat Model

At this point the Contacts view is empty because there is no underlying list of contacts to show; that is, Hyperbola does not have a model. A model that supports Hyperbola's chat domain will prove helpful as we work through building the application. You could go straight to a messaging library and start implementing the UI pieces on top of its model. But there is a danger that the UI work will get bogged down in the details of sending bytes around. What we really need is a simple chat model that has all the right entities and is sufficient to drive the UI parts of Hyperbola. When it comes time to use a real chat library, some rework will be needed, but we hope not too much.

The Hyperbola chat model shown in Figure 5-8 is very basic. A `Session` comprises the central object. It allows connecting to a messaging server and provides access to contacts, which are either groups or individuals. A `Session` has a reference to the root group for the logged-in user. Listeners can be attached to a `Session` and receive notifications when the root `ContactsGroup` changes.

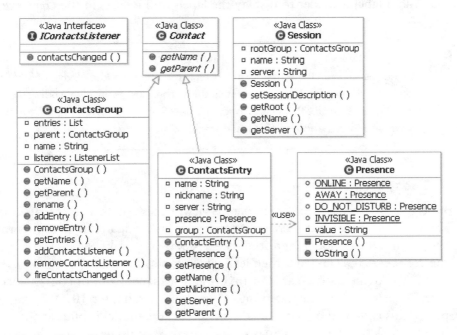

Figure 5–8 Classes in the prototype chat model

You can code the model yourself, or to save time you can copy the code for this chapter using the Samples Manager described in Section 3.4, "Sample Code." Here you want only part of the sample code, so copy just the package called `org.eclipsercp.hyperbola.model` by selecting the package in the top part of the compare editor and selecting **Copy to Workspace** from the context menu.

5.4 Filling in the Contacts View

Now that you have a model, you have something to put in the Contacts view. In the model, contacts are organized into groups of contact entries. A UI for this should be some sort of tree design that allows users to organize their contacts and groups. To help create that UI, this section shows you how to

○ Add a tree viewer to the `ContactsView` class

○ Initialize a `Session` object with test data

○ Add a content provider to populate the tree based on the contents of the contacts list

○ Add a label provider to display the labels and images in the `ContactsView`

NOTE

For the rest of the UI discussion, it is useful to have some knowledge of SWT and JFace. We do not go into great detail about their usage in Hyperbola since we want to focus on RCP-specific concepts. See Section 5.7, "Pointers," for more pointers to information on SWT and JFace.

5.4.1 The `ContactsView`

When the Workbench creates the Contacts view, it calls `createPartControl(Composite)` on the view so that it can create its controls. The code below does two things: It spoofs up a fake model, and it adds a `TreeViewer` to the view. Add the code to the `ContactsView` class and then let's take a look at it.

The fake model is created in `initializeSession()` out of convenience. Once a real chat model is integrated into Hyperbola in Chapter 10, "Messaging Support," this code will be removed. In any event, the model is built and is set as the input to the `TreeViewer`. The `TreeViewer` is also set up as a selection provider so that actions can determine the selection in this view.

org.eclipsercp.hyperbola/ContactsView
```
public class ContactsView extends ViewPart {
  public static final String ID =
      "org.eclipsercp.hyperbola.views.contacts";
  private TreeViewer treeViewer;
  private Session session;

  public ContactsView() {
    super();
  }
```

```
public void createPartControl(Composite parent) {
  initializeSession(); // temporary tweak to build a fake model
  treeViewer = new TreeViewer(parent,
      SWT.BORDER | SWT.MULTI | SWT.V_SCROLL);
  getSite().setSelectionProvider(treeViewer);
  treeViewer.setLabelProvider(new WorkbenchLabelProvider());
  treeViewer.setContentProvider(new BaseWorkbenchContentProvider());
  treeViewer.setInput(session.getRoot());
  session.getRoot().addContactsListener(new IContactsListener() {
    public void contactsChanged(ContactsGroup contacts,
        ContactsEntry entry) {
      treeViewer.refresh();
    }
  });
}

private void initializeSession() {
  session = new Session();
  ContactsGroup root = session.getRoot();
  ContactsGroup friendsGroup = new ContactsGroup(root, "Friends");
  root.addEntry(friendsGroup);
  friendsGroup.addEntry(new ContactsEntry(friendsGroup,
      "Alize", "aliz", "localhost"));
  friendsGroup.addEntry(new ContactsEntry(friendsGroup,
      "Sydney", "syd", "localhost"));
  ContactsGroup otherGroup = new ContactsGroup(root, "Other");
  root.addEntry(otherGroup);
  otherGroup.addEntry(new ContactsEntry(otherGroup,
      "Nadine", "nad", "localhost"));
}

public void setFocus() {
  treeViewer.getControl().setFocus();
}
}
```

TreeViewers do just what their name implies—display tree structures. This is done using two *providers*: the content provider and the label provider. Content providers supply the tree nodes (e.g., parents and children), and the label provider produces human-readable names and representative images for the nodes. TreeViewer .setInput(Object) tells a TreeViewer to build the tree using the supplied object. It is up to the configured content providers to interpret the object and make it look like a tree.

NOTE

Do not confuse views with JFace viewers. It's unfortunate that their names are so similar, but they are two separate concepts. A viewer is a model-based adapter for an SWT widget. A viewer can be used to show content within a view. Moreover, a view can contain multiple viewers, and even editors can contain viewers.

5.4.2 Content Providers Overview

TreeViewers require content providers that implement ITreeContentProvider, as shown below. This allows the viewer to query the structure of its input object using methods such as getChildren(Object) and getParent(Object).

```
org.eclipse.jface/ITreeContentProvider
public interface ITreeContentProvider extends
 IStructuredContentProvider {
  public Object[] getChildren(Object parentElement);
  public Object getParent(Object element);
  public boolean hasChildren(Object element);
}
```

The arguments to these methods are the elements being shown in the viewer. As shown in Figure 5-9, TreeViewer.setInput(Object) is called when ContactsView is created. This in turn uses the configured ITreeContentProvider.getChildren (Object) method to find the first level of elements to display. Notice that this means the root input object for the TreeViewer is never displayed—it provides the starting point from which the visible tree is built. The collaboration between the viewer and the content provider continues as more elements in the tree are expanded.

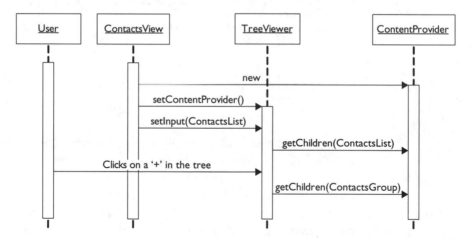

Figure 5–9   Content providers

Figure 5-9 shows how viewers and providers work together, but not how providers and input model objects interact. For example, how does the provider discover the children of a model object? There are several possible techniques:

o Make the model objects implement ITreeContentProvider.

○ Wrap the model objects with another object that an existing `ITreeContentProvider` understands.

○ Supply a customized content provider.

○ Extend the objects with the required provider function.

Adding the provider methods—for example, `getChildren(Object)` and `getParent(Object)`—to `ContactsEntry` and `ContactsGroup` is simple and straightforward. The methods simply expose the inherent structure of the underlying model objects. This approach has the drawback that it pollutes the chat model with UI concerns. It is better to keep the model and UI layers decoupled from one another.

Wrapping chat objects in provider-friendly objects gets around this limitation but introduces the overhead of having two objects for every model object. It also makes identity maintenance, such as equality checks, difficult, as more than one object—the model and the wrapper—can represent the same entity.

`TreeViewers` are customizable and allow you to supply your own content providers. We could simply implement providers that directly access model objects and navigate their object structure. This approach requires control over the providers and is not extensible as all object types handled must be known in advance.

The final approach is to use the Eclipse *adapter* mechanism to extend the behavior of the model objects. The Workbench defines a standard content provider called `BaseWorkbenchContentProvider` that knows how to navigate the `IWorkbenchAdaptable` type shown here:

org.eclipse.ui.workbench/IWorkbenchAdapter
```
public interface IWorkbenchAdapter {
  public Object[] getChildren(Object o);
  public ImageDescriptor getImageDescriptor(Object object);
  public String getLabel(Object o);
  public Object getParent(Object o);
}
```

If an object can adapt to `IWorkbenchAdapter`, it can be shown in a tree viewer using the standard content provider. In fact, objects that adapt to `IWorkbenchAdapters` can be shown in a wide range of viewers. All you have to do to enable this is have the model object implement `IAdaptable` and supply an adapter factory that produces `IWorkbenchAdapters` for the model objects.

5.4.2.1 Adding the `IWorkbenchAdapters`

Let's look at this in more detail. There are four things you have to do to use the adapter technique:

1. Configure the `TreeViewer` to use an instance of `BaseWorkbenchContentProvider` as its content provider.

2. Implement IWorkbenchAdapters for the chat model elements that need to be displayed.

3. Implement an adapter factory that returns an IWorkbenchAdapter for each model element.

4. Register the Hyperbola adapter factory with Eclipse.

The first point was covered in Section 5.4.1, "The ContactsView," when the TreeViewer was created. The HyperbolaAdapterFactory class below covers the next two requirements. It contains inner class implementations of IWorkbenchAdapter for ContactsGroup and ContactsEntry. The adapters do not maintain any state, so the same instances are used for all relevant model objects. When getAdapter(Object, Class) is called, the factory picks an adapter to return.

org.eclipsercp.hyperbola/HyperbolaAdapterFactory

```
public class AdapterFactory implements IAdapterFactory {

    private IWorkbenchAdapter groupAdapter = new IWorkbenchAdapter() {
        public Object getParent(Object o) {
            return ((ContactsGroup)o).getParent();
        }
        public String getLabel(Object o) {
            // to be filled in soon!
            return ((ContactsGroup)o).getName();
        }
        public ImageDescriptor getImageDescriptor(Object object) {
            // to be filled in soon!
            return null;
        }
        public Object[] getChildren(Object o) {
            return ((ContactsGroup)o).getEntries();
        }
    };

    private IWorkbenchAdapter entryAdapter = new IWorkbenchAdapter() {
        public Object getParent(Object o) {
            return ((ContactsEntry)o).getParent();
        }
        public String getLabel(Object o) {
            ContactsEntry entry = ((ContactsEntry)o);
            return entry.getName() + '-' + entry.getServer();
        }
        public ImageDescriptor getImageDescriptor(Object object) {
            // to be filled in soon!
            return null;
        }
        public Object[] getChildren(Object o) {
            return new Object[0];
        }
    };
```

```
public Object getAdapter(Object adaptableObject, Class adapterType) {
    if(adapterType == IWorkbenchAdapter.class &&
        adaptableObject instanceof ContactsGroup)
      return groupAdapter;
    if(adapterType == IWorkbenchAdapter.class &&
        adaptableObject instanceof ContactsEntry)
      return entryAdapter;
    return null;
  }

  public Class[] getAdapterList() {
    return new Class[] {IWorkbenchAdapter.class};
  }
}
```

The last step is to register the adapter factory with Eclipse when the
ContactsView is created and unregister it when the view is closed, as shown here:

org.eclipsercp.hyperbola/ContactsView
```
private IAdapterFactory adapterFactory = new HyperbolaAdapterFactory();

public void createPartControl(Composite parent) {
  treeViewer = new TreeViewer(parent, SWT.BORDER | SWT.MULTI
  Platform.getAdapterManager().
    registerAdapters(adapterFactory, Contact.class);
  ...
}
public void dispose() {
  Platform.getAdapterManager().unregisterAdapters(adapterFactory);
  super.dispose();
}
```

5.4.3 The Label Provider

The content provider gives you the tree structure to display, but not the labels and icons
needed to paint elements on the screen. This is the role of the label provider. When
the ContactsView was created in Section 5.4.1, a default WorkbenchLabelProvider was
configured as the TreeViewer's label provider. Like BaseWorkbenchContentProvider,
it used IWorkbenchAdapters to determine the label and image to show in the tree.

Minimally, you should update the adapter created in the adapter factory to
return the name of the group or contact it adapts. To make things a little more
interesting, the code below defines the label for group names to include the number of logged-in contacts in the group. Update the entry adapter as well, perhaps
to show contacts with a nickname followed by their real name and server. Decorating the entries with images is covered in the next section.

org.eclipsercp.hyperbola/HyperbolaAdapterFactory
```
private IWorkbenchAdapter groupAdapter = new IWorkbenchAdapter() {
  ...
```

```
public String getLabel(Object o) {
  ContactsGroup group = ((ContactsGroup) o);
  int available = 0;
  Contact[] entries = group.getEntries();
  for (int i = 0; i < entries.length; i++) {
    Contact contact = entries[i];
    if (contact instanceof ContactsEntry) {
      if (((ContactsEntry) contact).getPresence()
              != Presence.INVISIBLE)
        available++;
    }
  }
  return group.getName() +
      " (" + available + "/" + entries.length + ")";
}
```

Now Hyperbola is starting to look a bit more interesting, as shown in Figure 5-10.

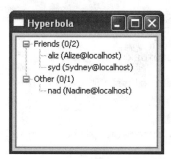

Figure 5–10   Hyperbola showing a mock-up Contacts view

5.5 Adding Images

A contacts list without images doesn't look quite right. Beyond aesthetics, images are useful for showing the status of each contact. In this section we

○ Add images to the Hyperbola plug-in

○ Add images to the Contacts view

The first thing is to create the needed images. Use your favorite image-editing program to create a couple of 16-x-16-pixel images in GIF format. Images used in trees and toolbars usually have a transparent background; as such, use a drawing tool that allows you to create GIF files with transparency. If you aren't much of an artist, copy the images we supplied with the code for this chapter.[1] Table 5-1 shows the images included in the prototype.

---

1. As you can see, we are not artistically inclined, but the images serve their purpose.

Table 5–1 Hyperbola Contacts View Icons

Image	Description
	User is logged in and is available for a chat.
	User is not logged in.
	User is away from the computer. You can chat, but the user may not respond right away.
	User is logged in but doesn't want to be disturbed.
	Groups.

Add the images to the standard Eclipse location in the Hyperbola plug-in—in a directory called icons at the root of the plug-in project. Next, identify the images in code so they can be referenced without having to remember where they are located on disk. A standard approach is to create an interface to track the image paths in your product. Create the IImageKeys interface shown here. The constants identify the relative path to each image in the icons directory.

```
org.eclipsercp.hyperbola/IImageKeys
public interface IImageKeys {
    public static final String ONLINE = "icons/online.gif";
    public static final String OFFLINE = "icons/offline.gif";
    public static final String DO_NOT_DISTURB = "icons/dnd.gif";
    public static final String GROUP = "icons/groups.gif";
    public static final String AWAY = "icons/away.gif";
}
```

Adding images to the Contacts view is easy; you simply update the appropriate IWorkbenchAdapters to provide an image for each item in the tree. In Eclipse there are two image representations: Images and ImageDescriptors.

Images—Images are graphical objects ready to be displayed. They maintain a handle to an underlying OS resource and as such are considered heavyweight objects. Care must be taken to dispose of these system resources when the image is no longer needed.

Image descriptors—Descriptors are lightweight representations of an image. They know where to find the image and can create images but do not do so immediately.

Descriptors are handy tokens you can use to talk about images before you actually need an Image object. The relationship is similar to the one between Java

File and, say, FileInputStream. Files are lightweight and are not directly associated with any OS resources, whereas FileInputStreams retain file handles and trigger disk access.

The code below shows how to create an ImageDescriptor. The code first uses Bundle.getEntry(String) to locate the image file and then calls createFromURL(URL) to create an instance of the descriptor.

```
public ImageDescriptor createImageDescriptorFor(String id) {
    URL url = Platform.getBundle("org.eclipsercp.hyperbola").
        getEntry(id);
    return ImageDescriptor.createFromURL(url);
}
```

Since this is such a common coding pattern, AbstractUIPlugin has a static helper called imageDescriptorFromPlugin(String, String) that looks in all the right places for the requested image and returns a descriptor. This method uses the Bundle instance to access files in the plug-in but does other bookkeeping that allows icons to be loaded from other locations. Since these and other methods need the plug-in's ID, it's a good time to create a constant for it. The ID is defined on the first page of the plug-in editor. Add the following to the Application class:

org.eclipsercp.hyperbola/Application
```
public static final String PLUGIN_ID = "org.eclipsercp.hyperbola";
```

TIP

Since plug-ins can be anywhere and can be in a directory or a JAR, you cannot access your plug-ins' files directly from disk (e.g., using java.io.File). Rather, the Eclipse Runtime provides several convenient methods for accessing files within particular plug-ins. See Bundle.getEntry(String) and related methods.

As we discussed earlier, images need to be managed because they represent OS resources. Fortunately, when using the IWorkbenchAdapter, the Workbench manages the images that are created and all you have to do is return the appropriate image descriptor.

The image shown for a ContactsEntry depends on each user's presence. Add the presenceToKey() method below to HyperbolaAdapterFactory. It should return the appropriate image key given the provided presence.

org.eclipsercp.hyperbola/HyperbolaAdapterFactory
```
private String presenceToKey(Presence presence) {
    if(presence == Presence.ONLINE)
        return IImageKeys.ONLINE;
```

```
    if(presence == Presence.AWAY)
      return IImageKeys.AWAY;
    if(presence == Presence.DO_NOT_DISTURB)
      return IImageKeys.DO_NOT_DISTURB;
    if(presence == Presence.INVISIBLE)
      return IImageKeys.OFFLINE;
    return IImageKeys.OFFLINE;
}
```

Also, change the Workbench adapters to return the image for both a contact group and a contact entry:

org.eclipsercp.hyperbola/HyperbolaAdapterFactory
```
public ImageDescriptor getImageDescriptor(Object object) {
  return AbstractUIPlugin.imageDescriptorFromPlugin(
    Application.PLUGIN_ID, IImageKeys.GROUP);
}
...
public ImageDescriptor getImageDescriptor(Object object) {
  ContactsEntry entry = ((ContactsEntry) object);
  String key = presenceToKey(entry.getPresence());
  return AbstractUIPlugin.imageDescriptorFromPlugin(
    Application.PLUGIN_ID, key);
}
```

Run Hyperbola and notice that the contacts have detailed labels and presence images, as shown in Figure 5-11—the UI is coming together.

Figure 5–11   Hyperbola with images in the Contacts view

5.6 Summary

In this chapter Hyperbola gained a simple model. You added the first view and learned about managing images. You should be getting more comfortable with using the RCP and doing plug-in development with Eclipse. If you were just skimming or had trouble, you can catch up by getting the completed code for this chapter as described in Section 3.4, "Sample Code."

5.7 Pointers

○ For more on perspectives, views, and editors, see Chapter 16.

○ To learn how to customize Workbench windows, see Chapter 19.

○ For customizing views and editors, see Chapter 20.

If you want to learn more about JFace and SWT, here are several good starting points:

○ Northover, Steve, and Mike Wilson. *SWT: The Standard Widget Toolkit*, vol. 1 (Addison-Wesley, 2004), ISBN 0321256638.

○ Clayberg, Eric, and Dan Rubel. *Eclipse Plug-ins*, 3rd ed. (Addison-Wesley, 2009), ISBN 0321553462.

○ Harris, Robert, and Rob Warner. *The Definitive Guide to SWT and JFACE* (Apress, 2004), ISBN 1590593251.

○ Eclipse **Help > Platform Plug-in Developer Guide > Programmer's Guide > Standard Widget Toolkit.**

○ Eclipse **Help > Platform Plug-in Developer Guide > Programmer's Guide > JFace UI Framework.**

○ SWT snippets: *http://eclipse.org/swt/snippets*.

CHAPTER 6

Adding Actions

In Eclipse, the term *action* is used to describe a visible element in an application that allows users to initiate a unit of work. You may notice several terms in Eclipse documentation that are used to describe units of work: *operations*, *actions*, *action delegates*, *commands*, and *jobs*. However, *actions* figure most prominently in RCP applications. The key concept is that when you click a menu or toolbar, or invoke a key sequence, an action is run. It's that simple.

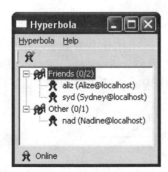

Figure 6–1 Hyperbola with actions and a status line

As you can imagine, actions are essential for most applications. Hyperbola doesn't have any actions yet, so it's difficult to see how the real product will look and feel (see Figure 6-1). In this chapter we show you how to

○ Add a top-level menu and toolbar

○ Add the standard **File > Exit** and **Help > About** actions

○ Create an action to add a contact and show it in the toolbar and menu

○ Add the Hyperbola icon to the task tray

○ Allow Hyperbola to minimize to the task tray

○ Add connection and presence status to the status line

6.1 Adding to the Menus and Toolbar

Actions are everywhere: in toolbars, top-level menus, context menus, status lines, and so on. In most applications the menu and toolbar play a supporting role for the main content area. When running an application for the first time, most users browse the top-level menu structure to find out what the application can do. This makes the top-level menu structure of your application very important.

Take a look at Hyperbola as it is now. Notice that it does not have a top-level menu. Let's fix that. The general pattern for making the toolbar, status line, or menu bar available is to configure the window before it is opened. This is done in `ApplicationWorkbenchWindowAdvisor.preWindowOpen()` by adding a call to methods such as `setShowMenuBar(boolean)`, as shown here:

```
org.eclipsercp.hyperbola/ApplicationWorkbenchWindowAdvisor
public void preWindowOpen() {
   IWorkbenchWindowConfigurer configurer = getWindowConfigurer();
   configurer.setInitialSize(new Point(250, 350));
   configurer.setShowMenuBar(true);
   ...
}
```

You should be familiar with this method—it's what you used to change the size of the window in a previous chapter. The `preWindowOpen()` method is called before the window's controls have been created, and it's the primary place for you to control which `WorkbenchWindow` parts are visible.

NOTE

For more advanced window customizations, refer to Chapter 19, "Customizing Workbench Windows," which explains how to customize the layout of `WorkbenchWindows` and how to let the user toggle the toolbar and status line.

The preceding code *enables* the menu bar but does not force it to be shown. It is shown only if it contains menu items. If you run Hyperbola now, the menu bar does not appear because it's empty.

6.1.1 Create a Top-Level Menu

Now that the top-level menu has been enabled, the next step is to create actions and add them to the menu. RCP applications have a dedicated advisor, called the ActionBarAdvisor, whose job is to create the actions for a window and populate the menu, toolbar, and status line. The ActionBarAdvisor is separate from the WorkbenchWindowAdvisor since an application often has hundreds of actions—this more clearly separates the concerns.

Figure 6-2 shows the call sequence between the WorkbenchWindow, the WorkbenchWindowAdvisor, and the ActionBarAdvisor. Notice that ActionBarAdvisor .makeActions() is called *before* the WorkbenchWindow's controls are created in createWindowContents(). This means that you cannot access any of the window's widgets when creating the actions—you cannot link the actions to any menus or other window parts.

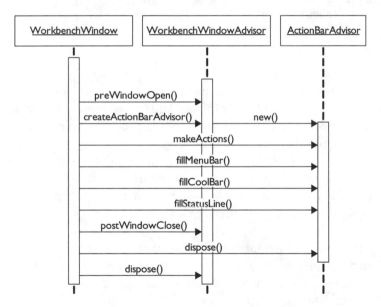

Figure 6–2 ActionBarAdvisor method sequencing

In Hyperbola we need two top-level menus: **Hyperbola** and **Help**. The **Hyperbola** menu should have general application actions and the **Help** menu some higher-level information related to Hyperbola itself (e.g., Help, About information, etc.). For now, let's just add **Exit** and **About** items to these menus.

Figure 6-2 shows that the steps for creating actions, makeActions(), and placing actions, fill*(), are separated. This allows you to create the actions just once and then place the same action objects in several locations, for example, in both the toolbar and a menu. This very useful coding pattern is shown in this code snippet:

```
org.eclipsercp.hyperbola/ApplicationActionBarAdvisor
public class ApplicationActionBarAdvisor extends ActionBarAdvisor {
  private IWorkbenchAction exitAction;
  private IWorkbenchAction aboutAction;
  protected void makeActions(IWorkbenchWindow window) {
    exitAction = ActionFactory.QUIT.create(window);
    register(exitAction);
    aboutAction = ActionFactory.ABOUT.create(window);
    register(aboutAction);
  }
  protected void fillMenuBar(IMenuManager menuBar) {
    MenuManager hyperbolaMenu = new MenuManager(
        "&Hyperbola", "hyperbola");
    hyperbolaMenu.add(exitAction);
    MenuManager helpMenu = new MenuManager("&Help", "help");
    helpMenu.add(aboutAction);
    menuBar.add(hyperbolaMenu);
    menuBar.add(helpMenu);
  }
}
```

When you created the skeleton RCP application, it included an `ActionBarAdvisor` implementation with empty `makeActions()` and `fillMenuBar()` methods. Now, modify the generated code as just shown to get top-level **Hyperbola** and **Help** menus with associated **Exit** and **About** actions.

Notice that `makeActions()` creates each action and saves it in a field. Each action is also *registered*. Registering actions ensures that they are deleted when the related Workbench window is closed—a very important characteristic. Registering actions also enables key bindings, as discussed in Chapter 12, "Adding Key Bindings."

Creating the **Exit** and **About** actions was easy because they already existed. The Workbench defines a set of common actions that are reusable in all RCP applications. Each of these actions is defined as an inner class of `org.eclipse.ui.actions.ActionFactory`. You instantiate them and use them as regular actions. They are preconfigured with a standard name, icon, and ID. The code snippet just shown demonstrates how this is done.

Run Hyperbola now and you should see the top-level menus and the new **Exit** and **About** actions, as shown in Figure 6-4 If you run the **Help > About** action, it displays an empty dialog, as shown in Figure 6-3. The **Installation Details** button shows the list of installed plug-ins. The **Configuration** tab within the **Installation Details** dialog shows information about your environment (e.g., the command-line arguments used to start Hyperbola, system properties, and user preferences).

Figure 6–3 Empty About dialog

Chapter 8, "Branding Hyperbola," shows you how to brand this dialog with an About image and some descriptive text.

NOTE

The **Installation Details** list is very handy for confirming which plug-ins are running as part of your application.

6.1.2 Menu Managers

Earlier, the **Exit** and **About** actions were added to a *menu manager*. A menu manager is responsible for keeping track of actions and submenus and allowing you to create logical structures of actions by grouping. It allows you to organize the actions you want to show without concerning yourself with how the menu is created. For example, the following modified version of the earlier code adds placeholders for actions. The real actions can then be added after the menu manager is created. This flexibility is quite powerful. For example, it lets you create menus that are filled in by other plug-ins.

```
org.eclipsercp.hyperbola/ApplicationActionBarAdvisor
protected void fillMenuBar(IMenuManager menuBar) {
   MenuManager hyperbolaMenu = new MenuManager(
       "&Hyperbola", "hyperbola");
   hyperbolaMenu.add(exitAction);
   hyperbolaMenu.add(new GroupMarker("other-actions"));
   ...
   hyperbolaMenu.appendToGroup("other-actions", aboutAction);
}
```

Menu managers can also be nested. This allows you to create multidimensional action structures such as cascading menus. Let's experiment with menu managers a bit. Change the ActionBarAdvisor with the following code snippet to add a **Help** cascading menu below the top-level **Hyperbola** menu, as shown in Figure 6-4:

```
org.eclipsercp.hyperbola/ApplicationActionBarAdvisor
protected void fillMenuBar(IMenuManager menuBar) {
    MenuManager hyperbolaMenu = new MenuManager(
        "&Hyperbola", "hyperbola");
    hyperbolaMenu.add(exitAction);
    MenuManager helpMenu = new MenuManager("&Help", "help");
    helpMenu.add(aboutAction);
    menuBar.add(hyperbolaMenu);
    hyperbolaMenu.add(helpMenu);
}
```

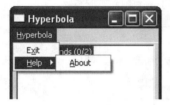

Figure 6–4   Cascading menu example

6.1.3 The Add Contact Action

The **Exit** and **About** actions are generic, so we used predefined actions. Of course, Hyperbola also needs some actions specific to instant messaging. Here we talk about how to

- ❍ Implement an action that adds a contact to the contacts list
- ❍ Ensure that the action is enabled only if a contact group is selected in the Contacts view
- ❍ Add the action to the top-level Hyperbola toolbar

Some actions should be available at all times and are independent of the current state of the application. **Exit** is a good example of this. Other actions should be available only when Hyperbola is in a certain state. For example, the **Add Contact** action you are about to add requires that a contact group be selected. Actions that do not make sense in the current state of Hyperbola should be disabled to indicate that they are not applicable.

First, create the **Add Contact** action as shown below. Don't worry about the compile errors; the missing `run()` and `selectionChanged()` methods are about to be added.

`org.eclipsercp.hyperbola/AddContactAction`
```
public class AddContactsEntryAction extends Action implements
    ISelectionListener, ActionFactory.IWorkbenchAction {
  private final IWorkbenchWindow window;
  public final static String ID =
    "org.eclipsercp.hyperbola.addContact";
  private IStructuredSelection selection;

  public AddContactAction(IWorkbenchWindow window) {
    this.window = window;
    setId(ID);
    setText("&Add Contact...");
    setToolTipText("Add a contact to your contacts list.");
    setImageDescriptor(
        AbstractUIPlugin.imageDescriptorFromPlugin(
        "org.eclipsercp.hyperbola", IImageKeys.ADD_CONTACT));
    window.getSelectionService().addSelectionListener(this);
  }
  public void dispose() {
    window.getSelectionService().removeSelectionListener(this);
  }
  // additional run() and selectionChanged() methods to be added
  // here
  ...
}
```

The constructor for this action is pretty standard; the action is given a name, an icon, a tool tip, and an ID. The ID is used to uniquely identify the action and is used by `ActionBarAdvisor.register(IAction)` to manage the action. The `IImageKeys.ADD_CONTACT` is a new image key that you must define. Alternatively, you can use an existing key just for now or import icons from the final code sample.

TIP

To make the examples clearer, we do not worry about translating the action labels. However, the Eclipse Java IDE comes with a handy wizard that helps *internationalize*, or *externalize*, the strings in your Java code. The tool can be run from **Source > Find Strings to Externalize...**.

The interesting part of the action is around the selection listener. In the constructor, the action is registered as a selection listener. Notice that the action implements `ISelectionListener`. This combination means that when the selection changes in

the window, the action is notified via its `selectionChanged(IWorkbenchPart,`
`ISelection)` method. An implementation of `selectionChanged()` is shown in the
following snippet:

org.eclipsercp.hyperbola/AddContactAction
```
public void selectionChanged(IWorkbenchPart part,
   ISelection incoming) {
   // selection containing elements
   if(incoming instanceof IStructuredSelection) {
     selection = (IStructuredSelection) incoming;
     setEnabled(selection.size() == 1 &&
         selection.getFirstElement() instanceof ContactsGroup);
   } else {
     // other selections (e.g., containing text or of other kinds)
     setEnabled(false);
   }
}
```

The code first checks that the incoming selection is structured. If it is not—
for example, if it's a text selection from an editor or something else—the selection
cannot affect the action's enablement state. If more than one item is selected, it
does not make sense for the user to add a contact, so the action is disabled. If the
incoming selection is structured and contains only one element and that element
is a `ContactsGroup`, the **Add Contact** action is enabled.

Notice that the new selection is remembered by the action so that if it is run,
it knows the group in which to add the new contact. Notice also that it only
makes sense to hang on to the selection if it caused the action to be enabled. All
other cases should make the selection field `null`.

We have not said where these selection events come from. You could bind the
listener to just the Contacts view, but what if there is another view or window that
shows contact groups? When its listener is added to the window's selection service,
the action hears about all selection changes made in that window. You can access a
window's selection service by calling `IWorkbenchWindow.getSelectionService()`.

The selection service doesn't generate selections on its own. For that purpose,
views and editors can register as selection *providers* and essentially publish their
selections to selection listeners. In the current Hyperbola, we expect most contact
group selection events to come from the Contacts view, so the Contacts view
needs to publish its selection events to the window! This needs to be done when
the contents of the Contacts view are created. Take a look at `ContactsView`
`.createContents(Composite)` and look for the line

```
getSite().setSelectionProvider(treeViewer);
```

This registers the `TreeViewer` (i.e., the contents of the Contacts view) as a selection provider.

The summary is that listening to the window instead of directly to a particular event source (e.g., a view) decouples actions from views and allows them to be used in other scenarios.

TIP

Notice that the action also implements `ActionFactory.IWorkbenchAction` and thus the `dispose()` method. When the action is disposed, it is essential that its selection listener be removed from the selection service. Failure to do this is a common cause of memory leaks—double-check to ensure that you always remove any listeners you register.

The action is configured and structured, so now add the `run()` method that does the real work. The code for this is shown below. Note that you can get the code for the dialog in the Samples Manager tool as described in Section 3.4, "Sample Code," or you can use a simple `InputDialog` to prompt for the contact information.

```
org.eclipsercp.hyperbola/AddContactAction
public void run() {
  AddContactDialog d = new AddContactDialog(window.getShell());
  int code = d.open();
  if (code == Window.OK) {
    Object item = selection.getFirstElement();
    ContactsGroup group = (ContactsGroup) item;
    ContactsEntry entry =
        new ContactsEntry(group, d.getNameText(), d.getNickname(),
            d.getServerText());
    group.addEntry(entry);
  }
}
```

The action needs the contact's name, nickname, and host server so it opens a dialog with three entry fields. The entered information is then used to create a `ContactsEntry` and add it to the previously selected group.

6.1.4 Adding the Add Contact Action

Now that you have created the **Add Contact** action, you need to add it to the top-level menu and toolbar. This part is easy since you did the same with the **Exit** and **About** actions. First, ensure that the action is created and registered in `ApplicationActionBarAdvisor.makeActions(IWorkbenchWindow)`. Remember to register the action to ensure that it is deleted when the window is closed. Minimizing a window does not close it; instead, a window is closed when its `Shell.close()` method is called.

```
org.eclipsercp.hyperbola/ApplicationActionBarAdvisor
protected void makeActions(IWorkbenchWindow window) {
    this.window = window;
    exitAction = ActionFactory.QUIT.create(window);
    register(exitAction);
    aboutAction = ActionFactory.ABOUT.create(window);
    register(aboutAction);
    addContactAction = new AddContactAction(window);
    register(addContactAction);
}
```

Update `fillMenuBar(IMenuManager)` and `fillCoolBar(ICoolBarManager)` to add the action to both the menu and toolbar as shown in the `ApplicationActionBar-Advisor` snippet below. Note that managing toolbars and menus is very similar.

NOTE

It's common jargon to refer to the top-level toolbar simply as the *toolbar*. But the methods in the `IWorkbenchWindowConfigurer` refer to it as the *coolbar*. This is an implementation detail that has leaked into the APIs. The toolbar is implemented using an SWT `CoolBar` to support dynamic positioning of its controls. In this chapter we refer to this area as the *top-level toolbar*.

```
org.eclipsercp.hyperbola/ApplicationActionBarAdvisor
protected void fillMenuBar(IMenuManager menuBar) {
    MenuManager hyperbolaMenu =
        new MenuManager("&Hyperbola", "hyperbola");
    hyperbolaMenu.add(addContactAction);
    hyperbolaMenu.add(new Separator());
    hyperbolaMenu.add(exitAction);
    MenuManager helpMenu = new MenuManager("&Help", "help");
    helpMenu.add(aboutAction);
    menuBar.add(hyperbolaMenu);
    menuBar.add(helpMenu);
}

protected void fillCoolBar(ICoolBarManager coolBar) {
    IToolBarManager toolbar = new ToolBarManager(coolBar.getStyle());
    coolBar.add(toolbar);
    toolbar.add(addContactAction);
}
```

Run the application and you should see an icon in the toolbar and an entry for **Add Contact** in the **Hyperbola** top-level menu. If you click the icon, you are prompted for the contact information, and after you click **OK,** the contact is created and appears in the contacts list. Notice that as you click around in the Contacts view, the action changes from enabled to disabled depending on the selection.

6.1.5 Customizable Toolbars

It is quite common for applications to allow customization of the toolbar. The Hyperbola toolbar is implemented in terms of the SWT CoolBar. Each ToolBarManager that is added to the ICoolBarManager is shown in a separate CoolItem group. As such, it can be separately positioned by the user. For example, toolbar managers can be moved onto separate rows or reordered within Hyperbola's toolbar. The Hyperbola in Figure 6-5 has two toolbar managers instead of one. Both managers have the **Add Contact** action. Since they are in separate managers, the actions can be moved independently within the toolbar. Experiment with this by adding the **Add Contact** action to multiple ToolBarManagers.

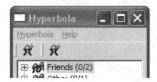

Figure 6–5 Top-level toolbar showing two cool items with the move handle

If you want your actions in the same toolbar group but separated, you can use JFace Separator instances to divide the actions into groups. An update that uses the Separator is shown here:

org.eclipsercp.hyperbola/ApplicationActionBarAdvisor
```
public void populateCoolBar(IActionBarConfigurer configurer) {
  ICoolBarManager mgr = configurer.getCoolBarManager();
  IToolBarManager toolbar = new ToolBarManager(mgr.getStyle());
  mgr.add(toolbar);
  toolbar.add(addContactAction);
  toolbar.add(new Separator());
  toolbar.add(addContactAction);
}
```

6.2 Adding to the Status Line

The status line at the bottom of the Hyberbola window is a great place to show information that is either global to the application or pertinent to the user's current task. Most instant messaging applications place an indicator in the status line to show the user's online status and presence. Since it's somewhat of a standard, Hyperbola should have it, too.

Figure 6-6 shows Hyperbola with an image that indicates whether or not the user is connected to a chat server and some text that indicates the current presence (e.g., available to chat, do not disturb). Eventually we want the icon and text to update automatically as the user's status changes, but for now, let's keep it simple.

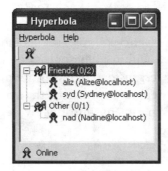

Figure 6–6   Hyperbola with a status line

Remember earlier when you enabled the toolbar and menu in `Application-WorkbenchWindowAdvisor.preWindowOpen()`? Go back there to enable the status line. From within the `preWindowOpen()` method, type `configurer.set` and then press **Ctrl+Space** to see all the setters. Then find the `setShowStatusLine()` method. This is a great use of Eclipse Java IDE's content assist—there are fewer mistakes, there is less to remember, and it's better than cut-and-paste.

org.eclipsercp.hyperbola/ApplicationWorkbenchWindowAdvisor
```
public void preWindowOpen() {
    IWorkbenchWindowConfigurer configurer = getWindowConfigurer();
    configurer.setInitialSize(new Point(250, 350));
    configurer.setShowCoolBar(true);
    configurer.setShowMenuBar(true);
    configurer.setShowStatusLine(true);
    configurer.setTitle("Hyperbola");
}
```

Double-check that this worked by running Hyperbola. The status line should be empty but nonetheless visible. Now you can add the icon and text using the following snippet for `ApplicationWorkbenchWindowAdvisor`. The `statusImage` is a field on the window advisor.

org.eclipsercp.hyperbola/ApplicationWorkbenchWindowAdvisor
```
public void postWindowOpen() {
```

```
    statusImage =
        AbstractUIPlugin.imageDescriptorFromPlugin(
        "org.eclipsercp.hyperbola",
        IImageKeys.ONLINE).createImage();
    IStatusLineManager statusline = getWindowConfigurer().
        getActionBarConfigurer().getStatusLineManager();
    statusline.setMessage(statusImage, "Online");
}
public void dispose() {
    statusImage.dispose();
}
```

Like the menu bar and toolbar, the status line is controlled by the Action-BarAdvisor. You may have noticed the fillStatusLine(IStatusLineManager) method in ActionBarAdvisor. IStatusLineManagers are regular contribution managers similar to IMenuManagers and IToolbarManagers. They include a handful of methods specific to status lines such as getProgressMonitor(), setMessage(Image, String), and setErrorMessage(Image, String).

There is one caveat about these additional methods: They can be called only after the status line's controls have been created. Since ActionBarAdvisor .fillStatusLine() is called before the status line has been created, you can't call these methods in the ActionBarAdvisor. Instead, a good place to set the message, for example, is in the WorkbenchWindowAdvisor.postWindowOpen() method, as shown in the previous snippet.

6.2.1 Status Line—A Shared Resource

As you have seen, it's very easy to add images and messages to the status line. Unfortunately, the status line is a shared resource and can be written to by any plug-in. If your application is small, like Hyperbola, you can simply centralize the use of the status line and avoid conflicts. This is not always feasible.

The status line is also special because it is configured with a predefined layout—the bar contains several reserved areas for standard controls, as shown in Figure 6-7.

Figure 6-7 Status line area breakdown

Fast views—The **Fast Views** area shows views that are removed from the window but can be accessed quickly from an icon docked in the fast view bar. For more information on fast views, consult the online Help.

Icon/message—You just used the **Icon/Message** area to show the user's connection and presence in Hyperbola. Consider this the status line contribution that any part is allowed to make when it has focus.

Progress—The first **Progress** area is used for showing modal progress. It is normally invisible until an `IWorkbenchWindow.run()` operation is invoked. When the operation is running, a progress indicator and **Cancel** button are made visible.

Contributions—The **Contributions** area is reserved for the Workbench advisor and active part contributions.

Jobs progress—The **Jobs Progress** area is hidden by default but can be enabled by calling `IWorkbenchWindowConfigurator.setShowProgressIndicator(boolean)`. See Sections 14.5, "Updating Hyperbola," and 17.8, "Reporting Progress," for more details.

Since the layout is somewhat fixed, it is not possible to left-align additional contributions to the status line—the reserved areas for the other items get in the way. However, when the **Jobs Progress** area is not shown, user contributions are right-aligned. You can make additions to the status line using `IStatusLineManager.add(IContributionItem)`.

In any event, there are many uses of the status line, and directly setting the **Icon/Message** area is very effective. For more advanced status line uses, see Section 17.7, "Adding Contributions to the Status Line."

6.3 System Tray Integration

Another common feature of instant messaging applications is integration into the system tray. Using this idea, we want Hyperbola to appear in the system tray as an icon representing the user's presence. This also allows Hyperbola to minimize to the system tray rather than continuing to be displayed in the task bar even though it is minimized. The tray items are also a popular location for adding actions related to your application. Figure 6-8 shows how this looks for Hyperbola.

Figure 6–8   Context menu on the Hyperbola task tray item

TIP

If you are going to use the system tray, it is good practice to make its use optional—if every application put itself in the system tray, it would get cluttered. When it is enabled, it should be used to display important status information to the user and provide a quick access point for running frequent actions.

Also, the system tray is not available on all platforms, so do not make it the focal point of your application's workflow. It should be used as an optional integration feature.

In this section we show you how to

○ Add the Hyperbola icon to the task tray

○ Allow Hyperbola to minimize to the task tray

○ Add the **About** and **Exit** actions to the context menu of the task tray item

6.3.1 Obtaining a Display

To get the system tray, you need a `Display`. A `Display` is an SWT object that represents the underlying graphics system. Typically, the `Display` is created before the Workbench is created via a call to `PlatformUI.createDisplay()`. Figure 6-9 shows the `WorkbenchWindow` lifecycle and highlights where the `Display` is available.

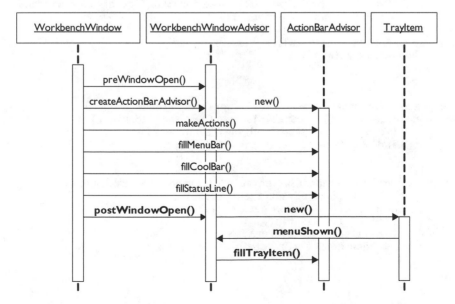

Figure 6–9 How the `ActionBarAdvisor` contributes actions to the task item

So, the first time a window is opened, the workbenchWindowAdvisor can get the Display via the window's shell and set up the system tray for Hyperbola. At this point the tray item is created and configured so that when its menu is shown, the ActionBarAdvisor populates the menu.

TIP

In any of the advisors, you can use IWorkbench.getDisplay() to get a valid display even before the windows are created.

6.3.2 Creating the Tray Item

The code snippet below from ApplicationWorkbenchWindowAdvisor shows how the system tray item is created and how it operates. First, the item is created and configured, and then listeners are added to support showing the menu and minimizing into the tray item. After the tray item is set up, a menu listener is added to it. That way, when the tray item is right-clicked, a context menu appears and is populated by the ActionBarAdvisor. Some platforms do not have system trays and initTaskItem() may return null. In that case the tray item is not created.

```
org.eclipsercp.hyperbola/ApplicationWorkbenchWindowAdvisor
public void postWindowOpen() {
  initStatusLine();
  final IWorkbenchWindow window = getWindowConfigurer().getWindow();
  trayItem = initTaskItem(window);
  if (trayItem != null) {
    hookPopupMenu(window);
    hookMinimize(window);
  }
}

private void hookMinimize(final IWorkbenchWindow window) {
  window.getShell().addShellListener(new ShellAdapter() {
    public void shellIconified(ShellEvent e) {
      window.getShell().setVisible(false);
    }
  });
  trayItem.addListener(SWT.DefaultSelection, new Listener() {
    public void handleEvent(Event event) {
      Shell shell = window.getShell();
      if (!shell.isVisible()) {
        shell.setVisible(true);
        window.getShell().setMinimized(false);
      }
    }
  });
}
```

```
private void hookPopupMenu(final IWorkbenchWindow window) {
    // Add listener for menu pop-up.
    trayItem.addListener(SWT.MenuDetect, new Listener() {
        public void handleEvent(Event event) {
            MenuManager trayMenu = new MenuManager();
            Menu menu = trayMenu.createContextMenu(window.getShell());
            actionBarAdvisor.fillTrayItem(trayMenu);
            menu.setVisible(true);
        }
    });
}

private TrayItem initTaskItem(IWorkbenchWindow window) {
    final Tray tray = window.getShell().getDisplay().getSystemTray();
    if (tray == null)
        return null;
    TrayItem trayItem = new TrayItem(tray, SWT.NONE);
    trayImage = AbstractUIPlugin.imageDescriptorFromPlugin(
        "org.eclipsercp.hyperbola", IImageKeys.ONLINE).createImage();
    trayItem.setImage(trayImage);
    trayItem.setToolTipText("Hyperbola");
    return trayItem;
}

public void dispose() {
    if(trayImage != null) {
        trayImage.dispose();
        trayItem.dispose();
    }
}
```

NOTE

The image and tray item area are saved as fields on the WorkbenchWindowAdvisor
so that they can be deleted when the window is closed.

Since the ActionBarAdvisor already manages all of Hyperbola's actions, it is
a good place to put the method that fills the system tray item's menu. This also
allows the tray item menu to reuse actions created in the ActionBarAdvisor. Add
the following snippet to ApplicationActionBarAdvisor:

org.eclipsercp.hyperbola/ApplicationActionBarAdvisor
```
protected void fillTrayItem(IMenuManager trayItem) {
    trayItem.add(aboutAction);
    trayItem.add(exitAction);
}
```

A shell listener is added in the hookMinimize() method to the window so that
the window is marked as hidden when minimized. This simulates minimizing the

window into the task bar. When the window is invisible, the only indication that Hyperbola is running is the system tray icon.

Another listener, also added in the `hookMinimize()` method, listens to the tray item to detect when it is selected. Selecting the task item is the cue that Hyperbola's window should be made visible if it had previously been minimized.

After setting this up, run Hyperbola and look for the system tray icon. Right-click it and the context menu appears. Minimize Hyperbola and notice that Hyperbola is completely gone except for the task tray icon. Click the tray icon and Hyperbola reappears.

6.4 Summary

There you have it—Hyperbola now has a minimal set of actions and some more advanced desktop integration. As we mentioned at the outset, actions are one of the key elements of building RCP applications. There are many ways actions can be used and placed in the Workbench. With the information in this chapter you are well on your way to mastering action definition and placement.

But What about Commands and Declarative Actions?

If you have some Eclipse plug-in development experience, you may be asking yourself why we haven't mentioned commands because you heard somewhere that actions were deprecated. As of Eclipse 3.5, actions aren't deprecated and they appear in many Eclipse applications still. Furthermore, in the context of a single small application, actions are easier to start with. In Chapter 12, "Adding Key Bindings," commands will be briefly introduced when adding key bindings to Hyperbola. In Chapter 18, "Commands," commands will be covered in depth along with the difference between actions and commands.

You may also be asking yourself why we have not used any of the Workbench's extension points for defining actions. After all, Eclipse is all about declarative contributions. This is a common question—when should an RCP application use the declarative Workbench extension points as opposed to simply creating the actions programmatically as in Hyperbola? In the context of a single small application, there is usually no need to use the extension point approach. In fact, an RCP application must minimally define a top-level menu structure using programmatic actions because without this, there would be no place to contribute actions declaratively.

However, there are advantages to using declarative actions. These are detailed later in the book but summarized here:

- They allow lazy loading of plug-ins by being shown in the UI without loading their associated plug-in. In large applications with many plug-ins this is very important.
- Declarative actions can be associated with perspectives and easily allow dynamic reconfiguration of top-level menus and toolbars based on the active perspective.
- They allow users to configure top-level menus and toolbars via the perspective customization dialog (refer to the `ActionFactory.EDIT_ACTION_SETS`).
- Declarative action contributions can be filtered out using *capabilities*.

Refer to Chapter 17, "Actions," and Chapter 18, "Commands," for examples of how to use declarative-style actions or commands in Hyperbola. Programmatic actions are used for the remainder of the Hyperbola tutorial for simplicity.

6.5 Pointers

This book contains many other action-related sections; if you are eager to learn more, you can skip ahead to any of these sections:

- To understand the differences between actions and commands, see Chapter 18.
- Adding key bindings to actions is discussed in Chapter 12.
- Mastering programmatic and declarative actions is covered in Section 17.2.
- For how to show progress for long-running actions, see Section 17.8.

CHAPTER 7

Adding a Chat Editor

Hyperbola is taking shape. Now you can pretty much define and manage users as well as track your status and integrate Hyperbola with the desktop. The only major item left is the chat area itself. Figure 7-1 shows the UI you are about to add. It's composed of a transcript area at the top and an input area at the bottom. Notice that unlike the Contacts view, the chat area is closable and has a title.

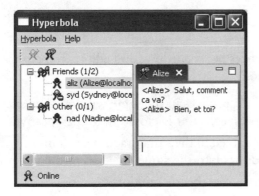

Figure 7–1 Chatting with Hyperbola

In this chapter we show you

❍ The difference between a view and an editor

❍ How to create a chat editor

❍ How to create an action that opens an editor

7.1 Views and Editors

Before getting into the details of how to create the chat editor, let's step back a bit and consider whether it should be a view or an editor. When you created the Contacts view in Chapter 5, "Starting the Hyperbola Prototype," we mentioned that views and editors contain the "real content" of your application. But how do you choose which one to use?

The rule of thumb is that editors are meant for the primary focus of attention while views provide supporting information for a given task. So, in Hyperbola, chatting is the primary task and browsing or managing contacts is a supporting function. This indicates that the Hyperbola chat area should be implemented as an editor.

Not all decisions are quite that clear-cut, however. Even the choice made here has been hotly discussed by the Hyperbola development team. It is, of course, technically possible to use a view to represent a unique chat instead of using the chat editor (an excellent exercise for the reader).

NOTE

The sample code for Chapter 23, "RCP Everywhere," shows how to display a chat in a window and in an editor.

Here is a short list of differences between views and editors to help you decide which to use for your application:

○ Editors are shared between perspectives in the same window. For example, if you close an editor in one perspective, it is closed in all perspectives.

○ Editors and views cannot be mixed in the same stack. For example, you can't drag and drop views and editors into the same location in the perspective.

○ Views can be detached from a Workbench window.

○ Views can be shown without a title.

○ Editors add contributions to the main toolbar and menu whereas views add contributions to their local toolbar and menu. You can, however, associate action sets to appear when a view is active.

○ It is possible to ask for the active editor even if the editor does not have focus. This makes it easier to synchronize views with editors, for example, linking outline-style views to the current editor.

7.2 Defining the Chat Editor

The first step in adding the chat editor is defining the editor extension. As we saw with the Contacts view in Chapter 5, first you define an extension, then you implement the class identified in the extension. Start by opening the Hyperbola plug-in editor and from the **Extensions** page click **Add....** Select the org.eclipse.ui.editors extension point from the list and click **OK**. This adds the extension point to the **All Extensions** list so that you can contribute extensions.

Next, right-click on the added org.eclipse.ui.editors item in the **All Extensions** list, and from the context menu select **New > Editor**. On the right side of the plug-in editor the details of the new extension are shown, as in Figure 7-2. Fill in the **id**, **name**, and **icon** fields.

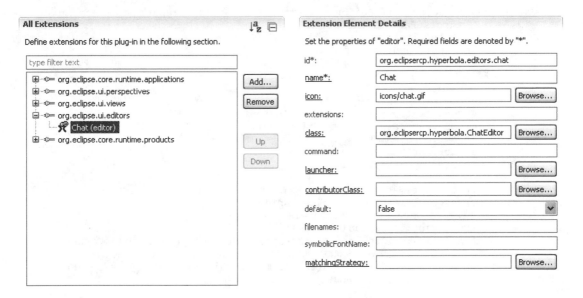

Figure 7–2   Adding the editor extension point to plugin.xml

The **class** field references a class that implements the chat editor. A trick for creating the class is to click on the **class** hyperlink in the plug-in editor. This launches the **New Class** wizard primed with the correct superclass (EditorPart) and various other settings. Enter the class name ChatEditor and click **Finish** to create the skeleton code for the editor. The generated skeleton will contain many TODOs. Browse the file to get a feel for the methods that need to be implemented.

Now let's look at each method individually and see how you should fill in the code. Keep in mind that any method we do not mention can be left as is. As

usual, it's good to define a constant to track the ID for the editor; this is the same
ID as defined in the editor extension. The first thing the editor needs to do is create the UI elements, such as the transcript area where the chat text appears and
the text entry area. The remainder of the editor code handles key presses and
transferring text to the transcript area from the entry area.

org.eclipsercp.hyperbola/ChatEditor

```
public class ChatEditor extends EditorPart {
  public static String ID = "org.eclipsercp.hyperbola.editors.chat";
  private Text transcript;
  private Text entry;

  // Always need a no-arg constructor.
  public ChatEditor() {
  }

  public void init(IEditorSite site, IEditorInput input)
      throws PartInitException {
    setSite(site);
    setInput(input);
    setPartName(getUser());
  }

  public void createPartControl(Composite parent) {
    Composite top = new Composite(parent, SWT.NONE);
    GridLayout layout = new GridLayout();
    layout.marginWidth = 0;
    layout.marginHeight = 0;
    top.setLayout(layout);

    transcript = new Text(top, SWT.BORDER | SWT.MULTI | SWT.WRAP);
    transcript.setLayoutData(new GridData(
        GridData.FILL, GridData.FILL, true, true));
    transcript.setEditable(false);
    transcript.setBackground(transcript.getDisplay().getSystemColor(
        SWT.COLOR_INFO_BACKGROUND));
    transcript.setForeground(transcript.getDisplay().getSystemColor(
        SWT.COLOR_INFO_FOREGROUND));

    entry = new Text(top, SWT.BORDER | SWT.WRAP);
    GridData gridData = new GridData(
        GridData.FILL, GridData.FILL, true, false);
    gridData.heightHint = entry.getLineHeight() * 2;
    entry.setLayoutData(gridData);
    entry.addKeyListener(new KeyAdapter() {
      public void keyPressed(KeyEvent event) {
        if (event.character == SWT.CR) {
          sendMessage();
          // Ignore the CR and don't add to text control.
          event.doit = false;
        }
      }
    });
  }
```

```
  public void setFocus() {
    if (entry != null && !entry.isDisposed()) {
      entry.setFocus();
    }
  }

  private String getUser() {
    return ((ChatEditorInput) getEditorInput()).getName();
  }

  private String renderMessage(String from, String body) {
    if (from == null)
      return body;
    int j = from.indexOf('@');
    if (j > 0)
      from = from.substring(0, j);
    return "<" + from + ">  " + body;
  }

  private void scrollToEnd() {
    int n = transcript.getCharCount();
    transcript.setSelection(n, n);
    transcript.showSelection();
  }

  private void sendMessage() {
    String body = entry.getText();
    if (body.length() == 0)
      return;
    transcript.append(renderMessage(getUser(), body));
    transcript.append("\n");
    scrollToEnd();
    entry.setText("");
  }
}
```

Editors need an IEditorInput before they can be opened. Editor inputs are a
lightweight description of the initialization information the editor uses to decide
what to show. The chat editor expects a ChatEditorInput that contains the user
name of the person at the other end of the chat. For now, just assume that a
ChatEditorInput exists while we continue reviewing the code for the editor. The
next section shows how to create the ChatEditorInput.

NOTE

In the real code, several methods are needed to support the **Save** and **Save As**
workflows. These are not shown here. You can simply use the defaults because
you won't need to save a chat when Hyperbola exits.

Editor implementations follow a common pattern that starts when `EditorPart`
`.createPartControl()` is called and the editor can create its widgets. `ChatEditor`
`.createPartControl(Composite)` creates two text fields: one that contains the
chat transcript and another to allow the user to enter and send messages.

In addition to creating the editor's widgets, an editor can update its title using
`EditorPart.setPartName()`. Even though a title was specified in the extension
description, it can be changed at any time. The last detail in the `ChatEditor` is a
constant called `ID`. This is the editor ID as defined in the editor extension and is
used to programmatically refer to this editor. This is going to be particularly useful when it comes time to write the action to show the editor.

The Life of an Editor

The general lifecycle of an editor is as follows:

○ The Workbench instantiates the editor, creates an editor site, then calls
`EditorPart.init(IEditorSite, IEditorInput)`. The editor site allows the
editor to access the Workbench's services. It is important that the editor class
have a public default constructor. The Workbench uses this to instantiate the
editor.

○ When the editor is made visible, the method `EditorPart.createControl`
`(Composite)` is called to create the editor's widgets.

○ Once the editor is created, the method `EditorPart.setFocus()` is called.

○ When the editor is closed, if the contents need to be saved, the method
`EditorPart.doSave(IProgressMonitor)` is called.

○ At the end of the editor lifecycle, the method `EditorPart.dispose()` is
called.

In addition to the temporal relationship between editors and the Workbench,
editors refer to and access parts of the Workbench. Figure 7-3 shows the key
characteristic that an `EditorPart` relates to the `WorkbenchWindow` via its site
(`IWorkbenchPartSite`). The site is the context that the editor uses to access the
Workbench and various Workbench services such as key bindings, the selection
service, and their action bars.

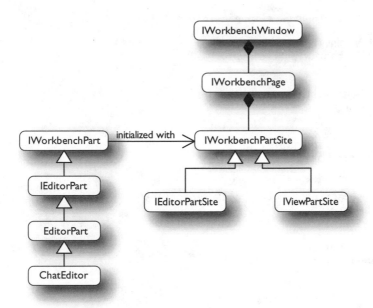

Figure 7–3 The chat editor in context

7.2.1 Editor Input

All editors are opened with an `IEditorInput` via the `IWorkbenchPage`, as shown below. We are going to add the action to open the editor in a bit, but for now we need a specific implementation of `IEditorInput`, to be called `ChatEditorInput`, so that Hyperbola can tell which editor it's talking to.

```
IWorkbenchPage.openEditor(IEditorInput input, String editorId)
```

The editor input is the model for the editor. Editor inputs are both initialization data for the editor, telling it what to show, and identification information for the Workbench, telling it which inputs have open editors. The latter point allows the Workbench to decide if an editor is already open for an input and to show it instead of opening a new one.

Create the `ChatEditorInput` as shown below. Most of the code here is bookkeeping. This editor input maintains a `participant`, the other person in the chat, and returns that value to identify the chat to be edited.

org.eclipsercp.hyperbola/ChatEditorInput
```
public class ChatEditorInput implements IEditorInput {
    private String participant;
```

```
public ChatEditorInput(String participant) {
  super();
  Assert.isNotNull(participant);
  this.participant = participant;
}

public boolean exists() {
  return false;
}

public String getToolTipText() {
  return participant;
}

public ImageDescriptor getImageDescriptor() {
  return null;
}

public String getName() {
  return participant;
}

public IPersistableElement getPersistable() {
  return null;
}

public boolean equals(Object obj) {
  if (super.equals(obj)) return true;
  if (!(obj instanceof ChatEditorInput))
    return false;
  ChatEditorInput other = (ChatEditorInput) obj;
  return participant.equals(other.participant);
}

public int hashCode() {
  return participant.hashCode();
}
}
```

7.2.2 The Chat Action

At this point the editor has been defined, but if you run Hyperbola, the ChatEditor cannot be shown. Editors are not opened automatically in a perspective but rather as the direct result of a user action. You need a ChatAction that initiates a chat based on the contact selected by the user. Use the **New Class** wizard to create a class named ChatAction, as shown in Figure 7-4. The action implements the ISelectionListener to track the selection to calculate enablement. It also implements IWorkbenchAction to make it disposable.

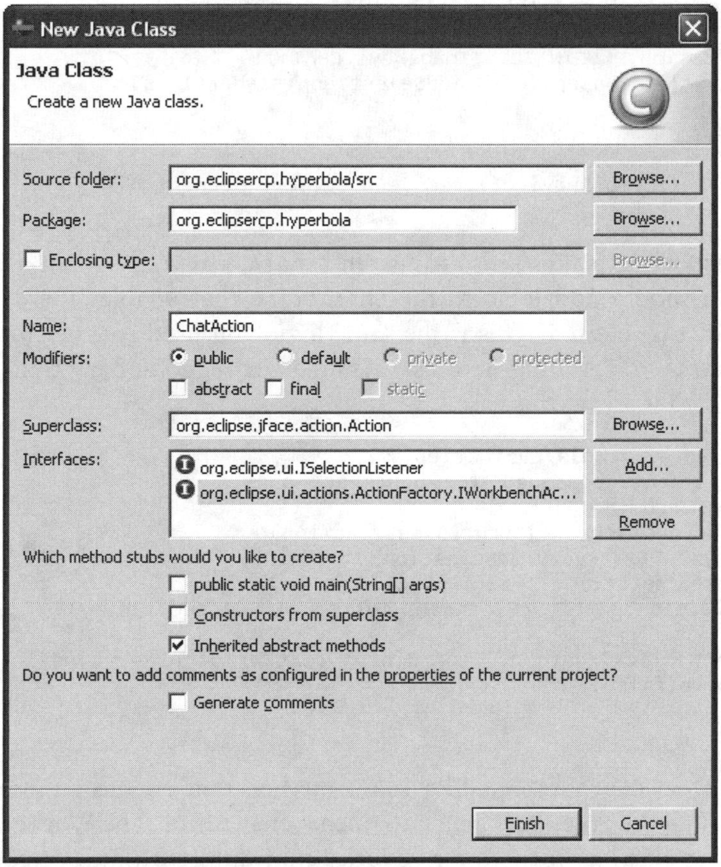

Figure 7–4 New Class wizard for creating the ChatAction

Once the skeleton action has been generated, add a constructor and a couple of instance variables to track the selection and window. This is almost identical to the AddContactAction you created in the previous chapter.

org.eclipsercp.hyperbola/ChatAction

```
public class ChatAction extends Action implements ISelectionListener,
    IWorkbenchAction {

private final IWorkbenchWindow window;
public final static String ID = "org.eclipsercp.hyperbola.chat";
private IStructuredSelection selection;

public ChatAction(IWorkbenchWindow window) {
  this.window = window;
  setId(ID);
  setText("&Chat");
```

```
    setToolTipText("Chat with the selected contact.");
    setImageDescriptor(AbstractUIPlugin.imageDescriptorFromPlugin(
        Application.PLUGIN_ID, IImageKeys.CHAT));
    window.getSelectionService().addSelectionListener(this);
}

public void dispose() {
    window.getSelectionService().removeSelectionListener(this);
}
```

In Hyperbola, it makes sense to use the ChatAction only when a contact is selected. You should add logic to the ChatAction that enables the action only when a contact is selected. This is the same logic you used for the **Add Contact** action in Chapter 6, "Adding Actions." As an exercise, go and get that code now and update it to work in this case.

org.eclipsercp.hyperbola/ChatAction
```
public void selectionChanged(IWorkbenchPart part,
    ISelection incoming) {
    if(incoming instanceof IStructuredSelection) {
        selection = (IStructuredSelection) incoming;
        setEnabled(selection.size() == 1 &&
            selection.getFirstElement() instanceof ContactsEntry);
    } else {
        // other selections(e.g., containing text or of other kinds)
        setEnabled(false);
    }
}
```

To round out ChatAction, add a run() method that creates an input for the selected user and asks the Workbench to open a chat editor. The Workbench takes care of finding existing open editors. Notice that different kinds of editors, like different kinds of views, are referenced by their IDs. This ID is the one you defined in the org.eclipse.ui.editors extension. It was also defined as a constant on the ChatEditor.

org.eclipsercp.hyperbola/ChatAction
```
public void run() {
    Object item = selection.getFirstElement();
    ContactsEntry entry = (ContactsEntry) item;
    IWorkbenchPage page = window.getActivePage();
    ChatEditorInput input = new ChatEditorInput(entry.getName());
    try {
        page.openEditor(input, ChatEditor.ID);
    } catch (PartInitException e) {
        // Handle error.
    }
}
```

The final step is to add the new action to the Hyperbola menu and toolbar. By now you have done this three or four times, so we leave it as an exercise for you.

Hint: Update the methods `makeActions()`, `fillMenuBar()`, and `fillCoolBar()` in the class `ApplicationActionBarAdvisor`.

7.3 Checkpoint

Now is a good time to run Hyperbola. Select a contact in the Contacts view and run the **Chat** action. A chat editor should open as shown in Figure 7-1. Notice that the chat editor is rather narrow. Even if you make the window bigger, the chat editor stays skinny. Remember all the way back to Chapter 5, when you defined the Hyperbola perspective? There we were not concerned about the editor area and we wanted the Contacts view to take up the whole window.

To fix this, first increase the default size of the Hyperbola window—we need more room now. Go to the `ApplicationWorkbenchWindowAdvisor`'s method `preWindowOpen()` and change the initial size of the window. The user can ultimately decide on the size of the window and all the views and editors, but it's always good to provide a good default layout.

Next, go to the `Perspective` class and change it to show the editor area. While you are there, shrink the relative size of the Contacts view by changing the ratio to .50f. These changes are shown here:

org.eclipsercp.hyperbola/Perspective
```
public void createInitialLayout(IPageLayout layout) {
   layout.setEditorAreaVisible(false);
   layout.setEditorAreaVisible(true);
   layout.addStandaloneView(ContactsView.ID, false,
       IPageLayout.LEFT, .50f, layout.getEditorArea());
}
```

The result of these changes is shown in Figure 7-5. The editor area is empty but shown, and the Contacts view takes up 50 percent of the page width.

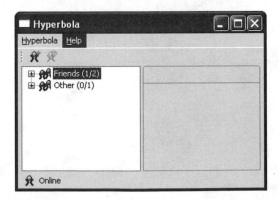

Figure 7–5 Hyperbola with the editor area shown

If you want to get fancy, you can show and hide the editor area automatically by adding an action that uses `IPartListeners` to listen for editors closing and then hides the area when the last editor is closed using `IWorkbenchPage.setEditor-AreaVisible(boolean)`.

7.4 Summary

You now have a running prototype of Hyperbola. Hyperbola is taking shape and is already far enough along to give people an idea of the end product and what is involved in making RCP applications. Along the way, you have become familiar with RCP and plug-in development in the Eclipse IDE.

The next chapters step back from the code and brand Hyperbola with a splash screen, custom executable, and icons to get it ready for shipping.

7.5 Pointers

○ For more on creating multiple instance views, see Section 16.2.1.

○ Drag and drop into the editor area is covered in Section 16.4.

○ Refer to Chapter 20 on customizing the look and feel of views and editors.

CHAPTER 8

Branding Hyperbola

Hyperbola is looking pretty good at this point—you can add contacts, initiate chats, and exercise the UI. Hyperbola shows images for the various online states, has actions in all the right places, and puts forward the look and feel we want. The people around you are in awe. But it still does not feel like a normal application—it is missing the splash screen, the images in the window title bar, a branded launcher, and other elements. We'll take care of that here. More generally, the goals of this chapter are to

○ Detail the branding for Hyperbola

○ Show how product configurations are created

○ Enumerate the various aspects of Eclipse product branding and how to configure them

○ Create a fully branded Hyperbola product

8.1 Defining the Hyperbola Product

Before you can do any branding or packaging of Hyperbola, you must define a *product configuration*. Product configurations gather all the information about splash screens, launcher icons, window images, About text, plug-in and feature lists, and so on into one place. Select the `org.eclipsercp.hyperbola` project and, if you are in the **Plug-in Development** perspective, use **File > New > Product Configuration** to start the **New Product Configuration** wizard as shown in Figure 8-1. Otherwise, use **File > New > Other... > Plug-in Development > Product Configuration**.

In the wizard, pick a location for the product configuration. The configuration file can go in any project associated with the product, but so far we have only one

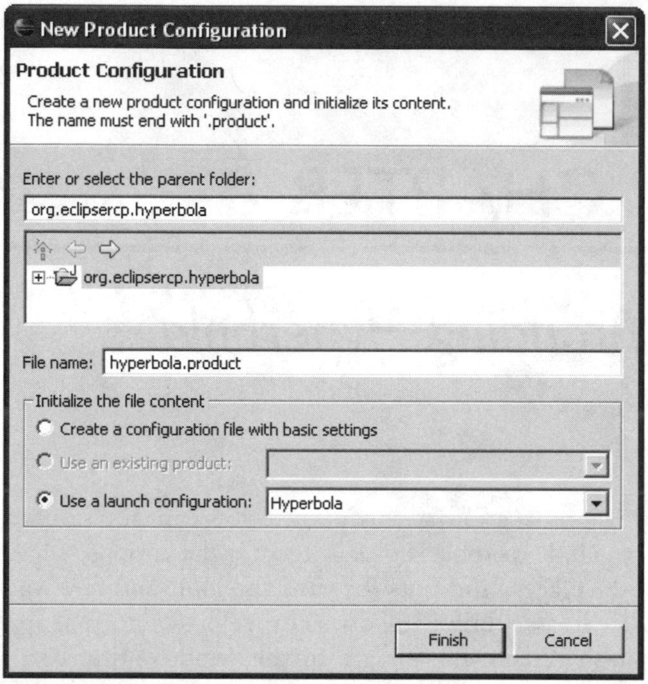

Figure 8–1   New Product Configuration wizard

project, so there's not much choice. Now give it a file name such as hyperbola
.product. The configuration file name must end in .product.

Next, choose a technique for initializing the configuration. The wizard can extract
information from an existing product or launch configuration or simply create a
basic product. If you have been following along, you already have a launch configuration called "Hyperbola" or "Eclipse Application." The currently defined configurations are listed in the **Use an existing launch configuration** drop-down. Enable
this option and pick a configuration you have already used and you know works.

NOTE

If you don't have a suitable launch configuration, launch Hyperbola by opening the
Hyperbola plug-in editor and clicking on one of the **Launch** links in the **Testing**
section of the **Overview** page. Then continue creating the product configuration.

When you click **Finish,** the wizard reads the launch configuration and uses it
to build a product definition. In particular, it gets the list of plug-ins and the ID

of the application extension used in the launch. The new product configuration is opened in an editor, as shown in Figure 8-2.

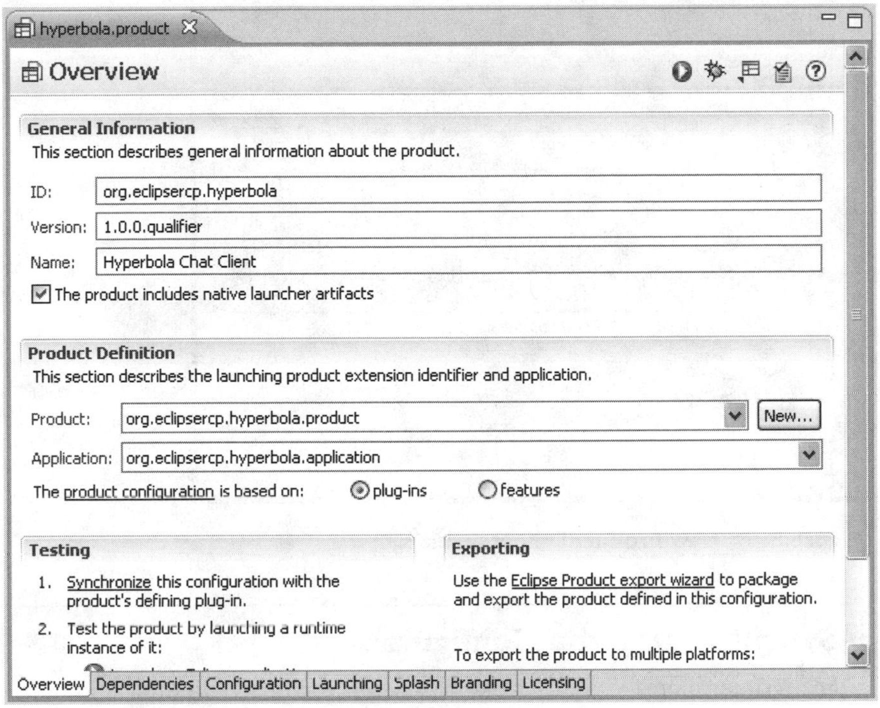

Figure 8–2 Hyperbola product overview

As with the plug-in editor, the product configuration editor gathers together information from many different files and presents it all in one place. The configuration information is grouped onto several tabs within the editor. The **Overview** page in Figure 8-2 shows the **Product Definition** section.

Here you specify the **ID**, the **Version**, and the **Name** of the product. Furthermore, you specify the **Product** and **Application** identifiers. You need a product definition and ID to tell Eclipse how to brand your application, so click **New...** to get the **New Product Definition** dialog shown in Figure 8-3.

As with applications, product extensions are contributed via extensions. They have an ID and identify the application to run when the product is run. Choose the Hyperbola plug-in and type product in the **Product ID** field. The Hyperbola application should already be selected, but it's worth checking. Click **Finish** to return to the product editor. The new product and application values show up on the **Overview** page.

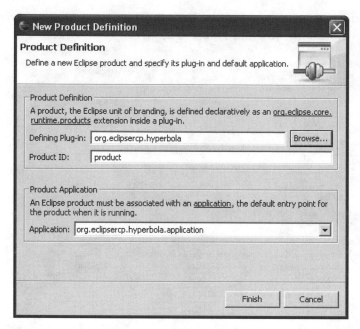

Figure 8–3   **New Product Definition** dialog

Synchronizing the Configuration

From time to time you may make changes in the product editor and then try them out only to find that they did not take effect. It is likely that the product configuration and its constituent files are not synchronized. As we mentioned at the outset, a product configuration is really an amalgam of information found in various files in the system. For example, the product extension is defined in the product plug-in's `plugin.xml` file. The application may be found in the same file or somewhere else. The information on the **Configuration** page may be found in the `config.ini` file or the product launcher's `.ini` file. Some of the branding information is stored in the product extension in the defining plug-in.

The product editor gives you the ability to explicitly synchronize the product configuration with the files it encompasses. The **Testing** section on the **Overview** page has a link that offers to **Synchronize** this configuration with the product's defining plug-in. You should click on this when you change the configuration.

PDE automatically synchronizes the configuration when you use the **Launch** links in the **Testing** section of the **Overview** page to run the product.

You still need to fill in the **Product Name**, Hyperbola Chat Client. This is the string that appears in the title bar of the Hyperbola windows. **Launch** the product using the links in the **Testing** section of the **Overview** page. Hyperbola should now look something like Figure 8-4.

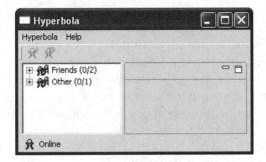

Figure 8–4 Ignored window title branding

Notice that the title bar of the window still says "Hyperbola." It should be "Hyperbola Chat Client" as you entered in the product configuration editor. Where's that coming from? Remember all the way back to Chapter 4, "The Hyperbola Application," when you first generated Hyperbola from the template? You entered "Hyperbola" in the template wizard and the string was embedded in the code snippet:

```
org.eclipsercp.hyperbola/ApplicationWorkbenchWindowAdvisor
configurer.setTitle("Hyperbola");
```

Go back and delete the setTitle() call and then run the application again. Figure 8-5 shows Hyperbola with a properly branded title bar label.

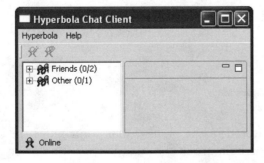

Figure 8–5 Good window title branding

You may not have noticed, but launching the product caused a new launch configuration to be created. Open up the launch configuration dialog (**Run > Run...**) and take a look at the list. There is Hyperbola, which you used as a base for the product configuration, and a new one called hyperbola.product (assuming that is the name you used for your product configuration file). The product editor uses this new configuration to launch your product. Since it is a normal launch configuration, you can run or debug it directly and use keyboard shortcuts such as **F11** to debug the last launched configuration.

PDE keeps the launch configuration and product configuration synchronized. If you change the list of plug-ins in the product configuration and save, the launch configuration is updated. This relationship is one-way—launching from or changing the launch configuration does not trigger any synchronization of the product configuration.

8.2 Window Images

Now that Hyperbola has a product configuration and the window title is set correctly, the next step is to add the graphical branding cues such as the splash screen, images, and icons. The next few sections go over each element of product branding.

Select the **Branding** page in the product editor and review the options for window images. Window images are the images that are typically shown at the top left corner of the window, in the task bar, and in other locations; it really depends on the window system you are running. Figure 8-6 shows the **Window Images** section of the **Branding** page. Here you identify two GIF images, one 16 × 16 and the other 32 × 32.

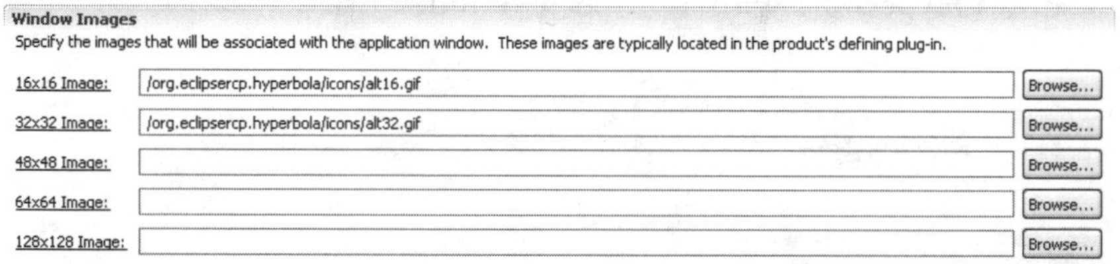

Figure 8–6   Window Images configuration

Typically, the images are stored in the plug-in that contributes the product extension. The images for Hyperbola are in the sample code for this chapter, as outlined in Chapter 3, "Tutorial Introduction." Use the Samples Manager to copy the contents of the org.eclipsercp.hyperbola/icons folder into the org.eclipsercp

.hyperbola project in your workspace and fill in the image locations as shown. Save the product configuration and then launch Hyperbola to see how the window images show up. Figure 8-7 shows the new look of Hyperbola.

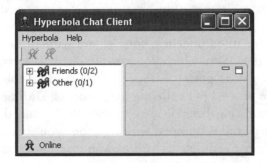

Figure 8–7   Window image branding

The running Hyperbola now looks like any other application on your system. The next step is to provide a custom launcher with proper icons.

8.3 Customizing the Launcher

The launcher is the program that end users run when they want to start Hyperbola, for example, hyperbola.exe on Windows. You could just use the launcher that comes with Eclipse, but of course you don't want to tell users to "double-click on eclipse.exe" to run Hyperbola—you want a hyperbola.exe for them to run. Furthermore, the Eclipse launcher has Eclipse icons associated with it. It makes more sense that these be Hyperbola-specific icons.

To set this up, use the **Program Launcher** section on the **Launching** page of the product editor as shown in Figure 8-8.

Program Launcher
Customize the executable that is used to launch the product.

Launcher Name: | hyperbola

Customizing the launcher icon varies per platform.

| linux | macosx | solaris | win32 |

A single XPM icon is required:

Icon: | /org.eclipsercp.hyperbola/branding/hyperbola.xpm [Browse...]

Figure 8–8   Launcher branding

The **Launcher Name** box allows you to enter the simple name of the launcher. You should not append .exe. That information is platform-dependent and PDE takes care of it when the product is exported.

The next section contains a series of entry fields for identifying the icons associated with Hyperbola's launcher. It turns out that each OS requires different image sizes and formats, so the product editor has a section for the supported OS. Figure 8-8 shows the sections for **linux, macosx, solaris**, and **win32**.

Fill in the image names for the OSs in which you are interested. The Hyperbola images are in the sample files you imported earlier in the branding folder. The launcher images are used in the process of exporting the products. During export, PDE creates a launcher program that behaves exactly like the standard Eclipse launcher but is named hyperbola and is branded with the icons you specified. We talk about launcher branding here to complete the branding story, but you cannot test it until the next chapter where you learn how to export Hyperbola.

8.4 Splash Screen

The splash screen is the first visible part of Hyperbola. Figure 8-9 shows the **Location** section of the **Splash** page in the product editor. Eclipse expects the splash screen to be called splash.bmp, so all you need to do is identify the plug-in that contains the file. You can get Hyperbola's splash screen from the sample code for this chapter. Note that if you leave this field blank, the splash screen is assumed to be in the same plug-in as the product. We recommend making an explicit choice here for completeness.

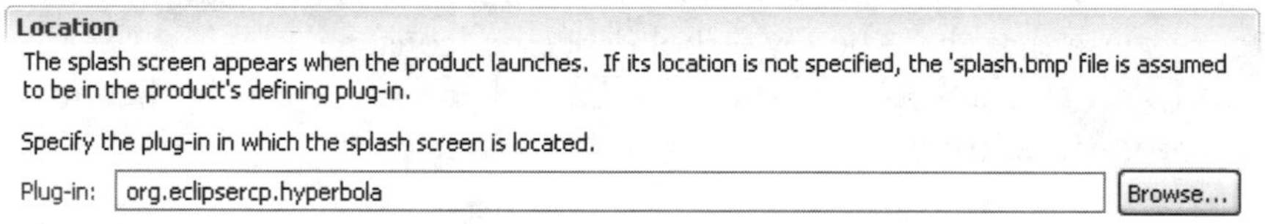

Location

The splash screen appears when the product launches. If its location is not specified, the 'splash.bmp' file is assumed to be in the product's defining plug-in.

Specify the plug-in in which the splash screen is located.

Plug-in: | org.eclipsercp.hyperbola | Browse...

Figure 8–9 Defining the splash screen

NOTE

Currently, the Eclipse launcher can only display splash screens that are saved as BMP images, the standard bit-mapped graphics format used on Windows. Although BMPs are a Windows standard, they can be saved and read on any platform.

Shipping Locale-Specific Files

If you need to have locale-specific splash screens or message catalogs, you have to put the relevant files into a locale-based directory structure, as shown in Figure 8-10. Under the nl directory, there is a structure that mimics the structure of Java locale strings. For example, the splash screen for the English locales is in the directory nl/en. The directories under nl/en contain data for English locale variations. Note that the root of the plug-in still contains splash.bmp and plugin.properties files. These are used when matching locale-specific files cannot be found.

The nl directory structure can be carved off and shipped separately in one or more *fragments*. When fragments are installed, their resources and code are seamlessly merged with those of their host plug-in. See Section 27.3, "Fragments," for more details on fragments. Using the fragment approach, the nl file structure in Figure 8-10 is simply moved to a set of fragments.

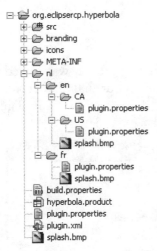

Figure 8–10   Locale-specific file structure

The locale-specific files in the structure are automatically searched when looking for translated strings. For example, many of the values in a plugin.xml are displayed in the UI and should be translated to support multiple locales. To enable this, %variables are used instead of the real text. The variable names correspond to keys in a plugin.properties file. The values in the file are translated for each locale and shipped separately in fragments. The text for the About dialog discussed later in this chapter is a good example of text that could be translated.

Now when you run Hyperbola, the splash screen appears. Hyperbola is a modest-size application and it comes up very quickly on average machines—so quickly, in fact, that there is barely time to read the splash screen. However, if the machine is slower or bogged down, or Hyperbola is installed on a network drive, the startup time may be longer. Without a splash screen, users may begin to wonder what, if anything, is happening. Including a splash screen helps set user expectations and gives your product a somewhat more polished feel.

8.5 About Information

Most applications have an *About* dialog that reports product version, license, and copyright information to the user. The Eclipse Workbench includes a standard dialog that presents this information and gives users access to configuration information that is useful if they need to report problems. You are, of course, free to ignore this dialog and write your own. If you want to use the standard About dialog, read on.

8.5.1 Product About Information

The **About** action, accessed via **Help > About Hyperbola**, was added to Hyperbola in Chapter 6, "Adding Actions," but the About dialog is currently empty. Let's add branding information to update the dialog, as shown in Figure 8-11.

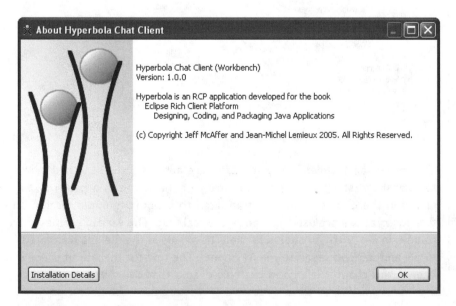

Figure 8–11   Hyperbola About dialog

The standard About dialog is branded by supplying an *About image* and some *About text*. The About image is the graphic shown at the left side of the dialog. This image can be anything you want, but it should be in GIF format. If the image is smaller than 250 × 330 pixels, the About text is shown at the right of the image in the dialog, as in Figure 8-11. If the image is larger, the About text is not shown and the image fills the entire top portion of the dialog. In any event, the image should be smaller than 500 × 330 pixels.

The branded About image and text are defined in the **About Dialog** section of the **Branding** page in the product editor, as shown in Figure 8-12. Notice that the About text has a value of %aboutText. You could put real text here. Using %aboutText indicates to Eclipse that the value is human-readable and the real text can be found in the plugin.properties file associated with the product plug-in. This allows the text to be adjusted to suit different locales. Create a plugin.properties file at the root of org.eclipsercp.hyperbola and add the following content:

org.eclipsercp.hyperbola/plugin.properties
```
aboutText=\n\nHyperbola Chat Client (Workbench)\n\
Version: 1.0.0\n\n\
Hyperbola is an RCP application developed for the book \n\
\tEclipse Rich Client Platform \n\
\t\tDesigning, Coding, and Packaging Java Applications \n\
\n\
(c) Copyright Jeff McAffer and Jean-Michel Lemieux 2005. \
All Rights Reserved.\n
```

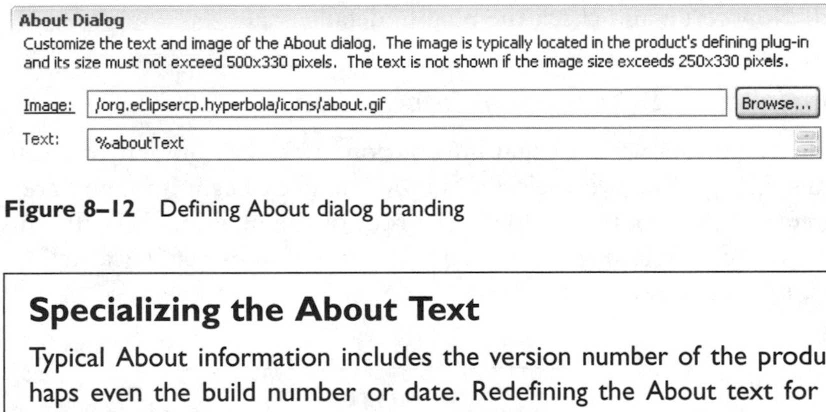

About Dialog
Customize the text and image of the About dialog. The image is typically located in the product's defining plug-in and its size must not exceed 500x330 pixels. The text is not shown if the image size exceeds 250x330 pixels.

Image: /org.eclipsercp.hyperbola/icons/about.gif   [Browse...]

Text: %aboutText

Figure 8–12 Defining About dialog branding

Specializing the About Text

Typical About information includes the version number of the product and perhaps even the build number or date. Redefining the About text for every build across all translations is challenging. Rather than forcing such values to be embedded in the text, the standard Eclipse About dialog does variable substitution in the About text string.

The About text is treated as a `java.text.MessageFormat` template, where values are supplied by the properties file called `about.mappings` in the product's plug-in. For example, change the Hyperbola `aboutText` shown in this section to have

```
Version: {0}\n\n\
```

and then add an `about.mappings` file in the Hyperbola product plug-in with the following line:

```
0=1.0.0
```

The net result is that the About dialog shows

```
"Hyperbola Version 1.0.0"
```

To move to the next version of Hyperbola, you only need to update the value of the key 0 in `about.mappings`. The downside to this approach is that the mapped values cannot be translated.

As one final check, run Hyperbola and open the About dialog. Don't forget to synchronize. Click on the **Installation Details** button. There should be a collection of Eclipse plug-ins and a single Hyperbola plug-in. Notice that our plug-in does not have a provider. Open the plug-in editor for Hyperbola by double-clicking on the `plugin.xml` file. On the **Overview** page, enter `eclipsercp.org` in the **Provider** field. Now rerun and check the plug-in details page.

8.5.2 Installation Details About Information

You may have noticed a **Legal Info** button at the bottom left of the installation details dialog. When you select a plug-in and click **Legal Info,** you are shown the contents of the `about.html` file in the root of the plug-in. Typically this contains detailed licensing information about the plug-in, but since it is a standard HTML page, it can present anything you like.

NOTE

If your plug-in is shipped as a JAR file and the `about.html` references other pages in the plug-in, the additional pages must be in a directory called `about_files` at the root of the plug-in. This is required because Eclipse extracts the files from the JAR before presenting the root file in the Web browser—browsers typically cannot see inside JARs.

8.6 Summary

Now you have a fully branded, somewhat functional Hyperbola product. There is enough here to give users a real idea of the look and feel of the final product on their desktop.

The only problem is that your office is getting crowded with all the people wanting to take Hyperbola for a spin. You really should distribute it for them to see. Unfortunately, Hyperbola is still in the laboratory—your workspace. Giving it to other users means giving them your entire workspace and getting them to install the full Eclipse SDK. That's where *product exporting*, the subject of the next chapter, comes in.

8.7 Pointers

○ The Eclipse User Interface Guidelines can help you with branding your application: *http://wiki.eclipse.org/User_Interface_Guidelines*.

CHAPTER 9

Packaging Hyperbola

The good news now is that you have a branded product configuration. But even though Hyperbola is fully branded, you still can't send it to your friends because it lives in your workspace. In this chapter we show you how to package that configuration and export it in various forms. The goal is to take Hyperbola from a laboratory prototype to a complete and ready-to-install Eclipse application. By the end of this chapter you will be able to impress your mother with the application you've written.[1] This chapter also covers

- ❍ The different shapes that RCP products can have
- ❍ Exporting Hyperbola and running it outside the workspace
- ❍ Exporting Hyperbola for other platforms
- ❍ Moving Hyperbola out of the laboratory and into the real world

9.1 Exporting Hyperbola

So far you have been running Hyperbola in place in the workspace. To export it, you have to identify what parts of the `org.eclipsercp.hyperbola` project go into the `org.eclipsercp.hyperbola` plug-in.

Open the plug-in editor for the Hyperbola plug-in and switch to the **Build** page. The **Binary Build** section shown in Figure 9-1 lists the set of development-time files and folders that are also part of the Runtime plug-in structure. PDE takes care of adding the compiled Java classes to the build output, but you have to manage

---

1. Don't laugh. The "Mom test" is actually quite challenging.

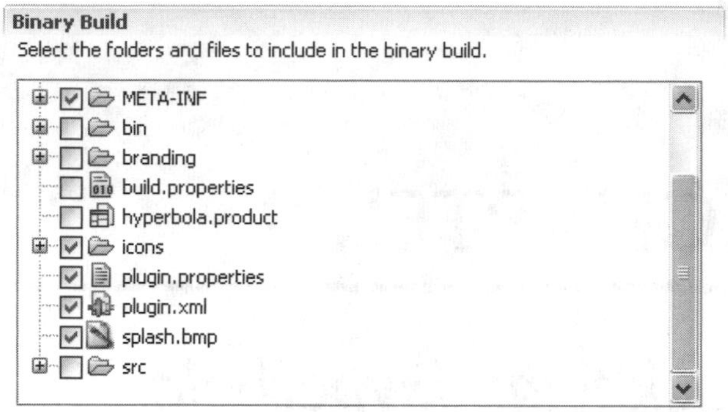

Figure 9–1   Binary build specification

the other files. For example, the whole META-INF directory and plugin.xml are required at runtime as they describe the plug-in. These were added to the list in Chapter 4, "The Hyperbola Application," when the project was first created.

In Chapters 5, "Starting the Hyperbola Prototype," and 8, "Branding Hyperbola," you added an icons directory, the splash.bmp file, the about.html file, and the plugin.properties file—all of which are runtime artifacts. Update the build specification for the Hyperbola plug-in by checking these resources in the list. If a resource is not checked, it is not included in the output.

TIP

Failure to correctly set up the **Binary Build** list is a very common source of errors. Typically, the plug-in works fine when run from the workspace, but when exported, various images, text messages, and other elements are missing. If this happens to you, first check the **Binary Build** list.

To start off, find the hyperbola.product file in the **Package Explorer** or **Navigator**. Right-click and choose **Export... > Eclipse product**. Alternatively, open the product editor, select the **Overview** page, and click on the **Product Export wizard** link. Either way, you should see the **Product Export** wizard, as shown in Figure 9-2.

First, ensure that the Hyperbola product configuration is selected in the **Configuration** drop-down. Then fill in the **Root directory**, the top-level directory that is embedded in the export output. For example, it is useful to set this to be the name of your product with the version number. This way, people can extract the product and it gets laid out on disk in a descriptive directory structure. For now, use "Hyperbola 1.0" in this field.

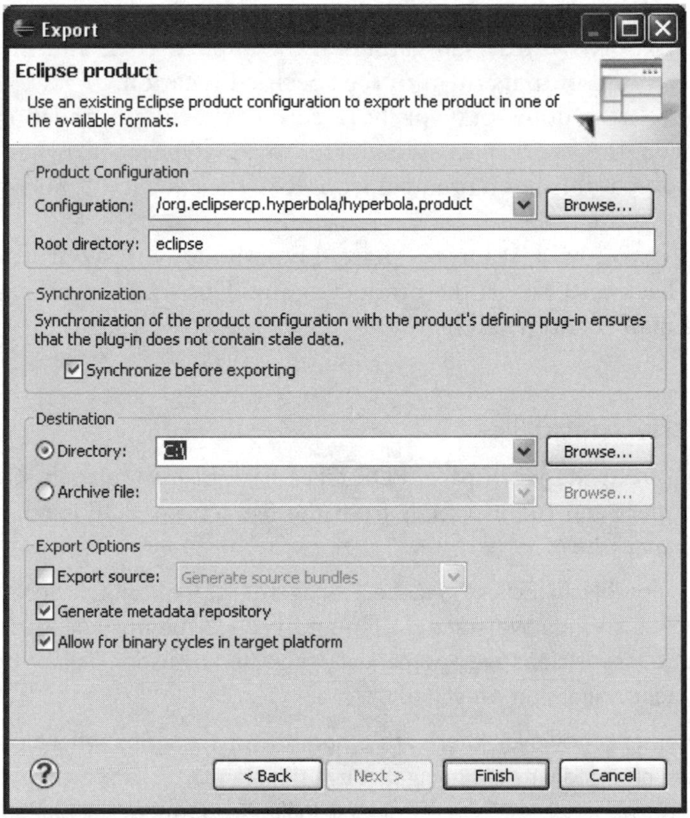

Figure 9–2   Product Export wizard

Earlier we talked about how the product configuration is an aggregation of information maintained in several different files. Checking the **Synchronization** check box ensures that the product configuration is properly synchronized before exporting. This helps avoid any surprising, and typically quite hard to debug, problems when running the exported product. Leaving this checked is *highly recommended*.

Next, pick the export **Destination** and set the shape of the export **Archive file** or **Directory**. This setting does not affect the content of the output—it is the same either way. Choose **Directory** so you can easily test what you are exporting. Later you can export as an archive to make Hyperbola easier to distribute. Put the output in any convenient location, but remember that the root directory entered earlier is appended to the location specified here.

Having set the various options, click **Finish** and PDE starts the export in the background (i.e., you can continue using Eclipse while the export completes).

First, it compiles the code from the workspace according to the configuration you described. The **Export** wizard then gathers the compiled code and the required parts of the target and outputs them to the specified location.

When the export is done, `c:\Hyperbola` contains a fully branded Hyperbola that runs outside the workspace. Navigate to `c:\Hyperbola\hyperbola.exe`. Notice that the executable has a branded icon. Run the executable and enjoy your completed RCP product!

Undoubtedly you will want to share Hyperbola with your friends and coworkers. Go back and export the product again. This time, specify an **Archive file** output and mail them the archive.

Cleaning the Install

When you run from the workspace, PDE takes care of many details. Once you export the product and run it directly from the file system, PDE is no longer in the loop and cannot help.

This crops up notably in Eclipse's cache management. Typically, Eclipse keeps a number of caches to improve startup time and reduce memory footprint. Since most production installations are not manually modified by users, Eclipse does only rudimentary cache validation on startup.

During development, however, there are a number of scenarios where previously installed files are changed without going through the standard channels. For example, if you export Hyperbola on top of a previous installation, some of the plug-in content may change but the plug-in was never "updated" or "uninstalled." Eclipse doesn't notice the change. To you it appears as though your changes are not being picked up.

The easiest way around this is to avoid overwriting or tweaking previous installs. Failing that, however, you can run Eclipse using the `-clean` command-line argument or put the `osgi.clean=true` system property in the product's `config.ini` or launcher initialization file.

Running this way during development is useful as it tells Eclipse to flush all of its caches and rebuild its state. Startup is a little slower, but you are guaranteed to get the latest information.

9.2 Exporting for Other Platforms

But what about your friends who use different operating or window systems or run on different hardware? They can't run the Hyperbola you just built because it contains platform-specific code. To package for other platforms, either you need to run on that platform, which is hard to manage, or you must have the code for those platforms on your machine. This is a typical cross-platform development scenario.

The first problem is to acquire all the platform-specific Eclipse code needed for these other platforms. Fortunately, the Eclipse platform team supplies a *delta pack* for every release. The delta pack contains all parts of the Eclipse SDK that are platform-specific. So, for example, if you are on Windows and want to export Hyperbola for Linux/GTK, you need the delta pack.

NOTE

The issue of platform-specific code shows up for several plug-ins in the Eclipse platform. SWT, for example, has a considerable amount of platform-specific code. Several other plug-ins have platform-specific fragments that deliver natives and Java code to support optimizations. In some cases the plug-ins work fine without the platform fragments, but with the fragments they are faster or support enhanced functionality.

Thankfully, in Chapter 3, "Tutorial Introduction," we already added the delta pack to the Hyperbola target definition. However, you can get the delta pack from the Eclipse downloads site, *http://eclipse.org/downloads*, by going to the Eclipse Platform downloads page. Scroll down to the section labeled **Eclipse RCP SDK** and download the **RCP delta pack**.

NOTE

In Chapter 3, "Tutorial Introduction," we talked about the importance of keeping your target and development Eclipse installs separate. Using the delta pack is a fine example that motivates that practice. If you were using the development Eclipse install as a target, the simple default setup, the preceding steps would have added the delta pack to the development install. As a result, the development environment would be cluttered with extra and irrelevant plug-ins.

Now your target has all the plug-ins, fragments, and launchers for every platform supported by Eclipse, but you have to set up your product to use them. Return to the Hyperbola product editor and switch to the **Dependencies** page. In the **Plug-ins and Fragments** section click **Add...** and select all the SWT-related elements listed, that is, all elements starting with `org.eclipse.swt`. These are the SWT implementations for all supported platforms. Since SWT is the only platform-specific part of Hyperbola, that is all you need. Save the product configuration and open the **Export** wizard from the **Overview** page.

Open the **Export** wizard as before and this time check the **Export for multiple platforms** option. Complete the first page of the wizard as before and click **Next** to get to the **Cross-platform export** page shown in Figure 9-3. Select the set of platforms for which you want to export and click **Finish**.

Figure 9–3   Cross-platform export

The export output goes to the archives or directories specific to the related platform. For example, the Windows output appears in the directory named `c:\win32.win32.x86\Hyperbola`.

9.3 Summary

Exporting Hyperbola is effectively the final step in branding the application. Without exporting, Hyperbola is just a wad of code in your workspace. Exported, Hyperbola becomes a full-fledged stand-alone application. PDE's exporting facilities make it easy to create these fully branded product packages—even across platforms. Now you have something to send to others.

9.4 Pointers

○ Chapter 24, "Building Hyperbola," describes how to automate this build process.

○ Chapter 26, "The Last Mile," details how to sign the output JARs and how to export for use in Java Web Start scenarios.

CHAPTER 10

Messaging Support

Eclipse RCP tooling makes creating RCP applications easy—there are wizards and editors that help automate the error-prone tasks of branding, exporting, and configuring an application. You could stop here, but the real fun of developing an RCP application is writing the domain-specific code. Hyperbola is no exception.

These tools and programming constructs are generic; they are not specific to application domains such as banking, stock trading, streaming video, instant messaging, or Mars space missions. That's where you come in. You will spend most of your time working on the code for your domain. Again, this is one of the benefits of Eclipse—it is essentially middleware that allows you to focus on your problems rather than on the infrastructure.

This chapter makes Hyperbola a real instant messaging client. The goal is to get Hyperbola into a state where you can chat and add more of the features you expect from an instant messaging application. As such, this chapter focuses somewhat more on the instant messaging domain and the details of getting set up to chat rather than generic RCP issues. Specifically, we show you how to

○ Integrate a third-party XMPP library called Smack
○ Replace the prototype model with Smack

NOTE

There are several places in this chapter that require more code changes or new code than we can detail in the text. Instead, the sample code for this chapter contains all the changes; we essentially take you on a tour of the code and highlight the points of particular interest. If you have the time, you may want to follow along and make the changes yourself.

10.1 Integrating a Third-Party Library

Alas, not all Java code is structured as Eclipse plug-ins. There is a vast array of useful Java code available in standard Java JAR files. Whether it is third-party libraries or in-house *legacy* functionality, reusing this code is extremely attractive and efficient. Fortunately, integrating these libraries into Eclipse is reasonably straightforward. The process of transforming non-Eclipse code libraries into Eclipse plug-ins is referred to as *bundling*.

10.1.1 Bundling Smack

Writing your own XMPP messaging library is quite a challenge. Fortunately, the folks at Jive Software (*http://jivesoftware.org*) wrote and open-sourced their Smack messaging library. We use this throughout the Hyperbola examples and have found it to be stable and easy to use.

The Fine Print

When you decide to reuse someone else's code, the first question to ask yourself is "Does the license allow me to repackage it and what are the exact terms of the license?" This is true regardless of whether or not you are working on open-source code or proprietary in-house software. Make sure you read and understand the license terms completely. You should not assume that just because you can look at it, you can use it, and just because you can use it, you can ship it.

It's not only what you can do with their code, but how does their license impact what you can do with *your* code and what your users can do with your product! You have to figure out what rights you are giving up by using a given library and how that affects your future users' use of the software.

In the case of Smack, the license is Apache, which is friendly to repackaging. The only note in its license is that the icons and images cannot be used outside of Smack.

First, download the Smack library from *www.igniterealtime.org/downloads/index.jsp*. At the time of this writing, the latest version was 3.1.0. Expand the archive somewhere convenient on disk.

Create a plug-in project using **File > New > Project... > Plug-in Development > Plug-in from existing JAR archives**. On the next page, identify the JARs you want in the plug-in. Click on **Add External...** and locate and select both smack.jar and smackx.jar from the Smack 3.1.0 install. Click **Next** to get the page shown in Figure 10-1.

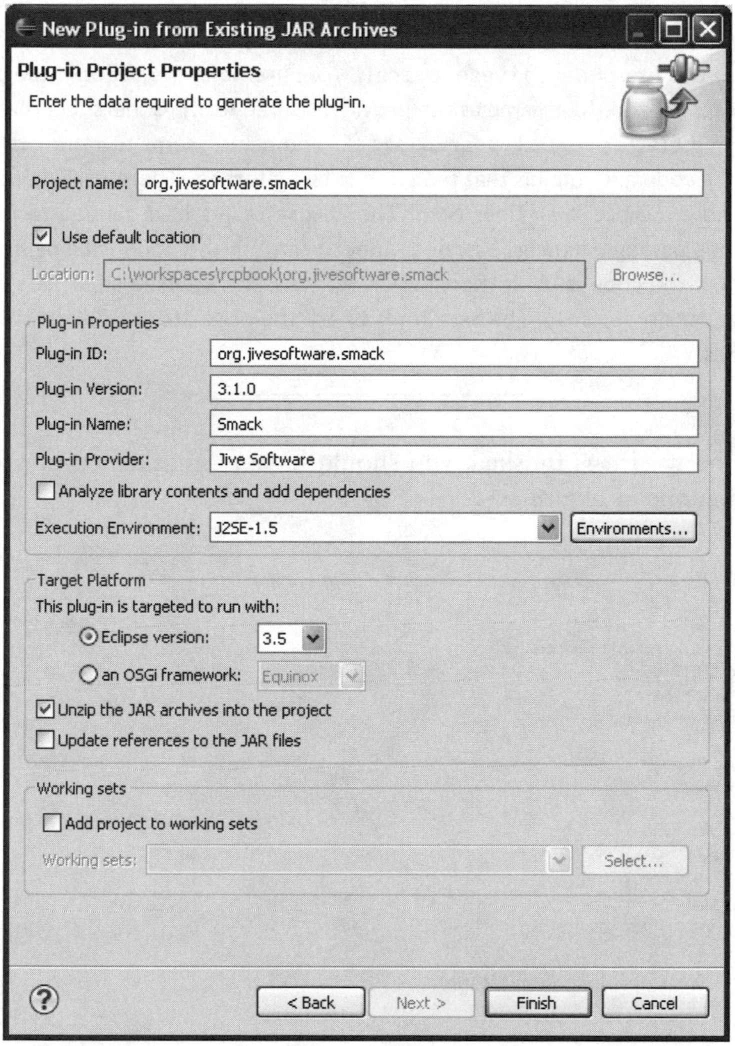

Figure 10–1 New plug-in project for bundling the Smack libraries

Fill in the **Project name** and **Plug-in ID**. As discussed previously, the plug-in ID and project name should match, and the plug-in ID should be based on the plug-in originator's Java package naming conventions. Here, the plug-in's code is coming from Jive Software, whose package naming convention for Smack is org.jivesoftware.smack. Use that as the project name. As you fill in the project name, the wizard automatically completes the plug-in ID. Update the plug-in version to 3.1.0 to match Smack's version and fill in the provider.

NOTE

Some see this use of `org.jivesoftware.*` (i.e., Jive Software's spot in the plug-in ID namespace) and their name as the provider as bad form. Others feel that using your own ID (e.g., `org.eclipsercp.smack`) and name seems to claim credit for the Smack code and implies that the code is being forked. There is likely no right answer here. Eclipse itself does both. The Eclipse teams have tended to use the originator's package naming (e.g., `org.apache.ant`) if the code is being included verbatim. If the code is being modified or adapted, the Eclipse namespace is used (e.g., `org.eclipse.ant`). The best bet is to ask the originator to deliver the code as bundles!

When the wizard is finished, you should have a Smack plug-in project that looks like the one in Figure 10-2.

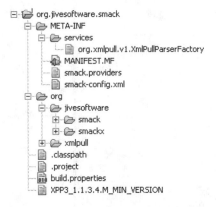

Figure 10–2   Smack project after creation

The option to unzip the JAR archives is useful if you want to ship the new plug-in as a JAR itself. Otherwise, the JARs would simply be copied into the plug-in and the plug-in would have to be shipped as a directory.

Aside from creating the project and exploding the JARs, the wizard generates a `MANIFEST.MF` file. The generated file is shown below. Notice that the various values you entered are embedded in the manifest. Notice also that there is a list of exported packages. These are all the packages the wizard discovered in the Smack JAR.

org.jivesoftware.smack/MANIFEST.MF
```
Bundle-Name: Smack
Bundle-SymbolicName: org.jivesoftware.smack
```

```
Bundle-Version: 3.1.0
Bundle-ClassPath: .
Bundle-Vendor: Jive Software
Export-Package: .,
 org.jivesoftware.smack,
 org.jivesoftware.smack.debugger,
 org.jivesoftware.smack.filter,
 org.jivesoftware.smack.packet,
 org.jivesoftware.smack.provider,
 org.jivesoftware.smack.util,
 ...
```

The Export-Package header lists those packages available to other plug-ins. Since the point of bundling is to make the library classes available to others, exporting them is a good thing. Note that without the exports, the Smack code would be usable inside the Smack plug-in, but not visible outside.

Notice that the bundling did not import any of the other files that were included in the Smack download. If you want the other files in the project, run the **Import** wizard and select the **File system** import option. Then browse to the expanded Smack directory and choose the files to import into the existing Smack plug-in project.

10.1.2 Testing the Bundling

It's a good idea to test your newly bundled Smack just to be sure everything is in order. The easiest way to do this is to create another plug-in that uses Smack and then ensure that you can compile against it and run with it. The Smack API is very convenient, so let's just create an RCP application that sends a message using the new Smack plug-in.

First, create a new plug-in project and call it smack.testing. Make it an RCP application, and on the **Templates** page select **Hello RCP**. This is similar to the procedure you followed in Chapter 4, "The Hyperbola Application," to create the Hyperbola shell. When the wizard is done, the smack.testing plug-in editor is left open. On the **Dependencies** page, add org.jivesoftware.smack to the **Required Plug-ins** list and save the file.

Dynamic Classpaths

One of the advantages of using plug-ins to manage the project dependencies is that it allows Eclipse tooling to manage your classpaths. Here you added Smack to the smack.testing plug-in's required list and automatically the content of the Smack plug-in was available on the smack.testing plug-in's classpath. The required plug-ins need not even be in the workspace—PDE and JDT take care of it for you.

You have already been working in this mixed mode throughout the previous chapters. The Hyperbola plug-in depends on the `org.eclipse.core.runtime` plug-in, but that plug-in has always been in your target. The Hyperbola plug-in compiles because it said it required the Runtime. PDE hides the details.

If at some point you check the Runtime out of CVS and into your workspace (e.g., to fix a bug or prototype a new feature), PDE updates the classpath and Hyperbola continues to compile and run.

We don't really care about a UI for our little test, so open the generated `Application` class and replace the `run()` method with this little Smack example:

```
smack.testing/Application
public Object start(IApplicationContext context) throws Exception {
  try {
    XMPPConnection con = new XMPPConnection("eclipsercp.org");
    con.connect();
    con.login("reader", "secret",
        Long.toString(System.currentTimeMillis()));
    Chat chat = con.getChatManager().createChat(
        "eliza@eclipsercp.org", this);
    chat.sendMessage("Hi There!");
    Thread.sleep(5000);
  } catch (XMPPException e) {
    e.printStackTrace();
  } finally {
    conn.disconnect();
  }
  return IApplication.EXIT_OK;

public void processMessage(Chat chat, Message message) {
    System.out.println("Returned message: " + message.getBody());
 }
}
```

As you type the code, notice that code completion works and classes are resolved by the Java editor. This is a good sign—the `smack.testing` plug-in can see the Smack classes. Ultimate proof comes when you save the `Application` class and it compiles without errors.

To run the test, right-click on the project, and from the context menu select **Run As > Eclipse Application**. If all goes well, the test code connects to the `eclipsercp.org` chat server as the user "reader" and sends a message to "eliza."

Eliza is actually a chat robot that responds to your messages in various ways. You should see her response in the regular Eclipse Console view. Depending on your

UI setup, you may have to open it using **Window > Show View > Other... > Basic > Console**.

```
Returned message: HI THERE!
```

Here, Eliza has simply changed your message to uppercase and sent it back. Even if you get a time-out, the test has proven itself—you were able to write a plug-in that compiled and ran with the bundled Smack library.

Bundling Smack was relatively easy. Other libraries may be more complicated depending on what they are doing and how they work. The typical problems encountered revolve around Eclipse's strong notion of component, class loading, and how the classpath is managed. Many libraries assume that all classes are available on the classpath, but Eclipse puts constraints on what classes are visible and from where. The most common programming patterns that can cause problems when bundling are the following:

○ Does the code use reflection, `Class.forName(String)`, or class references such as `Foo.class`?

○ Does the library use the context class loader?

○ Does it make assumptions about seeing classes from the Java Extensions class loader?

There are also some general issues to consider when bundling existing libraries:

○ Are the original JARs signed and is the signature important?

○ Does the license allow you to repackage?

○ Can multiple JARs be combined and still work? For example, are there overlapping package structures that rely on classpath ordering?

10.2 Refactoring the Model

It's time to refactor Hyperbola to use Smack rather than the prototype model. Doing this requires quite a number of minor but pervasive changes to accommodate new class and method names. Rather than detailing each of these changes, we take this opportunity to step back and show you how to use more Eclipse tooling, for example, code completion, organized imports, and refactoring. We also take you on a tour of the final code to highlight some of the transformation.

With the information provided here, it is quite feasible for you to do the refactoring yourself. Of course, if you would rather skip to the final code, you can compare the sample code for this chapter.

10.2.1 Introduction to Smack

Now that you have a Smack plug-in, let's look at the Smack APIs. Smack and XMPP are based on a few very simple concepts. The XMPP protocol is an IETF standard for instant messaging and presence awareness. The basic idea is that a client connects to a server. The server manages a list of contacts for each user and routes chat messages from one user to another.

Messages are sent to and from the server in packets that are simple blocks of XML. There are only three basic message types: `<message />`, `<presence />`, and `<iq />`. For example, the following XMPP message is sent by a client to indicate a presence change to "away" or that the user has been idle for some time. The details of the markup are not particularly interesting except to note that the protocol is extensible and packets can have subtypes. The XMPP specification process includes a number of Jabber[1] Enhancement Proposals (JEPs) that seek to add all manner of functionality such as file transfer.

```
<presence>
  <c
      node="http://exodus.jabberstudio.org/caps"
      ver="0.9.0.0"
      xmlns="http://jabber.org/protocol/caps"/>
  <show>away</show>
  <priority>1</priority>
</presence>
```

Of course, no one really wants to write code to parse XML and manage streams of packets. Smack does all of the message parsing and stream management for you. It also provides clients with APIs that hide the XMPP implementation details.

Smack provides helpful classes that take care of listening to common packets and maintain models of many of the basic messaging concepts such as chats (`Chat`), the contacts list (`Roster`), individual contacts (`RosterEntry`), groups of contacts (`RosterGroup`), and connections to the server (`XMPPConnection`). It's pretty easy to do things with Smack without intimate knowledge of XMPP—that is why we like it!

The typical workflow for a Smack client is to connect to the server and then send and receive messages while listening to packets sent and received using `Packet-Listeners`. The following code snippet illustrates how to use a `PacketListener` to look for incoming chat requests and tell the chat editor when one arrives:

org.eclipsercp.hyperbola/ApplicationWorkbenchAdvisor
```
XMPPConnection connection = session.getConnection();
```

---

1. Jabber is the historical name for XMPP.

```
if (connection != null) {
  PacketListener listener = new PacketListener() {
    public void processPacket(Packet packet) {
      Message message = (Message) packet;
      if (message.getType() == Message.Type.chat)
        startChat(message);
    }
  };
  PacketFilter filter = new PacketTypeFilter(Message.class);
  connection.addPacketListener(listener, filter);
}
```

The packet listener is added to the connection for a particular server. It is triggered when a message arrives from that server. This is a standard pattern in Smack: Register a listener and do something as a result of an incoming or outgoing message.

Another common example is listening for presence and contacts list changes. In XMPP, the server manages your contacts list. Changes to the list or the state of those in the list are sent to the client by the server. As such, you can use a PacketListener to track the state of the contacts list and the status of your contacts.

10.2.2 Design Objectives

When the Hyperbola prototype was created, the hope was that by decoupling the UI from the domain logic, we could ignore the details of messaging and eventually replace the prototype model with a real messaging library without major changes. Indeed, the Smack domain model is close to that of the original prototype. For example, in the prototype there are three main classes called Contacts, ContactsGroup, and ContactsEntry; in Smack, the equivalent classes are called Roster, RosterGroup, and RosterEntry.

There are two approaches to integrating the Smack infrastructure into Hyperbola:

○ Proxy all the Smack classes behind the existing prototype model and try to run without any changes to the actions and UI.
○ Delete the prototype model and replace it with Smack directly.

The proxy approach is attractive as it isolates the changes. Unfortunately, it creates duplicate classes and overhead for keeping the proxies synchronized with the Smack classes. It is an interesting approach if you have the requirements to support different XMPP libraries—that is not the case here. So instead, the Hyperbola model is replaced entirely by that of Smack. The Session class is retained as it is still useful and does not have a Smack equivalent.

10.2.3 Deleting Prototype Classes

To start the refactoring, add a dependency from the Hyperbola plug-in to the newly created org.jivesoftware.smack plug-in. This is what you did with the smack.testing plug-in a little earlier via the plug-in editor's **Dependencies** page. Be sure to include the org.jivesoftware.smack plug-in in the Hyperbola product by adding it to the **Plug-ins** list on the **Configuration** page of the product editor.

Now that the Smack classes are available in Hyperbola, it's time to change the code. The general strategy for the refactoring is to do all the following steps on each model class in turn:

1. Rename a model class to match the simple name of the related Smack class.
2. Delete the renamed model class.
3. Go to each file that has errors and organize the imports and fix-up methods that changed names or signatures.

Renaming and deleting are relatively easy. In the **Package Explorer**, right-click on the Contacts class and select **Refactor > Rename....** You are prompted for a new name and given the option to **Update references**. Ensure that that option is selected. You can also select some of the other update options, but they are not particularly needed here. Click **OK** and the tooling renames the class and updates all references. Use this to rename Contacts, ContactsEntry, and ContactsGroup to Roster, RosterEntry, and RosterGroup, respectively. You also need to rename IContactsListener to RosterListener. The Chat and Presence classes have equivalent names in Smack, so you can leave them alone. Note that you do not need to change the package name here. This step serves to update all the references to use the new short class names.

TIP

When "following the little red x's," it is convenient to use **Ctrl+.** to cycle between lines with compilation errors in the Java editor. Typically this is much easier than scrolling the file manually.

Next, delete all the renamed model classes except for Session. The Session class is still needed and is augmented with a ConnectionDetails class to track information about the user logged in. Then start working through the compile errors. For example, open the AddContactAction class and use **Source > Organize Imports** to fix the import list. Alternatively, click on the project or package in the **Package Explorer** and select the same operation to organize imports in all classes in the project or package. Then look at the remaining errors and fix the method calls. In general, the changes are just updates to referenced method names. For example, the following snippet shows the AddContactAction class's run() after being updated:

```
org.eclipsercp.hyperbola/AddContactAction
public void run() {
  Object item = selection.getFirstElement();
  if (item instanceof RosterGroup) {
    RosterGroup group = (RosterGroup) item;
    AddContactDialog d = new AddContactDialog(window.getShell());
    int code = d.open();
    if (code == Window.OK)
      try {
        Roster list =
            Session.getInstance().getConnection().getRoster();
        String user = d.getUserId() + "@" + d.getServer();
        String[] groups = new String[] { group.getName() };
        list.createEntry(user, d.getNickname(), groups);
      } catch (XMPPException e) {
      // Handle.
      }
  }
}
```

Once the refactoring is done, you are left with just Session in the original model package—Smack does not have an equivalent class. Smack does have an XMPPConnection class that manages the notion of server connections, but it connects to the server in its constructor. This makes it impossible to model connections before they are actually connected. When a connection field is added to Session, a session can simply have a null connection until the user has logged in.

For convenience, we also added a simple ConnectionDetails class as a data structure to store login information.

10.2.4 Adding Chats

Smack provides an object that models chats. To expose this in the UI, ChatEditors need to hook into Smack so that new chats cause an editor to be opened and incoming messages are directed to the correct ChatEditor.

Previously when we were introducing the PacketListeners, we showed an example of hooking a listener that calls startChat(Message) for all incoming chat messages. The following snippet shows the implementation of startChat(Message) and the logic for directing messages:

```
org.eclipsercp.hyperbola/ApplicationWorkbenchAdvisor
private void startChat(final Message message) {
  String user = StringUtils.parseBareAddress(message.getFrom());
```

```
    Chat chat = session.getChat(user, false);
    if (chat != null)
      return;
    IWorkbench workbench = getWorkbenchConfigurer().getWorkbench();
    workbench.getDisplay().asyncExec(new Runnable() {
      public void run() {
        openChatEditor(message);
      }
    });
  }
private void openChatEditor(Message message) {
    IWorkbenchPage page = findPageForSession(session);
    if (page != null) {
      String user = message.getFrom();
      ChatEditorInput editorInput = new ChatEditorInput(session, user);
      try {
        ChatEditor editor =
            (ChatEditor)page.openEditor(editorInput, ChatEditor.ID);
        editor.processFirstMessage(message);
      } catch (PartInitException e) {
        e.printStackTrace();
      }
    }
  }
}
```

The code first looks for a `Chat` object matching the sender of the current message. If one is found, a chat already exists and the related `ChatEditor` is already listening for messages. No further action is needed since the editor gets its own notification and has a chance to display the message.

If, however, this is a new chat, we have to open a new `ChatEditor`, as shown in `openChatEditor(Message)`. Note that since the new editor will have missed the first message—it didn't exist and so was not listening—we have to prime it with the first message.

NOTE

There is an important pattern shown in `startChat()`. All Eclipse UI drawing and interaction must take place on the UI thread. So, when a method can be run on any thread, you must ensure that any UI-related code is wrapped in either `Display.asyncExec(Runnable)` or `Display.syncExec(Runnable)`. Here the `startChat()` is called when an XMPP packet is received and there are no guarantees about the current thread. This pattern is very common in Eclipse applications using SWT.

10.3 Updating the UI

In Chapter 5, "Starting the Hyperbola Prototype," we saw that `TreeViewers` use content and label providers to determine what elements to show and how to show them. The setup there was quite straightforward:

- ❍ The chat model objects implemented `IAdaptable`.
- ❍ Hyperbola registered an adapter factory that produced different `IWorkbench-Adapters` for the different chat objects.
- ❍ The `TreeViewer` was configured with standard Workbench content and label providers that knew how to use instances of `IWorkbenchAdapter` to produce the information needed by the `TreeViewer`.

Now that we have moved to Smack model objects such as `RosterEntry` and `RosterGroup`, we no longer have `IAdaptables`. These classes cannot be modified to implement `IAdaptable` or extend `PlatformObject` as we did in the chat model. While it is still possible to map Smack model objects to `IWorkbenchAdapter`, the standard `TreeViewer` and provider infrastructure expect `IAdaptable` instances. In the next section we replace the standard providers with something more flexible.

Before doing that, let's update the adapter factory from Chapter 5, "Starting the Hyperbola Prototype," to adapt instances of `RosterEntry` and `RosterGroup` to `IWorkbenchAdapter`. While we're at it, we'll change the adapter factory to be registered declaratively using extensions rather than registering it programmatically as we did before. The snippet below shows the XML markup that identifies the `HyperbolaAdapterFactory` class as being able to supply `IWorkbenchAdapters` for the new Smack `RosterGroup` and `RosterEntry` model objects. This also highlights the fact that the factories and types being adapted need not be in the same plug-in.

org.eclipsercp.hyperbola/plugin.xml
```
<extension
    point="org.eclipse.core.runtime.adapters">
  <factory
      adaptableType="org.jivesoftware.smack.RosterGroup"
      class="org.eclipsercp.hyperbola.HyperbolaAdapterFactory">
    <adapter type="org.eclipse.ui.model.IWorkbenchAdapter"/>
  </factory>
  <factory
      adaptableType="org.jivesoftware.smack.RosterEntry"
      class="org.eclipsercp.hyperbola.HyperbolaAdapterFactory">
    <adapter type="org.eclipse.ui.model.IWorkbenchAdapter"/>
  </factory>
</extension>
```

10.3.1 The Content Provider

Now that we have Smack model objects adapted to be IWorkbenchAdapters, we should be able to use the default providers to populate the Contacts TreeViewer with RosterGroups and RosterEntrys. Unfortunately, the Workbench's built-in content and label provider classes require instances of IAdaptable, not just objects that can be adapted to IWorkbenchAdapter. This is a quirk of the implementation, not a design point. To work around this, we have to implement our own providers. Luckily this is reasonably easy.

The required content provider simply implements four methods that map almost directly onto the IWorkbenchAdapter methods. Go ahead and create the content provider as shown below. Notice that this content provider is completely generic and does not mention anything about Smack, chats, or Hyperbola. It just interprets IWorkbenchAdapters as needed by TreeViewers.

org.eclipsercp.hyperbola/HyperbolaContentProvider

```
public class HyperbolaContentProvider implements ITreeContentProvider {

    protected IWorkbenchAdapter getAdapter(Object element) {
        IWorkbenchAdapter adapter = null;
        if (element instanceof IAdaptable)
            adapter = (IWorkbenchAdapter) ((IAdaptable) element)
                .getAdapter(IWorkbenchAdapter.class);
        if (element != null && adapter == null)
            adapter = (IWorkbenchAdapter) Platform.getAdapterManager()
                .loadAdapter(element, IWorkbenchAdapter.class.getName());
        return adapter;
    }

    public Object[] getChildren(Object element) {
        IWorkbenchAdapter adapter = getAdapter(element);
        if (adapter != null)
            return adapter.getChildren(element);
        return new Object[0];
    }

    public Object[] getElements(Object element) {
        return getChildren(element);
    }

    public Object getParent(Object element) {
        IWorkbenchAdapter adapter = getAdapter(element);
        if (adapter != null)
            return adapter.getParent(element);
        return null;
    }

    public boolean hasChildren(Object element) {
        return getChildren(element).length > 0;
    }
}
```

10.3.2 The Label Provider

The label provider is a little more complex because it has to manage images, but as you can see from the snippet below, it otherwise follows exactly the same pattern as the content provider. Notice again that this provider is generic.

org.eclipsercp.hyperbola/HyperbolaLabelProvider

```
public class HyperbolaLabelProvider extends LabelProvider {
  private Map imageTable = new HashMap(7);

  protected IWorkbenchAdapter getAdapter(Object element) {
    IWorkbenchAdapter adapter = null;
    if (element instanceof IAdaptable)
      adapter = (IWorkbenchAdapter) ((IAdaptable) element)
        .getAdapter(IWorkbenchAdapter.class);
    if (element != null && adapter == null)
      adapter = (IWorkbenchAdapter) Platform.getAdapterManager()
        .loadAdapter(element, IWorkbenchAdapter.class.getName());
    return adapter;
  }

  public final Image getImage(Object element) {
    IWorkbenchAdapter adapter = getAdapter(element);
    if (adapter == null)
      return null;
    ImageDescriptor descriptor = adapter.getImageDescriptor(element);
    if (descriptor == null)
      return null;
    Image image = (Image) imageTable.get(descriptor);
    if (image == null) {
      image = descriptor.createImage();
      imageTable.put(descriptor, image);
    }
    return image;
  }

  public final String getText(Object element) {
    IWorkbenchAdapter adapter = getAdapter(element);
    if (adapter == null)
      return "";
    return adapter.getLabel(element);
  }

  public void dispose() {
    if (imageTable != null) {
      for (Iterator i = imageTable.values().iterator(); i.hasNext();)
((Image) i.next()).dispose();
      imageTable = null;
    }
  }
}
```

10.4 Chatting with Eliza

Now that Hyperbola has a real messaging library behind it, exercising it gets a little trickier. You need to have a real messaging server and someone to chat with. When you tested the bundled Smack, you connected to eclipsercp.org as "reader" and then chatted with "eliza@eclipsercp.org," a robot chat agent. Let's do the same thing with Hyperbola.

Open the Application class and modify run(Object) to call a login method before starting the Workbench as shown in the following snippet:

```
org.eclipsercp.hyperbola/Application
public class Application implements IApplication {
  public Object start(IApplicationContext context) throws Exception {
    Display display = PlatformUI.createDisplay();
    try {
      final Session session = Session.getInstance();
      if (!login(session))
        return IApplication.EXIT_OK;
      int returnCode =
          PlatformUI.createAndRunWorkbench(display,
              new ApplicationWorkbenchAdvisor());
      if (returnCode == PlatformUI.RETURN_RESTART)
        return IApplication.EXIT_RESTART;
      return IApplication.EXIT_OK;
    } finally {
      display.dispose();
    }
  }

  private boolean login(final Session session) {
    try {
      ConnectionDetails d =
          new ConnectionDetails("reader", "eclipsercp.org", "secret");
      XMPPConnection con = new XMPPConnection(d.getServer());
      con.login(d.getUserId(), d.getPassword(), d.getResource());
      session.setConnection(con);
      session.setConnectionDetails(d);
    } catch (XMPPException e) {
      return false;
    }
    return true;
  }
}
```

Add the login(Session) method as shown. This is basically the same code from when you were testing earlier. The code opens the connection, stashes it and the connection details in the given session, and returns. If the login fails, false is returned and Hyperbola exits.

Now start the Hyperbola application. You are automatically logged on to the server as "reader." Hyperbola shows you the contacts list that contains only one entry, "eliza." Select that entry and use **Hyperbola > Chat** to start chatting with Eliza, as shown in Figure 10-3.

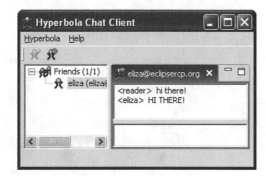

Figure 10–3   Chatting with Eliza

That's it. The Hyperbola application is now a functioning chat client.

10.5 Summary

This chapter covered a lot of details. Although most of it was specific to the Hyperbola application and XMPP, it's worthwhile to step back and see how the experiences apply more generally to your RCP applications:

- We can't say this enough: Separate the UI from the domain model. Build actions that manipulate the model and UIs that update accordingly. This makes your application easier to test and evolve. Many applications take this one step further and split the UI classes from the domain model classes into separate plug-ins. This is a popular pattern with Eclipse platform plug-ins, where related plug-ins are split and post-fixed with core and ui to differentiate them. We have not done this here just to keep things simple. The examples in Chapter 23, "RCP Everywhere," go into plug-in structuring in great detail.

- Your domain model is important and is something that is not addressed by Eclipse. Eclipse does, however, provide frameworks such as the extension registry and reusable UI components that make it easier to quickly get a product-quality application running. As we mentioned at the outset, this is the power of the Eclipse RCP. It is all the middleware code that you need to have but don't really want to write.

If you had trouble following along with all the code changes, import the code for this chapter and browse it to see the complete picture of changes that occurred.

10.6 Pointers

○ The Smack library is available at *www.igniterealtime.org/projects/smack/*.

CHAPTER 11

Adding a Login Dialog

At the end of Chapter 10, "Messaging Support," you hard-coded a login server and account so that you could test the newly enabled Hyperbola prototype. That was great for testing but clearly not realistic. In this chapter we walk through the creation and use of a login dialog and configuring Hyperbola to automatically log you in when it is started. In addition, we talk about how to

○ Display a login dialog before the Workbench starts
○ Ensure that the Hyperbola application's branding icon is shown on the dialog
○ Manually take down the splash screen before showing the login prompt
○ Add a preferences page
○ Remember login preferences
○ Store preferences securely using Equinox secure preferences

11.1 Adding the Login Dialog

The first thing to decide when adding a login prompt to an application is at what point in the application's lifecycle the prompt should actually appear. In this iteration of Hyperbola, we want to be logged in as soon as possible—even before the first Workbench window is shown. This has a number of advantages: It keeps the rest of the code simple since the connection information is assumed to be available and the connection open; the application can check licensing information; and the application can configure itself based on the logged-in user. For example, the name of the logged-in user can be used to determine what the UI looks like, what actions are available, and so on.

The first place that the Hyperbola application gets control is in the Application method start(IApplicationContext). This method simply creates an SWT Display and opens the Workbench using that Display. We want to prompt after creating the Display but before starting the Workbench. Note that there is no magic here—the run() method is not special. You are free to do as much UI work as you like before creating the Display or starting the Workbench. The only restriction is that you have to create the Display before anything can be drawn.

NOTE

Think of the Display as SWT's model. When a Display is created, it does not mean that a window or dialog has been opened. The Display is the single point of contact for all UI capabilities of SWT. It provides capabilities such as running the event loop, inter-thread communication, timers, fonts, and colors.

At the end of Chapter 10, you modified the Application's run(IApplicationContext) method to call login(Session). Now you have to change the login() method to prompt the user instead of automatically connecting with hard-coded connection details. You can write the login dialog yourself, or you can use the BasicLoginDialog class from the sample code for this chapter. You may notice another login dialog, LoginDialog, in the code for this chapter. This is the final version of the dialog as it appears at the end of the chapter. We included the BasicLoginDialog to help you get started. If you get the BasicLoginDialog from the code for this chapter, rename it LoginDialog.

Modify the login(Session) method to open the login dialog as shown below. Notice that whenever a dialog is shown before the first Workbench window is opened, it should not be parented. Here the BasicLoginDialog constructor takes a null argument. Dialogs without parents are managed by the windowing system and as such have an entry in the task bar. This means that users can tell that a dialog is open and can easily bring it to the front if needed.

```
org.eclipsercp.hyperbola/Application
private boolean login(final Session session) {
  while (session.getConnection() == null ||
        !session.getConnection().isAuthenticated()) {
    LoginDialog loginDialog = new LoginDialog(null);
    if (loginDialog.open() != Window.OK)
      return false;
    session.setConnectionDetails(loginDialog.getConnectionDetails());
    connectWithProgress(session);
  }
  return true;
}
```

The method `login(Session)` loops forever, prompting the user for login information and trying to log in using that information. The details of the `LoginDialog` are not particularly important here. It suffices to say that if the user clicks **OK** in the dialog, the login code gets the required information and attempts to log in by calling the `connectWithProgress(Session)` method. If the user clicks **Cancel**, the method returns and Hyperbola exits. If the login attempt fails, the user is prompted again.

Progress reporting during login is vital. In particular, during login you cannot be sure how long it will take to contact the remote server. Users appreciate feedback about the status of the login and expect the opportunity to cancel if it is taking too long.

As part of the refactoring in Chapter 10, a new login method that tracks progress during the initial connection and login was added to `Session`. The technique for reporting progress is to add an XMPP packet listener to the connection. The `Session` reports progress on an `IProgressMonitor` and checks for cancellation as packets are sent.

It's a good habit to ensure that long-running methods have some sort of feedback. In Hyperbola, the only thing we can tell the user is whether he or she is authenticating or receiving the roster from the server. The user can cancel between these operations.

org.eclipsercp.hyperbola/Session
```
public void connectAndLogin(final IProgressMonitor monitor)
    throws XMPPException {
  PacketListener progressPacketListener = new PacketListener() {
    public void processPacket(Packet packet) {
      if (monitor.isCanceled())
        throw new OperationCanceledException();
      String message = null;
      if (packet instanceof Authentication)
        message = "Authenticating...";
      if (packet instanceof RosterPacket)
        message = "Receiving roster...";
      if (message != null)
        monitor.subTask(message);
    }
  };
  try {
    monitor.beginTask("Connecting...", IProgressMonitor.UNKNOWN);
    String server = connectionDetails.getServer();
    monitor.subTask("Contacting " + server);
    connection = new XMPPConnection(server);
    connection.connect();
    connection.addPacketWriterListener(progressPacketListener,
        new OrFilter(new PacketTypeFilter(Authentication.class),
        new PacketTypeFilter(RosterPacket.class)));
```

```
    connection.login(connectionDetails.getUserId(),
        connectionDetails.getPassword(),
        connectionDetails.getResource());
} finally {
    if (connection != null)
        connection.removePacketWriterListener(progressPacketListener);
    monitor.done();
    }
}
```

The caller of `Session.connectAndLogin(IProgressMonitor)`—the `Application`, in our case—provides a monitor and displays the progress to the user. There's an existing dialog called `ProgressMonitorDialog` that shows progress that can be used for this purpose. The `connectWithProgress(Session)` method called from the application opens a progress dialog, then connects using the `Session`, as shown here:

org.eclipsercp.hyperbola/Application
```
private void connectWithProgress(final Session session) {
    ProgressMonitorDialog progress = new ProgressMonitorDialog(null);
    progress.setCancelable(true);
    try {
        progress.run(true, true, new IRunnableWithProgress() {
            public void run(IProgressMonitor monitor)
                throws InvocationTargetException {
                try {
                    session.connectAndLogin(monitor);
} catch (XMPPException e) {
    throw new InvocationTargetException(e);
                }
            }
        });
    } catch (InvocationTargetException e) {
    } catch (InterruptedException e) {
    }
}
```

Now when you run Hyperbola, it should appear as shown in Figure 11-1. Enter the user information used in Chapter 10—that is, the user is "reader," the server is `eclipsercp.org`, and use "secret" as the password. Click **Login** and you should once again be able to chat with Eliza. Of course, now you can log in to your own XMPP account and chat with your friends if you like.

You might have noticed that while the login dialog was up, the Hyperbola splash screen was showing. That seems a bit strange. Splash screens are there to reassure the user that something is happening. Once the Hyperbola application is up and interacting with the user, the splash screen is no longer needed. You can fix that by adding the following code just before calling `login(Session)` in `Application.run(IApplicationContext)`:

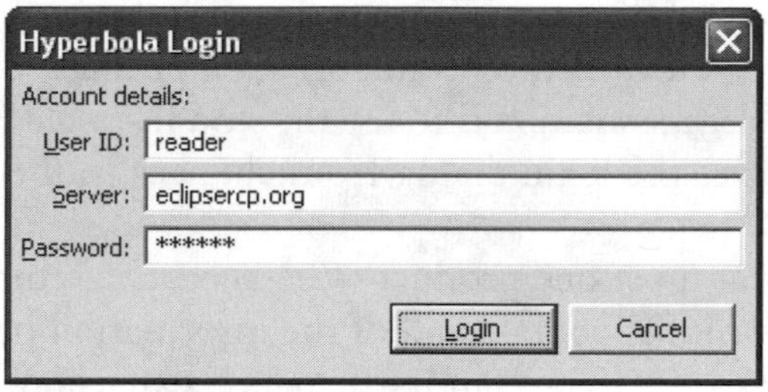

Figure 11–1   Login dialog

org.eclipsercp.hyperbola/Application
`context.applicationRunning();`

Note that the Workbench automatically closes the splash screen, if it is still up, when the startup sequence is completed. Once the splash screen is down, it cannot be redisplayed.

NOTE

It's actually possible to run code *before* the application is run. If you need to perform more advanced configuration, such as determining which plug-ins are loaded, see Chapter 27, "OSGi," for information about starting plug-ins from within the `config.ini` file using start levels.

11.1.1 Branding the Dialog

The best practice of setting the dialog's parent to `null` means that it does not inherit the icon set by the Workbench on the top-level window. Actually, there isn't even a Workbench or a top-level window. As a result, the Hyperbola icon is missing from the login dialog and the task bar entry, as shown in Figure 11-2.

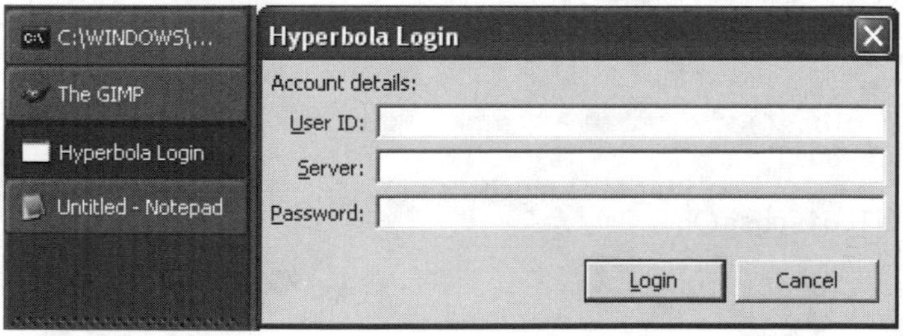

Figure 11–2   Task bar and dialog missing the Hyperbola icon

The quick fix for this is to directly access a Hyperbola icon and call
Dialog.setImage(Image). Since you've already configured the product icon via the
product configuration, a more elegant solution is to use the icon from the Hyperbola
product description. This isolates the login dialog from changes to the product's
branding.

Every running Eclipse has at most one product—the IProduct returned from
Platform.getProduct(). The product contains all of the information provided in
the related extension to the org.eclipse.runtime.product extension point. Of
course, getProduct() can return null since you can run an Eclipse application
directly without having a product.

Most of the information related to a product comes as free-form key/value
pairs. Eclipse defines some canonical keys such as the application name, the
About text, and so on in org.eclipse.ui.branding.IProductConstants. The
IProductConstants.WINDOW_IMAGES property is of particular interest here. The value
is a comma-separated list of image paths for different-size images that can be used to
represent product windows. Update the LoginDialog method configureShell(Shell)
to get the window images and use them for the dialog, as shown in the following
snippet:

```
org.eclipsercp.hyperbola/LoginDialog
protected void configureShell(Shell newShell) {
  super.configureShell(newShell);
  newShell.setText("Hyperbola Login");
  IProduct product = Platform.getProduct();
  if (product != null) {
    String bundleId = product.getDefiningBundle().getSymbolicName();
    String[] imageURLs = HyperbolaUtils.parseCSL(
      product.getProperty(IProductConstants.WINDOW_IMAGES));
    if (imageURLs.length > 0) {
      images = new Image[imageURLs.length];
      for (int i = 0; i < imageURLs.length; i++) {
        ImageDescriptor descriptor =
            AbstractUIPlugin.imageDescriptorFromPlugin(
                bundleId, imageURLs[i]);
        images[i] = descriptor.createImage(true);
      }
      newShell.setImages(images);
    }
  }
}
public boolean close() {
  if (images != null) {
    for (int i = 0; i < images.length; i++)
      images[i].dispose();
  }
  return super.close();
}
```

This code is doing more than you think. In particular, the `AbstractUIPlugin` static method `imageDescriptorFromPlugin(String, String)` isolates you from the form of the image paths. Contributed image paths can be a fully qualified uniform resource locator (URL) to the image or a relative path from within the declaring product plug-in. Here is an example of a fully qualified window image URL:

```
plugin.xml
<property
    name="windowImages"
    value="platform:/plugin/myplugin/icons/alt16.gif"/>
```

This example, on the other hand, shows the value as a relative image path:

```
org.eclipsercp.hyperbola/plugin.xml
<property
    name="windowImages"
    value="icons/alt16.gif"/>
```

Most of the images and icons contributed to UI extension points can take either relative or absolute URLs. This is useful as it allows you to put all your images and branding in one spot and then refer to them from wherever they are needed. Note, however, that if you are forcing or expecting other plug-ins to access your images, this effectively makes the image locations and names API—if you change them, the other plug-ins break.

11.2 Remembering Login Settings

If you have been following along and testing Hyperbola, you are likely tired of typing the same login information every time. These login settings should be saved between invocations of Hyperbola. In this section we augment the `Login-Dialog` to show a list of users and also save the list of users and their information for next time.

11.2.1 The Basics

You could just remember the last set of login information, but chat users often have several different identities. To accommodate this, Hyperbola needs a login dialog, as shown in Figure 11-3. The dialog has a list of user names instead of a single user. When a user name is selected in the **User ID** combo box, the **Server** and **Password** fields are updated with the information for that user. Furthermore, if you can add users, you should be able to delete them. The **Delete User** button allows users to delete the current account.

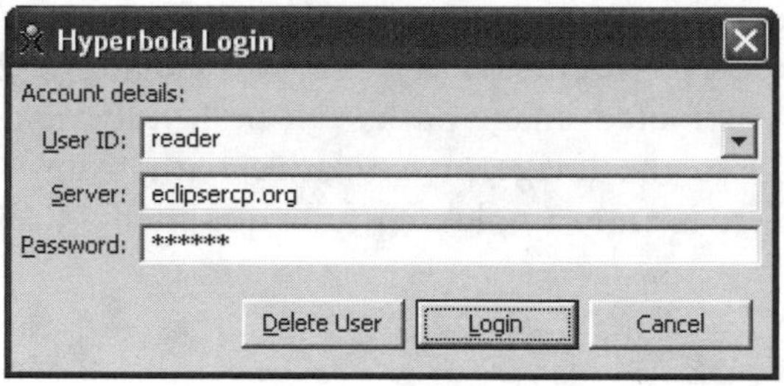

Figure 11–3   Improved login dialog

NOTE

To keep the code snippets concise, many of the details of building the UI and data structures have been omitted. The most interesting code is how to save and restore the list of users. Enough context is provided for you to understand the scope of the changes, but you should look at the sample code for this chapter for the complete story.

To minimize concurrent code changes, you should stage the implementation of this feature. First, refactor the dialog to accommodate several connection lists, and then add the code to save and restore the user information. This approach makes it easier to test and pinpoint problems since you are changing fewer things at once.

The LoginDialog class currently has a single ConnectionDetails field to track the login information for one user. You must refactor the dialog to support sets of connection details. Here is an overview of the refactoring:

1. Update the UI to allow selecting from a list of users. Replace the **User ID** text field with a combo box.

2. Add listeners to the **User ID** field to update the **Server** and **Password** fields when the user changes.

3. Update the data structures to track multiple user logins. Replace the ConnectionDetails field with a Map, called savedDetails, whose keys are user names and whose values are ConnectionDetails.

The first code snippet below shows the new savedDetails that track the connection information loaded and saved using the preferences mechanism—more on that a bit later. In addition, the userIdText field has been changed to a Combo. The code registers a listener on the Combo so that when the value is changed, the

serverText and passwordText values are updated based on the saved connection
information from savedDetails.

org.eclipsercp.hyperbola/LoginDialog
```
public class LoginDialog extends Dialog {
   private Combo userIdText;
   private Text serverText;
   private Text passwordText;
   private ConnectionDetails connectionDetails;
   private Map savedDetails = new HashMap();

   protected Control createDialogArea(Composite parent) {
     ...
     userIdText = new Combo(composite, SWT.BORDER);
     GridData gridData = new
         GridData(GridData.FILL, GridData.FILL, true, false);
     gridData.widthHint = convertHeightInCharsToPixels(20);
     userIdText.setLayoutData(gridData);
     userIdText.addListener(SWT.Modify, new Listener() {
       public void handleEvent(Event event) {
         ConnectionDetails d = (ConnectionDetails)
             savedDetails.get(userIdText.getText());
         if (d != null) {
           serverText.setText(d.getServer());
           passwordText.setText(d.getPassword());
         }
       }
   });
```

The user combo should be initialized with the list of known user names from
previous sessions and with the name used in the last session selected at startup. For
the time being, just add a couple of sample connection details to the savedDetails
field. The initializeUsers(String) method shown below can be called any time
after the combo is created, for example, at the end of createDialogArea(Composite).
It may be convenient to use this method in other scenarios to reset the list of
names in the combo.

org.eclipsercp.hyperbola/LoginDialog
```
protected void initializeUsers(String defaultUser) {
   userIdText.removeAll();
   passwordText.setText("");
   serverText.setText("");
   for (Iterator it = savedDetails.keySet().iterator(); it.hasNext();)
     userIdText.add((String) it.next());
   int index = Math.max(userIdText.indexOf(defaultUser), 0);
   userIdText.select(index);
}
```

Finally, the dialog refactoring is rounded out by adding the **Delete User** button to the button bar. When the button is clicked, the current user in the combo
is removed from the ConnectionDetails map and the combo is reinitialized.

org.eclipsercp.hyperbola/LoginDialog
```
protected void createButtonsForButtonBar(Composite parent) {
  Button deleteUser = createButton(parent,
      IDialogConstants.CLIENT_ID, "&Delete User", false);
  deleteUser.addSelectionListener(new SelectionAdapter() {
    public void widgetSelected(SelectionEvent e) {
      savedDetails.remove(userIdText.getText());
      initializeUsers("");
    }
  });
  createButton(parent, IDialogConstants.OK_ID, "&Login", true);
  createButton(parent, IDialogConstants.CANCEL_ID,
      IDialogConstants.CANCEL_LABEL, false);
}
```

Now you can test the new dialog by initializing the savedDetails map with a set of dummy users:

org.eclipsercp.hyperbola/LoginDialog
```
Public LoginDialog(Shell parent) {
  super(parent);
  savedDetails.put("reader",
      new ConnectionDetails("reader", "eclipsercp.org", "secret"));
  savedDetails.put("friend",
      new ConnectionDetails("friend", "eclipsercp.org", "secret"));
}
```

When you run the Hyperbola application, you should get the login dialog first. The dialog shows the sample users and allows you to delete users. Of course, Hyperbola does not remember your deletions yet—that's next.

11.2.2 Using Preferences

Now that the UI is mocked up, let's think about how to save connection information between sessions. There are many options for saving the user data from the login dialog. The brute-force approach is to use Platform.getStateLocation(Bundle). This gives you a location on the user's machine where the given plug-in can store any files it likes. This is useful if the plug-in needs to save large files or already has a persistence story. It is, however, a bit too heavyweight for storing simple preferences. All you really need here is a way to store a small set of key/value pairs. An easier approach is to use the preferences mechanism provided by the org.eclipse.equinox.preferences plug-in.

Preferences are key/value pairs where the key is an arbitrary name for the preference and the value is one of several types: boolean, long, int, String, float, or double. Preferences are stored and retrieved by the org.eclipse.equinox.preferences plug-in, so you don't have to be concerned with how this works. This makes it easier than having to write and read the file yourself.

NOTE

Eclipse preferences are very similar to `java.utils.prefs.Preferences` with additional support for searching, storing, and scoping. If you have already used Java Preferences, Eclipse preferences should be familiar.

Think of preferences as a hierarchical node structure where each node has a name and a unique and absolute path, as shown in Figure 11-4. Nodes in a preference tree are named and referenced in a similar manner to directories and files in a file system. The root node is referenced as "/" and children are referenced as absolute paths followed by the child's name. Each preference node has zero or more properties associated with it, where a property consists of a key and a value.

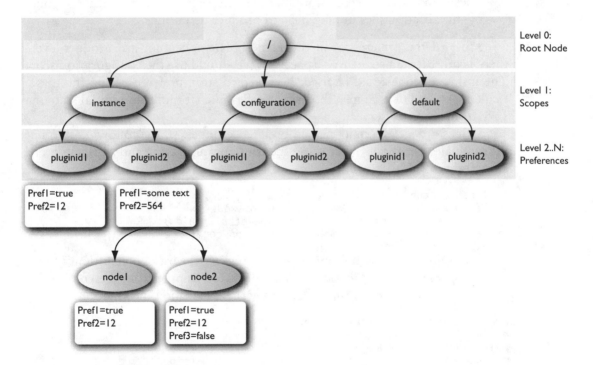

Figure 11–4   Preference node structure

The direct children of the root node are special and are referred to as *scopes*. Each scope is the root for all the preferences in that scope. The structure of the nodes in each scope is specified by the scope itself. Scopes are an open-ended set that controls the visibility and persistence of preferences. This means that the scope determines the location on the file system where preferences are stored. For example, in Hyperbola it may make sense to maintain some preferences on a per-user basis and some on a global, application basis. The set of scopes is extensible, but the Eclipse Runtime defines three basic scopes:

Instance scope—Preferences that are stored per workspace, or per running instance of Eclipse. If your product can run on different data sets, preferences stored in this type of scope are not available across the data sets.

Configuration scope—Preferences that are stored per Eclipse configuration. Such preferences are shared between multiple running instances of an Eclipse configuration. Configuration-scoped preferences are best suited for preferences that apply across the product regardless of the user or data set.

Default scope—Preferences that represent the default values for preferences. These are not changed or stored by the Eclipse Runtime but rather supplied by initialization files in plug-ins and product definitions.

Most of the preferences in the Hyperbola application are product-level—there is no real data set or workspace—so we should use the configuration scope. The instance scope could be used, however, to store preferences specific to particular servers. For example, the user's preferred chat mode and initial state may vary from server to server.

Scopes are just specially named preference nodes, so the following two lines are equivalent methods of accessing the configuration scope and getting a preference node called pluginid:

```
Preferences configurationScope =
  Platform.getPreferencesService().getRootNode().
      node(ConfigurationScope.SCOPE).node("pluginid");
Preferences preferences = new ConfigurationScope().getNode("pluginid");
```

Let's return to Hyperbola and store and retrieve the list of connection information using the configuration scope. The following snippet from the LoginDialog class shows the use of Preferences to save the connection information:

```
org.eclipsercp.hyperbola/LoginDialog
private static final String PASSWORD = "password";
private static final String SERVER = "server";
private static final String SAVED = "saved-connections";
private static final String LAST_USER = "last-connection";

public void saveDescriptors() {
    Preferences preferences = new ConfigurationScope()
        .getNode(Application.PLUGIN_ID);
    preferences.put(LAST_USER, connectionDetails.getUserId());
    Preferences connections = preferences.node(SAVED);
    for (Iterator it = savedDetails.keySet().iterator(); it.hasNext();) {
```

```
      String name = (String) it.next();
      ConnectionDetails d = (ConnectionDetails) savedDetails.get(name);
      Preferences connection = connections.node(name);
      connection.put(SERVER, d.getServer());
      connection.put(PASSWORD, d.getPassword());
    }
    try {
      connections.flush();
    } catch (BackingStoreException e) {
      e.printStackTrace();
    }
  }
}
```

The basic pattern when accessing Preferences is to start with the scope and then use your plug-in ID to isolate your preferences from those of other plug-ins. You can see this in the first line of saveDescriptors(). The last connection information is stored right on the node for the Hyperbola application in the configuration scope. This information is used to prime the login dialog with the previous selection the next time it is shown.

The hierarchical nature of Preferences is used to create a node for all saved connections. Effectively, this is a folder, just as you would use on the file system. In this node there is a node for each user. The node name is the user name and its map contains the server name and password.

WARNING

It is generally not a good idea to save passwords in preferences because they are stored as text and are easily read by anyone who has access to your machine. Since the Hyperbola application is sending its login information as text, we don't worry about this for now. If you need to store passwords on the user's machine, you can use the secure preferences mechanism in Eclipse, which saves passwords in a lightly encrypted file.

When the preferences have been created, calling Preferences.flush() ensures that they are saved to disk. The connection information is saved when the login dialog is closed. Overriding the Dialog.buttonPressed() method allows you to run arbitrary code based on the button that was pressed. It's important to eventually delegate to the overridden method so the standard behavior, such as closing the dialog, is still performed.

org.eclipsercp.hyperbola/LoginDialog
```
protected void buttonPressed(int buttonId) {
  String userId = userIdText.getText();
  String server = serverText.getText();
```

```
    String password = passwordText.getText();
    connectionDetails = new ConnectionDetails(userId, server, password);
    savedDetails.put(userId, connectionDetails);
    if (buttonId == IDialogConstants.OK_ID ||
        buttonId == IDialogConstants.CANCEL_ID)
      saveDescriptors();
    super.buttonPressed(buttonId);
  }
```

The LoginDialog must also load the preferences when it's created. Loading is a mirror image of storing, as shown in the LoginDialog snippet below. You simply ask for the same Preferences node and scan its properties and child nodes. You do not have to explicitly load the preferences from disk; they are loaded by the Eclipse Runtime as needed.

org.eclipsercp.hyperbola/LoginDialog
```
private void loadDescriptors() {
  try {
    Preferences preferences = new ConfigurationScope()
        .getNode(Application.PLUGIN_ID);
    Preferences connections = preferences.node(SAVED);
    String[] userNames = connections.childrenNames();
    for (int i = 0; i < userNames.length; i++) {
      String userName = userNames[i];
      Preferences node = connections.node(userName);
      savedDetails.put(userName, new ConnectionDetails(
          userName,
          node.get(SERVER, ""),
          node.get(PASSWORD, "")));
    }
    connectionDetails = (ConnectionDetails) savedDetails.get(
        preferences.get(LAST_USER, ""));
  } catch (BackingStoreException e) {
    e.printStackTrace();
  }
}
```

11.2.3 Storing Preferences Securely

Now that we have an idea of how to store preferences in general, how can we store user-sensitive information securely within Eclipse? Eclipse has an ISecurePreferences API that mimics the preferences mechanism discussed in the previous section. Logically speaking, the secure preferences API combines the functionality of a key ring with that of the normal preferences API. To access secure preferences, one simply calls the SecurePreferencesFactory in the org.eclipse.equinox.security plug-in.

```
ISecurePreferences preferences = SecurePreferencesFactory.getDefault();
ISecurePreferences connections = preferences.node("pluginid");
```

Let's return to the place we load preferences in Hyperbola. In the snippet below, the `SecureLoginDialog` obtains an `ISecurePreferences` node via the `SecurePreferencesFactory` instead of just a `Preferences` node. Otherwise, the code to load preferences is identical to what you did using the normal preferences mechanism in Eclipse.

org.eclipsercp.hyperbola/SecureLoginDialog
```
private void loadDescriptors() {
  try {
    ISecurePreferences preferences =
      SecurePreferencesFactory.getDefault();
    ISecurePreferences connections = preferences.node(SAVED);
    String[] userNames = connections.childrenNames();
    for (int i = 0; i < userNames.length; i++) {
      String userName = userNames[i];
      ISecurePreferences node = connections.node(userName);
      savedDetails.put(userName, new ConnectionDetails(
          userName,
          node.get(SERVER, ""),
          node.get(PASSWORD, "")));
    }
    connectionDetails = (ConnectionDetails) savedDetails.get(
        preferences.get(LAST_USER, ""));
  } catch (StorageException e) {
    e.printStackTrace();
  }
}
```

Secure preferences are stored in a similar fashion to normal preferences with one minor difference. When you store secure preferences in a node, there's an additional argument to specify whether you want the preferences encrypted or not using a password provider from Equinox security. The snippet below demonstrates encrypting the password for a connection but not the other information. If we deemed the other preferences important to encrypt, it's a matter of simply changing the `false` statement to `true` when storing the preferences.

org.eclipsercp.hyperbola/SecureLoginDialog
```
private void saveDescriptors() {
try {
    ISecurePreferences preferences =
            SecurePreferencesFactory.getDefault();
    preferences.put(LAST_USER, connectionDetails.getUserId(), false);
    ISecurePreferences connections = preferences.node(SAVED);
    for (Iterator it = savedDetails.keySet().iterator(); it.hasNext();) {
        String name = (String) it.next();
        ConnectionDetails d = (ConnectionDetails)
savedDetails.get(name);
        ISecurePreferences connection = connections.node(name);
        connection.put(SERVER, d.getServer(), false);
        connection.put(PASSWORD, d.getPassword(), true);
    }
```

```
        preferences.flush();
} catch (StorageException e) {
        e.printStackTrace();
} catch (IOException e) {
        e.printStackTrace();
}}
```

WARNING

Note that secure preferences are intended to store only relatively small amounts of data, such as passwords and other lightweight sensitive information. If you need to securely store large objects, consider encrypting such objects in a symmetric way using a randomly generated password and use secure preferences to store the password.

11.3 Adding Auto-login Preferences

Even though previously entered login information is now saved, users often appreciate the option of logging in automatically at startup. The Hyperbola application can present this option directly from the login dialog, as shown in Figure 11-5, or from a Preferences dialog, as shown in Figure 11-7. Let's do both!

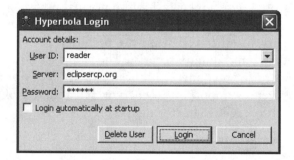

Figure 11–5   Login dialog with the auto-login preference

11.3.1 Creating a Preference Page

Preference pages contain a grab bag of application settings that users normally do not have to change. They are there to allow specific configuration of your application. Basic support for preference pages in Eclipse is provided by JFace. This support is extended by the Workbench to allow contributing preference pages in a plugin.xml. The Workbench also adds helper widgets that are useful in building preference pages.

To add a preference page for the auto-login preference, you first need to define a preference page extension for the Workbench's `org.eclipse.ui.preferencePages` extension point. Preference pages contributed this way automatically appear in the Workbench's standard Preferences dialog. You have added extensions a few times by now, so we will skim over it quickly here.

Open the Hyperbola plug-in editor, flip to the **Extensions** page, and click **Add....** Choose the `org.eclipse.ui.preferencePages` extension point and click **Finish**. That creates the extension. Right-click on the extension itself and choose **New > page**. Once you have the page element, fill in the details as shown in Figure 11-6. For the **class** field, use the normal trick of clicking on the **class** link to create a skeleton for the preference page class.

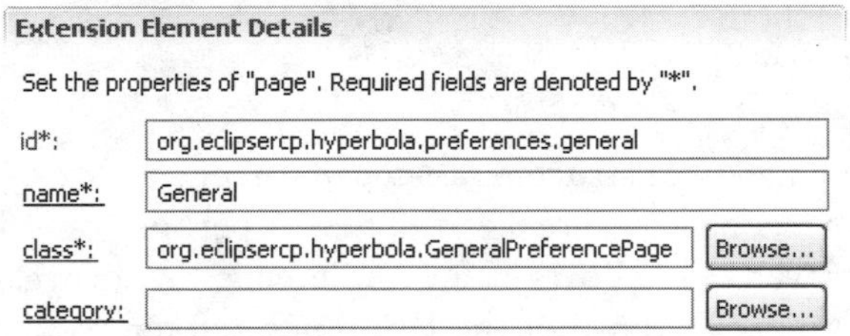

Extension Element Details

Set the properties of "page". Required fields are denoted by "*".

id*:	org.eclipsercp.hyperbola.preferences.general
name*:	General
class*:	org.eclipsercp.hyperbola.GeneralPreferencePage Browse...
category:	Browse...

Figure 11–6   Preference page extension point

All preference pages must implement the interface `IWorkbenchPreferencePage` by subclassing either `PreferencePage` or `FieldEditorPreferencePage`. The skeleton you created likely subclassed `PreferencePage`—change this to subclass `FieldEditorPreferencePage`. Field editors are very useful controls that are linked to underlying preferences. `FieldEditorPreferencePage` has various helpers for creating `FieldEditors`.

For the Hyperbola application, all we want to do is display a check box that allows toggling the auto-login preference. The resulting preference page is shown in Figure 11-7. The following code snippet shows the source for that preference page:

`org.eclipsercp.hyperbola/GeneralPreferencePage`
```
public class GeneralPreferencePage extends FieldEditorPreferencePage
    implements IWorkbenchPreferencePage {
  public static final String AUTO_LOGIN = "prefs_auto_login";
  private ScopedPreferenceStore preferences;
  public GeneralPreferencePage() {
    super(GRID);
    preferences = new ScopedPreferenceStore(
        new ConfigurationScope(),Application.PLUGIN_ID);
    setPreferenceStore(preferences);
  }
```

```
public void init(IWorkbench workbench) {
}
protected void createFieldEditors() {
  BooleanFieldEditor boolEditor = new BooleanFieldEditor(
      AUTO_LOGIN,
      "Login automatically at startup",
      getFieldEditorParent()
  );
  addField(boolEditor);
}
public boolean performOk() {
  try {
    preferences.save();
  } catch (IOException e) {
    HyperbolaUtils.log(
        "Unable to save general preference page preferences", e);
  }
  return super.performOk();
}
}
```

When the preference page is constructed, a ScopedPreferenceStore is created to wrap the configuration-scoped preferences for the Hyperbola plug-in. This is a backward-compatible layer that allows using preferences with FieldEditors. The FieldEditors APIs predate the use of the Runtime preferences and thus are not compatible without a helper class.

When the page is drawn, createFieldEditors() is called by the Workbench. The BooleanFieldEditor here is given the key for the auto-login preference. It then reads and writes that preference automatically. When the user clicks the **Apply** button, the preferences are saved to disk.

11.3.2 Adding the Action

Now that the preference page is defined, you have to add an action that opens the Preferences dialog. The Workbench provides an action called ActionFactory .PREFERENCES that opens the standard Preferences dialog and shows all registered preference pages. Update Hyperbola's ActionBarAdvisor to create and place the preferences action. The following snippet shows the relevant lines and leaves you to place them accordingly:

```
org.eclipsercp.hyperbola/ApplicationActionBarAdvisor
public void makeActions(IWorkbenchWindow window) {
  ...
  preferencesAction = ActionFactory.PREFERENCES.create(window);
  register(preferencesAction);
}

protected void fillMenuBar(IMenuManager menuBar) {
  MenuManager hyperbolaMenu = new MenuManager("&Hyperbola",
```

```
        "hyperbola");
    ...
    hyperbolaMenu.add(preferencesAction);
}
```

Start the Hyperbola application and select **Hyperbola > Preferences** to see the **Preferences** dialog, as shown in Figure 11-7.

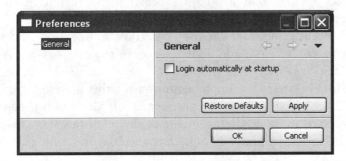

Figure 11–7   Standard **Preferences** dialog

11.3.3 Accessing Preferences

To implement auto-login, Hyperbola must be updated to check the preference value and react accordingly, as shown in this snippet:

```
org.eclipsercp.hyperbola/Application
private boolean login(final Session session) {
    boolean firstTry = true;
    LoginDialog loginDialog = new LoginDialog(null);
    while (session.getConnection() == null ||
            !session.getConnection().isAuthenticated()) {
        Preferences preferences = new
            ConfigurationScope().getNode(Application.PLUGIN_ID);
        boolean auto_login = preferences.getBoolean(
            GeneralPreferencePage.AUTO_LOGIN, true);
        ConnectionDetails details = loginDialog.getConnectionDetails();
        if (!auto_login || details == null || !firstTry) {
            if (loginDialog.open() != Window.OK)
                return false;
            details = loginDialog.getConnectionDetails();
        }
        firstTry = false;
        session.setConnectionDetails(details);
        ...
```

11.3.4 Default Preference Values

The preference page is up and working, but there is still one last detail to address—the default value of the auto-login preference.

The Workbench provides a default preferences scope called DefaultScope, which contains default values for preferences. Having a default scope and searching multiple scopes allows you to have defaults for a preference initialized in the DefaultScope but customized in another scope.

There is also an extension point called org.eclipse.runtime.preferences that can be used to register a class that initializes default preference values. The preference initializer ensures that a plug-in's preferences are initialized before another plug-in can access them.

Let's add a preference initializer for the Hyperbola application that sets the auto-login default to false. First, add an extension to the org.eclipse.runtime .preferences.initializer extension point. For the class attribute, create a class called PreferenceInitializer. The implementation for this preference initializer is shown below. Eclipse ensures that the preference initializer is run *before* any preferences are accessed in the node that matches this plug-in's ID. This implies that each plug-in is storing its preferences under a node with its plug-in ID.

org.eclipsercp.hyperbola/PreferenceInitializer
```
public class PreferenceInitializer extends
        AbstractPreferenceInitializer {
  public PreferenceInitializer() {
    super();
  }
  public void initializeDefaultPreferences() {
    IEclipsePreferences defaults = new
        DefaultScope().getNode(Application.PLUGIN_ID);
    defaults.putBoolean(GeneralPreferencePage.AUTO_LOGIN, false);
  }
}
```

11.3.5 Preferences on the Login Dialog

Although the auto-login preference is available in the Preferences dialog, it's convenient to also allow users to set this preference in context, for example, when they are using the login dialog. This is very easy to add. In the LoginDialog method createDialogArea(Composite), create an extra check box that is initialized with the preference value. Then we update the preference value when the check box state changes, as shown in the following snippet:

org.eclipsercp.hyperbola/LoginDialog
```
final Button autoLogin = new Button(composite, SWT.CHECK);
autoLogin.setText("Login &automatically at startup");
autoLogin.setLayoutData(
    new GridData(SWT.BEGINNING, SWT.CENTER, true, true, 2, 1));
autoLogin.addSelectionListener(new SelectionAdapter() {
    public void widgetSelected(SelectionEvent e) {
      IEclipsePreferences prefs =
          new ConfigurationScope().getNode(Application.PLUGIN_ID);
```

```
        prefs.putBoolean(
            GeneralPreferencePage.AUTO_LOGIN, autoLogin.getSelection());
    }
});
Preferences preferences =
    new ConfigurationScope(). getNode(Application.PLUGIN_ID);
boolean auto_login = preferences.getBoolean(
    GeneralPreferencePage.AUTO_LOGIN, true);
autoLogin.setSelection(auto_login);
```

11.4 Summary

The login dialog greatly improves the usability of Hyperbola. Here you learned how to add preferences to your application. Notice that again, Eclipse takes care of most of the hard work. The Eclipse RCP is full of frameworks for adding standard elements, such as preferences, to your application. Later chapters highlight additional facilities, but there are too many for us to cover them all. The online Eclipse Help is a good source of information on the ones we omit.

11.5 Pointers

○ Eclipse **Help > Platform Plug-in Developer Guide > Runtime overview**

○ Eclipse **Help > Platform Plug-in Developer Guide > Runtime overview > Security**

CHAPTER 12

Adding Key Bindings

All applications have actions that are initiated from the keyboard more often than from a toolbar or menu. Power users especially expect quick access to common actions using the keyboard. The Workbench includes an extremely flexible framework to manage actions and key bindings. This includes having locale- or function-grouped key binding configurations and key bindings that apply to only certain parts of the application.

You can add key bindings for all Hyperbola actions since there aren't that many. In general, however, you have to carefully select the actions to bind to key sequences. One rule of thumb comes from the observation that toolbars also contain frequently used actions. As such, consider providing key bindings for all of your toolbar items. Note also that actions often show up in various menus, so you can show their related key sequences there.

In this chapter we show you how to

○ Define key bindings for all the Hyperbola application's actions

○ Show key bindings in menus

○ Add key bindings for the reused **Quit** and **About** Workbench actions

○ Use key binding configurations to scope bindings

○ Add the Keys preference page to Hyperbola

12.1 Defining Commands

To assign a key binding to an action, you first have to create a command. Commands are the declarative components of an action and are independent of the implementation. They can be categorized and assigned key bindings. In Chapter 18, "Commands," we will cover them in more depth.

TIP

Why is it important to separate a command from an action implementation? A good example is when you need to provide key bindings for standard actions such as copy, cut, and paste. The implementation of these operations depends on the context, so the command must be separate from the implementation. A key binding can be defined for the command that applies regardless of the underlying implementation.

To start, let's add a key binding for the **Add Contact** action. Open the Hyperbola plug-in editor and create an `org.eclipse.ui.commands` extension. Once you've created a commands extension, take a look at the extension point description using the **Open extension point description** link in the **Extension Details** section. This gives you a good description of what the extension point does and, in the case of commands, the meaning of the fields for a commands extension. Notice that there are several different elements for a commands extension, such as commands, categories, and key bindings. In brief, a commands extension provides one-stop shopping for all your command needs.

It's good practice to group related commands together using *categories*. This helps users navigate the list of commands when managing key bindings. Start by creating a category, as shown in Figure 12-1. Click on the **commands** extension and from the context menu select **New > category**.

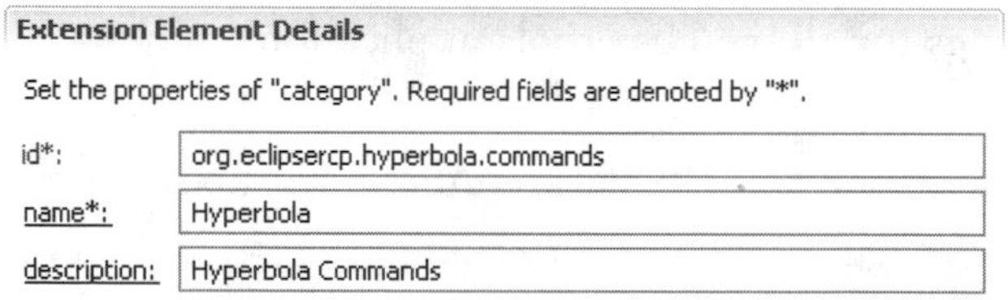

Extension Element Details

Set the properties of "category". Required fields are denoted by "*".

id*:	org.eclipsercp.hyperbola.commands
name*:	Hyperbola
description:	Hyperbola Commands

Figure 12–1 Category element details

Once the category is defined, create a command for the **Add Contact** action, as shown in Figure 12-2. Again, click on the **commands** extension and select **New > command**.

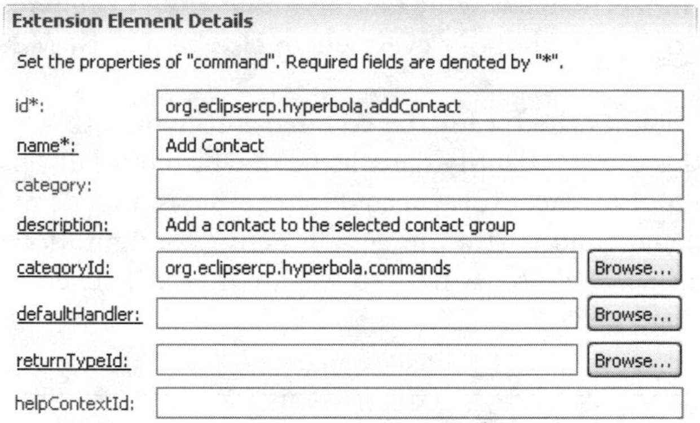

Extension Element Details

Set the properties of "command". Required fields are denoted by "*".

id*:	org.eclipsercp.hyperbola.addContact
name*:	Add Contact
category:	
description:	Add a contact to the selected contact group
categoryId:	org.eclipsercp.hyperbola.commands Browse...
defaultHandler:	Browse...
returnTypeId:	Browse...
helpContextId:	

Figure 12–2   Command element details

For the **id**, use the value defined in AddContactAction.ID. This is the unique identifier for this command. You should always have a constant for the command ID since it is needed to programmatically associate an action with a command. The **name** is a human-readable form that is displayed in a preference or configuration dialog. This name is not shown in menus and so it does not need a menu accelerator (e.g., "&" character). Last, the **categoryId** references the command category you just defined. The **category** element is deprecated and can be left empty. For simplicity, we will leave the other properties empty.

The next step is to add an org.eclipse.ui.bindings extension, add key bindings, and assign them to the proper command via the **commandId** attribute. Click on the org.eclipse.ui.bindings extension, and from the context menu select **New > key.**

The key details are shown in Figure 12-3. The most interesting part of the key element is the **sequence,** in this case, **M1+A.** *M1* in the sequence stands for "Meta 1."

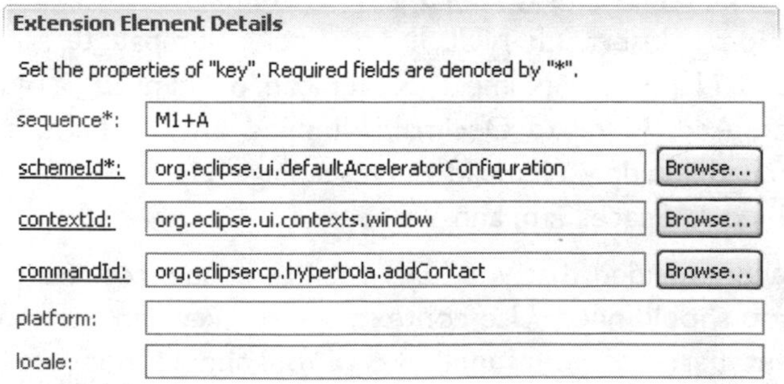

Extension Element Details

Set the properties of "key". Required fields are denoted by "*".

sequence*:	M1+A
schemeId*:	org.eclipse.ui.defaultAcceleratorConfiguration Browse...
contextId:	org.eclipse.ui.contexts.window Browse...
commandId:	org.eclipsercp.hyperbola.addContact Browse...
platform:	
locale:	

Figure 12–3   Key binding element details

This is the platform-independent way of talking about the "Command" key on the Mac and the "Ctrl" key just about everywhere else. Similarly, *M2* is "Shift" and *M3* is "Alt."

The **commandId** defines the ID for the command to which this key binding applies. The **schemeId** is used to identify the scheme in which this key binding lives. The `org.eclipse.ui.defaultAcceleratorConfiguration` is the default scheme created by the Workbench and is also the default active configuration. For now, the default scheme is fine. We discuss how to use an alternate scheme in Section 12.4, "Key Schemes."

Key Sequences

Key *sequences* are sets of *keystrokes* separated by spaces. A keystroke represents one or more keys held down at the same time. A keystroke can have zero or more modifier keys and exactly one other key. The keys are separated by the "+" character.

The recognized modifier keys are M1, M2, M3, M4, Alt, Command, Ctrl, and Shift. The "M" modifier keys are a platform-independent way of representing keys, and these are generally preferred. M1 is the "Command" key on MacOS X and the "Ctrl" key on most other platforms. M2 is the "Shift" key. M3 is the "Option" key on MacOS X and the "Alt" key on most other platforms. M4 is the "Ctrl" key on MacOS X and is undefined on other platforms. Since **M2+M3+<Letter>** (**Alt+Shift+<Letter>**) is reserved on MacOS X for writing special characters, such bindings are commonly undefined for `platform="carbon"` and redefined as **M1+M3+<Letter>**.

The actual key is generally specified simply as the ASCII character, in uppercase. So, for example, **F** and **,** are examples of such keys. However, there are some special keys that have no printable ASCII representation. The following is a list of the current special keys: Arrow_Down, Arrow_Left, Arrow_Right, Arrow_Up, Break, BS, Caps_Lock, CR, Del, End, Esc, F1, F2, F3, F4, F5, F6, F7, F8, F9, F10, F11, F12, F13, F14, F15, FF, Home, Insert, LF, NUL, Num_Lock, Numpad_0, Numpad_1, Numpad_2, Numpad_3, Numpad_4, Numpad_5, Numpad_6, Numpad_7, Numpad_8, Numpad_9, Numpad_Add, Numpad_Decimal, Numpad_Divide, Numpad_Enter, Numpad_Equal, Numpad_Multiply, Numpad_Subtract, Page_Up, Page_Down, Pause, Print_Screen, Scroll_Lock, Space, Tab, and VT.

It is also strongly recommended that you keep the key sequences short. One or two are the most you should need. Use contexts to give key sequences different meanings in different parts of your application. You should not use any key sequence that contains more than four keystrokes at the very most.

Now that you have defined the required extension elements, you must link the AddContactAction to its associated command. This is done by assigning the command ID to the action using the IAction method setActionDefinitionId(String). Update AddContactAction's constructor, as shown in the following code snippet:

org.eclipsercp.hyperbola/AddContactAction
```
public AddContactAction(IWorkbenchWindow window) {
  this.window = window;
  window.getSelectionService().addSelectionListener(this);
  setId(ID);
  setActionDefinitionId(ID);
  setText("&Add Contact...");
  setToolTipText("Add a contact to your contacts list.");
  setImageDescriptor(
      AbstractUIPlugin.imageDescriptorFromPlugin(
          Application.PLUGIN_ID, IImageKeys.ADD_CONTACT));
}
```

---

actionDefinitionId VERSUS ID

A common point of confusion is that the *ID* defined on an IAction is not the same as the action's *command ID*. The ID is used exclusively for supporting *retargetable actions*, while the actionDefinitionId is used to associate actions with commands. To reduce the complexity in your application, we recommend that you simply set both to the same value. It makes your life easier if you consider them to be the same and use a common constant for both.

Once the action is associated with the command ID, the action has to be registered with the Workbench. This tells the Workbench to call the action when the user inputs the key sequence. Hyperbola's actions are created in ApplicationActionBarAdvisor. Each action is registered by calling ActionBarAdvisor.register (IAction).

You might recall that actions are registered to ensure that they are properly deleted. Registering an action using ActionBarAdvisor.register(IAction) also registers the action's key binding. The following code snippet shows the register (IAction) method supplied by the Workbench. If you are already calling the method, no further effort is required. If not, change the code either to call register(IAction) or to call registerGlobalAction(IAction) directly.

org.eclipse.ui.workbench/ActionBarAdvisor
```
protected void register(IAction action) {
  Assert.isNotNull(action, "Action must not be null"); //$NON-NLS-1$
  String id = action.getId();
  Assert.isNotNull(id, "Action must not have null id");
```

```
      getActionBarConfigurer().registerGlobalAction(action);
      actions.put(id, action);
}
```

Just to be sure, go back to `ApplicationActionBarAdvisor.makeActions`
(`IWorkbenchWindow`) and confirm that the actions are being registered. When the
action definition ID is set in the `AddContactAction` constructor and the action is
registered with the Workbench, the action can participate in the key binding
mechanism. This is a useful pattern to use for all your actions.

org.eclipsercp.hyperbola/HyperbolaActionBarAdvisor
```
protected void makeActions(IWorkbenchWindow window) {
   exitAction = ActionFactory.QUIT.create(window);
   register(exitAction);
   aboutAction = ActionFactory.ABOUT.create(window);
   register(aboutAction);
   addContactAction = new AddContactAction(window);
   register(addContactAction);
   chatAction = new ChatAction(window);
   register(chatAction);
   ...
}
```

12.2 Checkpoint

At this point everything is in place to have the **Add Contact** action run when the
user inputs the **Ctrl+A** key sequence. Run Hyperbola now, try typing **Ctrl+A**, then
look at the **Hyperbola** menu and notice that the key binding is displayed at the
right of the menu, as shown in Figure 12-4.

Figure 12–4   Add Contact action with key binding in menu

12.3 Adding Key Bindings for Workbench Actions

Remember back when you added the **Exit** and **About** actions? They are defined
by the Workbench, and in the `ApplicationActionBarAdvisor` class you simply

created the actions and added them to the Hyperbola menu. Let's add some key bindings for them: **Ctrl+Q** to exit and **Ctrl+Shift+F1** to launch the About dialog.

Normally you would create a key binding for the actions as we did previously. But these are reusable actions from the Workbench and they likely already have commands. Unfortunately, the only way to find out if a command exists is by looking at the action's implementation to determine if the IAction method setActionDefinitionId(String) is being called. If it is, you don't need to define a new command. If a command is not defined, or you cannot tell, you must define one.

The following code snippets are what you would find if you browsed starting in the ActionBarAdvisor method makeActions(), then to the org.eclipse.ui .actions.ActionFactory, and finally into the QuitAction's constructor. Here you can see that the command ID for the **Quit** action is org.eclipse.ui.file.exit. Use this command ID to create a key binding for the action.

org.eclipsercp.hyperbola/HyperbolaActionBarAdvisor
```
protected void makeActions(IWorkbenchWindow window) {
   this.window = window;
   exitAction = ActionFactory.QUIT.create(window);
   register(exitAction);
}
```

org.eclipse.ui.workbench/ActionFactory
```
public static final ActionFactory QUIT = new ActionFactory("quit") {
   public IWorkbenchAction create(IWorkbenchWindow window) {
      if (window == null)
         throw new IllegalArgumentException();
      IWorkbenchAction action = new QuitAction(window);
      action.setId(getId());
      return action;
   }
};
```

org.eclipse.ui.workbench/QuitAction
```
public QuitAction(IWorkbenchWindow window) {
   this.workbenchWindow = window;
   setText(WorkbenchMessages.Exit_text);
   setToolTipText(WorkbenchMessages.Exit_toolTip);
   setActionDefinitionId("org.eclipse.ui.file.exit");
   window.getWorkbench().getHelpSystem().setHelp(this,
         IWorkbenchHelpContextIds.QUIT_ACTION);
}
```

After following through the code and finding the command ID, add a key binding for the **Quit** action and ensure that the ActionBarAdvisor method register(IAction) is called. The steps are the same as you used previously to register the **Add Contact** action.

Now that the **Quit** action has a key binding, as shown in Figure 12-5, rerun the same steps to add a key binding for the **About** action.

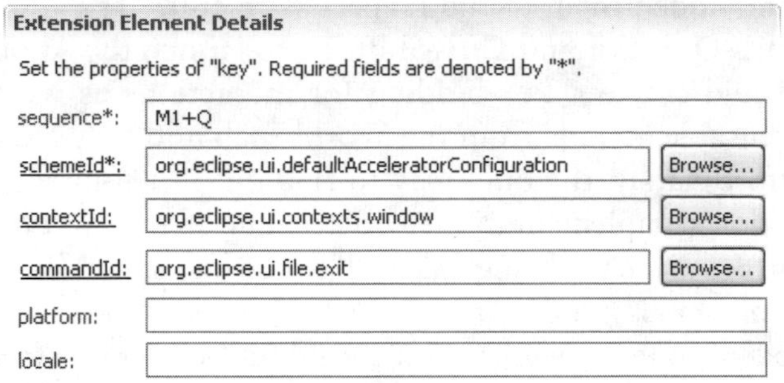

Extension Element Details

Set the properties of "key". Required fields are denoted by "*".

sequence*:	M1+Q
schemeId*:	org.eclipse.ui.defaultAcceleratorConfiguration	Browse...
contextId:	org.eclipse.ui.contexts.window	Browse...
commandId:	org.eclipse.ui.file.exit	Browse...
platform:	
locale:	

Figure 12–5   Key binding element details for existing Workbench actions

12.4 Key Schemes

You've seen that when defining a key binding, it must be assigned to a key scheme, and the binding is enabled only when the given scheme is active. The Workbench defines a scheme called `org.eclipse.ui.defaultAcceleratorConfiguration`, which is used as the scheme for all commands defined in the Workbench. It is also the default scheme used when the Workbench starts.

When defining key bindings in your RCP application, you have the choice of assigning them to this default key scheme with the caveat that there may be conflicts with existing bindings. An alternative is to define another key scheme using the `org.eclipse.ui.bindings` extension point and assigning all your key bindings to this scheme. You can even define key bindings to commands provided by the Workbench and assign them into this new scheme. The following example assigns the **Add Contact** command to the **M1+B** key instead of to **M1+A**, which was its value in the default key scheme:

org.eclipsercp.hyperbola/plugin.xml

```
<extension
  point="org.eclipse.ui.bindings">
  <scheme
      description="Keys for Hyperbola "
      id="org.eclipsercp.hyperbola.keyConfig"
      name="Hyperbola Keys"/>
  <key
      commandId="org.eclipsercp.hyperbola.addContact"
      contextId="org.eclipse.ui.contexts.window"
      schemeId="org.eclipsercp.hyperbola.keyConfig"
      sequence="M1+B"/>
</extension>
```

The new scheme, called `org.eclipsercp.hyperbola.keyConfig`, is not enabled by default. To enable it, you must add an entry to your plug-in customization file as follows (see Section 13.4, "Adding Help Content," for how to create a preference customization file):

```
org.eclipse.ui/KEY_CONFIGURATION_ID= org.eclipsercp.hyperbola.keyConfig
```

Alternatively, you can use the **Keys** preference page explained in the next section to switch between registered key schemes.

12.5 Keys Preference Page

The Workbench ships with a preference page that allows users to configure key sequences and toggle the active scheme. This preference page is called the **Keys** preference page. You can see it in action in the IDE by opening **Window > Preferences... > General > Keys**. The preference page shows all the commands in the selected scheme along with their bindings.

You can add this preference page to your application by defining an `org.eclipse.ui.preferences` extension with a special syntax. The Workbench includes an extension factory that provides access to these pages via a set of identifiers. An extension factory, or `IExecutableExtensionFactory`, is a parameterized executable extension that can create classes based on the parameters defined in the extension definition. This is useful for hiding implementation classes. The identifiers are used in preferences extensions as shown below. Notice that the markup is the same as for a regular preference extension, but instead of specifying the preference page's implementation class directly, `org.eclipse.ui.ExtensionFactory` is used and the **Keys** preference page identifier, `keysPreferencePage`, is given as a parameter.

```
org.eclipsercp.hyperbola/plugin.xml
<extension point="org.eclipse.ui.preferences">
   <view
       class="org.eclipse.ui.ExtensionFactory:keysPreferencePage"
       id="org.eclipsercp.hyperbola.preferences.keys"
       name="Keys"/>
</extension>
```

If you provide the **Keys** preference page in your application, you must define your own scheme, as defined in Section 12.4, because this preference page shows all the commands defined by the Workbench, even those that are not used in your application. Having a specific configuration will trim this list down to only those defined by your application. See Section 17.3, "Standard Workbench Actions," for more reusable preference pages and actions, and Section 11.3.2, "Adding the Action," for details on how to add the action to open the preferences page.

12.6 Summary

Key bindings are an essential part of your application's usability. You've seen that command IDs are the key to linking actions to key bindings. Many steps are required to link actions to key bindings. From the basic pattern you can see that it all comes down to everyone agreeing on the common currency—command IDs.

Always start by creating a set of constants for each of your actions. In Hyperbola they are added as static fields on each action. Then create associated commands for each using the IDs you've already defined, and add the key bindings that reference the commands. The final step is to associate an action with a command so that when a key sequence is pressed, the Workbench knows which action to run. A good rule of thumb is to configure each action in its constructor with its associated command ID by calling `IAction.setDefinitionId(String)`. Then register the action in the `ActionBarAdvisor` by calling `register(IAction)`, or if the action is defined within a view or editor, call `IActionBars.setGlobal-ActionHandler(String, IAction)`.

12.7 Pointers

○ Eclipse **Help > Platform Plug-in Developer Guide > Advanced workbench concepts > Workbench key bindings.**

○ There is a deep dive on commands in Chapter 18.

CHAPTER 13

Adding Help

Hyperbola is a complete though basic chat client. Even with its modest capabilities, users can run into trouble getting it configured or dealing with connections. Fortunately, the Eclipse Platform includes support for static, dynamic, and context-sensitive Help. Adding Help capabilities to Hyperbola gives its users a place to go for answers. This is an integral part of real-world applications. Also, adding Help support also marks the first time that you need to use plug-ins that are not included by default.

In this chapter we show how to

○ Set up your target environment to take advantage of Help support

○ Add Help support to Hyperbola

○ Add context-sensitive Help support

○ Create and structure Help content

13.1 Adding to the Target Platform

The Hyperbola prototypes in previous chapters used plug-ins that were found in the RCP SDK (in the target platform) and some of our own code (in the workspace). In this chapter we are looking to expand the target platform and use Eclipse plug-ins from outside the RCP SDK. To do this, we must get the plug-ins from somewhere and add them to the target.

Early in Chapter 3, "Tutorial Introduction," you set up separate IDE and target environments. This separation became important in Chapter 9, "Packaging Hyperbola," when we used the delta pack to the target platform to allow for cross-platform exporting. Here we'll see how the separation helps but also makes life a little harder.

13.1.1 Getting Plug-ins

At some point you will add capability to your application that you think someone else has already implemented. Instead of searching the Web, looking for plug-ins, you should start by looking at the list of plug-ins included in the Eclipse Platform. Over 100 plug-ins are included in the Platform, and many are useful in RCP applications. See Chapter 29, "Eclipse Ecosystem," for more information on which of the 100-plus plug-ins can actually be used in your RCP applications.

Chances are you already have an Eclipse Platform plug-in somewhere on your system. For example, if you did exactly as we described when creating your target platform and IDE setups, the target platform and IDE are based on the same version of Eclipse. That means your IDE has many plug-ins that can be used in your application. Since they are the same version levels of Eclipse, the plug-ins are all compatible with each other.

If your IDE and target versions do not match (as often happens at some point during a project), or you need plug-ins that do not happen to be in the IDE install, you must acquire them from somewhere. Typically, going to the originator is the best bet. For Eclipse plug-ins, that means returning to *http://eclipse.org/downloads*. Once there, find the archive that has the plug-ins you need. For example, the Platform SDK contains all the plug-ins you need for the Hyperbola example in this book. If you are using the EMF, GEF, or one of the other Eclipse projects, they typically have reasonably obvious SDK downloads.

13.1.2 Adding Plug-ins

Once you have the plug-ins on your machine, they need to be added to the target platform. This is done with the following steps:

○ In the target editor's **Definition** page click **Add…** and select **Software Site**. Click **Next**.

○ On the subsequent **Add Software Site** wizard page, choose **Galileo** in the **Work with** drop-down. If there is a more recent release repository available, feel free to choose it. If the site you want is not listed, click the **Add…** button and enter the **Name** and URL **Location** for the site. For example, the Galileo site is at *http://download.eclipse.org/releases/galileo*.

○ Once the site is selected, the content area of the wizard should fill in as shown in Figure 13-1. Uncheck the **Group by Category** box under the content area and then type "Help" in the filter area. Select **Eclipse Help System** to add Help support.

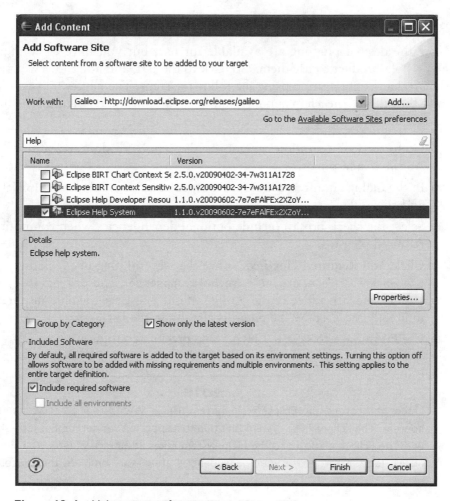

Figure 13–1   Help system software site

○ **Important!** You must **uncheck** the **Include required software** box at the bottom left of the wizard. Failure to do this will result in a bloated target that may not work for the Hyperbola scenario.

○ Click **Finish**.

13.2 Configuring the Help Plug-ins

Now the desired plug-ins are available for use, but you have to configure the Hyperbola product to use them. Go back to the IDE and add the new plug-ins to the product configuration using the following steps. The `org.eclipse.help` plug-in is the stub of the Help support and is already in the configuration since it is part of the RCP base.

❍ Go to the **Configuration** page of the Hyperbola product editor and click **Add...** to add plug-ins.

❍ In the dialog choose `org.eclipse.help.ui` and `org.eclipse.help.webapp` and click **OK**.

❍ Select the check box to **Include optional dependencies when computing required plug-ins.**

❍ Click **Add Required Plug-ins**. Notice that several plug-ins, including `org.apache.lucene`, `org.eclipse.help.appserver`, and `org.eclipse.help.base`, are added to the configuration. These are the plug-ins directly or indirectly required by the plug-ins already in the list.

❍ Use **File > Save** to save the Hyperbola product configuration.

NOTE

Under the covers, the Eclipse Help system uses a Web server to serve its Help content. The Eclipse Help system isn't tied to a specific Web server, but Jetty ships with the Eclipse platform so the Help system takes advantage of Jetty. You should notice Jetty in the list of your dependencies after you complete the preceding steps.

13.3 Add the Help Action

Now that the Help infrastructure is configured as part of the application, you are ready to add the **Help** actions and content. Hyperbola already has a **Help** menu (for the **About** action) to which you can add a **Help** action. The UI Workbench has a number of handy preconfigured actions (e.g., `ActionFactory.HELP_CONTENTS`) just for this purpose.

In the `ApplicationActionBarAdvisor.makeActions()` method, instantiate and register the Help contents action as follows:

```
org.eclipsercp.hyperbola/ApplicationActionBarAdvisor
helpAction = ActionFactory.HELP_CONTENTS.create(window);
register(helpAction);
```

TIP

When you added the create(IWorkbenchWindow) call, the helpAction field
was not declared so the editor marked the line with an error. Use the Eclipse
quick-fix feature to add the field. Click on the line and press **Ctrl+1**. Then pick
the **Create field 'helpAction'** quick fix. The helpAction field is added at the
top of the class.

Now add the action before the **About** action in the **Help** menu by updating
fillMenuBar() as shown here:

```
org.eclipsercp.hyperbola/ApplicationActionBarAdvisor
MenuManager helpMenu = new MenuManager("&Help","help");
helpMenu.add(helpAction);
helpMenu.add(aboutAction);
```

Save the file and run Hyperbola. You should see a **Help > Help Contents**
menu item. Select that item and you should get a dialog saying that the Help content is not installed.

13.4 Adding Help Content

Help content is written as a set of HTML documents and a set of table of contents (TOC) files that give the HTML structure. The easiest way to start adding
Help content is by using an extension template to generate a skeleton document
structure.

Open the Hyperbola plug-in editor, and on the **Extensions** page click on
Add... to add an extension. In the **New Extension** dialog, uncheck the **Show only
extension points from the required plug-ins** option. Then select the **Extension
Wizards** tab and pick **Extension Templates**. You should see something like Figure 13-2.

Select the **Help Content** template and click **Next**. This shows you the Help
template configuration page, as shown in Figure 13-3.

Enter "Hyperbola Help" in the **Label for table of contents** field. Select the
Primary check box to ensure that this Help is always shown at the top level in the
Help outline. You can enable a set of categories that makes sense to you. Don't
worry about this too much; it is easy to change them later. Click **Finish** to generate the various files and extensions.

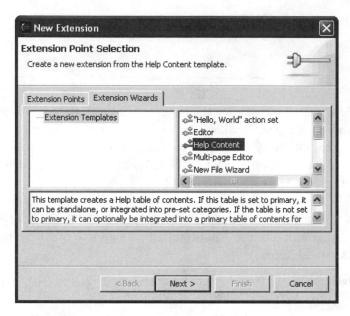

Figure 13–2   New Extension wizard

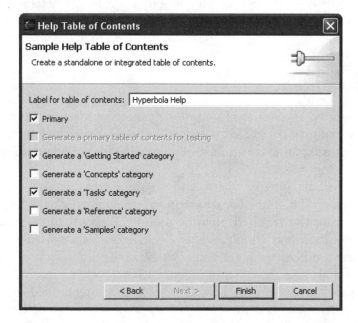

Figure 13–3   Help template configuration

Run Hyperbola again and select **Help > Help Contents**. Hyperbola spawns a separate window that looks like Figure 13-4. Notice here the table of contents structure down the left side with the categories you selected in the template. The template generated sample topics for each.

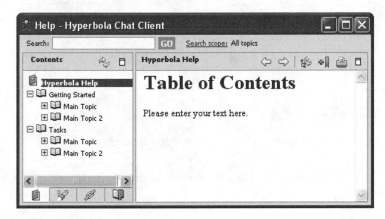

Figure 13–4 Initial Help content

When you ran the **Help > Help Contents** action, you likely saw a page on the right offering information on how to use the Eclipse Help system. This is the default Help home page. Fortunately, you can change this for Hyperbola by overriding a public Help preference in your product description.

Public preferences are used by many plug-ins to allow applications and products to tweak specific configuration options. For example, the Workbench has preferences to control things such as the perspective bar location, fast view bar location, traditional versus curvy tabs, and so on. Similarly, Help has preferences to control many aspects of the Help UI. For a complete list of Help preferences, refer to the section called "Help System Preferences" in the Eclipse IDE online Help. The particular preference to change the Help home page is called `org.eclipse.help.base/help_home`.

To override this Help preference, you need to specify a preference customization file and associate it with the Hyperbola product. Open Hyperbola's plug-in editor, and on the **Extensions** page select the **Hyperbola Chat Client** product extension to the `org.eclipse.core.runtime.products` extension point. Using its context menu, select **New > property** to add the `preferenceCustomization` property, as shown in Figure 13-5.

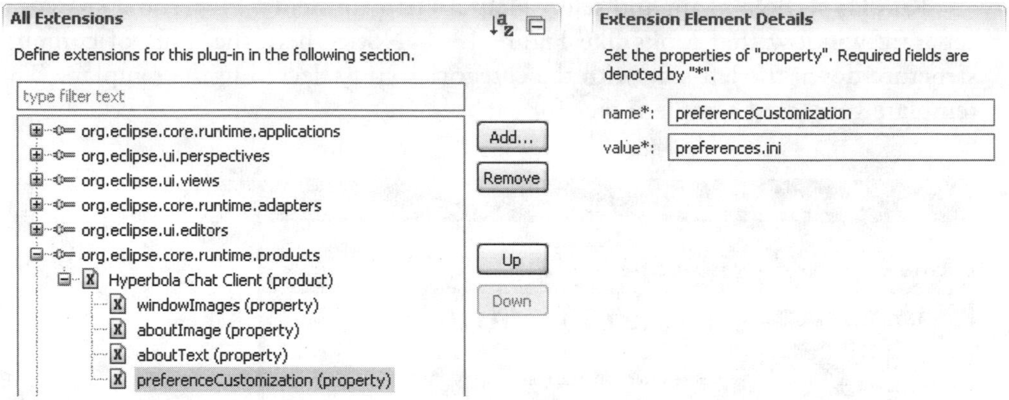

Figure 13–5   Adding the `preferenceCustomization` property to the product

Create the `preferences.ini` file in the root of the Hyperbola plug-in and add the following line:

```
org.eclipsercp.hyperbola/preferences.ini
org.eclipse.help.base/help_home=\
    /org.eclipsercp.hyperbola/html/help_home.html
```

The preferences customization file is a standard Java properties file where the keys are preference IDs encoded as `/plugin-id/preference-name` and the values are the new values for the preferences. Create the home page at the root Hyperbola's `html` directory and call it `help_home.html`. For now, you can simply show the Hyperbola splash screen, as shown here:

```
org.eclipsercp.hyperbola/html/help_home.html
<html>
  <body>
    <img src="../splash.bmp">
  </body>
</html>
```

Of course it's an HTML file, so you can make this as fancy as you like. Run Hyperbola again and launch Help. The first page shows the Hyperbola splash screen in the right pane. You could expand on the branding in this page to contain pointers on how to get started with Hyperbola.

NOTE

Adding Help to Hyperbola does not require that new dependencies be added. Notice that in the preceding steps you did not add any Help plug-ins to the Hyperbola plug-in's prerequisite list. All you did was add the Help-related plug-ins to the Hyperbola *product configuration*, thus ensuring that the Help infrastructure is shipped as part of Hyperbola.

The Help actions used are supplied by the UI Workbench plug-in, which is already a prerequisite. The Hyperbola Help content is contributed via extensions to a Help plug-in extension point. Contributing extensions to a plug-in's extension point does not imply that you depend on the plug-in.

13.5 Help Content Structure

The Help extension template added three things to the Hyperbola plug-in: a Help extension, an XML TOC, and HTML stub files for each Help page. You should think of the Help system as a mini Web site. The TOC files simply define the table of contents for HTML pages in the Help system. Of course, there is nothing hard-coded about this structure. You are free to set up whatever structure best suits your needs. You can have as many categories with whatever names and content you choose. Let's look at what the template generated.

The Help extension informs the Help system of all the TOC files. The Help system uses these to knit together diverse sets of Help into a coherent structure that is presented in the left pane of the Help window. This extension identifies three XML TOC files: toc.xml at the top level and one for each category selected when instantiating the template. The file toc.xml is marked as primary to ensure that it is always shown in the Help outline.

org.eclipsercp.hyperbola/plugin.xml
```
<extension point="org.eclipse.help.toc">
  <toc file="toc.xml" primary="true"/>
  <toc file="tocgettingstarted.xml"/>
  <toc file="toctasks.xml"/>
</extension>
```

The toc.xml file simply defines an *anchor* for each category. Anchors are locations to which other TOC files link and add their substructure. Below are the contents of toc.xml and toctasks.xml. Notice how toc.xml defines the "tasks" anchor and toctasks.xml links to that anchor. That setup inserts the toctasks.xml structure in the main table of contents at the "Tasks" entry.

org.eclipsercp.hyperbola/toc.xml
```
<toc label="Hyperbola Help" topic="html/toc.html">
  <topic label="Getting Started">
    <anchor id="gettingstarted"/>
  </topic>
```

```
      <topic label="Tasks">
        <anchor id="tasks"/>
      </topic>
</toc>
```

org.eclipsercp.hyperbola/toctasks.xml
```
<toc label="Tasks" link_to="toc.xml#tasks">
    <topic label="Main Topic" href="html/tasks/maintopic.html">
      <topic label="Sub Topic" href="html/tasks/subtopic.html"/>
    </topic>
    <topic label="Main Topic 2">
      <topic label="Sub Topic 2" href="html/tasks/subtopic2.html"/>
    </topic>
</toc>
```

From `toctasks.xml` you can infer that the template laid down an HTML structure, as shown in Figure 13-6. There is one directory for each category and a top-level `toc.html` file. The HTML files are just stubs, but they represent the real Help content shown in the right pane of the Help window. It is up to you to fill in and link together the relevant content.

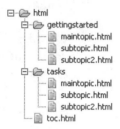

Figure 13–6   Help HTML content structure

13.6 Infopops or F1 Help

In Hyperbola we thought it would be good for users to be able to get context-sensitive Help. For example, when they are in a chat view, they should be able to find out how to send special messages, such as smileys. The *infopop* mechanism links UI elements such as views, menu items, and buttons to Help content. The user simply selects the element in question and presses the appropriate Help key—**F1** on Windows, **Ctrl+F1** on GTK. On older Macs there used to be a "Help" key but that has been replaced by going to the **Help** menu to request help. The associated Help is then displayed. Infopops are added by tagging UI elements (e.g., views and actions) with *Help contexts*. For example, the Contacts view is tagged by adding the following line in `ContactsView.createPartControl(Composite)`:

```
org.eclipsercp.hyperbola/ContactsView.createPartControl()
  PlatformUI.getWorkbench().getHelpSystem().setHelp(
    treeViewer.getTree(), "org.eclipsercp.hyperbola.contactsView");
```

The second argument to setHelp(Control, String) is a *context ID*. This is used as a key in a context table to look up Help content to display. The context table is maintained by the Help system and is constructed by gathering context extensions. The Hyperbola plug-in contributes the following context extension:

```
org.eclipsercp.hyperbola/plugin.xml
<extension point="org.eclipse.help.contexts">
  <contexts file="contexts.xml"/>
</extension>
```

The extension simply identifies contexts.xml as a file containing any number of context IDs to content mappings. Notice in the snippet below that the context ID, contactsView, matches the context ID assigned to the ContactsView after adding on the ID of the defining plug-in. The Help content for this context includes two topics.

```
org.eclipsercp.hyperbola/contexts.xml
<contexts>
  <context id="contactsView">
    <description>This is Contacts View</description>
    <topic
      label="Managing Contacts"/>
      href="html/tasks/managingContacts.html"
    <topic
      label="Grouping Contacts"/>
      href="html/tasks/groupingContacts.html"
  </context>
</contexts>
```

13.7 Exporting Plug-ins with Help

There is one final step to adding Help to Hyperbola. In the procedure described so far, we have added a number of files to the Hyperbola plug-in. These files need to be listed in build.properties so that PDE knows to include them when the plug-in is exported. Open Hyperbola's build.properties and check off the following files or folders:

○ html/

○ toc.xml

○ tocgettingstarted.xml

○ toctasks.xml

○ `preferences.ini`

○ `contexts.xml` (if needed)

Save the file, export Hyperbola, and run the application. Try accessing the various Help contents and make sure that everything works. If it doesn't, ensure that all the right files are in the exported Hyperbola.

13.8 Summary

Help is an important part of many applications. The Eclipse Help support is very easy to integrate and supports a wide range of options from static content to context-sensitive help. Help files can be shipped with an application or hosted remotely on a server.

13.9 Pointers

The Eclipse Help infrastructure supports many capabilities not discussed in this chapter. For an overview of these, refer to the following Eclipse IDE online Help topics:

○ **Platform Developer Guide > Programmer's Guide > Plugging in Help**

○ **Platform Developer Guide > Reference > Other reference information > Help System Preferences**

○ **Platform Developer Guide > Reference > Other reference information > Installing the stand-alone help system**

○ **Platform Developer Guide > Reference > Other reference information > Installing the help system as an infocenter**

○ Adding Eclipse Help to RCP applications article: *www.eclipse.org/articles/ article.php?file=Article-AddingHelpToRCP/index.html*

CHAPTER 14

Adding Software Management

Hyperbola is ready to ship. But what about the next version? What if there is a bug? And what about all this XMPP extensibility we talked about earlier? How can users get updates or find cool new features? The Eclipse Platform includes a provisioning component called Equinox p2 that discovers and installs updates to both existing functionality and totally new functionality. This is exactly what we need for Hyperbola in the long run.

In this chapter you will

❍ Learn about the end-user facilities provided by p2, including API

❍ Add update capabilities provided by p2 to the target platform and to Hyperbola

❍ Learn about features and create a feature for Hyperbola

14.1 Getting p2

Using the steps outlined in Chapter 13, "Adding Help," add **Equinox p2 SDK** to your target, as shown in Figure 14-1. Again, note the settings for the various check boxes.

Before we go into the exercise, we'll discuss the problem of manually dealing with collections of plug-ins and introduce the concept of features. Human error and miscommunication can cause you to get a few too many plug-ins, miss a few plug-ins, or pick up the wrong versions of plug-ins.

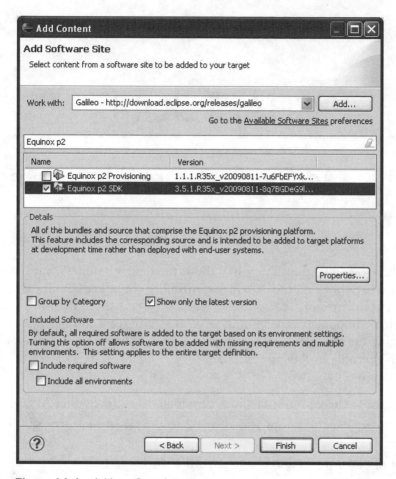

Figure 14–1   Adding p2 to the target

14.2 Features

Features allow you to abstract away the packaging details and talk about arbitrarily complex collections of plug-ins that can be built and deployed.

14.2.1 Uses of Features

Features can be used to manage plug-ins in the following ways:

> **Install/update**—Users and programs install and update features and, through the features, the listed plug-ins. Individual plug-ins are not updated directly.

Branding—Features can appear in a product's About dialog. This gives feature creators an opportunity to both make their presence known within a larger product setting and give users access to any required legal information.

Building—Features describe complete sets of plug-ins that make up a system. These plug-ins also need to be built and managed during development. Features play a central role in PDE's automated build process. Chapter 24, "Building Hyperbola," covers this in detail.

14.2.2 What Is a Feature?

A feature is a list of related plug-ins and other features. They are defined in a feature.xml file that lives in a feature directory. At its simplest, a feature contains an ID, a version, and a list of plug-ins. As with plug-in IDs, feature IDs typically follow Java package naming conventions, and their version numbers take the form major.minor.micro.qualifier.

The example below shows an abbreviated version of the feature.xml for the org.eclipse.rcp feature in your Eclipse target platform. The body of the feature lists the plug-ins that make up the RCP base. These plug-ins are said to be *included* in the feature. This means that if you install the RCP base feature, all listed plug-ins are installed.

org.eclipse.rcp/feature.xml
```
<feature id="org.eclipse.rcp" label="Eclipse RCP" version="3.5.0">
  <plugin id="com.ibm.icu" version="4.0.1"/>
  <plugin id="org.eclipse.core.commands" version="3.5.0"/>
  <plugin id="org.eclipse.core.expressions" version="3.4.0"/>
  <plugin id="org.eclipse.core.runtime" version="3.4.0"/>
  <plugin id="org.eclipse.core.databinding" version="1.2.0"/>
  <plugin id="org.eclipse.core.databinding.beans" version="1.2.0"/>
  <plugin id="org.eclipse.core.jobs" version="3.4.0"/>
  <plugin id="org.eclipse.osgi" version="3.5.0"/>
  <plugin id="org.eclipse.help" version="3.4.0"/>
  <plugin id="org.eclipse.swt" version="3.5.0"/>
  <plugin id="org.eclipse.jface" version="3.5.0"/>
  <plugin id="org.eclipse.jface.databinding" version="1.3.0"/>
  <plugin id="org.eclipse.ui" version="3.1.0"/>
  <plugin id="org.eclipse.ui.workbench" version="3.1.0"/>
  ...
</feature>
```

NOTE

It is important to note that features do not contain the plug-ins. Rather, features *reference* their constituent parts. This allows the same plug-in to appear in many features but be installed only once.

The preceding snippet shows the XML form of the feature—this reiterates the idea that a feature is really just a list of plug-ins and other features. In practice, you never have to edit the XML directly, as PDE includes a comprehensive feature editor. You can open the editor on the RCP feature using **File > Open File...** and navigating to the feature in your target or by double-clicking on the RCP base feature in the **Included Features** list of the Hyperbola feature. Either way, open the editor and flip to the **Plug-ins** page, as shown in Figure 14-2.

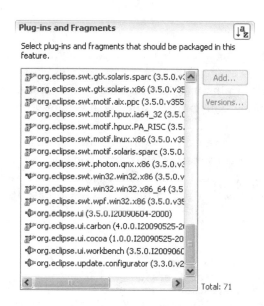

Figure 14–2   RCP feature plug-in list

Notice that the list shown has a number of entries related to SWT. These entries are the SWT fragments that contain the code specific to a given OS, window system, and processor architecture. If you install the RCP base feature on Windows, for example, the SWT fragment you need is different from the one you need on Linux using GTK. The **Plug-in Details** shown indicate that the selected fragment (`org.eclipse.swt.gtk.linux.x86`) is specific to `linux`, `gtk`, and `x86`. As such, p2 ignores this fragment on other configurations.

Only the relevant attributes need to be specified. For example, if your plug-in runs on all Cocoa systems, simply setting the **Window System** to cocoa is sufficient. Of course, if the plug-in or fragment includes native code, you must specify at least the **Operating System** and **Architecture** attributes.

NOTE

Notice also that the selected fragment is marked as *not* needing to be unpacked during installation. Plug-ins on a software site are stored as JARs. Traditionally, Eclipse has unpacked these JARs into plug-in directories after downloading. As of Eclipse 3.1, most plug-ins no longer need to be unpacked and therefore have this option deselected.

Now that you have the RCP base feature, you no longer have to laboriously list each of the RCP plug-ins when defining other features or products. Figure 14-3 shows the **Included Features** page for the Hyperbola feature editor. Included features are the RCP base feature and `org.eclipsercp.hyperbola.muc.feature`, an additional feature used to demonstrate the notion of *optional* features.

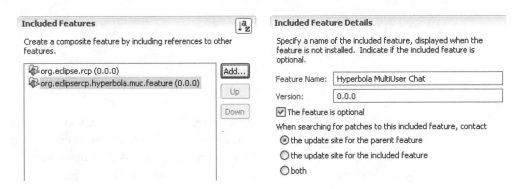

Figure 14–3   Including features

Here the **Included Feature Details** section shows the MUC feature marked as optional. Typically, a parent feature fails to install if some of its included features and plug-ins are not present. However, marking a feature as optional allows the parent to be installed even if the optional feature is not present or cannot be installed. This is ideal for defining products that are extensible according to user needs or OS facilities.

These examples illustrate the definition of feature content—features are made up of the plug-ins and features that are *included* in their definition. If you install a feature, all its constituents are also installed, if they are not already available.

This is powerful, but the inclusion characteristic is limiting. Typically, when you include some plug-ins or features, you are committing to shipping them. If your product is to be installed with others, it is better to simply state a dependency on the parts that are needed. For example, the Hyperbola feature could specify a *requirement* that the RCP feature already be installed. This does not commit you to delivering the RCP base, but it does express the dependency so that it can be checked. On the **Dependencies** page, you can list the features and plug-ins that must be present to successfully install your feature.

Figure 14-4 shows a feature that declares the RCP feature and p2 plug-ins as required but not supplied. Installing this feature makes no attempt to download or install the listed elements; rather, the information is used by the p2 UI to verify the correctness of a configuration.

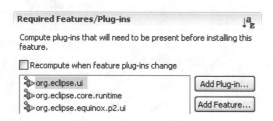

Figure 14–4   Feature dependencies

TIP

Features should have a license agreement. This agreement is shown to users as they go through the **Update/Install** wizard. To define the license, go to the **License Agreement** tab on the **Information** page of the feature editor. There you can fill in the license text and a URL to use when showing the license to the user.

14.3 Defining Features

Features collect sets of plug-ins that go together to form some coherent unit of functionality. Features have a very simple structure; they are a list of plug-ins and other features. They essentially constitute a bill of materials for a set of functions. This makes them very useful for organizing and managing systems.

NOTE

As discussed in Chapter 23, "RCP Everywhere," features are also very useful for keeping your team organized during the development of your product.

When we started out with the Hyperbola product definition in Chapter 8, "Branding Hyperbola," we chose to use a plug-in-based configuration (see the **Overview** page of the Hyperbola product editor). Let's change that now and use features. Go back to the Hyperbola product editor, and on the **Overview** page change the product configuration to be based on features, as shown in Figure 14-5.

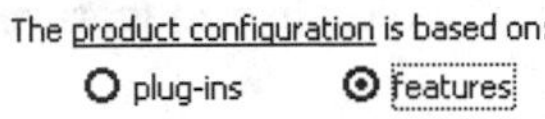

The product configuration is based on:

    ○ plug-ins   ⊙ features

Figure 14–5 A feature-based product configuration

Next, flip over to the **Configuration** page and click on the **New Feature...** button to start the **New Feature** wizard shown in Figure 14-6. You can also create features using **New > Project... > Plug-in Development > Feature Project**. Enter `org.eclipsercp.hyperbola.feature` for the project name. By default, the project name matches the feature ID just as with plug-ins. Fill in the feature properties, as shown in Figure 14-6.

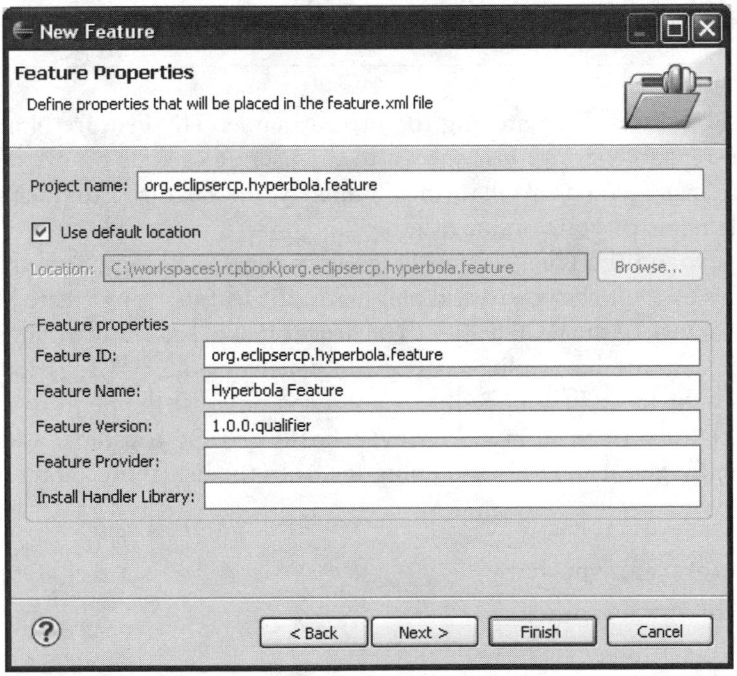

Figure 14–6 Defining the Hyperbola feature

Choosing Feature Identifiers

The feature and plug-in ID namespaces are distinct. As a result, you can have a plug-in and a feature with the same ID. This can be convenient, but it can also be confusing. At development time you may want to have both the feature and plug-in projects in your workspace at the same time. If you follow the recommended practice of matching the project names to the IDs, the plug-in and feature projects will collide and cannot be loaded together.

There are various conventions for naming features and feature projects. For historical reasons, the Eclipse platform feature IDs tend to overlap with the plug-in namespace, and feature project names are made up of the feature IDs followed by -feature. For example, the org.eclipse.platform feature is housed in a project called org.eclipse.platform-feature.

In this book we tend to avoid overlapping the feature and plug-in namespaces and use a naming convention that puts the word *feature* relatively early in the feature ID and matches project names to feature IDs. For example, using org.eclipsercp .hyperbola.muc.feature for both the ID and the project name distinguishes the MUC feature from the MUC plug-ins and results in all the Hyperbola feature projects sorting together in the repository and workspace.

Leave the **Feature ID** matching the project name. The **Feature Name** should be a human-readable string. It is shown to the user at various points when using the software management mechanisms. Similarly, the **Feature Provider** should be the readable name of your organization.

Click **Next** and the **Plug-ins and Fragments** page comes up, as shown in Figure 14-7. This page allows you to add plug-ins to the feature being created. Here you can take advantage of the RCP feature. The org.eclipse.rcp feature that is included with Eclipse lists the basic plug-ins (e.g., OSGi, Runtime, SWT, JFace, and UI) that make up the basic Eclipse RCP. So, you need only list the plug-ins either that you developed (e.g., org.eclipsercp.hyperbola) or that you have added to the target manually. Select the following plug-ins from the list (there should be three):

1. org.eclipse.ui.forms
2. org.eclipsercp.hyperbola
3. org.jivesoftware.smack

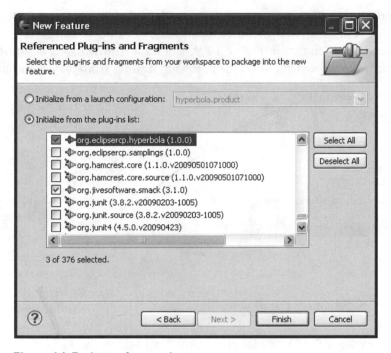

Figure 14–7   Listing feature plug-ins

Click **Finish**. The Hyperbola feature project is created and opened in a feature editor. On the **Overview** page of the editor there is a **General Information** section, as shown in Figure 14-8. Here you see the values that you just entered in the wizard.

General Information
This section describes general information about this feature.

ID:	org.eclipsercp.hyperbola.feature
Version:	1.0.0
Name:	Hyperbola
Provider:	eclipsercp.org
Branding Plug-in:	org.eclipsercp.hyperl [Browse...]
Update Site URL:	
Update Site Name:	

Figure 14–8   Filling in the feature information

The only thing left to do is connect the Hyperbola feature to a set of RCP features. Move over to the **Included Features** page and look for the **Included Features** section, as shown in Figure 14-9. Click on **Add...** to get a list of all the features known to the system. Select the following features from the list and click **OK**:

1. org.eclipse.equinox.p2.user.ui

2. org.eclipse.help

3. org.eclipse.rcp

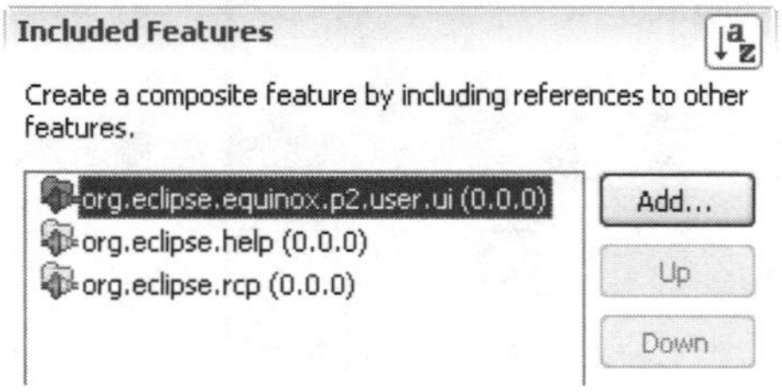

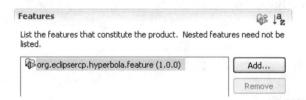

Figure 14–9   Adding the included features

That completes feature creation, so now go back to the Hyperbola product editor. Notice that the org.eclipsercp.hyperbola.feature you just created is listed in the **Features** section of the **Dependencies** page, as in Figure 14-10.

Figure 14–10   The Hyperbola product with its feature

Now you are back in exactly the same position you were in a few minutes ago, but the Hyperbola product is described in terms of features rather than just a list of plug-ins. This allows you to directly use the software management functionality to manage Hyperbola installs.

14.4 Branding Features

Since an Eclipse-based system is a composition of features and plug-ins from different sources, the standard About dialog exposes branding for individual features. This allows feature vendors to have a user-visible presence in the system. For example, after following the steps below, the Hyperbola feature branding seen via **Help > About Hyperbola** displays as shown in Figure 14-11.

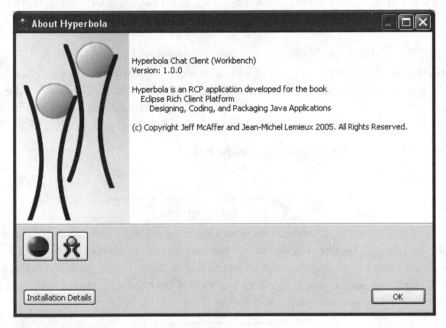

Figure 14–11   Hyperbola feature branding

The branding images and text are supplied by a *branding plug-in* defined in the **Overview > General Information > Branding Plug-in** field of the feature editor. The branding plug-in can be any plug-in included in the feature. Use the **Browse...** button and select org.eclipsercp.hyperbola as the branding plug-in.

The branding information is contained in a set of files, as shown below. The about.ini defines two properties: one for the informational About text and one for the feature image.

```
org.eclipsercp.hyperbola/about.ini
# Property "aboutText" contains blurb for feature details in the
# "About" dialog (translated).
# Maximum 15 lines and 75 characters per line.
aboutText=%blurb
```

The aboutText property gives the text that is displayed when the feature is selected in the feature details dialog. The main reason for this information being in a plug-in is to enable translation. As such, the value %blurb is defined in an associated about.properties file, which is shown here:

```
org.eclipsercp.hyperbola/about.properties
blurb=Hyperbola Chat Client Product\n\
Version: {featureVersion}\n\
Build id: {0}\n\
(c) Copyright Chris Aniszczyk, Jean-Michel Lemieux and Jeff McAffer.
All rights reserved.\n\
Visit http://eclipsercp.org/hyperbola
```

Translations of this value are then supplied in language-specific files in fragments of the Hyperbola plug-in as discussed in Section 8.4, "Splash Screen." The About text for features can be specialized for particular builds as described in Section 8.5, "About Information"; that is, the {0} in the About blurb can be replaced by values in an about.mappings file in the branding plug-in.

```
org.eclipsercp.hyperbola/about.mappings
0=1.0.0
```

WARNING

Feature branding information is separate from the product branding that is defined in org.eclipsercp.hyperbola. That branding is specified in the product extension and is displayed on the main About dialog. Because of a naming overlap, however, the about.mappings files are shared between the two. Care should be taken when assigning and using properties from this file.

Add these files as described and update the **Build** page in the Hyperbola plug-in editor to have all the about.* files checked in the **Binary Build** list. Reexport Hyperbola, then run it and check that your feature branding worked.

14.5 Updating Hyperbola

Now that we have a description of Hyperbola that p2 can manage, there are three common software management scenarios to support that are typical of any extensible RCP application:

Searching for updates to existing features—This finds and installs updates to existing features. For example, if you are running Hyperbola 1.0 and 1.1 is released, p2 allows you to update to the new version of Hyperbola.

Searching for new features—Hyperbola is based on XMPP and is thus very extensible. It makes sense to allow users to search for new features to install.

Managing the existing configuration of features—If users can install new features, it makes sense to allow them to enable, disable, or remove these features.

Up to now we've been using a default configuration of the p2 user interface that is provided by the `org.eclipse.equinox.p2.user.ui.sdk` plug-in. When we launch Hyperbola, we get the default p2 user interface available via the **Help > Install New Software...** menu.

TIP

When you are testing the software management facilities of Hyperbola, the easiest thing to do is export the product and run it as a normal application. Equinox p2 expects a particular setup on disk and typical workspace configurations are not suitable; that is, p2 does not initialize properly if you run out of the IDE unless you take special steps. These steps are a bit of a distraction to the current discussion. For now, simply export Hyperbola and run its launcher to test the update functionality.

All three of the preceding scenarios are supported by the existing p2 user interface. To search for updates to existing features, we can simply use the **Help > Check for updates** menu. To search for new features, we can use the **Help > Install New Software...** menu. To manage the existing configuration of features, we can use the **Help > About Hyperbola > Installation Details** menu.

14.6 Customizing the p2 UI

So far we have been reusing the existing p2 user interface with all of its defaults. However, the defaults may not be good enough depending on your application. To maximize reuse, the p2 user interface allows for various customizations. For example, if you want to customize the set of p2-related menu items, you can provide your own bundle that makes p2 UI contributions in lieu of the p2 UI bundle. This allows you to rearrange the way users encounter the install/update functionality or provide more precise control of what can be done by the user.

In addition, you may wish to expose a subset of functionality, such as permitting updating but not installing or uninstalling software, or you may wish to change what is visible on the installed software page, or what software is visible when browsing a site or even what sites are available to users.

The customization of the p2 user interface is accomplished via the `org.eclipse.equinox.internal.provisional.p2.ui.policy.Policy` class which controls different aspects of the UI. A default implementation is provided, but the policy allows you to control things such as

- Which repositories (sites) are visible to the user
- Whether the user can manipulate (add, enable, disable, remove) the sites
- What software is visible to the user when browsing software sites
- What software is shown as the root of the **Installed Software** page
- How licenses are remembered and stored

To provide your own customization, you create a `Policy` implementation and register it as an OSGi service. As part of your policy you can implement a variety of helper classes, such as

- `IUViewQueryContext`—manages what software is displayed to the user
- `LicenseManager`—represents how licenses are accepted and stored
- `RepositoryManipulator`—controls which repositories are visible to the user

For example, if you want to modify Hyperbola to expose only the ability to update and not install anything else, create a `HyperbolaPolicy` class that extends `Policy`. Then disable the ability to select repositories by calling `setRepositoryManipulator(null)`. Similarly, if you want the p2 user interface to show every potential update, create a new `IUViewQueryContext`, instantiate it with the `IUViewQueryContext.AVAILABLE_VIEW_FLAT` setting, and call `setQueryContext()` with the new query context as shown here:

org.eclipsercp.hyperbola/HyperbolaPolicy.java
```
public class HyperbolaPolicy extends Policy {
  public HyperbolaPolicy() {
    // Disable the ability to manipulate repositories.
    setRepositoryManipulator(null);

    // View everything in the repository.
    IUViewQueryContext context =
        new IUViewQueryContext(IUViewQueryContext.AVAILABLE_VIEW_FLAT);
    context.setVisibleAvailableIUProperty(null);
    setQueryContext(context);
  }
}
```

If you want to view updates by category, use the `IUViewQueryContext.AVAILABLE_VIEW_BY_CATEGORY` setting. The final step is to register and unregister the HyperbolaPolicy service. Registering the HyperbolaPolicy makes the p2 user interface aware of the policy so it can adapt to your customizations. This can be done in Hyperbola's Activator class as shown next or using Declarative Services (DS).

org.eclipsercp.hyperbola/Activator.java
```
public class Activator implements BundleActivator {
  ServiceRegistration registration;
  public void start(BundleContext context) {
    registration = context.register(Policy.class.getName(),
      new HyperbolaPolicy(), null);
  }
  public void stop(BundleContext context) {
    context.ungetService(registration.getReference());
    registration = null;
  }
}
```

Another customization point is the org.eclipse.ui.about.installationPages extension point that allows customization of the installation page contributions if some of the default pages are not relevant to your application.

14.7 Defining Categories

By default, the p2 user interface groups all installable software by repositories and categories and shows only categorized elements. In general, then, you have to categorize your software. Categories are created using a category definition. The first step is to create a category definition file using the **New > Project... > Plug-in Development > Category Definition** wizard. Leave the defaults and click **Finish**. Once the category definition file is open, select the default category created by the wizard and in the **Category Properties** section put org.eclipsercp.hyperbola .category in the **ID** field. In the **Name** field put "Hyperbola." After filling out the category properties, click the **Add Feature...** button and add the org.eclipsercp .hyperbola.feature to the **Hyperbola** category as shown in Figure 14-12.

Now the defined categories need to be put into the software site or repository containing the software. The easiest way to accomplish this is via the category publisher command-line application. The category publisher is invoked using the generic Eclipse and the command line shown here:

```
eclipse -application org.eclipse.equinox.p2.publisher.CategoryPublisher
    -metadataRepository file:/<some location>/repository
    -categoryDefinition file:/<some location>/category.xml
    -compress
```

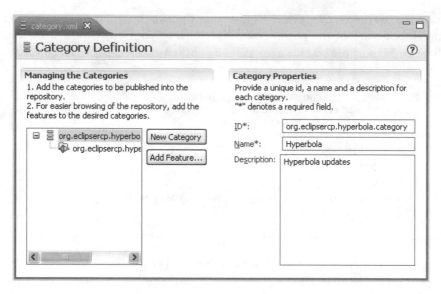

Figure 14–12   Hyperbola category definition

14.8 Automatic Updates

The p2 update facilities include the ability to periodically poll for updates to Hyperbola. In essence, it is simply a scheduler that runs according to a policy that you or the end user defines. For example, it's possible to check every day, on particular days of the week, or every time Hyperbola is started. Users are notified when updates are found. A preference controls whether or not p2 automatically downloads the updates for the user to install.

This functionality is included in the `org.eclipse.equinox.p2.ui.sdk.scheduler` plug-in that is already included in Hyperbola via the `org.eclipse.equinox.p2.ui` feature. Run Hyperbola and use **Hyperbola > Preferences... > Install/Update > Automatic Updates** to get to the preference page shown in Figure 14-13. These preferences can also be set in the Hyperbola product's preference initialization file, as discussed in Section 13.4, "Adding Help Content."

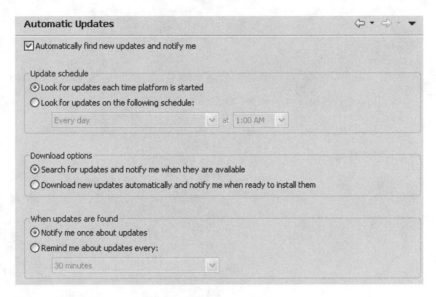

Figure 14–13 Automatic update preferences

14.9 Summary

With the addition of p2, Hyperbola is now future-proofed. Distributing bug fixes is easier—deployed clients can just download the new updates from the Hyperbola update site. The ability to update also allows new and optional features to be distributed over the Internet. All of this makes it easier and cheaper to manage.

This marks the end of the Hyperbola tutorial. Hyperbola is now a complete XMPP-based chat client that has an impressive feature list for such a small application (about 80K of source code). It has a pretty cool UI, is fully branded with its own launcher and splash screen, has integrated Help, and is packaged to enable updates.

14.10 Pointers

- ○ **Platform Developer Guide > Reference > Provisioning platform, p2.**
- ○ *http://wiki.eclipse.org/Equinox/p2.*
- ○ *http://wiki.eclipse.org/Equinox/p2/Adding_Self-Update_to_an_RCP_Applications.*
- ○ The OSGi and Equinox book contains another example of adding software management to an application using p2: McAffer, Jeff, Paul VanderLei, and Simon Archer. *OSGi and Equinox: Creating Highly Modular Java Systems* (Addison-Wesley, 2010), ISBN 0321585712.

PART III

The Workbench

The Workbench provides the UI building blocks that make Eclipse applications easy to write, easy to use, scalable, and extendable. One of the main advantages of using the Eclipse RCP is the benefit you get from reusing the UI building blocks—it allows you to focus on your domain without having to redesign the wheel. This is evident from the fact that the Hyperbola application developed in Part II required relatively little code.

But that work only scratched the surface of what is possible. The Workbench is much more powerful. It is made up of over 50 extension points and over 350 API classes. It would take an entire book to do justice to the functionality provided. Rather than attempt a broad partial coverage, the next few chapters focus on the parts of the Workbench that are essential for RCP applications. They dive into their API and use them to solve problems motivated by Hyperbola in various real-world scenarios.

You should come away from this part of the book with a solid understanding of the Workbench's structure and how you can control and customize its operation.

CHAPTER 15

Workbench Advisors

In Part II you got a glimpse of the ways in which the Workbench advisors are used in real applications, but you may have noticed that many of the advisors' methods were not used. This chapter explores these additional APIs and explains how they can be used in your application. Another area that you've started to get familiar with is the Workbench; we end this chapter with an overview of the Workbench and its extension points.

15.1 Workbench Advisors

You may recall from Part II that when the Hyperbola application starts, its main job is to call PlatformUI.createAndRunWorkbench(Display, WorkbenchAdvisor), as shown in the snippet below. This somewhat inconspicuous method bootstraps your UI by starting the Workbench. This leads to the creation, configuration, and opening of the application windows.

```
org.eclipsercp.hyperbola/Application
public class Application implements IApplication {
  public Object run(Object args) throws Exception {
    Display display = PlatformUI.createDisplay();
    try {
      int returnCode = PlatformUI.createAndRunWorkbench(display,
        new ApplicationWorkbenchAdvisor());
      if (returnCode == PlatformUI.RETURN_RESTART) {
return IApplication.EXIT_RESTART;
    }
    return IApplication.EXIT_OK;
  } finally {
    display.dispose();
  }
}
```

The Workbench, however, does not know how the application should behave or look—that's where the Workbench *advisors* come in. As their name implies, advisors give advice to the Workbench. In doing so, they influence what the UI contains and how it looks and feels.

Instead of changing the behavior of the Workbench, say, by subclassing, the Workbench aggregates the advisors and allows them to participate in the running of the Workbench. As you've seen in Hyperbola, when the Workbench opens a window, it asks an advisor to determine whether or not it should include a menu bar by calling the `WorkbenchWindowAdvisor.preWindowOpen()` method.

ADVISER OR ADVISOR?

The dictionary says that either spelling is correct, but common usage says that an *adviser* is someone defined by what he or she is doing: defined by a verb, one who is advising or dispensing advice. An *advisor* is someone defined by what he or she is—defined by what he or she continually does, someone in the position of providing advice.

There are three types of advisors, and each is characterized by the part of the Workbench to which it gives advice:

WorkbenchAdvisor—This advisor provides application-level advice. It participates in the startup and shutdown of the Workbench itself; there is one running Workbench per running Eclipse application.

WorkbenchWindowAdvisor—This advisor provides window-level advice. It participates in showing or hiding the menu, toolbar, and status line and in configuring the controls shown in the window. There is one `WorkbenchWindowAdvisor` instance for each window.

ActionBarAdvisor—This advisor provides window-level advice and helps define the actions that appear in the menu, toolbar, and status line of each window. There is one `ActionBarAdvisor` instance for each window.

Each advisor has an associated *configurer* that provides privileged access to the Workbench, Workbench window, and window's action bars (e.g., menu, toolbar, and status line). There's one configurer for each advisor type. Since the configurers provide privileged access to the Workbench, they should never be passed around to other plug-ins. The three different types of configurers are the `IWorkbenchConfigurer`, `IWorkbenchWindowConfigurer`, and `IActionBarConfigurer`. The following snippets demonstrate how each can be used within its associated advisor:

```
org.eclipsercp.hyperbola/ApplicationWorkbenchAdvisor
public void initialize(IWorkbenchConfigurer configurer) {
    configurer.setSaveAndRestore(true);
}
```

```
org.eclipsercp.hyperbola/ApplicationWorkbenchWindowAdvisor
public void preWindowOpen() {
    IWorkbenchWindowConfigurer configurer = getWindowConfigurer();
    configurer.setInitialSize(new Point(250, 350));
    configurer.setShowMenuBar(true);
    ...
}
```

```
org.eclipsercp.hyperbola/ApplicationActionBarAdvisor
protected void fillMenuBar(IMenuManager menuBar) {
    IMenuManager mainMenu = getActionBarConfigurer().getMenuManager();
    MenuManager hyperbolaMenu = new MenuManager(
        "&Hyperbola", "hyperbola");
    hyperbolaMenu.add(exitAction);
    MenuManager helpMenu = new MenuManager("&Help", "help");
    helpMenu.add(aboutAction);
    mainMenu.add(hyperbolaMenu);
}
```

The advisors have another very important role—they define top-level integration points for the product. For example, the advisors decide the names for the groups and separators within the top-level menu, toolbar, and status line. Plug-ins contributing to the product must use these names as integration points when defining and placing their own actions. This is discussed further in Section 17.2.2, "Allowing Contributions."

Advisors are very closely linked to the concept of a product. Although this relationship is not technically enforced—for example, the product extension point does not include details about the advisors—from the outside they are often seen as one. You typically have one set of advisors for each of your products. As you've seen, a product as defined by the product extension point refers to one application (e.g., IApplication), and each application is associated with one set of advisors.

15.1.1 Workbench Lifecycle

To understand the full scope of how advisors are used to configure the Workbench, let's take a look at the Workbench lifecycle and the points at which the different advisors participate.

Under the covers, when PlatformUI.createAndRunWorkbench() is called, the Workbench performs the following high-level steps:

○ Initializes an exception handler to trap uncaught exceptions.

○ Opens the main window, creating the default controls (toolbar, status line, perspective switcher, perspective), and restores any saved state.

❍ Takes down the splash screen.

❍ Opens one or more windows and initializes them with UI settings that have been saved from the last session.

❍ Runs the SWT event loop.

❍ When `IWorkbenchWindow.close()` is called, the windows' states are saved, then the windows are closed.

Figure 15-1 shows the typical runtime interaction between the Workbench and the various advisors.

When the Workbench runs, it allows the `WorkbenchAdvisor` to participate from the very beginning by calling `WorkbenchAdvisor.initialize()`. This happens before any windows are opened. As each window is opened, a `WorkbenchWindowAdvisor`

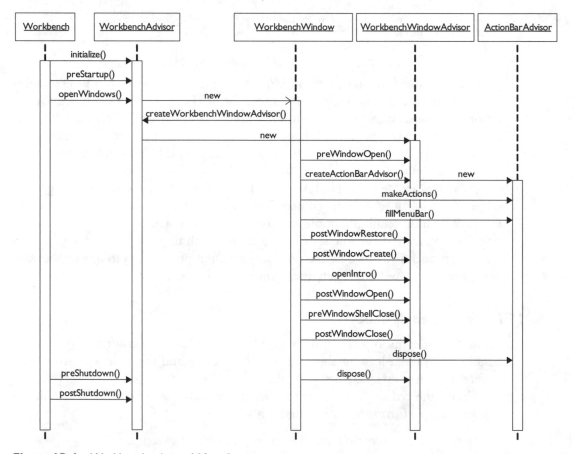

Figure 15–1   Workbench advisors' lifecycle events

is created and associated with that window instance. This workbenchWindowAdvisor instance is consulted throughout the window's lifecycle. The ActionBarAdvisor is created by the WorkbenchWindowAdvisor *before* the window is opened and participates in populating the menu, toolbar, and status line of each window. The next sections reveal more detail about the lifecycle and APIs for each type of advisor.

15.2 WorkbenchAdvisor

The WorkbenchAdvisor in Hyperbola played only a small part in the overall application. It initialized settings in the WorkbenchAdvisor method initialize() and then hooked the chat listener to process incoming chats. This is very typical of a WorkbenchAdvisor—initializing application lifecycle settings and cleaning up when the Workbench shuts down.

It is tempting to use the lifecycle methods in your WorkbenchAdvisor to trigger initialization of additional parts of your application. Resist that urge! The work done here sits squarely in the path of displaying the application's first window—the more work you do, the longer your users wait to see your application. This can't be stressed enough: Do as little as possible in the WorkbenchAdvisor's initialization code.

NOTE

A good technique for minimizing initialization costs is to initialize resources only when first accessed. For example, do not bother creating fonts or images until they are needed. This has the added benefit of saving space since only those resources being used are allocated. Note also that this approach applies to the initialization of model data structures and references to other plug-ins.

The WorkbenchAdvisor's API methods fall into three categories:

Lifecycle—allows the advisors to participate in startup and shutdown of the application

Exception and idleness—allows the advisor to participate when an exception occurs and when the application is idle

Configuration—allows the advisor to determine default values for global application settings

15.2.1 Lifecycle API

You should use the lifecycle methods to initialize, restore, and then save and shut down aspects of your application. The description of each method in Table 15-1 provides a hint as to the type of work typically done in each method.

Table 15–1   Workbench Lifecycle Events

Method	Description
initialize(IWorkbenchConfigurer)	This marks the beginning of the advisor's lifecycle and is called during Workbench initialization prior to any windows being opened. This is a good place to parse the command line and register adaptors. Most applications call IWorkbenchConfigurer .setSaveAndRestore(true) to ensure that the Workbench settings are saved on exit. See Section 15.2.1.1, "IWorkbench-Configurer," for information on the IWorkbenchConfigurer.
preStartup()	Called after the Workbench has been initialized and just before the first window is about to be opened. This is a good place to configure settings that affect the perspectives, views, and editors to be shown, for example, when overriding the initial perspective.
openWindows()	Called by the Workbench to restore the Workbench state and open the Workbench windows. This method is rarely overridden.
restoreState(IMemento)	Called from within openWindows() when the Workbench is starting. The given memento contains settings that have been saved during the last shutdown from saveState().
createWorkbenchWindowAdvisor (IWorkbenchWindowConfigurer)	Called before each Workbench window is opened to create the WorkbenchWindowAdvisor for the window.
postStartup()	Performs arbitrary actions after the Workbench windows have been opened or restored but before the main event loop is run. This is a good place to start any background jobs such as auto-update daemons.
preShutdown()	Called immediately prior to Workbench shutdown before any windows have been closed. The advisor may veto a regular shutdown by returning false. Advisors should check IWorkbenchConfigurer.emergencyClosing() before attempting to communicate with the user.
postShutdown()	Called during Workbench shutdown after all windows have been closed. Advisors should check IWorkbenchConfigurer .emergencyClosing() before attempting to communicate with the user.

(continues)

Table 15–1   Workbench Lifecycle Events (*Continued*)

Method	Description
saveState(IMemento)	Called when the Workbench is shutting down and allows the WorkbenchAdvisor to save state that is persisted to disk. This state is available to the restarted application via restoreState(IMemento).

15.2.1.1 IWorkbenchConfigurer

When the WorkbenchAdvisor method initialize(IWorkbenchConfigurer) is called, it's provided with an IWorkbenchConfigurer. The configurer is used to configure the Workbench and provides privileged access to it, for example, telling it to save Workbench settings or registering images with the Workbench. The configurer can be accessed after the initialize() method is called by calling the WorkbenchAdvisor method getWorkbenchConfigurer().

The IWorkbenchConfigurer is mostly used to

❍ Set and get properties on the configurer using the setData(String, Object) and getData(String) methods. This is useful for passing data from the WorkbenchAdvisor to the WorkbenchWindowAdvisor or ActionBarAdvisor.

❍ Close the Workbench in case of emergency and find out if it's closing via the emergencyClose() and emergencyClosing() methods.

❍ Determine if the Workbench should exit when the last window is closed via the setExitOnLastWindowClose(boolean). If the Workbench does not exit and the event loop keeps running, you can either open another window using IWorkbench.openWorkbenchWindow(String, IAdaptable) or close the Workbench by calling IWorkbench.close().

Because advisors have privileged access to the Workbench, it's best to keep both the configurers and the advisors private and not pass them to other plug-ins.

15.2.1.2 Closing the Workbench

The Workbench can be closed any time after the WorkbenchAdvisor method initialize() is called. There are three ways of closing the Workbench:

IWorkbench.close()—This method performs a normal shutdown. In Hyperbola the ActionFactory.QUIT_ACTION calls this method to exit the Workbench.

IWorkbench.restart()—This method performs a normal shutdown and causes the application to restart immediately.

IworkbenchConfigurer.emergencyClose()—This method causes Eclipse to exit gracefully but immediately. It is called when a fatal error occurs and the application cannot risk a normal shutdown. The Workbench attempts to at least save the user's settings.

15.2.1.3 Workbench Preferences

In addition to configuration settings available on the `IworkbenchConfigurer`, there are additional Workbench preferences to control the look and feel of the application. These include setting the perspective bar's location, the fast view bar's location, and the use of traditional versus curvy tabs. Table 15-2 lists the most popular public preferences for RCP applications. See the `org.eclipse.ui.IworkbenchPreferenceConstants` interface for a complete list.

The `WorkbenchAdvisor` can set preferences in the `initialize()` method as shown here:

```
PlatformUI.getPreferenceStore().setValue(
    IworkbenchPreferenceConstants.SHOW_TRADITIONAL_STYLE_TABS, true);
```

Table 15–2 Useful Workbench Customization Preferences Defined by `org.eclipse.ui`

Preference Name	Description
PRESENTATION_FACTORY_ID	Overrides the presentation used to display editors and views. See Chapter 20, "Customizing the Presentation of Views and Editors," for a detailed look at changing the look and feel of editors and views.
SHOW_TRADITIONAL_STYLE_TABS	This preference is used to switch between rectangular (traditional) and curved tabs. Note that the IDE application sets this preference to `false` by default. By default, this preference is set to `true`.
EDITOR_MINIMUM_CHARACTERS	Sets the minimum number of characters shown on editor tabs before they get shortened when many editors are opened. This preference's default value is 8.
KEY_CONFIGURATION_ID	Sets the default key configuration to use for key bindings. This preference's default value for RCP applications is `org.eclipse.ui.defaultAcceleratorConfiguration`. See Section 12.4, "Key Schemes," for an example of using this preference.
SHOW_PROGRESS_ON_STARTUP	If this preference is enabled, shortly after the splash screen is shown a progress window appears, showing which plug-ins are being loaded. By default, this preference is set to `false`.

As described in Section 13.4, "Adding Help Content," preferences can also be initialized using the product preference customization file. For example, add the following to your product's preferences customization file to show the perspective bar and fast view bar on the left and to use curvy tabs. The advantage of using a customization file is that it allows different products that may be built from your application to have different values for these preferences.

org.eclipsercp.hyperbola/preferences.ini
```
org.eclipse.ui/DOCK_PERSPECTIVE_BAR=left
org.eclipse.ui/SHOW_TEXT_ON_PERSPECTIVE_BAR=false
org.eclipse.ui/SHOW_TRADITIONAL_STYLE_TABS=false
```

15.2.2 Exceptions and Idleness API

The Workbench runs a standard SWT event loop. It is possible that bugs in the application, a constituent plug-in, or critical situations (e.g., running out of memory) in the system can cause exceptions to be thrown into the event loop code. When this happens, the Workbench's event loop calls WorkbenchAdvisor.eventLoopException(), as shown in the snippet below. Table 15-3 also lists the exception and idleness methods available on the WorkbenchAdvisor.

org.eclipse.ui.workbench/Workbench
```
while (loopShell != null && !loopShell.isDisposed()) {
  try {
    if (!display.readAndDispatch())
      display.sleep();
  } catch (Throwable e) {
    wb.getAdvisor().eventLoopException(e);
  }
}
```

Table 15–3   Workbench Event Loop Methods

Method	Description
eventLoopException(Throwable)	This method is called when an unchecked exception propagates to the Workbench's event loop. The default implementation logs the exception and keeps the Workbench running. The Workbench also tracks how many times this method was called since fatal recursive exceptions (out of memory, stack overflow) may have occurred and, instead of prompting many times, allows the user to close the Workbench. Call IWorkbench.emergencyClose() from this method.
eventLoopIdle(Display)	This method is called when there are no more events on the queue. It is safe to call IWorkbench.close() from this method.

Even though this usually means that the application is in an invalid state, the WorkbenchAdvisor's default implementation logs the exceptions and allows the application to keep running. Your advisor can extend this exception handling by, for example, prompting the user to take some action such as logging a bug report, or by shutting down the application. To shut down the Workbench in an emergency, the WorkbenchAdvisor should call the IWorkbenchConfigurer method emergencyClose().

To avoid causing such emergencies, you should write your code defensively—catching and handling exceptions locally. This can be challenging since you do not have control over the exceptions thrown during calls to third-party code. To help, the Runtime provides the platform method run(ISafeRunnable), a convenient mechanism for safely running untrusted code.

The ISafeRunnable interface contains two methods: run() and handleException (Throwable). You simply wrap calls to untrusted code in the run() method. When ISafeRunnable is executed, the platform catches all exceptions and allows the handleException() method to handle them. Since the platform automatically logs exceptions, your handleException() should focus on recovering from the problem if possible. The snippet below shows a typical use of ISafeRunnable when notifying listeners. If the listener fails, the code moves on to the next listener, trusting that the failure has been logged.

```
for (int i = 0; i < listeners.length; i++) {
  final ContentTypeChangeEvent event =
      new ContentTypeChangeEvent(type);
  final IContentTypeChangeListener listener =
      (IContentTypeChangeListener) listeners[i];
  ISafeRunnable work = new ISafeRunnable() {
    public void handleException(Throwable exception) {
      // already logged in Platform#run()
    }
    public void run() throws Exception {
      listener.contentTypeChanged(event);
    }
  };
  Platform.run(work);
}
```

15.2.3 Configuration API

When a Workbench window is opened for the first time, it asks the WorkbenchAdvisor for the settings that are used to create the initial perspective and page input. Without this information, your application does not start. The information is provided by the methods listed in Table 15-4. These are used only once to initialize the setting. Subsequent runs use the values saved with the Workbench settings.

Table 15–4 Workbench Configuration Methods

Method	Description
getInitialWindowPerspectiveId()	Returns the initial perspective ID. In Hyperbola this method returns org.eclipsercp.hyperbola.perspective, used for new Workbench windows. If this method returns null, the Workbench window is considered empty and the control returned from WorkbenchWindowAdvisor.createEmptyWorkbenchWindow (Composite) is shown instead of the contents of a perspective.
getMainPreferencePageId()	Returns the preference page that should be displayed first in the list. Defaults to null, indicating that pages should be arranged alphabetically.
getDefaultPageInput()	Returns the page input—an opaque IAdaptable—that is passed to new IWorkbenchPage objects when they are opened. The page input is then available to all views and editors on the page via IWorkbenchPart.getSite().getPage().getInput(). This mechanism is handy for passing a context to all components of a perspective.
getWorkbenchErrorHandler()	Returns the Workbench error handler for the advisor. Can also be contributed declaratively via the org.eclipse.ui.status-Handler extension point.

15.3 WorkbenchWindowAdvisor

In Hyperbola, WorkbenchWindowAdvisor plays a more visible role than Workbench-Advisor. It configures the window's title, the visibility of the menu bar, toolbar, and status line, and many more things. Essentially, this advisor controls the appearance of each Workbench window.

The methods on WorkbenchWindowAdvisor relate to the lifecycle of the window instead of the Workbench's lifecycle. Within the lifecycle methods, the advisor can configure the window via its IWorkbenchWindowConfigurer. Think of the configurer as providing special APIs that allow the advisor to fine-tune elements of the WorkbenchWindow that are not available via the standard IWorkbenchWindow APIs. As such, the configurer has several useful methods such as setInitialSize(Point), setShowToolbar(boolean), setTitle(String), and setShowMenuBar(boolean). The following snippet shows a typical use of this advisor:

```
org.eclipsercp.hyperbola/ApplicationWorkbenchWindowAdvisor
public void preWindowOpen() {
    IWorkbenchWindowConfigurer configurer = getWindowConfigurer();
    configurer.setInitialSize(new Point(400, 300));
    configurer.setShowCoolBar(true);
```

```
        configurer.setShowStatusLine(true);
        configurer.setShowMenuBar(true);
}

public void dispose() {
    statusImage.dispose();
    trayImage.dispose();
    trayItem.dispose();
}

public void postWindowOpen() {
    initStatusLine();
    final IWorkbenchWindow window = getWindowConfigurer().getWindow();
    trayItem = initTaskItem(window);
    if (trayItem != null) {
        hookPopupMenu(window);
        hookMinimize(window);
    }
}
```

The Hyperbola `WorkbenchWindowAdvisor` overrides a few methods, such as these:

`prewindowOpen()`—configures the parts of the window that should be visible and sets the initial window size, as shown in the previous snippet

`postWindowOpen()`—configures things that need the window to be created, for example, to set up system tray integration

Working through the tutorial in Part II is the best way to understand how a `WorkbenchWindowAdvisor` is used. For more advanced Workbench window customization, see Chapter 19, "Customizing Workbench Windows."

15.3.1 `IWorkbenchWindowConfigurer`

As shown in the previous code snippet, the window's configurer is most often used in the `WorkbenchWindowAdvisor` to show and hide items in the window. It can also be used to

○ Set and get properties on the configurer using the `setData(String, Object)` and `getData(String)` methods. This is useful for passing data from this advisor to the `ActionBarAdvisor`.

○ Allow the advisor to create the menu, toolbar, and status line itself and arrange these controls in different ways. See Chapter 17, "Actions," for examples of using these methods with Hyperbola.

○ Configure the drag-and-drop behavior of the editor's area. See Section 16.4, "Drag and Drop with Editors."

15.4 **ActionBarAdvisor**

The ActionBarAdvisor is responsible for the actions shown in the top-level menu, toolbar, and status line of your application. As you saw in Chapter 6, "Adding Actions," this advisor has a very straightforward lifecycle. It creates the actions when makeActions(IWorkbenchWindow) is called and positions the actions in their respective areas when fillMenuBar(), fillCoolBar(), and fillStatusLine() are called. When the window is closed, the dispose() method is called so it can clean up. The following snippet shows a typical use of this advisor:

```
org.eclipsercp.hyperbola/ApplicationActionBarAdvisor
protected void makeActions(IWorkbenchWindow window) {
   exitAction = ActionFactory.QUIT.create(window);
   register(exitAction);
   aboutAction = ActionFactory.ABOUT.create(window);
   register(aboutAction);
   addContactAction = new AddContactAction(window);
   register(addContactAction);
   ...
}

protected void fillMenuBar(IMenuManager menuBar) {
   MenuManager hyperbolaMenu =
     new MenuManager("&Hyperbola", "hyperbola");
   hyperbolaMenu.add(addContactAction);
   hyperbolaMenu.add(chatAction);
   hyperbolaMenu.add(new Separator());
   hyperbolaMenu.add(preferencesAction);
   hyperbolaMenu.add(new Separator());
   hyperbolaMenu.add(exitAction);
   MenuManager helpMenu = new MenuManager("&Help", "help");
   helpMenu.add(helpAction);
   ...
}
```

The following points describe the responsibility of the ActionBarAdvisor:

○ Creates the fixed menu, toolbar, and status line structure for the application

○ Adds placeholders for contributed actions and menus

○ Creates the static actions and registers them with the Workbench to enable key bindings

Reading Chapter 6 and seeing how it is used in building Hyperbola is the best way to learn about ActionBarAdvisor. Chapters 18 and 19 contain more advanced examples.

15.4.1 `IActionBarConfigurer`

As shown in the previous code snippet, the action bar's configurer is used only in `ActionBarAdvisor` to access the areas in the window that can accept actions and contributions.

15.5 Workbench Overview

There is much more to the Workbench than the advisors. In Part II you saw that much of the Workbench configuration is done by adding extensions to the many Workbench extension points. This section provides a quick overview of the overall role of the Workbench and a reference to its many extension points.

As JFace adds structure to SWT, so the Workbench adds presentation and coordination to JFace. Consider the Workbench as providing the following functionality to your application:

Configures and manages windows—The first Workbench window is opened using `PlatformUI.createAndRunWorkbench(Display, IWorkbenchAdvisor)` during application startup. This also runs the event loop and manages all subsequent windows. An RCP application has special status with the Workbench— it provides a set of Workbench advisors that participate in the management of the Workbench and the windows that it opens. This part of the Workbench is specific to RCP applications since only one application plug-in can define the running of the Workbench.

Defines a UI paradigm—Chapters 5, "Starting the Hyperbola Prototype," and 7, "Adding a Chat Editor," introduced the RCP basic building blocks of the Workbench UI: perspectives, views, and editors. These common UI components define the way application content is shown to the user. A *perspective* is a visual container for a set of *views* and *editors*—everything shown to the user is in a view or editor and is laid out by a perspective. There are many APIs available to manage and control these components of the UI.

Provides contribution-based extensibility—While JFace defines the notions of actions, preferences, wizards, windows, and so on, the Workbench defines extension points that expose these elements. For example, the Workbench's wizard and preference page extensions are just thin veneers over the related JFace constructs.

The use of extension points to build UIs has a fundamental impact on the scalability of the interface in terms of both complexity and performance. Since all these extensions are handled lazily, applications scale better with respect to performance. As the UI gains views, editors, actions, and so forth, the additional contributions are available but are not loaded or executed until they are required—no code is loaded before its time.

The use of extension points allows multiple unrelated plug-ins to coexist within the same dialogs and menus—UI elements do not need to know about each other to be integrated.

Browsing the Workbench

Since the Workbench contains a significant body of code and extension points, it's worth a few words on how to browse the code and discover its capabilities.

Online Help

The Eclipse IDE online Help shown in Figure 15-2 contains a complete set of reference materials for both APIs and Workbench extension points. While this is a good place to look for information on standard Workbench features, most of the content is general-purpose and does not focus on RCP issues—that is why you have this book!

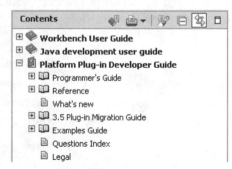

Figure 15–2 Platform Developer Guide reference section

Browsing the Source

You can also browse the Workbench code from within the IDE and take advantage of the search facilities such as **Search > Search...** and **Navigate > Open *** to see how other plug-ins use the Workbench facilities. This is a very effective means of learning how to use the APIs.

You can browse the extension point documentation using the `plugin.xml` editor. Open the Plug-ins view using **Window > Show View > Other ... > PDE > Plug-ins**, and from there you can open a plug-in editor on any plug-in in your target or workspace. Both the **Extensions** and **Extension Points** pages have an **Open extension point description** line that opens the documentation for the extension point.

15.5.1 Workbench Extension Point Reference

Throughout the tutorial in Part II, you encountered most of the important extension points defined by the Workbench. For example, in Chapters 5 and 7 you added a view, an editor, and a perspective to Hyperbola. This section gives you a quick overview of all the Workbench extension points, to provide context for the following chapters and a reference for extension points that are not described later but that may be useful in your RCP application.

NOTE

Some extension points are not fully covered in this book because they are covered well in existing documentation or are not specific or key to RCP use cases.

Although the list of over 42 Workbench extension points looks daunting, categorizing them makes it much more tractable. The next sections (including Tables 15-5 through 15-9) summarize the categories and give short descriptions of each of the Workbench's extension points. When possible, pointers to other chapters in the book are provided in an extension point's description.

15.5.2 Actions

The extension points in Table 15-5 support adding menus, menu items, and toolbar buttons to windows, editors, and views. Also, as shown in Chapter 12, "Adding Key Bindings," you can use them to add key bindings to existing actions.

Table 15–5 Action Extension Points at a Glance

Extension Point	Description
actionSets	Used to add menus, menu items, and toolbar buttons to the common areas in the Workbench window. These contributions, collectively known as an *action set*, appear in a Workbench window when added to a perspective. See Chapter 16, "Perspectives, Views, and Editors," for how to add action sets to a perspective, and Chapter 17, "Actions," for how to define and use actions sets in RCP applications.
actionSetPartAssociation	Used to define an action set to be added to a perspective when a part (view or editor) is opened in the perspective. In the case of an editor, the action set remains visible while the editor has focus. In the case of a view, the action set is visible when the view has focus.

(continues)

Table 15–5 Action Extension Points at a Glance (*Continued*)

Extension Point	Description
commands	Used to declare commands and command categories and assign key sequences to commands. Commands are useful for assigning key bindings and menus. See Chapters 12, 17, and 18.
menus	Used to declare menu contributions with commands. See Chapter 18.
dropActions	Used to allow drag and drop between unrelated plug-ins. Because of the UI layering imposed by the plug-in design, views are often not aware of the content and nature of other views. This mechanism delegates the drop behavior back to the originator of the drag operation.
editorActions	Used to add actions to the menu and toolbar for editors registered by other plug-ins.
popupMenus	Used to add new actions to context menus owned by other plug-ins. The plug-in defining the context menu has to explicitly register with the Workbench to accept contributions from other plug-ins. See Chapter 17. Note: It's recommended to use the menus extension point since this one may be deprecated in the future.
viewActions	Used to add actions to the pull-down menu and toolbar for views registered by other plug-ins.

15.5.3 Scalability

The extension points described in Table 15-6 support the creation of large-scale applications. For example, activities are used to automatically or manually hide certain elements of the UI.

Table 15–6 Scalability Extension Points at a Glance

Extension Point	Description
activities	Used by the Platform to filter contributions from the Workbench until such time as a user expresses interest in them. This allows the Workbench to dynamically reveal contributions based on the usage pattern of a user. It's important to note that only UI elements contributed declaratively via extensions can be filtered.
elementFactories	Used to add element factories to the Workbench. An element factory, IElementFactory, is used to re-create IAdaptable objects that are persisted during Workbench shutdown, for example, to restore editors or persist objects during drag-and-drop operations. See Section 16.4 for a drag-and-drop example.

(continues)

Table 15–6 Scalability Extension Points at a Glance (*Continued*)

Extension Point	Description
themes	Allows the definition of colors, fonts, and other presentation theme preferences. Themes allow applications to selectively override default color and font specifications for particular uses. See IThemeManager and ExtensionFactory.COLORS_AND_FONTS_PREFERENCE_PAGE.
workingSets	Used to define a working set wizard page. Working sets contain a number of elements of type IAdaptable and can be used to group elements for presentation to the user or for operations on a set of elements. A working set wizard page is used to create and edit working sets that contain elements of a specific type.

15.5.4 Contributions

The extension points in Table 15-7 allow the contribution of pages, wizards, and other standard elements to the UI.

Table 15–7 Contribution Extension Points at a Glance

Extension Point	Description
decorators	Used to add label decorators to JFace viewers in other unrelated plug-ins, for example, to add CVS decorations into the Navigator and Package Explorer.
exportWizards	Used to register export wizard extensions. Export wizards appear as choices in the Export dialog and are used to export artifacts from the Workbench. See ActionFactory.EXPORT.
importWizards	Used to register import wizard extensions. Import wizards appear as choices in the Import dialog and are used to import artifacts into the Workbench. See ActionFactory.IMPORT.
newWizards	Used to register element creation wizard extensions. Creation wizards appear as choices within the new dialog. See ActionFactory.NEW and Section 17.5, "Consolidating Declarative Actions," for examples.
preferencePages	The Workbench provides a common dialog box for preferences. The purpose of this extension point is to allow plug-ins to add pages to the Preferences dialog box. When the Preferences dialog is opened, usually from the menu bar, it's populated with contributed pages. See Chapter 11, "Adding a Login Dialog," for an example.
propertyPages	Used to add additional property pages for objects of a given type. RCP applications can open a generic properties dialog by using the ActionFactory.PROPERTIES actions defined by the Workbench.

(continues)

Table 15–7   Contribution Extension Points at a Glance (*Continued*)

Extension Point	Description
statusHandlers	The Workbench provides a status handling facility that shows problems to users. This facility can be customized via an extension point that allows new status handlers for a specific product. This handler is associated to a product and is intended to present problems in a useful manner to a user.
systemSummarySections	The Workbench provides an About dialog that can be branded and reused by client product plug-ins. This dialog can show other dialogs containing configuration details. Clients can add their own information in this summary by contributing to this extension point. See ActionFactory.ABOUT.

15.5.5 Perspectives

The extension points in Table 15-8 are used to define the basic components of the UI in terms of views, editors, and perspectives. Most RCP applications have at least one perspective and minimally one view. Perspective extension points are meant to allow plug-ins to contribute to perspectives contributed from other plug-ins.

Table 15–8   Perspective Extension Points at a Glance

Extension Point	Description
editors	Used to add new editors to the Workbench. An editor is a visual component within a Workbench page. It is typically used to edit or browse a document or input object. See Chapters 7 and 17.
perspectiveExtensions	Used to extend perspectives registered by other plug-ins.
perspectives	Used to add perspective factories to the Workbench. A perspective factory is used to define the initial layout and visible action sets for a perspective. See Chapters 5, 7, and 17.
presentationFactories	Used to register a presentation factory. A presentation factory defines the overall look and feel of the Workbench, including how views and editors are presented. See Chapter 20.
views	Used to define additional views for the Workbench. A view is a visual component within a Workbench page.

15.5.6 Startup

The extension points in Table 15-9 relate to the behavior of the Workbench when the application starts up.

Table 15–9   Startup Extension Points at a Glance

Extension Point	Description
intro	This extension point is used to register implementations of special Workbench parts, called *intro parts*. Intro parts are responsible for introducing a product to new users. An intro part is typically shown the first time a product is started.
startup	Used to register plug-ins that want to be activated on startup.

15.6 Summary

In this chapter you got a glimpse of the Workbench features available to you when building RCP applications. The features in the Workbench exist because they were needed when building the Eclipse IDE product—not because the Eclipse RCP needed a UI framework; that is, they address real, concrete problems but are general enough to be used in other situations. After all, the IDE is essentially a very sophisticated RCP application!

The next couple of chapters are dedicated to uncovering the essential RCP-specific Workbench features.

15.7 Pointers

○ Eclipse **Help > Platform Plug-in Developer Guide > Advanced workbench concepts**

CHAPTER 16

Perspectives, Views, and Editors

The Hyperbola UI described in Part II is purposely simple, but it still touches on most of the central features of the Workbench's UI paradigm, in particular, *perspectives*, *views*, and *editors*. If you take a careful look at the Eclipse IDE's UI, you can see that much more can be done with these building blocks than what we've used so far in Hyperbola. For example, as shown in Figure 16-1, the Workbench allows multiple windows to be opened and each window to have multiple perspectives. You can also define perspectives that are fully customizable by the user—views can be moved, minimized, closed, or arranged as *fast views*. RCP applications can use this power to provide a rich user experience and many layers of functionality without overwhelming the user.

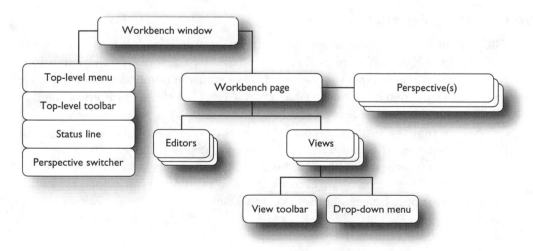

Figure 16–1   Runtime composition of perspectives, views, and editors

In this chapter we extend Hyperbola to have multiple perspectives and multiple windows, and to use advanced view manipulation techniques. Specifically, we show you how to

○ Add perspectives

○ Use the programmatic perspective and view APIs

○ Use multiple instances of a view and sticky views

○ Open and track multiple Workbench windows

○ Connect parts together

○ Add drag-and-drop support to the editor area

16.1 Perspectives

Perspectives group together and organize UI elements that relate to a specific task or workflow. For example, in the Eclipse IDE, the Java perspective contains views for editing Java source files, while the Debug perspective contains views for debugging Java programs. You can have multiple perspectives in the same window, allowing you to switch tasks without having to change windows.

To show how perspectives can be used in RCP applications, let's walk through the steps required to add two new perspectives, "Free Moving" and "Debug," to Hyperbola. The Free Moving perspective allows the user to move around the Contacts view. The Debug perspective, as shown in Figure 16-2, shows a console with the XMPP output of all incoming and outgoing messages.

16.1.1 Adding Perspectives

The first step is to define the new perspective extensions and perspective factory classes. Open Hyperbola's plug-in editor and add two new perspective extensions to the existing `org.eclipse.ui.perspectives` extension point, as shown in Figure 16-3. The steps are the same as in Chapters 4, "The Hyperbola Application," and 5, "Starting the Hyperbola Prototype."

Notice that the original Hyperbola perspective does not have an icon. An icon was not needed because the perspective concept was never exposed—users just saw the Hyperbola window. In this new Hyperbola perspectives are exposed; therefore, you need icons. For each of the new perspectives and for the default perspective, supply a meaningful name and icon.

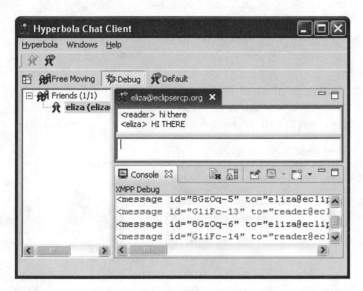

Figure 16–2   The Debug perspective in Hyperbola

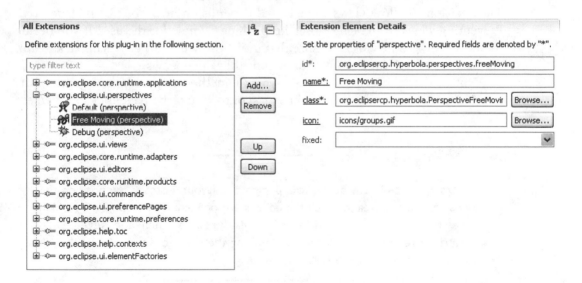

Figure 16–3   Two new perspectives added to Hyperbola

The **class** attribute defines an IPerspectiveFactory that generates the initial page layout and visible action sets for a page. You can use the usual trick of clicking on the **class** attribute to launch the **New Class** wizard. Name the perspective classes PerspectiveFreeMoving and PerspectiveDebug.

The Free Moving perspective is the same as the original Hyperbola perspective except that the Contacts view has a title bar and is movable. So, instead of calling IPageLayout.addStandaloneView(), call IPageLayout.addView() as shown here:

org.eclipsercp.hyperbola/PerspectiveFreeMoving
```
public class PerspectiveFreeMoving implements IPerspectiveFactory {
    public void createInitialLayout(IPageLayout layout) {
        layout.addStandaloneView(ContactsView.ID, false,
            IPageLayout.LEFT, 0.33f,layout.getEditorArea());
        layout.addView(ContactsView.ID, IPageLayout.LEFT, 0.33f,
            layout.getEditorArea());
        layout.getViewLayout(ContactsView.ID).setCloseable(false);
    }
}
```

By default, Eclipse views are closable. To override this behavior, the Free Moving perspective retrieves the IViewLayout and calls setCloseable(false). The decision to allow views to be closed depends on how your UI is structured. Preventing views from being closed keeps things simple for the user. If you decide to allow views to be closed, ensure that users know how to get them back again. See Section 16.2.1 for examples of actions that open views.

Notice that the createInitialLayout() method is passed an IPageLayout. The perspective uses the layout object to control how the page looks and where views go.

NOTE

Editors are not directly added to a perspective layout; instead, you position the views around the area in which the editors are opened. It's also possible to hide the editor area. It can be made visible later via the IWorkbenchPage.setEditor-AreaVisible(boolean) method or by using the org.eclipse.ui.workbench.ActionFactory.SHOW_EDITOR action.

16.1.2 Adding the Debug Perspective and Console View

The Eclipse Platform includes a very useful Console plug-in that can be used to add a console to your RCP application. Here we use the Console view contributed by this plug-in in the Debug perspective. The console supports advanced features such as line coloring and hyperlinks. To add the console to Hyperbola, follow the instructions in Chapter 13, "Adding Help," for adding plug-ins to your target, but instead of adding the Help plug-ins, add the following:

- ○ org.eclipse.text
- ○ org.eclipse.jface.text
- ○ org.eclipse.ui.console
- ○ org.eclipse.ui.workbench.texteditor

Then, to implement a console that displays all outgoing and incoming XMPP message in raw XML, create the DebugConsole class as follows:

org.eclipsercp.hyperbola/DebugConsole

```java
public class DebugConsole extends MessageConsole {
  private MessageConsoleStream outMessageStream;
  private MessageConsoleStream inMessageStream;

  private PacketListener outListener = new PacketListener() {
    public void processPacket(Packet arg0) {
      outMessageStream.println(arg0.toXML());
    }
  };

  private PacketListener inListener = new PacketListener() {
    public void processPacket(Packet arg0) {
      inMessageStream.println(arg0.toXML());
    }
  };

  public DebugConsole() {
    super("XMPP Debug", null);
    outMessageStream = newMessageStream();
    outMessageStream.setColor(Display.getCurrent().getSystemColor(
        SWT.COLOR_BLUE));
    inMessageStream = newMessageStream();
    inMessageStream.setColor(Display.getCurrent().getSystemColor(
        SWT.COLOR_RED));

    Session.getInstance().getConnection().
        addPacketWriterListener(outListener, null);
    Session.getInstance().getConnection().
        addPacketListener(inListener, null);
  }

  protected void dispose() {
    Session.getInstance().getConnection().removePacketWriterListener(
        outListener);
    Session.getInstance().getConnection().removePacketListener(
        inListener);
  }
}
```

Add the new `DebugConsole` to the console manager in the `ApplicationWorkbench-`
`Advisor`'s `initialize(IWorkbenchConfigurer)` method as follows:

`org.eclipsercp.hyperbola/ApplicationWorkbenchAdvisor`
```
public void initialize(IWorkbenchConfigurer configurer) {
  ...
  ConsolePlugin.getDefault().getConsoleManager().addConsoles(
      new IConsole[] { new DebugConsole(session) });
}
```

Alternatively, you can use the `org.eclipse.ui.console.consoleFactories`
extension point to register the Debug console with the Console view. This
approach is good if you expect to ship Hyperbola without a console and have it
added by another plug-in. In this case, decoupling the advisor from the console
is a good idea.

The Debug perspective is very similar to the original Hyperbola perspective,
but it adds a Console view below the chat editor area:

`org.eclipsercp.hyperbola/PerspectiveDebug`
```
public class PerspectiveDebug implements IPerspectiveFactory {
  public void createInitialLayout(IPageLayout layout) {
    layout.addStandaloneView(ContactsView.ID, false,
        IPageLayout.LEFT, 0.33f, layout.getEditorArea());
    layout.addView(IConsoleConstants.ID_CONSOLE_VIEW,
        IPageLayout.BOTTOM, 0.70f, layout.getEditorArea());
  }
}
```

The `IPageLayout.BOTTOM` flag is used to place the Console view below the editor area. The Console view's ID is defined by the Console plug-in and is available
from `IConsoleConstants`.

16.1.3 `IPageLayout` Reference

Our use of `IPageLayout` has been straightforward, but in fact there are many
additional useful methods. These methods can be grouped into two categories:

View placement—Methods meant for placing views in the perspective, for
example, methods that stack views together or add placeholders for views to
be opened after the perspective is shown. See Table 16-1 for a complete list.

Perspective configuration—Methods to configure other elements associated
with a perspective, for example, which wizards or action sets are shown when
the perspective is activated. Refer to Chapter 17, "Actions," for how to
define and use action sets and new wizards. See Table 16-2 for a complete
listing of perspective configuration methods.

Table 16–1 `IPageLayout` Placement Methods

Method	Description
`addFastView(String id)`	Adds a view to the page layout. By default the view is hidden and shown in the perspective's fast view bar.
`addPlaceholder(String id, int relationship, float ratio, String refPartId)`	Adds a placeholder for a view with the given ID to this page layout. View placeholders are used to define the position of a view before the view appears. Initially, the placeholder is invisible; however, if the user ever opens a view with the same ID as a placeholder, the view replaces the placeholder as it is made visible.
`addStandaloneView(String id, Boolean showTitle, int relationship, float ratio, String refPartId)`	Adds a stand-alone view with the given ID to this page layout. A stand-alone view cannot be docked together with other views. A stand-alone view's title can optionally be hidden. If hidden, any controls typically shown with the title (such as the **Close** button) are also hidden.
`addView(String id, int relationship, float ratio, String refPartId)`	Adds a view with the given ID to this page layout. Placement of the view is specified using the `relationship`, `ratio`, and `refPartId`.
`createFolder(String id, int relationship, float ratio, String refPartId)`	Creates and adds a folder with the given ID to this page layout. A folder is an area that contains several views in the same location. To the user, this shows as a set of views stacked together.
`createPlaceholderFolder(String id, int relationship, float ratio, String refPartId)`	Creates and adds a placeholder for a folder with the given ID to this page layout. The placeholder folder allows a set of views to be described that can be stacked together without having the views added to the perspective when the perspective is opened. This is commonly used with `IPlaceHolderFolderLayout.addPlaceholder(String id)`.

NOTE

The user can manually detach movable views from a Workbench window by dragging them, but there is no programmatic or declarative support for creating a detached view using `IPageLayout`.

Table 16-2 `IPageLayout` Configuration Methods

Method	Description
addActionSet(String actionSetId)	Adds an action set to the current layout. The action set must have been previously contributed to the Workbench via the org.eclipse.ui.actionSets extension point. Another way of associating an actionSet with a perspective is to use the org.eclipse.ui.perspectiveExtensions extension point. The perspectiveExtensions allows you to selectively make an action set visible in a specific perspective as opposed to visible at all times.
addNewWizardShortcut(String wizardId)	Adds a new wizard shortcut to the page layout. These are typically shown in the UI to allow rapid navigation to appropriate new wizards.
addPerspectiveShortcut(String perspId)	Adds a perspective shortcut to the page layout. These are typically shown in the UI to allow rapid navigation to appropriate new wizards. The shortcuts are useful only if you are using the ContributionItemFactory.PERSPECTIVES_SHORTLIST menu. See Section 16.1.5, "Perspective Menu," for more details.
addShowInPart(String viewed)	Adds an item to the **Show In** prompter. These are typically added to allow quick navigation from an element in one view to an element in another view. See ContributionItemFactory.VIEWS_SHOW_IN.
setEditorAreaVisible(boolean)	Shows or hides the editor area. The editor area is empty when the perspective is created, but on subsequent starts of the application it may contain editors that have been persisted from the last session.
setFixed(boolean)	Resides in a fixed layout, where parts cannot be moved or zoomed and the initial set of views cannot be closed. You can also make individual views nonclosable by calling IViewLayout.setCloseable(boolean).

NOTE

Many of these methods take view identifiers, for example, as the base for relative positioning. IPageLayout includes constants for view identifiers. They are listed mostly for convenience and backward compatibility. We recommend that you define your layout relative to the editor area and use your own view IDs instead of these. It's entirely possible that these predefined view IDs are contributed plugins (e.g., IDE plug-ins) that are not included in your application.

If you have more complex layout requirements or want to allow users to drag and stack views together, refer to the APIs available on IPageLayout, IViewLayout, and IFolderLayout.

16.1.4 Perspective Bar

Hyperbola's two new perspectives are defined, but they are not available to the user yet—users have no way of opening them. For most applications, providing a way to switch between perspectives is sufficient. The Workbench provides a perspective switching bar that is hidden by default in RCP applications. It has to be enabled from the WorkbenchWindowAdvisor to appear, as shown in Figure 16-4.

```
org.eclipsercp.hyperbola/ApplicationWorkbenchWindowAdvisor
public void preWindowOpen() {
    IWorkbenchWindowConfigurer configurer = getWindowConfigurer();
    configurer.setInitialSize(new Point(600, 500));
    configurer.setShowCoolBar(true);
    configurer.setShowMenuBar(true);
    configurer.setShowStatusLine(true);
    configurer.setShowPerspectiveBar(true);
    ...
}
```

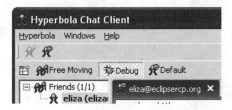

Figure 16–4 Perspective bar

The perspective bar allows switching between open perspectives and includes the ability to open new perspectives. Its context menu contains several useful options for manipulating perspectives and the perspective bar itself. You can show or hide perspective text, close individual or all perspectives, as well as customize, reset, and change the location of the bar. The perspective bar's default location is just below the toolbar, but it can be placed in the top right or on the left using the IWorkbenchPreferenceConstants.DOCK_PERSPECTIVE_BAR preference. You can set this in the Hyperbola preferences.ini file as follows:

```
org.eclipsercp.hyperbola/preferences.ini
org.eclipse.ui/DOCK_PERSPECTIVE_BAR=TOP_RIGHT
```

16.1.5 Perspective Menu

Instead of, or in addition to, the perspective switching bar, you can use the **Perspective** menu. The **Perspective** menu displays a list of perspective shortcuts that have been configured for the active perspective and an **Other...** item, as shown in Figure 16-5. The **Other...** item shows a dialog allowing the user to open any other perspective. If you do not like the wording or the prompting dialog, you can always write a custom menu and dialog using the perspective APIs discussed in Section 16.1.6, "Programmatic Perspective Control." But if you want to use it as is, simply add the contribution item to an existing menu in the `ActionBarAdvisor`.

```
org.eclipsercp.hyperbola/ApplicationActionBarAdvisor
protected void makeActions(IWorkbenchWindow window) {
    perspectivesMenu =
       ContributionItemFactory.PERSPECTIVES_SHORTLIST.create(window);
}

protected void fillMenuBar(IMenuManager menuBar) {
    MenuManager layoutMenu = new MenuManager("Switch Layout", "layout");
    layoutMenu.add(perspectives);
    menuBar.add(layoutMenu);
}
```

Figure 16–5   Using the **Perspective** menu

The menu shows the list of perspective shortcuts that have been added to the perspective layout via the `IPageLayout` method `addPerspectiveShortcut(String)`. To keep menus and toolbars scalable as your application grows, it's important to allow the perspective to control the available set of actions, perspectives, and view shortcuts. In the case of Hyperbola, each perspective should add a shortcut for each of the other perspectives, as shown here, so users can get to any perspective from any other perspective:

```
org.eclipsercp.hyperbola/Perspective
public class Perspective implements IPerspectiveFactory {
  public static final String ID =
  "org.eclipsercp.hyperbola.perspective";
  public void createInitialLayout(IPageLayout layout) {
    layout.addStandaloneView(ContactsView.ID, false, IPageLayout.LEFT,
        0.33f, layout.getEditorArea());
    layout.addPerspectiveShortcut(PerspectiveDebug.ID);
    layout.addPerspectiveShortcut(PerspectiveFreeMoving.ID);
  }
}
```

In large applications, shortcuts are added for the most frequently used transitions, and the **Other...** category is used to navigate to the others. A common performance blooper is to reference perspectives from other plug-ins in the perspective factory. This causes the other plug-ins to be loaded at startup.

16.1.6 Programmatic Perspective Control

If the perspective bar and menu give users too much control over your application, you can hide the bar and add your own actions to switch between perspectives. You may not even want to expose the term *perspective*. One common pattern is to add an action that shows a particular set of views that matches a workflow the user understands to the top-level menu or toolbar. To the user, it is a set of arranged views; to the application, it is a perspective.

The snippet below shows a sample action that shows a given perspective in a given window. This might surface in Hyperbola, for example, as a simple "Debug" menu entry. The action uses the perspective's ID to find the perspective descriptor from the registry. The descriptor contains the label and icon that were defined in the perspective extension. If you prefer to have perspectives open in a separate window, you can set the IWorkbenchPreferenceConstants.OPEN_PERSPECTIVE_WINDOW preference to true, and then IWorkbench.showPerspective() opens all new perspectives in their own windows.

```
org.eclipsercp.hyperbola/SwitchPerspectiveAction
public class SwitchPerspectiveAction extends Action {
  private final IWorkbenchWindow window;
  private final String id;
  private IPerspectiveDescriptor desc;

  public SwitchPerspectiveAction(IWorkbenchWindow window, String id) {
    this.window = window;
    this.id = id;
    desc = PlatformUI.getWorkbench().
        getPerspectiveRegistry().findPerspectiveWithId(id);
    if(desc != null) {
```

```
      setText(desc.getLabel());
      setImageDescriptor(desc.getImageDescriptor());
    }
  }

  public void run() {
    try {
      PlatformUI.getWorkbench().showPerspective(id, window);
    } catch (WorkbenchException e) {
      MessageDialog.openError(window.getShell(), "Error",
          "Error opening perspective:" + e.getMessage());
    }
  }
}
```

All defined perspectives are stored by the Workbench perspective registry and are accessed by a unique ID. Given an ID, the following classes offer APIs for manipulating, querying, and observing perspectives within the Workbench:

IWorkbenchPage—The Workbench page has methods for opening, closing, and reverting perspectives.

IPerspectiveRegistry—The registry provides access to the perspectives known to the Workbench. A perspective descriptor has the information described in the extension point such as ID, name, and icon.

IPerspectiveListeners—You can register to receive perspective notifications using the IWorkbenchWindow.addPerspectiveListener() method. Three separate listener interfaces are available: IPerspectiveListener, IPerspectiveListener2, and IPerspectiveListener3. A common use of perspective listeners is to update the title of the application window when a perspective is changed. See org.eclipse.ui.workbench.PerspectiveAdapter.

TIP

You may notice when debugging perspectives that you modify the perspective, but the changes do not appear when you relaunch. We saw this in Chapter 5. It is because the Workbench saves perspective layouts between launches. If you modify a perspective in code, you may have to reset the perspective to see your changes. You can reset a perspective using the context menu on the perspective bar or by calling IPerspectiveRegistry.revertPerspective(IPerspectiveDescriptor) in your code.

16.2 Views and Editors

While developing Hyperbola in Part II, you learned the basics of using views and editors and the differences between the two. Typically, an editor shows the main content of your application, whereas views support this with additional navigation or context-sensitive information related to the task being done with the editor.

If you are familiar with the Eclipse IDE, you already know that in Hyperbola we have hidden a couple of the standard IDE mechanisms for managing views and editors. For example, the idea of a user opening an arbitrary view is not exposed, whereas in the Eclipse IDE there's a **Window > Show View** menu entry that allows the user to open any view.

As with many things related to perspectives, views, and editors, it's up to the individual RCP application to decide how to expose these to the end users. The goal of this section is to review some of the advanced RCP-related view and editor features.

16.2.1 Multiple Instances of the Same View

As we have seen in Hyperbola, it's possible to open multiple instances of an editor each with its unique editor input. It's also possible to open multiple instances of a view. Imagine a more advanced Hyperbola that allows you to connect to multiple servers at once. Users can then manage different contacts lists or different logins within the same application. To present this, however, Hyperbola would need a Contacts view for each connection.

There are two techniques for opening multiple instances of the same view in the same perspective. Regardless of the technique used, the first step is to edit Hyperbola's plug-in definition and change the `enableMultiple` property of the Contacts view extension point to `true`.

Once that is done, multiple views can be opened directly in the perspective factory, as shown below. The view ID argument of the `addView()` method can take a qualified view format as `primary-id:secondary-id`. The secondary ID must be unique within the perspective.

```
org.eclipsercp.hyperbola/Perspective
public void createInitialLayout(IPageLayout layout) {
    layout.addStandaloneView(ContactsView.ID + ":1", false,
        IPageLayout.LEFT, 0.33f, layout.getEditorArea());
    layout.addView(ContactsView.ID + ":2",
        IPageLayout.BOTTOM, 0.70f, layout.getEditorArea());
    layout.addView(ContactsView.ID + ":3",
        IPageLayout.BOTTOM, 0.70f, layout.getEditorArea());
}
```

The second technique is to open the secondary views via an action. The following `OpenViewAction` is generically defined to open a new instance of a given view ID, and the action is added to Hyperbola as **Hyperbola > New Contacts View**:

org.eclipsercp.hyperbola/OpenViewAction
```
public class OpenViewAction extends Action {
  private final IWorkbenchWindow window;
  private int instanceNum;
  private final String viewId;

  public OpenViewAction(IWorkbenchWindow window, String viewId) {
    this.window = window;
    this.viewId = viewId;
  }

  public void run() {
    try {
      window.getActivePage().showView(viewId,
          Integer.toString(instanceNum), IWorkbenchPage.VIEW_ACTIVATE);
          instanceNum++;
    } catch (PartInitException e) {
      // Handle exception.
    }
  }
}
```

Notice that the view is created with both a view ID and a secondary unique instance ID. The secondary ID must be remembered if you need to refer to individual views. In this Hyperbola example the secondary ID does not need to be remembered.

If you run Hyperbola and trigger the **New Contacts View** action, a new Contacts view opens at a default location, at the bottom right of the editor area in the perspective. This can be improved. Just as you can define a perspective that contains multiple instances of the same view, so you can define placeholders for these views in the layout. When the views are opened, they are placed in the predefined placeholder locations. The following snippet shows how the Free Moving perspective is set up to ensure that all Contacts views are opened together in the same stack:

org.eclipsercp.hyperbola/Perspective
```
public void createInitialLayout(IPageLayout layout) {
  IFolderLayout folder = layout.createFolder("contacts",
      IPageLayout.LEFT, 0.33f, layout.getEditorArea());
  folder.addPlaceholder(ContactsView.ID + ":*");
  folder.addView(ContactsView.ID);
  IViewLayout viewLayout = layout.getViewLayout(ContactsView.ID);
  viewLayout.setCloseable(false);
  layout.addPerspectiveShortcut(Perspective.ID);
  layout.addPerspectiveShortcut(PerspectiveFreeMoving.ID);
}
```

Notice that the Contacts view placeholder uses a multi-instance view format of `primaryId:secondaryId` and a * wildcard for the secondary ID. This indicates that any Contacts view with a secondary ID should be placed in the folder. Wildcards are also supported for the primary ID.

16.2.2 Sticky Views

A *sticky view* is a view that stays open across perspective switches. Once open in one perspective, the sticky view remains open in all perspectives hosted in that Workbench window. This is true even for perspectives that do not define that view as part of their layout. Sticky views were added to support instructional aids that can span perspectives such as Help, Intro, and Cheat Sheets.

Sticky views are defined using the `stickyView` tag in an `org.eclipse.ui.views` extension, as shown in this snippet:

```
org.eclipsercp.hyperbola/plugin.xml
<extension point="org.eclipse.ui.views">
  <view
      class="org.eclipsercp.hyperbola.ContactsView"
      icon="icons/groups.gif"
      id="org.eclipsercp.hyperbola.views.contacts"
      name="Contacts"/>
  <stickyView
      closeable="false"
      id="org.eclipsercp.hyperbola.ContactsView"
      location="LEFT"
      moveable="false"/>
</extension>
```

The sticky view extension adds a placeholder for the view in the Workbench page but does not show the view. The given ID must be that of an existing view. When the existing view is opened, it becomes sticky. Think of this extension as adding the *sticky* attribute to an already defined view.

Sharing Views and Editors

When multiple perspectives are open in the same window, it's common to have the same views open in multiple perspectives. If two or more perspectives have the same view open, they share the same view instance. For example, open the Java and the Java Browsing perspectives in the same window. Then open the Package Explorer in the two perspectives. Expand some nodes in the Package Explorer in one perspective and notice that the other perspective for the Package Explorer has the exact same expansion state. Notice, however, that if you close the view in one perspective, it is not closed in the others.

Editors are very similar to views in terms of sharing the same instances, but in addition to being the same instance in all perspectives, closing an editor in one perspective closes it in all perspectives. For perspectives in different Workbench windows, neither editors nor views are shared.

16.2.3 Showing Contributed Views

It's quite easy to open specific views if the application knows in advance about all the possible view IDs. In applications that allow views to be contributed by other plug-ins, you may want to allow users to open views manually.

The Workbench exposes a *view shortlist* mechanism that you can use to show users a list of available views. This is similar to the **Window > Show View** menu entry found in the Eclipse IDE. Set this up by creating a contribution item in the ActionBarAdvisor and adding it to any menu. In the following example, the item is added to the Hyperbola main menu:

```
org.eclipsercp.hyperbola/ApplicationActionBarAdvisor
protected void makeActions(IWorkbenchWindow window) {
  views =
     ContributionItemFactory.VIEWS_SHORTLIST.create(window);
}

protected void fillMenuBar(IMenuManager menuBar) {
  MenuManager viewsMenu = new MenuManager("Open View", "views");
  viewsMenu.add(views);
  menuBar.add(viewsMenu);
}
```

The initial list of views shown in the menu consists of the view shortcuts defined by the active perspective. This list is configured by a perspective using IPageLayout.addShowViewShortcut(String).

16.2.4 View Registry

Of course, if you don't like the predefined view menus or features, you can consult the view registry and customize how views are managed in your application. The view registry is accessed using the IWorkbench method getViewRegistry() and has several useful methods for querying registered views. Each view is described using an IViewDescriptor that includes the view's name, icon, ID, and other properties defined in the view's extension point.

16.2.5 Connecting Parts Together

There's a good chance that your UI parts—the views and editors—will need to communicate. For example, the Hyperbola Contacts view could show a contact in bold when a chat editor for that contact is active.

In the Workbench there are three techniques for communicating between parts. First let's review the techniques, then we'll look at how to use one of these techniques to implement contact entry bolding.

Using the selection—The ISelectionService allows views and editors to register their selection with the Workbench, thus allowing other parts to listen to selection changes and respond appropriately. To publish selections, use the IWorkbenchSite method setSelectionProvider(ISelectionProvider), and to subscribe to selections, use the ISelectionService method addSelectionListener(ISelectionListener). This is a good technique because it allows parts to be decoupled. We've already used this technique to connect the Hyperbola actions to the Contacts view and ensure that when the selection changes, the actions are enabled correctly.

Part listeners—You can also connect parts together by listening to the events that are fired when a part is closed, opened, and hidden. Use IPartService to register for part events. Again, this is a good technique because it keeps the parts decoupled. This is the technique that is used below to implement the Hyperbola bolding of the contact example.

Direct communication—Whereas the selection and part service allows any part to listen and react to changes, you can also use a direct connection by having specific views call back to or open other views or editors (e.g., using the methods on IWorkbenchPage to open or close parts). For example, the Hyperbola bolding feature can be implemented by allowing the ChatEditor to notify the ContactsView when it opens. This technique is not ideal because it places a tight coupling between the parts.

To implement bolding of contacts when a chat is in progress, the Contacts view has to know when a chat editor is opened and closed and bold the appropriate contact accordingly. The best technique is for the Contacts view to register a part listener using the IPartService and remember which chat editors are open. The label provider is refreshed when a part is opened or closed, and the active chat list is consulted to decide whether or not a contact should be bold.

The code changes are simple and are described here:

❍ Add a part listener to the Contacts view to track which chat editors are opened and closed.

❍ Register and unregister the part listener.

❍ Change the label decorator to set the font of an item, and use the list of active chat editors to determine the font for a contact.

The part listener is added as a field of ContactsView. It remembers the set of open chats in openEditors and refreshes the labels when a chat editor is opened or closed.

org.eclipsercp.hyperbola/ContactsView
```
private IPartListener partListener = new IPartListener() {
  public void partOpened(IWorkbenchPart part) {
    trackOpenChatEditors(part);
  }

  public void partClosed(IWorkbenchPart part) {
    trackOpenChatEditors(part);
  }

  private void trackOpenChatEditors(IWorkbenchPart part) {
    if (! (part instanceof ChatEditor)) return;
    ChatEditor editor = (ChatEditor) part;
    ChatEditorInput input = (ChatEditorInput) editor.getEditorInput();
    String participant = input.getParticipant();
    if (openEditors.contains(participant)) {
      openEditors.remove(participant);
    } else {
      openEditors.add(participant);
    }
    treeViewer.refresh(true);
  }
  ...
};
```

The part listener is registered with the Workbench when the Contacts view is created and unregistered when it's closed.

org.eclipsercp.hyperbola/ContactsView
```
public void createPartControl(Composite parent) {
  ...
  getSite().getWorkbenchWindow().
    getPartService().addPartListener(partListener);
}

public void dispose() {
  getSite().getWorkbenchWindow().
    getPartService().removePartListener(partListener);
}
```

The existing label provider is augmented with a special decorating label provider that allows other label decorators to participate in label decorations. The new ContactsDecorator consults the list of opened chat editors and makes the contacts that have open editors show as bold. It also implements an `IFontProvider` as an indication that it can change the font in addition to providing text and images. The original `HyperbolaLabelProvider` is still used, but it is wrapped in the `DecoratingLabelProvider` instance.

org.eclipsercp.hyperbola/ContactsView

```
private class ContactsDecorator implements
  ILabelDecorator, IFontDecorator {
  ...
    public Font decorateFont(Object element) {
      if(element instanceof RosterEntry) {
        RosterEntry entry = (RosterEntry)element;
        if(ContactsView.this.openEditors.contains(entry.getUser()))
          return JFaceResources.getFontRegistry().
              getBold(JFaceResources.DEFAULT_FONT);
      }
      return null;
    }
  }

  public void createPartControl(Composite parent) {
    treeViewer = new TreeViewer(parent, SWT.BORDER | SWT.MULTI
        | SWT.V_SCROLL);
    getSite().setSelectionProvider(treeViewer);
    HyperbolaLabelProvider hyperbolaLabelProvider =
      new HyperbolaLabelProvider();
    DecoratingLabelProvider decorator =
      new DecoratingLabelProvider(hyperbolaLabelProvider,
        new ContactsDecorator());
    treeViewer.setLabelProvider(decorator);
    ...
  }
}
```

The result of these changes is shown in Figure 16-6.

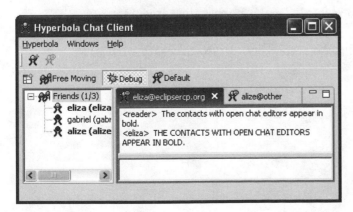

Figure 16–6   Contacts view with bold contacts

Approaches such as this are very powerful. One of the key points here is that the chat editor did not require modification. You can imagine adding other plug-ins to Hyperbola that also connect to existing parts without needing to modify those parts; that is, plug-ins have opportunities to integrate with your application without you needing to know about them.

16.3 Multiple Workbench Windows

The Workbench supports opening multiple top-level windows. These windows are managed by the Workbench, and the WorkbenchWindowAdvisor participates in each window's lifecycle. There are two techniques for opening a new Workbench window from an RCP application:

❍ Use the ActionFactory.OPEN_WINDOW or the OpenInNewWindow action. These actions open a new window using the perspective currently showing in the window in which the action is run.

❍ Call the IWorkbench method openWorkbenchWindow(String, IAdaptable). This method opens a new window and shows the identified perspective.

16.3.1 Window Navigation Menu

When an application allows multiple windows to be created, it should provide an easy way of navigating between the windows. The Workbench provides a reusable menu that displays a list of open windows. Selecting a window causes it to get focus. To add the windows list menu to your application, add the Contribution-ItemFactory.OPEN_WINDOWS item to a menu, as shown in the following snippet and in Figure 16-7:

```
org.eclipsercp.hyperbola/ApplicationActionBarAdvisor
protected void makeActions(IWorkbenchWindow window) {
  openWindows =
    ContributionItemFactory.OPEN_WINDOWS.create(window);
}

protected void fillMenuBar(IMenuManager menuBar) {
  ...
  windowsMenu.add(openWindows);
}
```

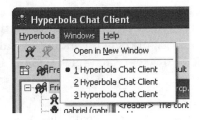

Figure 16–7   Window list menu in action

16.4 Drag and Drop with Editors

Each Workbench window has an editor area that is optionally visible. When the editor area is visible, it can be used as a target for drag-and-drop operations. For example, this is used by the IDE to open an editor on a file dropped on the editor area. This is possible even if the editor area is blank. Drag and drop on the editor area is set up using the `IWorkbenchWindowConfigurer` for a particular window.

To show how this works, let's enhance Hyperbola to allow dragging contacts from the Contacts view into the editor area to initiate a chat. There are four main parts involved in making this happen:

- ○ Decide which *transfer types* are to be supported by the editor area and implement them. In Hyperbola the transfer type is an `IEditorInput` that describes the editor to be opened when the drop completes. Since drag and drop can occur between applications, a transfer type is used to serialize the required information. Even if the drag and drop occurs within the same application, a transfer type is needed.

- ○ Because editor inputs are serialized when they are transferred in a drag-and-drop event, the `ChatEditorInput` must be modified to implement `IPersistableElement`.

- ○ Add a *drop adapter* that knows the actions to take when an `IEditorInput` transfer type is dropped onto the editor area. Drop adapters are simple—they perform actions based on the transfer type dropped. In the Hyperbola case, the drop adapter opens an editor.

- ○ Enable the Contacts view to initiate a drag operation. The Contacts view also has to create the editor inputs that are dropped in the editor area.

The next sections step through the code needed for each of these four parts. The transfer type for dragging editor inputs from one part to another is already defined in the Workbench and is called `EditorInputTransfer`. This is the class that serializes the editor inputs into a byte array that is then added to the drag-and-drop events. The transfer is added to the Workbench window by calling the `IWorkbenchWindowConfigurer` method `addEditorAreaTransfer(Transfer)` from the `WorkbenchAdvisor`, as shown here:

org.eclipsercp.hyperbola/ApplicationWorkbenchWindowAdvisor
```
public void preWindowOpen(IWorkbenchWindowConfigurer configurer) {
  ...
  configurer.addEditorAreaTransfer(EditorInputTransfer.getInstance());
  configurer.configureEditorAreaDropListener(
    new EditorAreaDropAdapter (configurer.getWindow());
}
```

Notice that this also configures a `DropTargetListener` to listen for drops in the editor area. The drop adapter registered is Hyperbola's `EditorAreaDropAdapter`, shown below. It processes the drop event and opens an editor if the transfer type is an editor input. The adapter can open multiple editors if the transfer contains an array of editor inputs. You can extend its behavior to accept application-specific objects as well. The editor area for each window can be individually configured and reconfigured with additional editor area transfers and drop listeners at any time.

org.eclipsercp.hyperbola/EditorAreaDropAdapter
```
public class EditorAreaDropAdapter extends DropTargetAdapter {
  public void handleDrop(IWorkbenchPage page, DropTargetEvent event) {
    if (EditorInputTransfer.getInstance().
        isSupportedType(event.currentDataType)) {
      EditorInputTransfer.EditorInputData[] editorInputs =
          (EditorInputTransfer.EditorInputData []) event.data;
      for (int i = 0; i < editorInputs.length; i++) {
        IEditorInput editorInput = editorInputs[i].input;
        String editorId = editorInputs[i].editorId;
        openEditor(page, editorInput, editorId);
      }
    }
    ...
  }
}
```

Once the editor area is configured to accept drop requests, the next step is to enable dragging from the Contacts view. Add the following method to the `ContactsView` and call it from `createPartControl()`:

org.eclipsercp.hyperbola/ContactsView
```
protected void initDragAndDrop(final StructuredViewer viewer) {
  int operations = DND.DROP_COPY;
  Transfer[] transferTypes = new
    Transfer[]{EditorInputTransfer.getInstance()};
```

```
    DragSourceListener listener = new DragSourceAdapter() {
      public void dragSetData(DragSourceEvent event) {
        if (EditorInputTransfer.getInstance().isSupportedType(
          event.dataType)) {
          String[] names = getNames();
          EditorInputTransfer.EditorInputData[] inputs =
            new EditorInputTransfer.EditorInputData[names.length];
          if (names.length > 0) {
            for (int i = 0; i < names.length; i++)
              inputs[i] = EditorInputTransfer.createEditorInputData(
                ChatEditor.ID,
                new ChatEditorInput(getSession(), names[i]));
            event.data = inputs;
            return;
          }
        }
        event.doit = false;
      }
      public void dragFinished(DragSourceEvent event) {}
      public void dragStart(DragSourceEvent event) {
        super.dragStart(event);
      }
    };
    viewer.addDragSupport(operations, transferTypes, listener);
}
```

The method adds drag-and-drop support to the ContactsView's TreeViewer. When a drag is started, the listener initializes the event by creating an editor input for each of the contacts selected in the viewer. The selection is obtained using getNames(). If the event does not support EditorInputTransfers, the drag is canceled by setting event.doit to false.

The last step is to modify ChatEditorInput to implement IPersistableElement. The IPersistableElement allows the input to be serialized during a drag and drop. Drag-and-drop transfers are always serialized, even when the drop occurs inside the application.

This requires two changes; the first is to implement saveState(IMemento) and getFactoryId(). The next is to implement a factory that can deserialize the chat editor inputs. Since the chat editor input is simple, all it takes to serialize the input is to remember the user name. The factory can create a new input using the name.

org.eclipsercp.hyperbola/ChatEditorInput
```
public class ChatEditorInput
  implements IEditorInput, IPersistableElement {
  public String getFactoryId() {
    return ChatEditorInputFactory.ID;
  }

  public void saveState(IMemento memento) {
    memento.putString(KEY_NAME, getParticipant());
  }
```

```
    ...
}
public class ChatEditorInputFactory implements IElementFactory {
  public static final String ID = "org.eclipsercp.hyperbola.chatinput";

  public IAdaptable createElement(IMemento memento) {
    String name = memento.getString(ChatEditorInput.KEY_NAME);
    if (name != null)
      return new ChatEditorInput(Session.getInstance(), name);
    return null;
  }
}
```

With these changes Hyperbola is drag-and-drop-enabled. We set up only the Contacts view to initiate drags, but it's easy to see how other views could be similarly set up. If you want to learn more about drag and drop, read the articles listed in Section 16.6, "Pointers."

16.5 Summary

The one thing to remember when designing your RCP application is that the Workbench provides a default implementation for many useful features that are designed to scale. Perspectives, views, and editors provide a rich UI model that you do not have to reinvent. In places where the standard features do not apply to your application, the Workbench tries to allow you to write your own custom solution using the provided APIs.

16.6 Pointers

- ○ Arthorne, John (IBM). "Drag and Drop in the Eclipse UI," August 25, 2003 (*http://eclipse.org/articles/Article-Workbench-DND/drag_drop.html*).
- ○ Irvine, Veronica (IBM). "Drag and Drop—Adding Drag and Drop to an SWT Application," August 25, 2003 (*http://eclipse.org/articles/Article-SWT-DND/DND-in-SWT.html*).

CHAPTER 17

Actions

There is much more to the notion of actions than we've covered in our examples so far. Chapter 6, "Adding Actions," ended with an explanation of why Hyperbola does not use declarative actions, a standard technique in Eclipse. To recap, the actions in Hyperbola are defined and placed programmatically by the `ActionBarAdvisor`. This technique is simple and ideal for small, closed applications. In Chapter 14, "Adding Software Management," we talked about updating deployed applications and adding new plug-ins. How do these new plug-ins add their actions? The answer lies in the Workbench's support for declarative actions.

This chapter is split into two parts. The first explains when and how to use declarative actions, and the second gives useful tips and tricks for writing product-quality actions. Specifically in this chapter we show you how to

- ○ Decide between using declarative and programmatic actions
- ○ Add declarative actions to Hyperbola
- ○ Use retargetable actions to define pluggable behavior
- ○ Write actions that correctly track selection
- ○ Show progress for long-running actions
- ○ Use actions in alternate ways, such as showing text, creating multirow toolbars, and adding controls to toolbars
- ○ Add contributions to the status line

17.1 Overview

Before introducing declarative actions, let's take a step back and look at what an action is all about. The primary role of actions is to expose application behavior to the user. When you click on a menu item or toolbar item or invoke a key sequence, an action is run. Furthermore, you can set up a system so that the same action is placed in a menu and a toolbar and bound to a key sequence—actions allow you to separate behavior from placement. Actions also determine if they are enabled, figure out what elements to work on, run the work, and display the results.

Below is a list of the basic responsibilities of actions. As you explore the various ways of defining and using actions, remember that these responsibilities apply regardless of how or where they are defined and used—only the syntax is different.

Placement—Actions can be placed in many areas of the Workbench: in views, editors, context menus, and top-level menus and toolbars. When they are created, they are given a reference to the container in which they are placed, allowing them to query for selection or access other information.

Rendering—There are several types of actions, for example, menus, toolbar buttons, radio buttons, drop-down menu buttons, and so on. When you create an action, you have to decide what type of action it is and how it will be rendered in the UI. Actions also contain basic information, such as a label, an icon, and a tool tip, which display and describe the action to the user.

Input and enablement—Actions usually perform work on a set of objects. The input to an action is defined by the selection in the related UI part. For example, if an action is in a view, the related selection is that of the widgets in the view. An action in the Workbench window uses the selection that comes from the active view or editor. As an action's context changes (e.g., its input changes or its container state changes), the action must update its enablement state.

Behavior—When an action is eventually run, it performs some operation on its input. If the action is long-running, it should show progress to the user.

Binding—An action can be controlled by the keyboard instead of by its explicit UI element. Actions can also be bound to other mechanisms that control when they are run.

When you add an action, you have to implement each of these responsibilities. Figure 17-1 shows how the **Build** action from the IDE product implements these responsibilities.

The **Build** action is *placed* in the top-level toolbar and menu, it is *rendered* as a push button with a name and image, it's *enabled* when at least one project is

```
// org.eclipse.ui.actions.BuildAction
class BuildAction extends Action implements ISelectionListener (
  private IWorkbenchWindow window;
  public BuildAction(WorkbenchWindow window) {
    super(?&Build?, IAction.AS_PUSH_BUTTON);
    this.window = window;
    window.getSelectionService().addSelectionListener(this);
  }
  public void run() {
    // do some work
  }
  public void selectionChanged(IWorkbenchPart part, ISelection selection)
  {
    setEnabled(doesSelectionContainProject(selection));
  }
  public void dispose() {
    window.getSelectionService().removeSelectionListener(this);
  }
};
?
// Somewhere in another class that creates the action and places it
IAction action = new BuildAction(window);
action.setImageDescriptor(imageDescriptor);
action.setTooltipText(?Build the selected project?);
Action.setDefinitionId(?org.eclipse.ui.build?);
ICoolBarManager mgr = configurer.getCoolBarManager();
IToolBarManager toolbar = new ToolBarManager(mgr.getStyle());
toolbar.add(action);
```

Labels pointing to the code: Placement, Rendering, Behavior, Input and Enablement, Rendering, Binding, Placement, Rendering

Figure 17–1 Action responsibilities

selected, and its *input* is the selected project. Its *behavior* is to build the selected project.

17.2 Declarative Actions in Hyperbola

Imagine a scenario where Hyperbola is extended by the Debug and MUC (multiuser chat) plug-ins. Ideally, the actions defined by these plug-ins are placed side by side in some top-level menu, and the fact that they originate from different sources is hidden. This promotes the added behavior as an integral part of Hyperbola rather than as something tacked onto the side.

Here we focus on this scenario and talk about

○ The different kinds of declarative actions
○ Extending the ActionBarAdvisor to support action contributions into the top-level menu and toolbar

○ Using an action set to add two declarative actions, **Export Contacts** and **Import Contacts**, to Hyperbola's top-level menu and toolbar in several locations to demonstrate placement control

○ Adding a context menu with **Export** and **Import** actions to the Contacts view

17.2.1 Declarative Actions

One of the Workbench's main roles is as an integration point. Plug-ins contribute actions, views, and the like to the Workbench, and the Workbench structures, places, and manages them. Diverse sets of plug-ins are thus integrated and the user experience is improved. To participate in the integration, however, plug-ins must supply their contributions declaratively rather than programmatically.

The Workbench supports the following extension points into which plug-ins make action contributions, describing the action's implementation, placement, icon, and label. Armed with a set of extensions to these extension points, the Workbench inserts the actions into existing menus and toolbars.

`org.eclipse.ui.actionSets`—This extension describes a set of menus and actions that is added to the top-level menu and toolbar. Action sets are enabled and disabled as a group.

`org.eclipse.ui.popupMenus`—This extension point is used to contribute actions to context menus that have been registered with the Workbench.

`org.eclipse.ui.editorActions`—This extension point is used to add actions to the top-level menu and toolbar when a particular editor is enabled.

`org.eclipse.ui.viewActions`—This extension point is used to add actions to the local menu and toolbar for views.

Within the context of a small application, such as Hyperbola, there is usually no need to use declarative actions. However, there are benefits of using declarative actions that should be considered:

○ Declarative actions are shown in the UI without loading their associated plug-in. In large applications with many plug-ins, this is crucial to scalability.

○ Dynamic reconfiguration of top-level menus and toolbars based on the active perspective is enabled by associating action sets with perspectives.

○ Users can configure top-level menus and toolbars via the perspective customization dialog (see the `ActionFactory.EDIT_ACTION_SETS` action).

The downside of declarative actions is that they cannot build on one another, and their ordering within a menu is controlled by the Workbench. In other words, you cannot deterministically order two actions sets within the same menu. The other issue is that toolbar and menu paths are error-prone. It's hard to find the right paths, and when you get it wrong, menus just do not show up.

17.2.2 Allowing Contributions

To take advantage of the benefits of declarative actions, RCP applications should define a top-level menu and toolbar skeleton in the `ActionBarAdvisor` and use declarative actions for everything else.

Even if you choose not to use declarative actions for your part of the application, you should design your application so that other plug-ins can extend its menus and toolbars. This way, third parties can add functions and you can ship additional functions after the main product ships.

The first step is to add *placeholders* into the top-level menus and toolbars. This is where the declarative actions will plug in. Placeholders are added to `IContributionManager` instances, such as `ToolbarManager` or `MenuManager`. They are named entities that are referenced from declarative action definitions.

Hyperbola already has a named top-level menu. In the `ActionBarAdvisor` method `fillMenu()`, the Hyperbola menu is created as a `MenuManager` using the snippet below. The first parameter to the constructor is the menu name, as shown in the UI, and the second, `hyperbola`, is the ID of the menu.

org.eclipsercp.hyperbola/ApplicationActionBarAdvisor
```
MenuManager hyperbolaMenu = new MenuManager("&Hyperbola", "hyperbola");
```

You can define placeholders using the `hyperbola` menu as part of the path (e.g., `hyperbola/placeholder`). Once the placeholders are defined, the Workbench takes care of the rest—it decides which contributed actions are applicable and automatically inserts them when the toolbar or menu is shown.

The Workbench supplies a standard placeholder ID that is used to mark the location in a contribution manager where contributions are added. The constant `IWorkbenchActionConstants.MB_ADDITIONS` is used in the code snippets below to identify placeholders. It is then used in `plugin.xml` files of plug-ins contributing action sets to link actions into menus and toolbars.

org.eclipse.ui/IWorkbenchActionConstants
```
/**
 * name of group for adding new top-level menus (value "additions")
 */
public static final String MB_ADDITIONS = "additions";
```

Let's change Hyperbola's `ActionBarAdvisor` to allow contributed actions in the following areas:

○ On the menu bar, between the **Hyperbola** and **Help** menus

○ In the **Hyperbola** menu, between the first two groups

○ At the end of the toolbar

○ In the Contacts view's context menu

We cover the first three actions next and the context menu action in Section 17.2.4, "Context Menus."

There's no magic when adding placeholders; you simply add them the same way that actions are added. The following code snippet from Hyperbola's ActionBarAdvisor adds a placeholder to the **Hyperbola** menu as well as to the menu bar and the end of the toolbar:

```
org.eclipsercp.hyperbola/ApplicationActionBarAdvisor
protected void fillMenuBar(IMenuManager menuBar) {
   // top-level menu called Hyperbola with ID 'hyperbola'
   MenuManager hyperbolaMenu =
      new MenuManager("&Hyperbola", "hyperbola");
   hyperbolaMenu.add(addContactAction);
   hyperbolaMenu.add(removeContactAction);
   hyperbolaMenu.add(chatAction);
   // Placeholder within the 'hyperbola' menu called 'additions'. This
   // can be referenced as 'hyperbola/additions'.
   hyperbolaMenu.add(new Separator(
      IWorkbenchActionConstants.MB_ADDITIONS));
   hyperbolaMenu.add(new Separator());
   hyperbolaMenu.add(preferencesAction);
   hyperbolaMenu.add(new Separator());
   hyperbolaMenu.add(exitAction);
   ...
   menuBar.add(hyperbolaMenu);
   // top-level menu placeholder with ID 'additions'
   menuBar.add(new Separator(IWorkbenchActionConstants.MB_ADDITIONS));
   menuBar.add(helpMenu);
}

protected void fillCoolBar(ICoolBarManager coolBar) {
   IToolBarManager toolbar = new ToolBarManager(coolBar.getStyle());
   coolBar.add(toolbar);
   toolbar.add(addContactAction);
   toolbar.add(removeContactAction);
   toolbar.add(chatAction);
   // top-level toolbar placeholder with ID 'additions'
   coolBar.add(new Separator(IWorkbenchActionConstants.MB_ADDITIONS));
}
```

Placeholders are added as either Separators or GroupMarkers. Separators surround all contributions by the appropriate separators, whereas contributions to a GroupMarker are added as is, without any additional separators.

TIP

To support action contributions to menus anywhere in your application, not just at the top level of menus, you must document the menu and group IDs defined by your application. The Workbench provides a list of commonly used menu IDs in IWorkbenchActionConstants. The IDE product uses these, but you are free to use your own identifiers instead. These IDs effectively become API and so should be documented and maintained.

17.2.3 Declaring Actions

Now that the placeholders are in place, let's declaratively add some action sets to Hyperbola. In this example the two actions called **Export Contacts** and **Import Contacts** are added to the three placeholders we just defined. In practice, placing an action in one or two spots is enough, but here we want to demonstrate all the cases.

The following action set adds a menu called **Tools** to the top-level menu bar and adds the **Import** and **Export** actions to that menu:

```
org.eclipsercp.hyperbola/plugin.xml
<extension point="org.eclipse.ui.actionSets">
   <actionSet
       id="org.eclipsercp.hyperbola.actionSet1"
       label="Hyperbola Tools"
       visible="true">
     <menu
         id="org.eclipsercp.hyperbola.tools"
         label="&amp;Tools"
         path="additions">
       <groupMarker name="group1"/>
     </menu>
     <action
         class="org.eclipsercp.hyperbola.actions.ExportContactsAction "
         icon="icons/export.gif"
         id="org.eclipsercp.hyperbola.exportContacts"
         label="&amp;Export Contacts"
         menubarPath="org.eclipsercp.hyperbola.tools/group1"
         style="push"/>
     <action
         class="org.eclipsercp.hyperbola.actions.ImportContactsAction "
         icon="icons/import.gif"
         id="org.eclipsercp.hyperbola.importContacts"
         label="&amp;Import Contacts"
         menubarPath="org.eclipsercp.hyperbola.tools/group1"
         style="push"/>
   </actionSet>
</extension>
```

The first thing in an action set is its ID. An ID must be globally unique relative to all other action set IDs. The easiest way to ensure uniqueness is to prefix the ID with the ID of the contributing plug-in.

Action sets are not normally shown to the user. The actionSet element's label attribute is used to represent the action set in the perspective configuration dialog (see ActionFactory.EDIT_ACTION_SETS). The actionSet element's visible attribute determines if the action set should be visible in all perspectives. If this is set to false, perspectives determine which action sets to show using IPageLayout .addActionSet(String). When true, the action set can be hidden by the user only if the perspective customization dialog is shown, or by calling the IWorkbenchPage method hideActionSet(String).

The menu element defines a top-level menu into which actions can be placed. The menu element's path attribute causes the menu to be placed in the menu bar in the additions placeholder that we defined in the code earlier. The menu element's label attribute defines the text that is shown in the UI to represent the menu. This menu element also defines a groupMarker element that defines a placeholder for actions. The menu element's menu ID is important because it is used to place the actions defined in the containing actionSet element. Again, the menu element's ID should be unique among menus.

The action elements carry enough information to support displaying an action without running any code. That information includes the label, icon, and action style (e.g., push button, toggle, radio). The location of the action is determined by the action element's menubarPath attribute. The path consists of multiple menu IDs with a terminating group ID. In this example the menu and group happen to be defined by the action set's menu, and the menu itself is placed in the menu bar.

The implementation of an action is defined by its class attribute. The supplied class must implement an interface that is particular to the extension point to which the action is being added. For example, here the class must implement IWorkbenchWindowActionDelegate. This gives the action a Workbench window as context for its operation. If the action was added to a view or editor, it would have to implement a different interface. All these interfaces extend IActionDelegate. Let's take a look at the ImportContactsAction:

org.eclipsercp.hyperbola/ImportContactsAction
```
public class ImportContactsAction implements
 IWorkbenchWindowActionDelegate {
  private IWorkbenchWindow window;

  public void dispose() {
  }
```

```
public void init(IWorkbenchWindow window) {
  this.window = window;
}

public void run(IAction action) {
  HyperbolaUtils.import();
}

public void selectionChanged(IAction action, ISelection selection) {
  }
}
```

Action classes for declarative actions are very similar to a regular IAction, but they have additional methods such as init() and selectionChanged(). An IAction is not used directly because the Workbench is lazy. It places proxy IAction instances into menus and toolbars instead of instantiating declared actions. The proxy actions keep a reference to the action delegate for which they are serving as a proxy.

Notice that run(IAction) and selectionChange(IAction) take an action argument—this is the proxy. Under the covers, the proxy is the action that is part of the menu. As such, changing how the action appears (e.g., its enablement or label) requires changing the proxy action. The proxy action uses the information from the declarative action's description to display, perform basic enablement, and then ultimately run the action.

Adding these actions to the **Hyperbola** menu and the toolbar follows the same pattern. The only difference is that the menubarPath attribute has a different value. For example, adding the following action to the action set places the **Import** and **Export** actions, as shown in Figure 17-2.

org.eclipsercp.hyperbola/plugin.xml
```xml
<action
    class="org.eclipsercp.hyperbola.actions.ExportContactsAction"
    icon="icons/export.gif"
    id="org.eclipsercp.hyperbola.action2"
    label="&amp;Export Contacts"
    menubarPath="hyperbola/additions"
    style="push"
    toolbarPath="additions"/>
```

Here the hyperbola/additions menu path and additions toolbar path refer directly to the names of the menus and placeholders we added to the Hyperbola ActionBarAdvisor earlier.

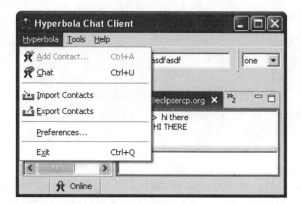

Figure 17–2 **Import** and **Export** declarative actions in the menu and toolbar

17.2.4 Context Menus

It is often convenient for users to act directly on a UI element using a context menu or by double-clicking, for example, initiating a chat in Hyperbola by double-clicking on a contact in the Contacts view. So far Hyperbola does not have any context actions, let alone any extensible structure for adding them. In this section we add a context menu and then add some declarative actions to it.

The snippet below shows the ContactsView method makeActions(). This method is called from the ContactsView method createControlPart() and does the following:

○ Adds a context menu.

○ Adds the chat action to the menu.

○ Adds the MB_ADDITIONS placeholder to the menu.

○ Registers the menu with the Workbench.

○ Initializes double-click behavior on the tree viewer.

org.eclipsercp.hyperbola/ContactsView
```
private void makeActions() {
  chatAction = new ChatAction(getSite().getWorkbenchWindow());

  // Initiate a chat on double-click.
  treeViewer.addDoubleClickListener(new IDoubleClickListener() {
    public void doubleClick(DoubleClickEvent event) {
      chatAction.run();
    }
  });
```

```
    // Create the context menu and register it with the Workbench.
    MenuManager menuMgr = new MenuManager("contactsPopup");
    manager.add(chatAction);
    manager.add(new Separator(IWorkbenchActionConstants.MB_ADDITIONS));
    Menu menu = menuMgr.createContextMenu(viewer.getControl());
    treeViewer.getControl().setMenu(menu);
    getSite().registerContextMenu(menuMgr, treeViewer);
}
```

The ChatAction used here is the same one that was added to Hyperbola's top-level menu in Chapter 7, "Adding a Chat Editor." The context menu is defined using the MenuManager in the same way as the top-level menus defined previously.

The registerContextMenu() method is used to hook the menu into the Workbench and its declarative action mechanisms. When a registered menu is shown, the Workbench adds any related declarative contributions. In the case of a context menu, contributions to the org.eclipse.ui.popupMenus extension point that apply to the current selection are added.

The last step is to define the declarative actions for **Export** and **Import** that place them in the context menu. The snippet below adds an org.eclipse.ui.popupMenus extension that applies to any instance of RosterEntry. Notice that here the action is not placed in a particular menu. Rather, it is scoped so that when a RosterEntry (e.g., a contact) is selected, the action is available and is added to any open context menu.

```
org.eclipsercp.hyperbola/plugin.xml
<extension point="org.eclipse.ui.popupMenus">
    <objectContribution
        adaptable="false"
        id="org.eclipsercp.hyperbola.objectContribution1"
        objectClass="org.jivesoftware.smack.RosterEntry">
      <action
          class="org.eclipsercp.hyperbola.actions.ExportContactsAction"
          icon="icons/export.gif"
          id="org.eclipsercp.hyperbola.action1"
          label="&amp;Export Contacts"/>
    </objectContribution>
</extension>
```

Apart from the objectContribution element, the actions in this example are described in the same manner as action sets. The existing ExportContactsAction implementation is even reused after one small change—the action class must implement IObjectActionDelegate in addition to IWorkbenchWindowActionDelegate. The new interface is needed so the action can track its context. In the case of a context menu action, the context is the UI part that is showing the context menu.

17.3 Standard Workbench Actions

In Chapter 6 you saw that the Workbench defines a set of reusable actions. These actions are defined as inner classes of `org.eclipse.ui.actions.ActionFactory` and are instantiated and used as regular actions.

```
exitAction = ActionFactory.QUIT.create(window);
```

The reusable actions have preconfigured names, icons, IDs, and action definition IDs, but any of these attributes can be overridden after the action is created.

```
exitAction.setText("&Quit"); // Change from Exit to Quit.
```

All actions created from the `ActionFactory` are instances of `IWorkbenchAction`. `IWorkbenchAction` extends `IAction` and adds the `dispose()` method since instances must be deleted when their associated window is closed.

Before implementing an action in your application, check to see if the `ActionFactory` defines a related action. Reusing these standard actions gives your application a more consistent look and feel. A partial list of reusable actions is given in Table 17-1.

Table 17–1   Partial List of Actions Available from `ActionFactory`

Method	Description
ABOUT	Opens the standard Workbench About dialog.
CLOSE	Closes the active editor.
CLOSE_ALL	Closes all open editors.
EXPORT	Opens the **Export** wizard.
HELP_CONTENTS	Displays the registered Help contribution. This is a no-op until you have added a Help provider to your application. See Chapter 13, "Adding Help," for more details on adding Help to your application.
IMPORT	Opens the **Import** wizard.
OPEN_NEW_WINDOW	Opens a new Workbench window using the same perspective as the one currently showing in the originating window. If you need to open another window using another perspective, you can directly call the `IWorkbench` method `openWorkbenchWindow()` with a perspective ID.
PREFERENCES	Opens the Workbench Preferences dialog, composed of pages contributed via the `org.eclipse.ui.preferencePages` extension point.

(continues)

Table 17–1   Partial List of Actions Available from `ActionFactory` (*Continued*)

Method	Description
PROPERTIES	Opens the Properties dialog and primes it with the property pages for the current selection. The pages shown are those contributed via the `org.eclipse.ui` `.propertyPages` extension point.
QUIT	Exits the Workbench.
SAVE	Saves the active Workbench part if it implements `ISaveablePart`.
SAVE AS	Allows the active part to save its contents to another object.
SAVE_ALL	Saves all open editors that have unsaved changes.

Reusable Preference Pages and Views

The Workbench also provides a set of reusable preference pages and views. The complete list can be found on the `org.eclipse.ui.ExtensionFactory` class. It includes common things such as the Keys, Colors and Fonts, and Decorators preference pages, as well as the Progress view.

The extension factory provides access to these pages and views via a set of identifiers. The identifiers are used in view extensions as shown below. Notice that the markup is the same as for a regular view extension, but instead of specifying the view's implementation class directly, the `ExtensionFactory` is used and the view identifier is provided after the ":".

```
<extension point="org.eclipse.ui.views">
  <view
      class="org.eclipse.ui.ExtensionFactory:progressView"
      icon="icons/progress.gif"
      id="org.eclipsercp.hyperbola.views.progress"
      name="Progress"/>
</extension>
```

See `IExecutableExtensionFactory` for how to define your own factories.

17.4 Retargetable Actions

The Workbench defines yet another special type of actions called *retargetable actions*. Retargetable actions are similar to regular actions except they do not have behavior. Instead, their behavior is supplied by another action. Hyperbola does not have a particularly compelling use case for retargetable actions, so to illustrate the concept we look at implementing **Back** and **Forward** buttons in an RCP-based Web browser application.

NOTE

The source code for an RCP Web browser that uses retargetable actions is available in the Eclipse Platform CVS repository, in the `org.eclipse.ui.examples.rcp.browser` project.

The Web browser application uses several views, each with its own browser widget. The main toolbar has **Back** and **Forward** actions that control the active browser. If there is only one set of actions in the toolbar, how do they control the view that happens to be active?

One way to implement this is to create two regular actions that can be accessed statically from the views and implement the views to hook themselves to the actions when they become active. When the actions run, the current view gets called and performs the required behavior. The views also have to unregister themselves when they are deactivated.

This is essentially what retargetable actions do, with the benefit that the Workbench provides the management of binding actions to retargetable actions as Workbench parts are activated and deactivated.

NOTE

Some of the reusable actions defined on `ActionFactory` are retargetable actions (e.g., COPY, PASTE, CUT, NEXT, PREVIOUS, RENAME, and DELETE). By using these actions, your application exposes standard icons, labels, and key bindings that are familiar to users.

The following snippet shows how the **Forward** retargetable action is added to the toolbar in the `ActionBarAdvisor`. Notice that retargetable actions are added in exactly the same way as regular actions.

org.eclipse.ui.examples.rcp.browser/BrowserActionBarAdvisor
```
RetargetAction action = new RetargetAction("myapp.forward","Forward");
action.setImageDescriptor(forwardImage);
action.setToolTipText("Forward");
toolbar.add(action);
```

When creating a retargetable action, you have to specify the ID for the action and the default label. The ID is used to match the action that implements the behavior to the retargetable action that places it.

Now that the **Forward** action is in the toolbar, the Browser view needs to register its implementation of the **Forward** action with the Workbench. To do this, it implements an IAction and registers it as a *global action handler* with the Browser view's action bars. This is usually done when the part creates its actions and controls, as shown in the next snippet. The ID of the retargetable action specified earlier is used to link in the new action.

```
org.eclipse.ui.examples.rcp.browser/BrowserView
public class BrowserView extends ViewPart {
   ...
  public void createPartControl(Composite parent) {
    IAction nextAction = new Action("Forward") {
      public void run() {
        browser.forward();
      }
    };
    // Add global action handlers.
    getViewSite().getActionBars()
        .setGlobalActionHandler("myapp.forward", forwardAction);
}
```

The Workbench handles the details of ensuring that the retargetable action is associated with the active view or editor. When retargetable actions are not linked with an action, they are automatically disabled.

17.5 Consolidating Declarative Actions

The Workbench offers some facilities for aggregating and presenting similar actions. For example, the **New** wizard dialog presents a set of wizards and allows users to choose the one they want. Plug-ins hook into this facility by contributing extensions to the relevant Workbench extension points. The Workbench exposes chooser dialogs or menus for preference pages, property pages, new wizards, import wizards, and export wizards. See Section 15.5.3, "Scalability," for the complete extension point reference.

This approach is powerful for applications as they can expose common access points for exporting, importing, and creating new things without having to know or determine what kinds of new things or exports and imports are supported. The mechanism is useful for plug-in writers as their actions are integrated into the host application, alongside other related functions.

The actions that show dialogs or menus are available on `ActionFactory` as `ActionFactory.EXPORT`, `ActionFactory.IMPORT`, `ActionFactory.NEW`, `ActionFactory` `.PREFERENCES`, and `ActionFactory.PROPERTIES`. The following snippet from Chapter 11, "Adding a Login Dialog," shows how these actions are added to toolbars or menus:

org.eclipsercp.hyperbola/ApplicationActionBarAdvisor
```
protected void makeActions(IWorkbenchWindow window) {
  preferencesAction = ActionFactory.PREFERENCES.create(window);
  register(preferencesAction);
  ...
}
```

If the standard dialogs and menus are not suitable, you can access the contributions directly and build your own UI. The extension registries for the contributions to the **Import**, **Export**, and **New** wizards are accessed by calling the appropriate `IWorkbench` method, `get[New|Import|Export]WizardRegistry()`.

The Workbench also exposes a handy **New** menu that is similar to the **Perspectives** and **Views** menus shown in Chapter 16, "Perspectives, Views, and Editors." This is a cascading menu with quick access to the list of contributed new wizards. You can add this menu using the `ContributionItemFactory.NEW_WIZARD_SHORTLIST` helper, as shown here:

org.eclipsercp.hyperbola/ApplicationActionBarAdvisor
```
protected void makeActions(IWorkbenchWindow window) {
  MenuManager newMenu = new MenuManager("New", "new");
  perspectives =
    ContributionItemFactory.NEW_WIZARD_SHORTLIST.create(window);
}
protected void fillMenuBar(IMenuManager menu) {
  newMenu.add(perspectives);
}
```

To keep menus short, the quick access list of wizards shown is the set of new wizards explicitly defined by the active perspective. Perspectives configure the list using the `IPageLayout` method `addNewWizardShortcut(String)`.

17.6 Toolbar Action Tricks

Desktop applications often need to show more than buttons in the toolbar. This adds a bit of polish and usability to the look and feel of the application. In this section we show you how to tweak your toolbar actions and have them show text, wrap on multiple lines, and host various controls.

17.6.1 Showing Images and Text

Showing both images and text for certain toolbar items is a common requirement. The text is generally placed either to the right of or below the image for the
action, as shown in Figure 17-3. This improves usability for new users who do
not know the meanings of the images. The Workbench supports mixing images
and text, but only with programmatic actions.

Figure 17–3   Toolbar actions with text

Let's walk through how this is done. When an application contributes actions
to the top-level toolbar, it adds them to an `ICoolBarManager`. The `ICoolBarManager`
interface extends `IContributionManager` and can manage both `IActions` and
`IContributionItems`. Contributed items wrap the SWT controls that are shown
in the contribution manager and are ultimately responsible for rendering the
items in a menu, a composite, or a coolbar.

JFace provides a helper class called `ActionContributionItem` for directly adding actions to a contribution manager. Contributed action items effectively transfer the properties of an action down to an SWT control. As such, they can be used
to configure whether or not text is shown on the toolbar.

To control the `ActionContributionItem` for an action, first create the toolbar
with a style flag that includes `SWT.BOTTOM` or `SWT.RIGHT` to indicate where to show
the text. Then, for each action, create an `ActionConfigurationItem` and set its
mode to `ActionContributionItem.MODE_FORCE_TEXT`. Next, call `ToolBarManager`
`.add(IContributionItem)` to add the contribution item to the toolbar. The following code shows how to do this in Hyperbola's `ActionBarAdvisor`:

```
org.eclipsercp.hyperbola/ApplicationActionBarAdvisor
protected void fillCoolBar(ICoolBarManager coolBar) {
  IToolBarManager toolbar =
      new ToolBarManager(coolBar.getStyle() | SWT.BOTTOM);
  coolBar.add(toolbar);

  ActionContributionItem addContactCI = new
      ActionContributionItem(addContactAction);
  addContactCI.setMode(ActionContributionItem.MODE_FORCE_TEXT);
  toolbar.add(addContactCI);
```

```
ActionContributionItem removeContactCI = new
    ActionContributionItem(removeContactAction);
removeContactCI.setMode(ActionContributionItem.MODE_FORCE_TEXT);
toolbar.add(removeContactCI);

ActionContributionItem chatActionCI = new
    ActionContributionItem(chatAction);
chatActionCI.setMode(ActionContributionItem.MODE_FORCE_TEXT);
toolbar.add(chatActionCI);

coolBar.add(new Separator(IWorkbenchActionConstants.MB_ADDITIONS));
}
```

17.6.2 Adding Controls to the Toolbar

Another common feature is to place SWT controls in the toolbar instead of in buttons. Again, the key here is to put an IContributionItem into the toolbar instead of an IAction. This works because both ToolItems and CoolItems allow controls to be set as their contents. JFace includes a helper class, ControlContribution, that supports adding controls to toolbars and coolbars. The code for Control-Contribution is shown here:

org.eclipse.jface/ControlContribution
```
public abstract class ControlContribution {
  protected abstract Control createControl(Composite parent);

  public final void fill(Composite parent) {
    createControl(parent);
  }

  public final void fill(Menu parent, int index) {
    Assert.isTrue(false, "Can't add a control to a menu");
  }

  public final void fill(ToolBar parent, int index) {
    Control control = createControl(parent);
    ToolItem item = new ToolItem(parent, SWT.SEPARATOR, index);
    item.setControl(control);
    item.setWidth(computeWidth(control));
  }
}
```

To add your own control, subclass ControlContribution and implement createControl(Composite) to return the desired control. The returned control is added to the toolbar by placing it in a dedicated tool item. The following snippet from Hyperbola's ActionBarAdvisor shows how to place a combo box into the Hyperbola main toolbar:

org.eclipsercp.hyperbola/ApplicationActionBarAdvisor
```
protected void fillCoolBar(ICoolBarManager coolBar) {
```

```
IToolBarManager toolbar = new ToolBarManager(coolBar.getStyle());
coolBar.add(toolbar);

IContributionItem comboCI = new ControlContribution() {
  protected Control createControl(Composite parent) {
    Combo c = new Combo(parent, SWT.READ_ONLY);
    c.add("one");
    c.add("two");
    c.add("three");
    return c;
  }
};
toolbar.add(comboCI);
}
```

17.7 Adding Contributions to the Status Line

In Chapter 6 you added a presence indicator to Hyperbola's status line. You may have noticed that as parts are activated—for example, activating the Contacts view, then a chat editor—this status line indicator disappears. This happens because the indicator was added to the shared message area of the status line (refer to Chapter 6 for an overview of the areas in the status line). A better approach is to add the indicator to the contribution area so that it remains visible across part switches.

Actions or contribution items can be added to the status line in the Action-BarAdvisor method fillStatusLine(). To maintain some stability in the status line, you should add contributions to predefined named groups that are defined on StatusLineManager as BEGIN_GROUP, MIDDLE_GROUP, and END_GROUP. This enables aligning global contributions to the right or left of the contribution area.

Status line contributions are very similar to the ControlContribution classes used in the last section. Instead of adding a control to a toolbar, they add controls to a composite—the status line is really just a fancy composite.

The sample code for this chapter includes a custom contribution item called StatusLineContribution, which uses a CLabel control to show its contents. A CLabel is a custom SWT control that displays both an image and a label together. The fill(Composite) method in StatusLineContribution is called to add the contribution to the status line. You can add just about anything you like at this point. Here we use two CLabels, the first to show a separator and the other to show an icon followed by text:

org.eclipsercp.hyperbola/StatusLineContribution
```
public void fill(Composite parent) {
  Label separator = new Label(parent, SWT.SEPARATOR);
  label = new CLabel(parent, SWT.SHADOW_NONE);
```

```
    GC gc = new GC(parent);
    gc.setFont(parent.getFont());
    FontMetrics fm = gc.getFontMetrics();
    Point extent = gc.textExtent(text);
    if (widthHint > 0)
      widthHint = fm.getAverageCharWidth() * widthHint;
    else
      widthHint = extent.x;
    heightHint = fm.getHeight();
    gc.dispose();

    StatusLineLayoutData statusLineLayoutData =
      new StatusLineLayoutData();
    statusLineLayoutData.widthHint = widthHint;
    statusLineLayoutData.heightHint = heightHint;
    label.setLayoutData(statusLineLayoutData);
    label.setText(text);
    label.setImage(image);
    ...
}
```

The `StatusLineLayoutData` is a special layout used to tell the status line how much room is needed for the contribution area. These areas cannot be resized dynamically, so you must commit to a size when they are created.

To add the contribution to the status line, create the contribution in the `ActionBarAdvisor` method `makeActions()` and add it as follows:

org.eclipsercp.hyperbola/ApplicationActionBarAdvisor
```
protected void fillStatusLine(IStatusLineManager statusLine) {
    statusLine.add(statusContribution);
}
```

17.8 Reporting Progress

In a perfect world, actions run at the speed of light and the user never has to wait. However, in reality, many actions may take a noticeable amount of time to complete. Without feedback to the user, these actions make your application look unresponsive. Adding progress reporting to actions is therefore critical.

The simplest feedback option is to show a busy cursor, as shown here:

org.eclipsercp.hyperbola/ProgressAction
```
public void run() {
    BusyIndicator.showWhile(display, new Runnable() {
      public void run() {
          // Perform action's work here.
      }
    });
}
```

This is great for operations that are not instant but are likely to take less than about two seconds. If the action takes longer than two seconds, the busy cursor does not provide enough feedback—it appears that the UI is blocked and there is no possibility of canceling the action.

The Runtime's IProgressMonitor interface is useful for reporting progress and allowing cancellation. The following is an example of running a long operation while showing a progress dialog:

org.eclipsercp.hyperbola/ProgressAction
```
ProgressMonitorDialog pd =
  new ProgressMonitorDialog(window.getShell());
pd.run(true /*fork*/, true /*cancelable*/,
  new IRunnableWithProgress() {
    public void run(IProgressMonitor monitor) throws
        InvocationTargetException, InterruptedException {
      monitor.beginTask("Long running action", 100);
      for (int i = 0; i < 10; i++) {
        if (monitor.isCanceled())
          return;
        monitor.subTask("working on step " + i);
        Display.asyncExec(new Runnable() {
          public void run() {
            textField.setText("New work: " + i);
          }
        });
        monitor.worked(10);
        sleep(1000);
      }
      monitor.done();
    }
  });
```

The progress dialog runs the given runnable and displays the main task name, optional subtask names, and a progress bar. A **Cancel** button allows the user to cancel the action. The ability to cancel an action depends on how often the action checks the IProgressMonitor for cancellation.

This example forks the operation. Forking a long-running action is highly desirable because it allows the UI to repaint and process events while the action is running—the application looks more responsive. It does mean, however, that the action's code must use Display.syncExec(Runnable) or Display.asyncExec(Runnable) to do any drawing since the action is run outside the main UI thread.

The problem with progress dialogs is that they flicker and flash when the operation runs quickly. A better solution is to show a busy cursor and show the progress dialog only if the action has been running for more than a specified amount of time. The IProgressService provides this functionality and unifies progress reporting in the Workbench.

The progress service tries to achieve a balance between a busy cursor and a dialog. The coding pattern is very similar to that of the progress dialog except that the `IRunnableWithProgress.run()` method is always forked. The progress service displays a busy cursor first, then pops up a progress dialog when the operation runs for more than a specified threshold. The threshold for switching between a busy cursor and the progress dialog is hard-coded into the Workbench; it's currently 800ms. The following snippet shows how the service is accessed via the `IWorkbench`:

```
PlatformUI.getWorkbench().getProgressService().
    busyCursorWhile(new IRunnableWithProgress() {
        public void run(IProgressMonitor monitor) {
            // Do the work.
        }
    });
```

The progress service also handles the case when a foreground action is blocked by a background action. In this case the service displays a list of the actions that may be blocking the foreground action and allows them to be canceled by the user.

17.8.1 Nonmodal Progress

The Runtime provides a *jobs* mechanism that is useful for managing background tasks. The `Job` class is a cross between a `java.lang.Runnable` and a `java.lang.Thread`. Jobs require less overhead than threads because they are pooled. They also support progress and cancellation and can be configured with varying priorities and scheduling rules that describe how they interact with other jobs. Here is a simple job that does some fake work:

org.eclipsercp.hyperbola/ProgressAction
```
Job job = new Job("long running action") {
  protected IStatus run(IProgressMonitor monitor) {
    monitor.beginTask("Long running action", 100);
    // Do some work.
    return Status.OK_STATUS;
  }
};
job.setUser(true);
job.schedule();
```

As with actions, the user probably wants to know about running jobs, but not in a way that interrupts or blocks the UI. Not all jobs are alike, and the progress presentation depends on how the job is created. There are three categories of jobs:

○ **User-initiated jobs**—These are jobs that the user has triggered. The Workbench automatically shows user jobs in a modal progress dialog with a button to allow the user to run the job in the background and continue working. Jobs are marked as user jobs using the Job method setUser(boolean).

○ **Automatically triggered jobs**—These jobs have meaning for the user but are not initiated directly by the user. They are shown in the progress view and in the status line, but the modal progress dialog is not shown.

○ **System operations**—These are jobs that are not triggered by the user and can be considered as platform implementation detail. They are created by setting the system flag using the Job method setSystem(boolean).

The Workbench shows progress for user jobs using an area in the status line, as shown in Figure 17-4, and supplies a modal dialog that contains a **Run in background** button. The background job progress area has to be explicitly enabled in WorkbenchWindowAdvisor.preWindowOpen() as follows:

```
configurer.setShowProgressIndicator(true);
```

When this is enabled and a background job is run, the user is presented with a progress dialog. If the user selects **Run in background**, the dialog is dismissed and progress is shown in the progress area in the status line.

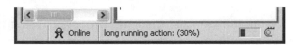

Figure 17–4   Showing job progress in the status line

NOTE

The sample code for this chapter includes an example action that runs several long-running actions using the different progress feedback mechanisms. The last action is run as a job. The action can be found in the main menu as **Tools > Long running action example**.

17.8.2 Progress View

The Workbench also provides a view that displays progress for multiple jobs simultaneously. It complements the status line progress by providing more detailed status information about running jobs as well as the ability to cancel jobs.

In everyday usage, users are not expected to use the Progress view since background jobs should complete reasonably quickly and users can keep working while background jobs run. Nevertheless, if you want to include the Progress view in your application, add the following view extension to your plugin.xml file:

```
org.eclipsercp.hyperbola/plugin.xml
<extension point="org.eclipse.ui.views">
  <view
      class="org.eclipse.ui.ExtensionFactory:progressView"
      icon="icons/progress.gif"
      id="org.eclipsercp.hyperbola.views.progress"
      name="Progress"/>
</extension>
```

You can give the view any name and still use the implementation provided by the Workbench's ExtensionFactory. Don't forget to update your perspective to show the Progress view, as shown here:

```
org.eclipsercp.hyperbola/Perspective
public class Perspective implements IPerspectiveFactory {
  public void createInitialLayout(IPageLayout layout) {
    layout.addStandaloneView(ContactsView.ID, false,
        IPageLayout.LEFT, 0.33f, layout.getEditorArea());
    layout.addView("org.eclipsercp.hyperbola.views.progress",
        IPageLayout.BOTTOM, 0.22f, layout.getEditorArea());
  }
}
```

You can control a job's icon and various other job properties using the constants in IProgressConstants and the Job method setProperty(QualifiedName, Object).

17.8.3 Customizing Progress

Job progress support in Eclipse is tailored for large-scale IDE applications, in which the type of background jobs is not known at design time. A quick survey of existing non-Eclipse-based products confirms that there are no standard ways of showing background progress—the chosen solution is often domain-specific and highly integrated.

Here is a list of different ways applications can show background progress:

Web browser—Web browsers load pages in the background and show an animated icon but do not lock the UI. In many applications this image is branded. Status text is often shown in the status line.

Nonblocking progress dialogs—Some applications allow concurrent operations and display their progress by showing a nonmodal progress dialog for each separate operation. The advantage of this approach is that the user can easily cancel individual background tasks without hunting for a Progress view.

Specific task progress—Progress reporting for specific types of operations is also common. For example, a word processor may use one animated image when saving a file, another for checking spelling and grammar, and yet another when loading large files.

Context progress—Applications using a tabbed browsing paradigm often show progress on each tab to indicate the status of the background tasks initiated from a certain tab. In other words, progress is shown in multiple locations in the application.

If you decide that you don't like the background progress support in Eclipse, it's possible to implement a custom solution. To demonstrate, let's work through an example of replacing the existing support with an implementation that shows progress for background jobs in separate nonmodal dialogs. When the background job is finished, the dialog is automatically closed.

Jobs are created by the user and run by the Platform. The `IProgressMonitor` passed to the job's `run()` method is used to report the job's progress. Here is an example of a job reporting progress:

```
Job job = new Job("Working") {
  protected IStatus run(IProgressMonitor monitor) {
    monitor.beginTask("Calculating things", 1000);
      for (int i = 0; i < 1000; i++) {
        monitor.worked(1);
        monitor.subTask("doing " + i);
        if (monitor.isCanceled())
          return Status.CANCEL_STATUS;
      }
      monitor.done();
      return Status.OK_STATUS;
  }
};
job.setUser(true);
job.schedule();
```

To write your own progress reporting, first implement a subclass of `org.eclipse.core.runtime.jobs.ProgressProvider` and then register the provider with the Workbench. The provider is responsible for creating `IProgressMonitor` instances for use by the job framework when running jobs. This, combined with notifications about the lifecycle of jobs, allows you to implement background progress reporting. The Workbench registers its progress provider only if progress support is enabled; otherwise, you can register your own in the `WorkbenchAdvisor` method `preStartup()`.

```
Platform.getJobManager().setProgressProvider(new DialogProgressProvider());
```

17.8.4 Writing a `ProgressProvider`

The most interesting method on the `ProgressProvider` is `createMonitor(Job)`. This method returns the progress monitor that is passed to the running job. In the following example, a nonmodal progress monitor dialog is created every time a new job is run:

```
org.eclipsercp.hyperbola/DialogProgressProvider
public class DialogProgressProvider extends ProgressProvider {
   public IProgressMonitor createMonitor(final Job job) {
      final IProgressMonitor[] m = new IProgressMonitor[]{
         new NullProgressMonitor()};
      Display.getDefault().syncExec(new Runnable() {
         public void run() {
            final ProgressMonitorDialog dialog =
               new NonBlockingProgressMonitorDialog(
                  Display.getDefault().getActiveShell());
            dialog.setBlockOnOpen(false);
            dialog.setCancelable(true);
            dialog.open();
            job.addJobChangeListener(new JobChangeAdapter() {
               public void done(IJobChangeEvent event) {
                  // What if the job returned an error?
                  close(dialog);
               }
            });
            m[0] = new AccumulatingProgressMonitor(
               dialog.getProgressMonitor(), Display.getDefault());
         }
      });
      return m[0];
   }

   private void close(final Dialog d) {
      Display.getDefault().asyncExec(new Runnable() {
         public void run() {
            if (d != null && ! d.getShell().isDisposed())
               d.close();
         }
      });
   }
}
```

The essential part of this snippet is the subclass of `ProgressMonitorDialog` that makes the progress dialog nonmodal. The new dialog is used to create an `IProgressMonitor` that shows progress using an indicator with status messages and task names. When a job completes, the dialog is closed.

To keep this example simple, the error status of the job is not checked—it is possible to check the return status and prompt the user or provide an indication that an error has occurred. The dialog's progress monitor is wrapped with another progress monitor, `AccumulatingProgressMonitor`, that ensures all calls to the `IProgressMonitor` methods by the background job are run in the UI thread. This is important because the dialog assumes that it is being called from the UI thread, whereas jobs are always run in a non-UI thread.

WARNING

The progress view relies on the Workbench's progress provider. If you add your own provider, the progress view stops working as only one progress provider can be registered at a time.

17.9 Summary

The main difference between RCP development and regular plug-in development is the level of control and responsibility you have when writing an RCP application. RCP application writers have full control over the structure of the menus and toolbars, and whether to allow contributions and where they are added. Plug-in writers have it easy—they plug into an existing application in well-defined ways. RCP application writers, in essence, define the ways in which others can plug in.

In this chapter you learned when and how to use declarative actions and how to open up your application to accept them. This, in combination with the general tips and tricks, gives you a solid base for adding well-behaved, well-integrated, and responsive actions to your application.

CHAPTER 18

Commands

In Chapter 12, "Adding Key Bindings," we were first introduced to commands as a way to add key bindings. The introduction was brief on purpose as actions were still being introduced and not covered in depth as we just did in Chapter 17. One thing that wasn't mentioned was that the actions and commands frameworks are two different frameworks that accomplish the same thing: contributing bits of functionality to the Workbench. Another thing that wasn't mentioned was that the actions framework has been around since the very early release of Eclipse and has aged considerably. The actions framework outgrew its initial use cases as the Eclipse platform expanded into new territories. Furthermore, there are many weaknesses in the API, but the main weakness is that the UI and handling of an action are *coupled*. So an effort was made in Eclipse 3.1 to provide a modern alternative to actions with the introduction of the *commands framework*. As of Eclipse 3.3, the commands API stabilized and offered a viable alternative to the actions framework.

This chapter is split into two parts. The first explains commands, and the second part upgrades Hyperbola to use commands instead of actions. Specifically in this chapter we'll show you how to

- ○ Understand the problems surrounding the actions framework
- ○ Use commands to provide menu contributions
- ○ Decide between using commands and actions
- ○ Replace certain actions in Hyperbola with commands

18.1 The Problem with Actions

The deficiencies of the actions API were identified a while ago and documented in Bug 36968. In Chapter 17 some of the complexities involved in using actions as a Workbench contribution mechanism should have become evident. To understand the basics of the problem, it's best to look at the IAction interface:

org.eclipse.jface/IAction

```
...
public void run();
public void setAccelerator(int keycode);
public void setEnabled(boolean enabled);
public void setImageDescriptor(ImageDescriptor image);
public void setText(String text);
...
}
```

From the IAction interface, it's evident that many aspects of an action are tightly coupled that shouldn't be. The user interface bits of the action (text and image) are coupled to the actual implementation of the action (run). This coupling makes the action framework less flexible, for example, if you wanted to provide different implementations of the same action depending on the context. How can the action's enablement be dynamically computed based on some external properties or workflow? What happens if you need to maintain several customizable keyboard accelerator codes? Furthermore, the existing action extension points—org.eclipse.ui.actionSets, org.eclipse.ui.popupMenus, org.eclipse.ui.editor-Actions, and org.eclipse.ui.viewActions—specify both their placement and visibility criteria.

The limitations of actions become apparent if you use them in a large, complex application. Because of these limitations, there was a need for a new framework. This new framework needed to unify the concept of contributions across the Workbench and also have a clean separation between behavior and presentation. The commands framework is the incarnation of this new framework.

ARE ACTIONS DEPRECATED?

As of Eclipse 3.5, the actions framework isn't deprecated. It may be deprecated in a future release of Eclipse, but that's doubtful given its widespread usage. In this book we cover both the actions and commands frameworks because both frameworks are used widely.

18.2 Commands

In essence, a command represents the abstraction between presentation and behavior. A command itself doesn't represent the presentation or the behavior. In concrete terms, a command binds one or more menu contributions (presentation) with one or more handlers (behavior) as shown in Figure 18-1.

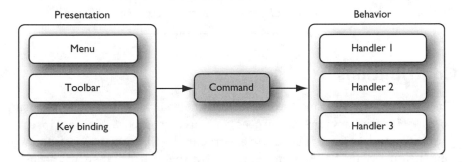

Figure 18–1   A command in pictures

In Chapter 12, "Adding Key Bindings," we created our first command in Hyperbola that represented the notion of adding a contact to Hyperbola. This was required in order to take advantage of the key binding support in Eclipse via the `org.eclipse.ui.bindings` extension point. To understand how to define a command, let's look at an example:

```
org.eclipsercp.hyperbola/plugin.xml
<extension
        point="org.eclipse.ui.commands">
    <category
        description="Hyperbola Commands"
        id="org.eclipsercp.hyperbola.commands"
        name="Hyperbola"/>
    <command
        categoryId="org.eclipsercp.hyperbola.commands"
        description="Add a contact to the selected contact group"
        id="org.eclipsercp.hyperbola.addContact"
        name="Add Contact"/>
</extension>
```

The first step was to define a command *category* which is a grouping mechanism for commands. A category has an associated *name* and *description*. The next step was to define a command with a unique identifier of `org.eclipsercp.hyperbola`
`.addContact`. The optional `categoryId` defines the ID for the category to which this command applies. The `name` and `description` fields represent human-readable

text. Note that there is no reference to a specific implementation, key binding, or menu contribution.

TIP

To observe the execution of commands in the commands framework, you can register an `IExecutionListener` via the `ICommandService`. Note that the listener is merely an observer of commands so it can't veto or modify them.

18.3 Contributions

In Chapter 17, "Actions," we discussed the four action-related extension points: `org.eclipse.ui.actionSets`, `org.eclipse.ui.popupMenus`, `org.eclipse.ui.editorActions`, and `org.eclipse.ui.viewActions`. In the commands framework, these extension points have been replaced by the `org.eclipse.ui.menus` extension point. The `org.eclipse.ui.menus` extension point is used to define placement and visibility of a command. Specifically, the `locationURI` attribute dictates the placement of the command. The `visibleWhen` child element specifies the visibility of the command.

18.3.1 Menu Contributions

Hyperbola already has a named top-level menu. In the `ActionBarAdvisor` method `fillMenu()`, the **Hyperbola** menu is created as a `MenuManager` using the snippet below. The first parameter to the constructor is the menu name, as shown in the UI, and the second, hyperbola, is the ID of the menu.

org.eclipsercp.hyperbola/ApplicationActionBarAdvisor
```
MenuManager hyperbolaMenu = new MenuManager("&Hyperbola", "hyperbola");
```

To place the **Hyperbola** menu contribution in a declarative fashion using the `org.eclipse.ui.menus` extension is straightforward via this example:

org.eclipsercp.hyperbola/plugin.xml
```
<extension
      point="org.eclipse.ui.menus">
   <menuContribution
         locationURI="menu:org.eclipse.ui.main.menu?after=additions">
      <menu
            id="org.eclipsercp.hyperola.menus.main"
            label="Hyperbola"
            mnemonic="&amp;Y">
      </menu>
```

```
        </menuContribution>
    </extension>
```

The `menuContribution` element specifies the placement of the menu via the `locationURI` attribute. The `locationURI` has a special syntax and can be broken down into three parts as shown in Figure 18-2: scheme, identifier, and arguments.

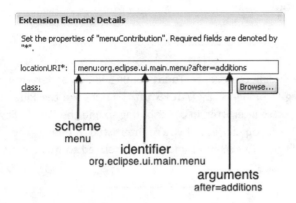

Figure 18–2 `locationURI` syntax

The scheme of the `locationURI` identifies the type of menu contribution. The valid types are

menu—the main application menu or a view pull-down menu

popup—a pop-up (context) menu in a view or editor

toolbar—the main application toolbar or a toolbar within a view

The identifier of the `locationURI` specifies the unique identifier of the contribution. In the preceding example we added the **Hyperbola** menu item to the Eclipse main menu using the `org.eclipse.ui.main.menu` identifier. A list of common `locationURI` identifiers is provided here:

org.eclipse.ui.main.menu—the main menu

org.eclipse.ui.main.toolbar—the main toolbar

org.eclipse.ui.views.ProblemView—the Problems view

org.eclipse.ui.views.ContentOutline—the Outline view

org.eclipse.ui.popup.any—any context menu

The final aspect of the `locationURI` is the arguments. Arguments represent the specific location within a given menu, pop-up, or toolbar where a contribution lives. The arguments are composed of the placement of the contribution, which can be before or after, an equals sign ("="), and the identifier of some item in the menu, pop-up, or toolbar. The identifier additions can be used to indicate that the contribution placement should happen in the default location within the given menu, pop-up, or toolbar.

· TIP

If you're having trouble finding the proper `locationURI` identifier for your contribution, consider using the Plug-in Spy (**Alt+Shift+F1**). Invoke the Plug-in Spy over an editor or view you're interested in contributing to and the Plug-in Spy will present you with identifiers you can use. If you're interested in menus, the Menu Spy (**Alt+Shift+F2**) will give you relevant information related to menu contribution identifiers.

In Hyperbola the **Add Contact** command is placed in two locations, the main menu and the toolbar. To place the **Add Contact** command in the main menu, we simply need to add a new menu element under the **Hyperbola** menu element as shown here:

```
org.eclipsercp.hyperbola/plugin.xml
<extension
        point="org.eclipse.ui.menus">
    <menuContribution
        locationURI="menu:org.eclipse.ui.main.menu?after=additions">
        <menu
            id="org.eclipsercp.hyperola.menus.main"
            label="Hyperbola"
            mnemonic="&amp;Y">
            <menu
                commandId="org.eclipsercp.hyperbola.addContact"
                label="Add Contact"
                tooltip="Add a contact">
        </menu>
        <menu>
    </menuContribution>
</extension>
```

To add the **Add Contact** command to the toolbar, we need to specify a new `locationURI` that represents the toolbar location `org.eclipse.ui.main.toolbar` as shown here:

```
org.eclipsercp.hyperbola/plugin.xml
<extension point="org.eclipse.ui.menus">
  <menuContribution
    locationURI="toolbar:org.eclipse.ui.main.toolbar?after=additions">
      <menu
        commandId="org.eclipsercp.hyperbola.addContact"
        label="Add Contact"
        tooltip="Add a contact">
      </menu>
  </menuContribution>
</extension>
```

18.3.2 Standard Workbench Contributions

In Hyperbola we created and registered standard Workbench actions like **Exit** with the ActionFactory class in the makeActions(IWorkbenchWindow window) method as demonstrated in the following snippet:

```
org.eclipsercp.hyperbola/ApplicationActionBarAdvisor
exitAction = ActionFactory.QUIT.create(window);
register(exitAction);
aboutAction = ActionFactory.ABOUT.create(window);
register(aboutAction);
helpAction = ActionFactory.HELP_CONTENTS.create(window);
```

We registered these actions by using the ActionBarAdvisor.register(IAction) method as demonstrated below. Under the covers, this took care of things like registering the standard action's respective key binding. In terms of presentation, we placed the actions in the ActionBarAdvisor method fillMenu().

```
org.eclipsercp.hyperbola/ApplicationActionBarAdvisor
MenuManager hyperbolaMenu = new MenuManager("&Hyperbola", "hyperbola");
...
hyperbolaMenu.add(new Separator());
hyperbolaMenu.add(exitAction);
```

The commands framework requires a different approach. For example, if we look at the **Exit** action, we can replicate the behavior and placement using the org.eclipse.ui.menus extension point. To place the **Exit** action in the proper location, we add a menu child element relative to the **Hyperbola** menu we defined earlier. To represent the proper exit behavior, we can reuse the existing **Exit** command identifier provided by the Workbench, org.eclipse.ui.file.exit, as shown in this snippet:

```
org.eclipsercp.hyperbola/plugin.xml
<extension
        point="org.eclipse.ui.menus">
    <menuContribution
            locationURI="menu:org.eclipse.ui.main.menu?after=additions">
        <menu
```

```
            id="org.eclipsercp.hyperola.menus.main"
            label="Hyperbola"
            mnemonic="&amp;Y">
            <menu
                commandId="org.eclipse.ui.file.exit"
                label="Exit"
                tooltip="Exit Hyperbola">
            </menu>
        <menu>
    </menuContribution>
</extension>
```

This pattern can be applied to the other standard Workbench actions like Preferences and Help. To find existing command identifiers, we recommend that you take a look at the IWorkbenchActionConstants and IIDEActionConstants classes. An even easier way to find existing command identifiers is to use the extension editor and click the **Browse...** button to bring up a command identifier selection dialog as shown in Figure 18-3.

Figure 18–3 Browsing for command identifiers using the extension editor

18.3.3 Contribution Visibility

The visibility of contributions needs to be controlled. For
plug-in developers contributed top-level menu items without a..,
they should be visible? The user interface would get cluttered quickly.
bola the **Add Contact** command should be visible only when a RosterGroup e..
is selected. To accomplish this, we need to add a visiblewhen child element to the
respective **Add Contact** menu element.

```
org.eclipsercp.hyperbola/plugin.xml
<extensionpoint="org.eclipse.ui.menus">
   <menuContribution
     locationURI="menu:org.eclipse.ui.main.menu?after=additions">
     <menu
       id="org.eclipsercp.hyperbola.menus.main"
       label="Hyperbola"
       mnemonic="&amp;Y">
     <menu
       commandId="org.eclipsercp.hyperbola.addContact"
       icon="icons/add_contact.gif"
       label="Add Contact">
        <visibleWhen checkEnabled="false">
          <with variable="selection">
            <or>
              <instanceof
                value="org.jivesoftware.smack.RosterGroup">
              </instanceof>
            </or>
          </with>
        </visibleWhen>
     </menu>
   </menu>
</extension>
```

In the visiblewhen expression in this snippet, the selection variable evalu-
ates its child element, or. The or element expresses that the object must be an
instance of RosterGroup via the instanceof element.

18.4 Handlers

The behavior of a command is specified via a handler, specifically via the
org.eclipse.ui.handlers extension point. Using the org.eclipse.ui.handlers
extension point, you can associate one or more classes that implement IHandler
and represent the behavior of your command.

PROGRAMMATIC COMMANDS AND HANDLERS

To programmatically associate a handler with a command, you can use the IHandlerService which is obtained from a view site. To programmatically define or execute a command, you can obtain the ICommandService.

In Hyperbola we can refactor the **Add Contact** action into a command handler by making AddContactAction extend AbstractHandler instead of Action as shown in the following snippet:

org.eclipsercp.hyperbola/AddContactAction

```
public class AddContactAction extends AbstractHandler {
    public final static String ID = "org.eclipsercp.hyperbola.addContact";

    public AddContactAction() {
        // Do nothing.
    }

    public Object execute(ExecutionEvent event) throws ExecutionException {
        IWorkbenchWindow window = HandlerUtil.getActiveWorkbenchWindow(event);
        AddContactDialog d = new AddContactDialog(window.getShell());
        int code = d.open();
        IStructuredSelection selection =
            (IStructuredSelection) HandlerUtil.getCurrentSelection(event);
        RosterGroup group = (RosterGroup) selection.getFirstElement();
        if (code == Window.OK) {
            Roster list = Session.getInstance().getConnection().getRoster();
            String user = d.getUserId() + "@" + d.getServer();
            String[] groups = new String[] { group.getName() };
            try {
                list.createEntry(user, d.getNickname(), groups);
            } catch (XMPPException e) {
                e.printStackTrace();
            }
        }
        return null;
    }
}
```

The main differences between the old and new AddContactAction is that the logic that was previously in the run() method is now in the execute(ExecutionEvent event) method which is required by extending AbstractHandler. Furthermore, since the Workbench window is no longer passed in as part of the constructor, we have to use the HandlerUtil class to obtain the current Workbench window and selection. When working with handlers, we recommend using the HandlerUtil class for things like acquiring the active editor and current selection.

Now that we have defined a proper handler, the next step is to make the commands framework aware of our handler by using the `org.eclipse.ui.handlers` extension point as shown here:

org.eclipsercp.hyperbola/plugin.xml
```
<extension
        point="org.eclipse.ui.handlers">
    <handler
          class="org.eclipsercp.hyperbola.AddContactAction"
          commandId="org.eclipsercp.hyperbola.addContact">
    </handler>
</extension>
```

The handler element acts as the glue between a defined command and the behavior. The class attribute defines a class that implements `IHandler` or extends `AbstractHandler`. The `commandId` attribute represents an identifier that is used to reference an existing command.

TIP

If you have an existing action, you can use the `ActionHandler` class to convert it into an instance of an `IHandler`.

Restricting the execution of a handler is done in a similar fashion to the way we restricted menu contributions via `visiblewhen` expressions, discussed in Section 18.3.3. Within the context of handlers, we have the option of `enabledwhen` and `activewhen` expressions. We recommend always specifying an `activewhen` expression to avoid unnecessary plug-in loading. For a handler to be loaded, the command must be selected and the `enabledwhen` and `activewhen` expressions must be satisfied.

18.5 Summary

In this chapter you learned about the existing problems of the actions framework and how the commands framework solves those problems. We even modified existing actions in Hyperbola to take advantage of the commands framework. When you are starting an application from scratch, it's highly recommended that you use the commands framework instead of the actions framework.

18.6 Pointers

The Eclipse wiki contains a breadth of information regarding the commands framework:

○ *http://wiki.eclipse.org/Platform_Command_Framework*

○ *http://wiki.eclipse.org/Command_Core_Expressions*

○ *http://wiki.eclipse.org/Menu_Contributions*

The Eclipse Platform team has a useful example illustrating different aspects of the commands framework. It's available in CVS under the `org.eclipse.ui.examples` name:

○ *http://dev.eclipse.org/viewcvs/index.cgi/org.eclipse.ui.examples.contributions/*

CHAPTER 19

Customizing Workbench Windows

A side effect of creating applications with a UI framework is that they tend to look somewhat similar. This may be a good thing; as more applications share a UI model, they become familiar in their look and feel and it is easier to learn new applications.

In reality, the modern desktop is a far cry from being an example of uniformity. Even though each OS provides a standard set of native widgets, an increasing number of applications attempt to distinguish themselves by looking different, providing nonrectangular windows, having different layout mechanisms (e.g., tabbed browsing with custom-drawn tabs), and often their own widget sets. It is very common for applications to promote brand recognition based on a specific look.

The next two chapters are dedicated to developers who want to create applications that do not look and feel like Eclipse. In this chapter you'll learn to

o Understand the different customization options available

o Understand their limitations

o Extend Hyperbola to allow the toolbar and status line to be hidden and add a new quick bar to the window layout

o Make Hyperbola run in a nonrectangular window

19.1 Customization Defined

Eclipse is all about plug-ins and extensibility. In a perfect world, the entire Workbench would be pluggable in every possible way. For practical reasons, the Workbench is designed to meet specific extensibility requirements, and these do not include fine-grained customizations of Workbench windows or the assembly and painting of every UI element.

Before the Eclipse RCP opened up new opportunities for the Workbench, this level of customization was not needed. The Workbench's focus was to support an IDE platform. The capabilities found in the Eclipse Workbench are now being used for much more than IDEs. To support this, the Eclipse team has enhanced the Workbench's UI to be customizable in the following ways:

Customize a window's contents—A Workbench window's default layout includes a toolbar, perspective bar, docking trim, content area, and status line. workbenchWindowAdvisors, however, can override all aspects of Workbench window creation and change the location of elements as well as add or remove elements.

Customize a window's shape—By default, Workbench windows are rectangular. Nonrectangular Workbench windows can be created by overriding how windows are created.

Customize the drawing and behavior of views and editors—Views and editors provide much of the look and feel of applications. You can provide your own implementation of view and editor management and drawing and fundamentally change the look and feel of an application.

The next two chapters cover these three Workbench customization options in more detail, providing both background information and examples.

NOTE

You can do a lot with SWT without ever programming to the graphics interface or implementing a custom layout—the supplied widgets handle the painting of icons, text, and other data for you. However, when customizing the Workbench look and feel, it's useful to understand how to draw objects and be creative with layouts. Our discussion here assumes some familiarity with SWT concepts and operation.

19.2 Customizing a Workbench Window

The Workbench opens and configures Workbench windows based on the configuration information provided by a workbenchWindowAdvisor. The typical behavior when a Workbench window is created is that the following controls are created: a menu bar, a toolbar, a trim that is used to place fast views and the perspective bar, a page content area, and a status line. Figure 19-1 shows a typical Workbench window's contents.

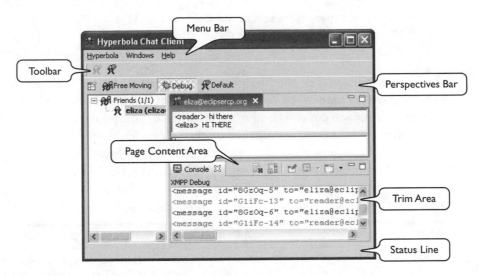

Figure 19–1 Typical Workbench window's contents

The creation of these controls can be changed using the following techniques:

○ Change the visibility of the standard controls by calling the IWorkbenchWindow-Configurer method setShow*() from the WorkbenchWindowAdvisor method preWindowOpen(). These methods control the initial visibility only and do not hide/show the controls once the window is opened.

○ Override the creation of the window's controls by implementing the WorkbenchWindowAdvisor method createWindowContents(). This moves the responsibility for creating a window's controls to the advisor.

For most applications, the setShow*() methods available on IWorkbench-WindowConfigurer are sufficient. To provide further customization, however, the WorkbenchWindowAdvisor needs to create a window's contents from scratch. To give you an idea of how this works, the following snippet shows a customized createWindowContents(Shell) method that creates a window in a manner very similar to the Workbench:

```
org.eclipsercp.hyperbola/ApplicationWorkbenchWindowAdvisor
public void createWindowContents(Shell shell) {
    IWorkbenchWindowConfigurer configurer = getWindowConfigurer();
    Menu menu = configurer.createMenuBar();
    shell.setMenuBar(menu);
    FormLayout layout = new FormLayout();
    layout.marginWidth = 0;
    layout.marginHeight = 0;
    shell.setLayout(layout);
```

```
    toolbar = configurer.createCoolBarControl(shell);
    page = configurer. createPageComposite(shell);
    statusline = configurer.createStatusLine(shell);
}
```

Notice that most of the work is done by a set of helper methods on IWork-benchWindowConfigurer (see Table 19-1 for a complete list). These methods create the typical Workbench controls and make it easier to compose a custom layout from standard parts. The controls supplied by the helpers are untyped and are not meant to be changed in any way. For example, do not downcast them and tweak the underlying control because the control type is not API. Just place them in the layout.

Table 19–1   IWorkbenchWindowConfigurer Control Creation Methods

Method	Description
createMenuBar(Composite)	Creates the top-level menu with style SWT.BAR. The created control is assigned as the menu bar for a shell using the Decorations method setMenuBar(menu). This menu is managed by the Workbench.
createCoolBarControl(Composite)	Creates the top-level toolbar that is managed by the Workbench. There are no parenting restrictions on this control, and it can be positioned anywhere.
createPageComposite(Composite)	Creates the area in which views and editors are shown. This method *must* be called from createWindow-Contents() or the Workbench will not run.
createStatusLine(Composite)	Creates the status line that is managed by the Work-bench. There are no parenting restrictions on this control, and it can be positioned in areas other than under the top-level menu.

These methods are more than just conveniences. If the Workbench creates the controls, it can also add in declarative contributions. We saw this in Chapter 17, "Actions," where menus and toolbars needed to be managed by the Workbench if contributions were to be added.

If your application does not need action contributions in the menu, toolbar, or status line, you can leave out these calls completely or replace them. Of course, this may prevent some plug-ins from integrating into your application as they expect a menu bar and toolbar into which they can contribute actions.

In any event, createPageComposite(Composite) must be called for the Workbench to run properly. It can be called at any time within the createWindowContents() method.

NOTE

There are limitations as to when you can override the Workbench window. The Workbench's default implementation of `createWindowContents()` creates controls that are not available to clients, such as the job progress area, the trim that docks fast views, and the perspective bar. When you override `createWindowContents()`, you lose these areas.

19.2.1 Example: Hide and Show

To demonstrate the customization of a window's content, let's modify Hyperbola so that users can hide and show the toolbar and status line. The Workbench does not directly support this—you can add or remove the toolbar and status line when the window is created, but you cannot change the visibility afterward.

While we're at it, let's include a quick search panel that appears below the page content area when **Ctrl+F** is pressed and hidden when the **Esc** key or **Close** button is pressed. The quick search panel is not a view or an editor but a custom area that is completely controlled by Hyperbola.

Figure 19-2 shows the result of this customization. The toolbar and status line are hidden, and the quick search panel is visible at the bottom of the window. There are actions in the main menu that toggle the visibility of each.

Figure 19–2 Example of new panel with toolbar and status line hidden

19.2.2 FormLayout

The key to getting the flexibility we need in this scenario is the use of SWT's `FormLayout`. A `FormLayout` can be used to describe complex layouts and make it easy to add or remove controls. A `FormLayout` is based on `FormAttachments`.

There is an attachment for each side of a control. Each attachment specifies how its side of the control is attached to other controls or the control's parent composite.

Window creation in the `WorkbenchWindowAdvisor` method `createWindowContents()` is simple. The `FormLayout` is added to the shell, and then the toolbar, page, and status line are created using the appropriate `IWorkbenchWindowConfigurer` methods. Notice that each control is stored as a field on the `WorkbenchWindowAdvisor`—this is needed to allow changing the layout of the controls as they are hidden and shown.

org.eclipsercp.hyperbola/ApplicationWorkbenchWindowAdvisor
```
public void createWindowContents(Shell shell) {
  IWorkbenchWindowConfigurer configurer = getWindowConfigurer();
  Menu menu = configurer.createMenuBar();
  shell.setMenuBar(menu);
  FormLayout layout = new FormLayout();
  layout.marginWidth = 0;
  layout.marginHeight = 0;
  shell.setLayout(layout);
  toolbar = configurer.createCoolBarControl(shell);
  page = configurer.createPageComposite(shell);
  statusline = configurer.createStatusLineControl(shell);

  // The layout method does the work of connecting the
  // controls together.
  layoutNormal();
}
```

After the controls are created, they are connected together in the `layoutNormal()` method. Here the attachments are specified either as a percentage of the space available in the parent or as a direct connection to a neighboring control. Once the layout is configured, the shell must be told to lay out its controls.

org.eclipsercp.hyperbola/ApplicationWorkbenchWindowAdvisor
```
private void layoutNormal() {
  // toolbar
  FormData data = new FormData();
  data.top = new FormAttachment(0, 0);
  data.left = new FormAttachment(0, 0);
  data.right = new FormAttachment(100, 0);
  toolbar.setLayoutData(data);
  // status line
  data = new FormData();
  data.bottom = new FormAttachment(100, 0);
  data.left = new FormAttachment(0, 0);
  data.right = new FormAttachment(100, 0);
  statusline.setLayoutData(data);
  // page contents
  data = new FormData();
  data.top = new FormAttachment(toolbar);
  data.left = new FormAttachment(0, 0);
  data.right = new FormAttachment(100, 0);
```

```
    data.bottom = new FormAttachment(statusline);
    page.setLayoutData(data);
    getWindowConfigurer().getWindow().getShell().layout(true);
}
```

19.2.3 Hiding the Toolbar

With this setup, hiding a control is a matter of making it invisible and then rewiring the controls to which it is attached. For example, the code snippet below, from Hyperbola's workbenchWindowAdvisor, shows how to hide and show the toolbar from Figure 19-1. To hide the toolbar, it is made invisible and its bottom neighbor, the page area, has its top wired to the top of the parent composite. The toolbar disappears and the page area snaps up to take its place. Showing the toolbar is the reverse. This same pattern is used to control the layout of the status line.

org.eclipsercp.hyperbola/ApplicationWorkbenchWindowAdvisor
```
public void setShowToolbar(boolean visible) {
  if (visible) {
    if (toolbar.isVisible())
      return;
    FormData data = (FormData) page.getLayoutData();
    data.top = new FormAttachment(toolbar, 0);
    page.setLayoutData(data);
    toolbar.setVisible(true);
  } else {
    if (!toolbar.isVisible())
      return;
    FormData data = (FormData) page.getLayoutData();
    data.top = new FormAttachment(0, 0);
    page.setLayoutData(data);
    toolbar.setVisible(false);
  }
  getWindowConfigurer().getWindow().getShell().layout(true);
}
```

19.2.4 Adding the Toggle Actions

Now that the window and its controls have been created, we need actions that toggle the visibility of these controls. The setShow*() methods on the workbenchWindowAdvisor can be used to toggle the controls—all that is left is to create a set of actions that call these new methods. Hyperbola's ActionBarAdvisor's constructor is modified to take an extra argument of type workbenchWindowAdvisor. This allows it to call back and control the visibility, as shown in the snippet below. As usual, actions are created and managed by the ActionBarAdvisor.

org.eclipsercp.hyperbola/ApplicationActionBarAdvisor
```
protected void makeActions(IWorkbenchWindow window) {
  ...
```

```
toggleToolbar = new Action("Toolbar", IAction.AS_CHECK_BOX) {
    public void run() {
        windowAdvisor.setShowToolbar(!windowAdvisor.getShowToolbar());
    }
};
}
```

There is a subtle implementation issue to consider: As you can see in Figure 19-3, the actions are created before the window. Actions whose enablement depends on the state of a control in the window must be initialized after the window is created rather than when the action bars are created.

Figure 19-3 also shows an easy solution to this problem—code your WorkbenchWindowAdvisor and ActionBarAdvisor to coordinate when the window's contents have been created. See the call to updateEnablements() below.

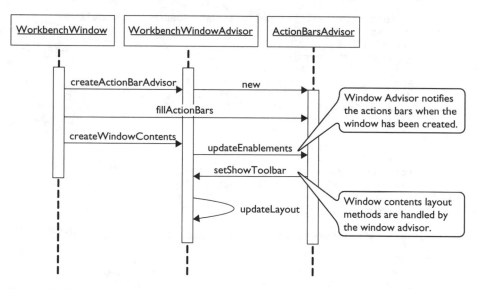

Figure 19–3   Example method sequence

The code for updateEnablements(), shown below, is straightforward. It sets the state of the actions according to the current visibility of the associated controls.

org.eclipsercp.hyperbola/ApplicationActionBarAdvisor
```
private void updateEnablements() {
    toggleToolbar.setChecked(windowAdvisor.getShowToolbar());
    toggleStatusLine.setChecked(windowAdvisor.getShowStatusline());
    toggleQuickSearch.setChecked(windowAdvisor.getShowSearchPanel());
}
```

In addition to using this method when the window is created, it is handy to call the toggling actions to update the action, as shown in the following snippet from the `ActionBarAdvisor` method `makeActions()`:

```
org.eclipsercp.hyperbola/ApplicationActionBarAdvisor
toggleQuickSearch = new Action("Search Panel", IAction.AS_CHECK_BOX) {
   public void run() {
      windowAdvisor.setShowSearchPanel(
         !windowAdvisor.getShowSearchPanel());
      updateEnablements();
   }
};
```

19.2.5 Quick Search Panel

So far you've seen how to toggle controls that the Workbench creates. Adding controls to a Workbench window is handled the same way. Most of the work required is in designing the controls and deciding on an appropriate SWT layout. The following snippet sketches the quick search panel:

```
org.eclipsercp.hyperbola/QuickSearchPanel
public class QuickSearchPanel extends Composite {
   private Image nextImage;
   private Image previousImage;
   private Image closeImage;

   public QuickSearchPanel(Composite parent,
     final ICloseable closeable) {
      super(parent, SWT.NONE);
      GridLayout layout = new GridLayout();
      layout.marginHeight = 3;
      layout.marginWidth = 5;
      layout.numColumns = 4;
      setLayout(layout);
      Label l = new Label(this, SWT.NONE);
      l.setText("Find Contact: ");
      ...
}
```

To add the quick search panel, create the control and wire it into the window's layout. In our example the quick search panel does not show at startup but is instead shown when explicitly toggled via the keyboard or menu item. The next snippet shows how the layout must consider the visibility of the status line in determining where to attach the bottom of the search panel:

```
org.eclipsercp.hyperbola/ApplicationWorkbenchWindowAdvisor
public void setShowSearchPanel(boolean visible) {
   if (visible) {
      if (searchPanel != null)
         return;
```

```
        searchPanel = new QuickSearchPanel(
            getWindowConfigurer().getWindow().getShell(), null);
        FormData data = (FormData) page.getLayoutData();
        data.bottom = new FormAttachment(searchPanel, 0);
        page.setLayoutData(data);
        data = new FormData();
        data.left = new FormAttachment(0, 0);
        data.right = new FormAttachment(100, 0);
        if (statusline.isVisible()) {
          data.bottom = new FormAttachment(statusline, 0);
        } else {
          data.bottom = new FormAttachment(100, 0);
        }
        searchPanel.setLayoutData(data);
      } else {
        ...
      }
    }
```

19.2.6 Checkpoint

Overriding the Workbench window's content creation is possible but not free. If you rely on things such as the perspective bar, fast views, and the background progress area, you should think twice about this approach. In fact, it's really only fast views that are lost when replacing the window's contents because in Chapter 16, "Perspectives, Views, and Editors," you saw how to implement your own perspective bar and in Chapter 17 how to implement your own background progress indicator.

The reason for showing the quick search panel was to emphasize that once you control the creation of the window's content area, anything is possible. The next section shows another example of this when we override createWindowContents() to create a completely new window shape.

19.3 Custom Window Shapes

Another common technique for branding an application is the use of nonrectangular windows. An application window can be curved and have transparent areas. Here we skim the surface of creating custom windows to whet your appetite.

The simplest approach to customizing the window shape is to modify the shell created by the WorkbenchWindowAdvisor and then add widgets, such as toolbars and lists, directly to the shell. Ideally, the widgets you add are crafted to match the custom look of the shell. Here we stick to the standard widgets used in Hyperbola and end up with the Hyperbola shown in Figure 19-4.

Figure 19–4 Hyperbola has got the blues

NOTE

The elements of the new Hyperbola may be rectangular, but the overall shell mask is the union of the three rectangular components—this forms a nonrectangular whole. (As you can tell, we are not graphic artists, but this shape demonstrates our point.)

Manipulating SWT regions and shells is the key to creating nonrectangular windows. Shells have styles that determine how a window is rendered, for example, with a border, with **Maximize** and **Minimize** buttons, resizable, and so on. The area of the window that is visible to the user is controlled by setting the shell's region. A region is a collection of polygons in the *x-y* coordinate system. A region can be as complex or as simple as you need.

NOTE

The region of a shell can be specified only if its trim (i.e., the border and title area) is not shown. This is controlled using the SWT.NO_TRIM flag on shell creation.

```
Shell shell = new Shell(null, SWT.NO_TRIM);
Region region = new Region();
region.add(new Rectangle(0, 0, 400, 600));
Shell.setRegion(region);
```

You can even call `setRegion(Region)` multiple times to change the shape of the shell dynamically. This is how the famous "paper clip" animation is implemented. By changing the shape of the shell based on a timer, you can effectively create an animated window with transparent areas.

NOTE

The sample code for this chapter includes both the "hide and show" example and this nonrectangular window example. The login dialog includes a check box to select the example to run.

19.3.1 Creating the Shape

Simple shapes that can be defined as a set of rectangles are easy to set up—simply create a region and add the various rectangles. More complex regions, however, are hard to describe explicitly. In the end, it is easier to build a region from an image.

For example, you can use any drawing tool to draw an image that is a template for your window. Design the image with spots for the various controls you need in the application. From this you get two things: the look of your application and a mask that defines the region. The mask is made up of every pixel in the rectangular image that is not transparent. For example, Figure 19-5 shows the mask for our Hyperbola example from Figure 19-4.

Figure 19–5 Mask layer used to define a region

You can load the mask and define the region at the same time as the application template image is loaded using the code in the following snippet:

```
org.eclipsercp.hyperbola/ImageUtilities
static void loadRegionsAndImages(Display display,
    ImageData[] datas, Image[] images, Region[] regions) {
  for (int i = 0; i < datas.length; i++) {
    Region region = new Region(display);
    ImageData data = datas[i];
    ImageData mask = data.getTransparencyMask();
    Rectangle pixel = new Rectangle(0, 0, 1, 1);
    for (int y = 0; y < mask.height; y++) {
      for (int x = 0; x < mask.width; x++) {
        if (mask.getPixel(x, y) != 0) {
          pixel.x = data.x + x;
          pixel.y = data.y + y;
          region.add(pixel);
        }
      }
    }
    images[i] = new Image(display, datas[i]);
    regions[i] = region;
  }
}
```

Here the template image is loaded and its getTransparencyMask() scanned to create the region. The region ends up being a collection of 1-x-1 rectangles, each representing one nontransparent pixel in the mask. Of course, the underlying implementation merges these rectangles.

Notice that this method handles the loading of several templates and regions. This is useful if your application allows switching the window shape or animating the window.

NOTE

The image used in this example has a fixed size. To create a resizable nonrectangular window based on an image requires more work than we can include in this example.

19.3.2 Creating the Window

Once regions are initialized with images, you need to configure the application's shell from the WorkbenchWindowAdvisor. The shell has to be configured with the SWT.NO_TRIM style bit before it is created. This is done in the WorkbenchWindowAdvisor method prewindowOpen():

```
org.eclipsercp.hyperbola/ApplicationWorkbenchWindowAdvisor
public void prewindowOpen() {
  getWindowConfigurer().setShellStyle(
      SWT.NO_TRIM | SWT.ON_TOP | SWT.NO_BACKGROUND);
}
```

Next, you must update the method postWindowCreate() to configure the shell in the following ways:

○ Load the regions and images and add a paint listener to the shell to draw the shell border. This is much easier than drawing it programmatically using SWT graphics context (GC) calls.

○ Add support for dragging the shell with the mouse. The usual method of moving shells with the title bar is not available here since the shell uses the NO_TRIM style.

○ Set the size and region for the shell.

```
org.eclipsercp.hyperbola/NonRectWorkbenchWindowAdvisor
public void postWindowCreate(IWorkbenchWindowConfigurer configurer) {
  datas = loadImages();
  images = new Image[datas.length];
  regions = new Region[datas.length];
  final Shell shell = configurer.getWindow().getShell();

  loadRegionsAndImages(shell.getDisplay(), datas, images, regions);

  Listener listener = new Listener() {
    int startX, startY;
    public void handleEvent(Event e) {
      if (e.type == SWT.MouseDown && e.button == 1) {
        startX = e.x;
        startY = e.y;
      }
      if (e.type == SWT.MouseMove &&
        (e.stateMask & SWT.BUTTON1) != 0) {
        Point p = shell.toDisplay(e.x, e.y);
        p.x -= startX;
        p.y -= startY;
        shell.setLocation(p);
      }
      if (e.type == SWT.Paint) {
        ImageData data = currentData
        e.gc.drawImage(currentImage, data.x, data.y);
      }
    }
  };
  shell.addListener(SWT.MouseDown, listener);
  shell.addListener(SWT.MouseMove, listener);
  shell.addListener(SWT.Paint, listener);
```

```
    currentData = datas[0];
    currentImage = images[0];
    currentRegion = regions[0];
    ImageData data = datas[0];
    Point location = shell.getLocation();
    shell.setSize(data.x + data.width, data.y + data.height);
    shell.setRegion(currentRegion);
}
```

Don't forget to dispose of the images when the window is closed.

19.3.3 Defining the Window Contents

The last step is to place the controls in the custom-shaped window. Unfortunately, SWT does not provide a predefined layout that can help here. Instead, since the window is a fixed size, you can simply place the controls at absolute locations within the shell. Using the drawing application you used to create the image templates, identify the coordinates for different locations in the image, and then use these to set the bounds of the controls. This is brittle, but it works.

In this example, three controls are placed in the window. A combo box is added to the top, the page content area is added in the middle, and the toolbar is added to the floating area at the bottom:

```
org.eclipsercp.hyperbola/NonRectWorkbenchWindowAdvisor
public void createWindowContents(
    IWorkbenchWindowConfigurer configurer, Shell shell) {
  int x = 26;
  int y = 66;

  Combo box = new Combo(shell, SWT.DROP_DOWN);
  box.setBounds(34, 40, 150, 20);

  Control page = configurer.createPageComposite(shell);
  page.setBounds(x, y, 499 - x, 391 - y);

  Control coolBar = configurer.createCoolBarControl(shell);
  coolBar.setBackground(
    new Color(coolBar.getDisplay(), new RGB(159,159,169)));
  coolBar.setBounds(29, 428, 499 - 29, 21);
}
```

You can also set the background color for controls to make them blend into the window's colors.

COLORS THAT CAN'T BE CHANGED

Some of the widgets created in the page composite area are drawn by the Workbench. These include the background area beside the tabs and the trim shown between views and editors that allow resizing. Refer to Chapter 20, "Customizing the Presentation of Views and Editors," for information on customizing the look and feel of these areas.

19.4 Summary

This chapter should have opened your eyes to some of the UI customization options available in Eclipse. The Workbench is extremely flexible, and where it is less obviously customizable, it offers ways of overriding its mechanisms and letting you do what you want. Going off the beaten track is always more work, but as we have shown here, the cost of getting radically different looks is relatively modest.

The next chapter covers another set of customizations: changing how views and editors look and behave. Those facilities, in concert with the ones described here, remove all limits to customization of the Workbench.

19.5 Pointers

The presentation API is covered well in this presentation:

○ *http://dev.eclipse.org/viewcvs/index.cgi/*checkout*/org.eclipse.ui.examples .presentation/eclipsecon2005-presentationsAPI.ppt?rev=1.1&content- type=application/powerpoint*

CHAPTER 20

Customizing the Presentation of Views and Editors

Much of the "look and feel" of Eclipse applications is defined by the way editor and view tabs are shown. Most of the Eclipse IDE uses native widgets, such as toolbars, dialogs, and menus. There are some Workbench components, however, that use custom widgets. For example, native tab widgets don't support drag-and-drop reordering, focus highlighting, and **Close** buttons. As such, Eclipse uses a custom widget called `CTabFolder` for view and editor tabs.

As you saw in Chapter 19, "Customizing Workbench Windows," there are many good reasons to customize the look of RCP applications. Changing how editors and views are shown has a significant impact. Fortunately, you can provide your own implementation of view and editor rendering and navigation. If the standard look or behavior does not match your needs, you can change it. This chapter shows you how to use a presentation and how to write your own.

20.1 Presentations

The Workbench uses the term *presentation* to define the set of Workbench classes that is responsible for managing and displaying editors and views. Presentations do more than paint widgets—they are not just *skin* for the application. They also provide behavior for widgets. Presentations control the look of tabs—the very fact that tabs are used at all—as well as toolbars, menus, and how parts are dragged from place to place.

Presentations manage stacks of *presentable parts* such as views and editors. They allow collections of like parts to be stacked together and control the presentation and behavior of the stack. The Workbench may instantiate several presentations for a given page depending on the perspective layout. In essence, each hole that you define in your perspective is filled with a presentation that stacks views or editors in the hole.

Figure 20-1 shows what Hyperbola would look like if you could remove presentation from the Workbench. This isn't a mock-up; it is using a presentation that does not do much. The look resembles a perspective in which all views and editors are stand-alone. The most obvious quirk is that the chat editors and Console views no longer show their tabs. From the example you can see that presentations play an important role in the Workbench and in defining the overall look and feel of your application.

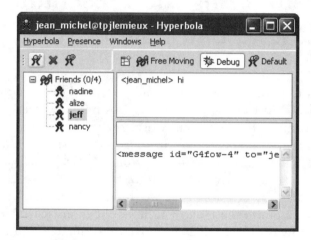

Figure 20–1   Hyperbola without a presentation

20.2 Sample Presentations

Eclipse comes with a couple of sample presentations that you can use if the standard presentation is not suitable for your application. They also provide a good example of writing presentations. In this section we show you how to use these existing presentations in your application.

To use an existing presentation, identify your preferred presentation factory as outlined below. First, find the ID for the presentation. This is the ID of its extension to the `org.eclipse.ui.presentationFactories` extension point. Look for it in the `plugin.xml` file of the plug-in providing the presentation. An example of the R21 extension is shown here:

```
org.eclipsepresentations.r21/plugin.xml
<extension point="org.eclipse.ui.presentationFactories">
  <factory
    name="R21"
```

```
      class="o.e.ui.internal.presentations.R21PresentationFactory"
      id="org.eclipse.ui.internal.r21presentationFactory">
   </factory>
</extension>
```

Next, set the UI's `presentationFactoryId` preference to this ID. You can do this either in the product preference initialization file, as described in Section 13.4, "Adding Help Content," which is preferred, or in code. Both techniques are shown in the snippets below:

org.eclipsercp.hyperbola/preferences.ini
```
org.eclipse.ui/presentationFactoryId=\
    org.eclipse.ui.internal.r21presentationFactory
```

Setting the preference in code effectively overrides the Workbench's default presentation. Note that the preference must be set before the first Workbench window is created.

```
IPreferenceStore store =
    PlatformUI.getWorkbench().getPreferenceStore();
store.put(IWorkbenchPreferenceConstants.PRESENTATION_FACTORY_ID,
    "org.eclipse.ui.internal.r21presentationFactory");
```

20.2.1 The R21 Presentation

The first presentation, called "R21," provides the look and feel of Eclipse as it was in Eclipse 2.1. The look and feel of Eclipse underwent an overhaul during the development of Eclipse 3.0, but some people still prefer the old presentation. Figure 20-2 shows Hyperbola using the R21 presentation.

If you like the retro look, you can use the R21 presentation plug-in available in the Eclipse SDK in a plug-in called `org.eclipse.ui.presentations.r21`. The Eclipse team provides this presentation as more of an example than a full-featured presentation. For example, it does not support stand-alone views. To use the R21

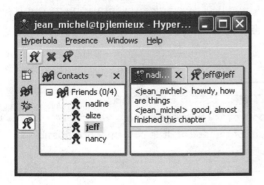

Figure 20–2 Hyperbola with the R21 look

presentation, add the `org.eclipse.ui.presentations.r21` plug-in to your target and set up the presentation as described previously.

20.2.2 *Example Presentations*

In addition to the R21 presentation, there is a plug-in that contains example presentations. This plug-in can be found on *http://dev.eclipse.org* in the `/home/cvs/org.eclipse.ui.examples.presentations` plug-in. When you check out this project from CVS, have a look in the `plugin.xml` for the list of registered presentation factories and their IDs.

20.3 Writing a Presentation

Presentations are, of course, entirely customizable. This section guides you through the classes and coding tricks needed to implement a custom presentation. The presentations API is relatively small but quite detailed and involved. We start with a short introduction and then show you how to build your own simple presentation.

Workbench windows delegate the creation of the part stacks to a registered `AbstractPresentationFactory`. As you saw in the previous section, this is contributed by an extension to the `org.eclipse.ui.presentationFactories` extension point. The factory to use is identified via the UI's `presentationFactoryId` preference.

The factory provides methods for creating the different stack types: stand-alone view, regular view, and editor. Each stack is an instance of a `StackPresentation` and is assigned a number of parts to show. It is completely up to the stack to decide how to display these parts to the user. The stacks *do not* create a part's widgets; they simply define where and how the part is shown.

At creation time, stacks are given a presentation site, an instance of `IStackPresentationSite`. The site is used to send events and requests from the `StackPresentation` to the Workbench. The stack presentation site controls stack-related behavior such as dragging and dropping of the stack and minimize/maximize.

MULTIPLE PAGE EDITORS

The Workbench provides support for multipage editors where each page is represented by a tab at the bottom of the editor. It is currently not possible to override this behavior with a presentation.

Figure 20-3 shows the primary classes in the `org.eclipse.ui.presentations` package. To get started, you need to provide two concrete implementations shown in gray: a stack presentation and a presentation factory.

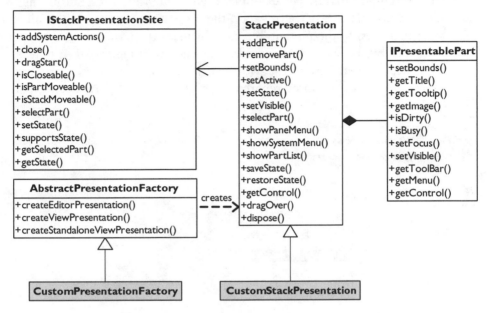

Figure 20–3 Presentation classes

At runtime, when a window is created, the presentation factory is called by the Workbench and asked to create a stack presentation. The factory is straightforward—it simply creates the stack presentation instance providing both a parent composite and an `IStackPresentationSite`.

Subsequently, the Workbench tells the presentation its bounds (i.e., its size) using `setBounds(Rectangle)`, and the presentation is given a part to show via `addPart(IPresentablePart)`. The simplest presentation ensures that the bounds of the parts it's showing are set using the `IPresentablePart` method `setBounds(Rectangle)`, and the part is made visible using the `IPresentablePart` method `setVisible(boolean)`.

Presentation sites provide helper methods to support dragging and querying the page layout for settings such as whether or not the stack is movable or closable. Presentations should honor these configuration settings.

20.3.1 *Widget Hierarchy*

A full understanding of widget hierarchy is essential when implementing a presentation. It's not complicated, but it provides insight into many design points in the presentation APIs. For example, even though the presentation has a method called addPart(IPresentablePart), the presentation does not actually parent the widget related to the presentable part. Instead, the part's control and toolbar are parented by the Workbench window, as shown in Figure 20-4; that is, the Runtime widget hierarchy of the Workbench does not reflect the presentation class hierarchy. This is to allow reparenting and moving of parts between stacks.

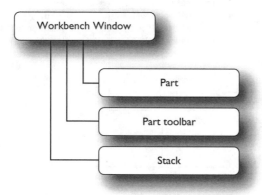

Figure 20–4   Runtime widget parenting

Similarly, a presentation should never reference a presentable part's control because a part can be shown simultaneously in several stacks. Instead, presentations should call the IPresentablePart method setBounds(Rectangle) and the IPresentablePart method setVisible(boolean) to control the placement of the part's controls.

The stacks do parent some widgets, however. Normally they create a number of widgets to display tabs or other UI pieces used for inter-part navigation. These parts should be parented by the stack itself.

20.3.2 StackPresentation

A StackPresentation contains the bulk of a presentation's definition. Its main responsibilities are to control the visibility of its presentation parts, to supply the trim around the presentable parts, and to show the part's toolbar.

Although most users expect presentations to support the behavior provided by the Workbench's default presentation, much of that behavior is optional. Your presentation needs to support only the features required by your application. Table 20-1 provides a brief overview of the features provided by the Workbench's built-in presentation. This is a good guide to what a full-featured presentation should support.

Table 20–1 Workbench's Default Presentation Features

Feature	Description
Borders and trim	The stack presentation creates a trim that is displayed around the stack.
Closing parts	The stack should allow the user to select a part and close it. To close a part, call the IStackPresentationSite method closePart().
Disposal	The stack must set a listener on the composite it creates and delete the stack when its composite is deleted or when the stack's dispose() method is called. The stack cannot assume that disposal occurs only when the stack's dispose() method is called since there are times when the StackPresentation method dispose() is not called and instead the stack's control is simply destroyed.
Focus	A stack can listen to focus changes and highlight itself based on its focus. The stack site can set the active state via the StackPresentation method setActive().
Location	The stack must set the bounds of the presentable part so the part can be drawn in the appropriate location. The stack doesn't actually parent the presentable part's widget; it simply informs the part where it can display itself. A stack selects a part by calling the IStackPresentationSite method selectPart().
Ordering parts	You can allow the user to reorder parts within the stack.
Part menu	The stack should display the part menu provided by the IPresentablePart method showMenu().
Part property changes	Presentable parts have several properties that can dynamically change (e.g., name, image, dirty, and busy states). Stacks should listen for changes to a part and update themselves accordingly.
Parts list	The stack can display a part picker that is shown when the **Open Editor Drop-Down** key is pressed. It can also provide a button in the stack to show the drop-down.
Persistence	A stack can persist and restore information related to its parts using the StackPresentation methods restoreState() and saveState(). For example, the stack can remember the parts that it contains and automatically re-create the parts using the IPresentationSerializer factory when the stack is re-created.

(continues)

Table 20–1   Workbench's Default Presentation Features (*Continued*)

Feature	Description
Themes	The stack uses theme colors via the `IworkbenchThemeConstants` when providing focus and selection highlights to parts. It can also listen to changes to the theme and update appropriately.
Toolbars	Determines the visibility and location of the toolbar for a part when the part is visible.

20.4 Example Presentation

This section illustrates how to code some of the features in Table 20-1 to implement the simple presentation shown in Figure 20-5. Rather than showing all the code here, we highlight the most important parts. The complete version is available in the sample code for this chapter.

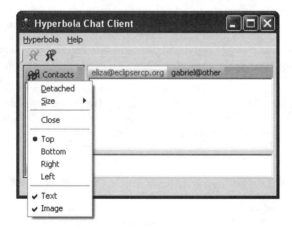

Figure 20–5   Hyperbola's new look

Let's start by defining the requirements:

○ The presentable part tabs must appear at the top of the stack and allow the user to switch between parts. The active part's tab must be shown in green and the hidden parts shown in white.

○ The part tabs must wrap to another line if there are too many parts to show on one line.

○ Toolbars and view menus must be supported.

○ To close a part, there must be a **Close** action in the context menu for a tab. In addition, there are actions to customize the look and location of the tabs (e.g., bottom, right, left).

○ The user must be able to drag and drop parts from one stack to another and move the stacks around. In this example, layout preferences such as stand-alone and nonclosable are to be ignored.

○ The presentation border and trim must be drawn to highlight the active stack.

20.4.1 The Presentation Factory

The first thing to do is declare the presentation factory and register it with the org.eclipse.ui.presentationFactories extension point, as shown here:

org.eclipsercp.hyperbola/plugin.xml
```
<extension point="org.eclipse.ui.presentationFactories">
  <factory
    class="o.e.hyperbola.presentation.HyperbolaPresentationFactory"
    name="Hyperbola Presentation"
    id="org.eclipsercp.hyperbola.presentation"/>
</extension>
```

The implementation of the factory is straightforward—it simply creates the stack presentation instances as shown in the next code snippet. Notice that this is where the stack presentation gets access to the IStackPresentationSite and the Composite, with which it can parent its controls. These are passed to the factory by the Workbench and are simply forwarded to the stack presentations. For simplicity in our example, all the methods return the same StackPresentation. An alternative is to create different types for editors, views, and stand-alone views.

org.eclipsercp.hyperbola/HyperbolaPresentationFactory
```
public class HyperbolaPresentationFactory
    extends AbstractPresentationFactory {
  public StackPresentation createEditorPresentation(Composite parent,
      IStackPresentationSite site) {
    return new HyperbolaPresentation(parent, site);
  }

  public StackPresentation createViewPresentation(Composite parent,
      IStackPresentationSite site) {
    return new HyperbolaPresentation(parent, site);
  }

  public StackPresentation createStandaloneViewPresentation(
      Composite parent,
      IStackPresentationSite site, boolean showTitle) {
    return new HyperbolaPresentation(parent, site);
  }
}
```

20.4.2 The Stack Presentation

Again, the stack is the meat of any presentation. In our example, the meat is in the HyperbolaStackPresentation class. The main task in creating a presentation is to design its layout and pick the UI widgets needed for switching between presentable parts, showing the part contents, the part toolbar, and any other widgets that appear in the presentation. Figure 20-6 shows a sketch of our example presentation with the widgets that are used to place the different elements of an IPresentablePart. At the top is the titleArea, which contains the tabs that allow switching between parts. This is a simple Composite with a RowLayout that wraps children if necessary. When a part is added to the presentation, a composite that shows the part's name and icon is added to the titleArea.

NOTE

Using Composites for the tabs is a bit heavyweight; instead, we could have used org.eclipse.swt.widgets.items. Whereas Composites can contain other controls, items can't. The main reason we used Composites was that the existing SWT layouts work with Composites and not items. We didn't want to add more complexity to the example by having to write a custom layout. For an example of how to use items, see SWT's CTabFolder, CTabItem, and CTabLayout.

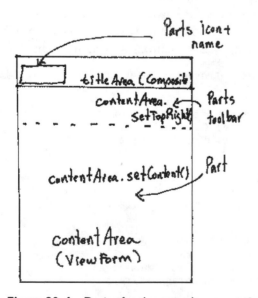

Figure 20–6   Design for the example presentation

The contentArea is where the IPresentablePart can be displayed. It's implemented as a ViewForm, which is a handy SWT class that allows the layout of three controls at the top and one content control below. If an IPresentablePart has a toolbar, it's shown in the ViewForm's top right slot.

The bulk of a presentation involves laying out the controls in the presentation and calculating in which area the part should be shown when calling IPresentablePart .setBounds(Rectangle). However, the first thing the presentation does is create the widgets shown in Figure 20-6, adding a dispose listener to the topmost control in the presentation.

org.eclipsercp.hyperbola/HyperbolaStackPresentation
```
public HyperbolaStackPresentation(Composite parent,
    IStackPresentationSite stackSite) {
  // Create a top-level control for the presentation.
  presentationControl = new Composite(parent, SWT.NONE);
  titleArea = new Composite(presentationControl, SWT.NONE);

  contentArea = new ViewForm(presentationControl, SWT.NONE);
  clientArea = new Composite(contentArea, SWT.NONE);
  clientArea.setVisible(false);

  // Add a dispose listener. This will call the presentationDisposed()
  // method when the widget is destroyed.
  presentationControl.addDisposeListener(new DisposeListener() {
    public void widgetDisposed(DisposeEvent e) {
      // Remove any listeners or resources that were created.
      presentationDisposed();
    }
  });
}

public void dispose() {
  presentationDisposed();
}
```

Note here that the presentation has a dispose() method, but it is not guaranteed to be called. Since each presentation creates a top-level control, the disposal of that control indicates that it is safe to clean up any resources held by the presentation. Without this structure, it is very easy to leak presentations as stacks are closed.

The titleArea is used to show view and editor tabs. A simple Composite with a RowLayout is enough here. The tabs that are added as children of the titleArea use the RowLayout's wrapping behavior.

org.eclipsercp.hyperbola/HyperbolaStackPresentation
```
public HyperbolaStackPresentation(Composite parent,
    IStackPresentationSite stackSite) {
  ...
  titleArea.addListener(SWT.MenuDetect, menuListener);
  RowLayout rowLayout = new RowLayout ();
```

```
      rowLayout.marginLeft = 0;
      rowLayout.marginRight = 0;
      rowLayout.marginTop = 0;
      rowLayout.marginBottom = 0;
      rowLayout.spacing = 0;
      titleArea.setLayout (rowLayout);
      ...
}
```

It is standard practice for presentations to draw an outline of the stack area and differentiate the part switching (i.e., tab) area from the area that shows the presentable parts themselves. To do this, a paint listener is added to the topmost control.

org.eclipsercp.hyperbola/HyperbolaStackPresentation
```
public HyperbolaStackPresentation(Composite parent,
    IStackPresentationSite stackSite) {
    ...
    presentationControl.addPaintListener(new PaintListener() {
        public void paintControl(PaintEvent e) {
            Rectangle clientArea = presentationControl.getClientArea();
            e.gc.setLineWidth(getBorderWidth());
            e.gc.setForeground(getBorderColor());
            e.gc.drawRectangle(clientArea.x, clientArea.y,
                clientArea.width-1, clientArea.height-1);
            Rectangle contentAreaBounds = contentArea.getBounds();
            int ypos = contentAreaBounds.y - 1;
            e.gc.drawLine(clientArea.x, ypos,
                clientArea.x + clientArea.width - 1, ypos);
        }
    });
}
```

20.4.3 Size and Position

When the presentation is told to update its size, it lays out its controls and initializes the bounds for the presentable part, as shown below. The presentable part needs to be told where, relative to the presentation, to draw.

org.eclipsercp.hyperbola/HyperbolaStackPresentation
```
public void setBounds(Rectangle bounds) {
    Rectangle newBounds = Geometry.copy(bounds);
    // Set the bounds of the presentation widget.
    presentationControl.setBounds(newBounds);
    // Update the bounds of the currently visible part and the title area.
    // Determine the inner bounds of the presentation.
    Rectangle presentationClientArea =
        presentationControl.getClientArea();
    presentationClientArea.x += getBorderWidth();
    presentationClientArea.width -= getBorderWidth() * 2;
    presentationClientArea.y += getBorderWidth();
    presentationClientArea.height -= getBorderWidth() * 2;
    Point p = titleArea.computeSize(
```

```
        presentationClientArea.width, SWT.DEFAULT);
   titleArea.setBounds(x, y, presentationClientArea.width, p.y);
   contentArea.setBounds(presentationClientArea.x, yy,
        presentationClientArea.width,
        presentationClientArea.height - p.y);
}
```

Usually, the presentable part's placement depends on the other widgets shown in the presentation. In this example, the size of the titleArea dictates the size of the contentArea—the tabs take priority over the part content. The thickness and shape of the border must also be considered.

The setBounds(Rectangle) method gives you full control. The layout can be as complicated or as simple as you need. The only restriction is that only *one* part can be visible at a time within the same stack. Beyond that, you can put the tabs at the bottom or down the sides; have big tabs, small tabs, no tabs; and so on— you have complete control.

20.4.4 Adding, Selecting, and Removing Parts

Now that the widgets are created and laid out, the presentation has to handle part manipulation. This requires implementations of the following StackPresentation methods: addPart(IPresentablePart), removePart(IPresentablePart), and showPart(IPresentablePart). This example shows presentation parts as rectangles in the title area. Clicking on a rectangle switches to the part associated with that rectangle.

As shown in the next snippet, when a part is added, a PartTab composite is created and parented by the titleArea. The new part is attached to the PartTab and the PartTab is initialized using the image and text from the IPresentablePart. All the PartTab does is add the image and text and decide how to render the tab. As shown here, the PartTab does all of its work in a paint listener:

org.eclipsercp.hyperbola/PartTab
```
public PartTab(Composite parent) {
   super(parent, SWT.NONE);
   addPaintListener(this);
}

public void paintControl(PaintEvent e) {
   Rectangle titleRect = getClientArea();
   int x = titleRect.x + VERT_SPACING;
   GC gc = e.gc;
   setBackground(getParent().getBackground());
   fill(gc, titleRect.x, titleRect.y,
      titleRect.width - 1, titleRect.height);
   // Draw the image and text.
   ...
}
```

```
public void setSelected(boolean selected) {
  this.selected = selected;
  redraw();
}

public Point computeSize(int wHint, int hHint) {
  int width = VERT_SPACING; int height = HORIZ_SPACING;
  GC gc = new GC(this);
  if (image != null && showImage) {
    Rectangle imageBounds = image.getBounds();
    height = imageBounds.height + HORIZ_SPACING;
    width += imageBounds.width + VERT_SPACING;
  }
}
...
```

Our PartTab is relatively simple. There are many other properties that could be shown, for example, the part's content description or busy state. Your presentation can show these and others however you like.

The snippet below shows the creation and initialization of a PartTab when a new part is added. Notice that a property listener is added to the presentation part. This allows the PartTab to be updated when a part property changes. Properties are things such as the part's text, icon, tool tip, and dirty state—essential data to show in the tab. See IPresentablePart for a complete listing of supported properties.

org.eclipsercp.hyperbola/HyperbolaStackPresentation
```
public void addPart(IPresentablePart newPart, Object cookie) {
  PartTab item = new PartTab(titleArea);

  // Initialize the PartTab with the image, text... from the part.
  updatePartItem(item, newPart);

  item.setData(PART_DATA, newPart);

  // This will update the ToolItem to reflect changes in the part.
  newPart.addPropertyListener(childPropertyChangeListener);

  // Attach a dispose listener to the item.
  item.addDisposeListener(tabDisposeListener);

  // Listen to selection events in the new tool item.
  item.addMouseListener(mouseListener);
  ...
}
```

TIP

Remember to remove listeners when they are no longer needed to avoid memory leaks.

The preceding snippet added a mouse listener to the new tab. This is used to detect when tabs are selected and then to make parts visible. The next snippet shows the listener and highlights the importance of remembering the part with its associated tab. Otherwise, how would you find the part that matches the event?

```
org.eclipsercp.hyperbola/HyperbolaStackPresentation
private MouseListener mouseListener = new MouseAdapter() {
  public void mouseDown(MouseEvent e) {
    PartTab toolItem = (PartTab) e.widget;
    IPresentablePart item = getPartForTab(toolItem);
    if (item == null)
      return;
    // Clicking on the active tab gives focus to the current part.
    if (item == current)
      item.setFocus();
    getSite().selectPart(item);
    selectPart(item);
    Point toDisplay = toolItem.toDisplay(new Point(e.x, e.y));
    if (e.button == 3)
      showSystemMenu(toDisplay);
    ...
};
```

20.4.5 Menus

There are three basic menus that should be handled by a presentation: the system menu, the part list menu, and the view pane menu. The system menu normally contains actions related to the presentation; the part list menu should allow the user to navigate between the parts in the stack; and the view pane menu is the menu returned by the IPresentablePart method getMenu().

In our example only the system menu is needed. The presentation is responsible for creating and showing the menu but must allow the IStackPresentation site to add standard actions such as **Move, Size,** and **Detach** actions to the menu.

```
org.eclipsercp.hyperbola/HyperbolaStackPresentation
Menu aMenu = systemMenuManager.createContextMenu(titleArea);
getSite().addSystemActions(systemMenuManager);
systemMenuManager.update(true);
aMenu.setLocation(displayPos.x, displayPos.y);
aMenu.setVisible(true);
```

20.5 Summary

In this chapter you learned that *presentations* are responsible for managing and drawing a stack of views or editors. A presentation instance is created for each stack of views or editors in a perspective. These instances do not actually parent the widgets created for the view or editor; rather, they simply control the size and location of the views and editors in the stack. With an understanding of the basic implementation patterns from Section 20.4 and the responsibilities of a presentation from Table 20-1, you should have enough background to write your own presentation.

The best way to write your own presentation is to start with an existing one, then modify it to suit your needs. There is actually quite a bit more to the implementation than shown here. The full example included in the sample code for this chapter adds support for dragging; closing parts; moving the tabs to the bottom, right, or left of the content area; and much more. It should serve as a good starting point for creating your own presentations. The example presentations in `org.eclipse.ui.examples.presentations` can also serve as a base for your own presentations.

20.6 Pointers

The presentation API is covered well in this presentation:

○ *http://dev.eclipse.org/viewcvs/index.cgi/*checkout*/org.eclipse.ui.examples .presentation/eclipsecon2005-presentationsAPI.ppt?rev=1.1&content-type= application/powerpoint*

PART IV

Development Processes

The creation of a rich client application is as much about the actual code that needs to be written as it is about how to structure, package, and deliver it. Part IV of the book introduces you to an array of topics from integrating third-party libraries to creating dynamic systems that run in a wide variety of operating environments to running automated builds and delivering RCP applications.

CHAPTER 21

Installing and Updating with p2

In Chapter 14, "Adding Software Management," you defined a *feature* for the Hyperbola plug-ins and added software management support to allow a user to install new features and update existing features. That discussion did not include the details of what is happening under the covers, especially with regard to how p2 operates.

p2 is the provisioning system developed by the Equinox project at eclipse.org. It is a powerful replacement for the original Eclipse Update Manager included with the Eclipse Platform. While retaining much of the original functionality, p2 allows system designers greater flexibility in how they define, structure, and deploy their systems. Fundamentally p2 is a provisioning platform; that is, it is not just one provisioning system but rather a collection of provisioning technologies on top of which you can build a fit-for-purpose provisioning solution. Of course, p2 comes with quite a number of preconfigured pieces to make the creation of your solution as straightforward as possible. This chapter digs deeper and

○ Introduces the various roles of the p2 component

○ Describes the p2 architecture and terminology

○ Demonstrates how to use the p2 provisional API with Hyperbola

○ Describes how to manage metadata and repositories

○ Describes how to install plug-ins using the p2 director

21.1 The Roles of p2

Installation and updates are managed in Eclipse by the provisioning platform called p2. You can use p2 to install or manage any aspect of your application, from the physical plug-ins and native code, to the configuration of the installed software (e.g., file permissions, command-line arguments, etc.). Installation with p2 does more than simply add and remove files in the file system—p2 captures a sequence of events that must occur to lay down and configure a system so that it is ready to run. Core aspects of p2 include the following:

○ Automatic resolution of dependencies between software components. With p2, you state the root set of items you want installed or uninstalled, and p2 computes the complete set of required system changes automatically.

○ Transport of software components and configuration data from remote repositories to the system being installed. p2 includes sophisticated algorithms for performing multithreaded transfers, including support for mirrors and automatic rebalancing of transfers based on network state.

○ An extensible mechanism for instructing p2 how to install and configure various kinds of software. By default p2 knows how to install and configure Eclipse plug-ins, features, and basic native integration such as setting permissions and creating symbolic links.

○ A graphical user interface integrated into the Eclipse platform, to allow end users to examine and manage the application.

○ A suite of command-line tools and Ant tasks, to allow developers and release engineers to build and configure p2-enabled applications.

21.2 Architecture

The centerpiece of the architecture is the *agent*. The agent is a notional concept—there is no actual agent object. Rather the agent is the logical entity that reasons about *metadata* to manage *profiles* by coordinating the downloading of *artifacts* from *repositories* and using an *engine* to manipulate the profiles. Figure 21-1 shows an overview of the agent, the large box in the middle, and how the various parts fit together.

The Hyperbola application is represented by a profile, a runnable configuration of software. The artifacts being installed and updated are mostly bundles, and the metadata being reasoned about is the dependency information extracted from the constituent bundle manifests and product configuration files. The integrated runtimes include the OS and Equinox/Eclipse.

The p2 architecture is quite loosely coupled. The metadata and artifact repositories are independent, the director and engine can be remote, profiles can be distributed, and so on. This allows for great flexibility in putting together provisioning solutions. This chapter shows you how p2 fits together and how the different parts interact to support software management in Hyperbola.

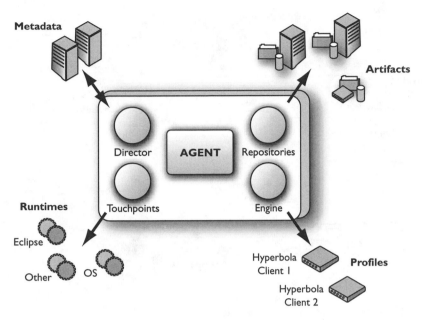

Figure 21–1   Architecture of p2

21.2.1 Installable Units

One of the key characteristics of p2 is its separation of metadata from the artifacts being manipulated. Managing these separately allows p2 to reason about vast numbers of artifacts without having to download any. It also allows for the addition of nonfunctional information to the provisioning setup without modifying the artifacts themselves.

All metadata is captured in *installable units* (IUs). Figure 21-2 shows the structure of an IU. An IU has an ID and a version, the combination of which must be globally unique. IUs also have an open set of key/value properties used to capture information such as name and type.

The basis of the p2 dependency structure is an IU's generic *capability* mechanism. IUs provide and require capabilities. A capability is simply an ID and version number in a *namespace*. For example, a bundle that exports the `org.eclipsercp.hyperbola` package at version 1.0 is said to provide a capability with ID `org.eclipsercp.hyperbola` and version 1.0 in the `java.package` namespace. Similarly, a bundle that imports that package is said to require the corresponding capability. IUs requiring capabilities can specify a version range. Since the set of namespaces is open, the p2 metadata structure can be used to represent all manner of relationships.

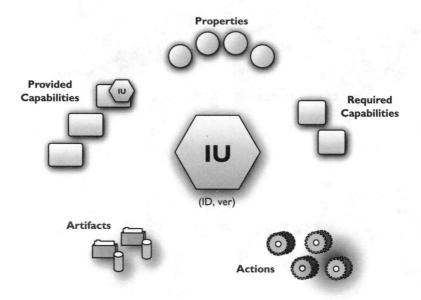

Figure 21–2   The structure of an installable unit

In addition to the dependency information, each IU has a number of related artifacts that are installed when the IU is installed and a set of actions that are executed when the IU goes through an install, configure, unconfigure, and uninstall lifecycle.

21.2.2 Artifacts

p2 treats artifacts as opaque blobs of data and knows only about the metadata used to describe them. That being said, p2 is able to store the same artifact in multiple forms and do a number of interesting optimizations to reduce bandwidth and disk space requirements.

21.2.3 Repositories

All artifacts and metadata are stored in repositories in a p2 system. p2 specifies an API for repositories but not their internal representation. A repository may be on disk, in memory, structured using XML or in a database, or pretty much in any other form. For example, p2 includes repository definitions that integrate legacy Eclipse update sites unchanged. Metadata and artifact repositories are often colocated for convenience but need not be. p2 includes several tools for publishing to repositories and mirroring repositories.

21.2.4 Profiles

As mentioned previously, p2 defines profiles to represent runnable configurations of software. Technically profiles are just descriptions of the system; that is, they list the IUs installed in them. During the actual install operation the relevant artifacts are fetched, installed, and configured into the system. On completion, the fact that the artifact has been installed is recorded in the profile. A p2 agent can manage many profiles representing many different systems.

21.2.5 Director

The director is the brains of the p2 operation. It is responsible for working with the metadata available in the known repositories, the profile being managed, and the provisioning request supplied to it to come up with a set of install, uninstall, and update operations. These operations are then passed to the p2 engine for execution.

NOTE

On the surface the director's job seems reasonably straightforward, but it turns out to be one of those very challenging (i.e., NP-complete) computer science problems. Fortunately, p2 includes a pseudo-Boolean constraint solver, SAT4J, to help with formulating provisioning solutions.

21.2.6 Engine

The engine's job is simply to execute a given set of install, uninstall, and update operations. The engine walks through a set of *phases* and executes the relevant part of each operation in each phase. For example, when an IU is installed, its related artifacts must first be fetched, then installed, and finally configured. Each phase is executed for all involved IUs before proceeding to the next phase.

The engine is assisted in executing these phases by a set of *touchpoints*. A touchpoint is the interface between p2 and some runtime or configuration system. For example, when a bundle is installed into an Equinox system, its start level and auto-start state need to be configured. This is done by the Equinox touchpoint. If p2 were being used to install a WAR or RPM, the relevant operations would be carried out by, say, a Tomcat or RPM touchpoint, respectively.

21.3 Using the p2 API

p2 exposes a set of provisional APIs that can be used to fully customize the install experience for your application. The reason for this is that many applications need full control of how p2 works. For example, a developer may want to show an application-specific wizard to guide users through the update process, or nothing at all. To support these different workflows, p2 provides the mechanics and leaves it up to you to write the supporting code. To use advanced p2 functionality in Hyperbola, we first have to use some of the p2 provisional API:

- ○ IProfileRegistry—manages the list of profiles
- ○ IInstallableUnit—represents what to install (e.g., a feature or a plug-in)
- ○ IPlanner—creates the provisioning plans needed when manipulating profiles
- ○ IEngine—executes provisioning plans to effect the actual install or uninstall of software
- ○ IMetadataRepositoryManager—tracks metadata repositories
- ○ IArtifactRepositoryManager—tracks artifact repositories

21.3.1 Adding Repositories

The first step in updating Hyperbola is to ensure that there is a place to grab updates from. In p2 terminology, this ensures that there is an available metadata and artifact repository for Hyperbola to pull updates from. To advise where Hyperbola will search for updates, we can use a touchpoint advice file (p2.inf) to augment the metadata that is generated.

```
org.eclipsercp.hyperbola/p2.inf
instructions.configure=\
  addRepository(type:0,location:http${#58}//eclipsercp.org/updates);\
  addRepository(type:1,location:http${#58}//eclipsercp.org/updates/);
```

In Section 21.4 we cover in depth the various ways you can customize p2 metadata using touchpoint instructions and advice files. Touchpoint instructions are very flexible and allow you to do such things as add repositories, copy files, and set file permissions.

21.3.2 Loading Repositories

Now that the proper repositories are defined, we can load the metadata repository and begin structuring a query using the p2 API. To load repositories, we need to obtain the IMetadataRepositoryManager and get the list of known repositories to load:

```
org.eclipsercp.hyperbola/P2Util.java
IMetadataRepositoryManager manager = (IMetadataRepositoryManager)
ServiceHelper.getService(
   Activator.bundleContext, IMetadataRepositoryManager.class.getName());
// Get the list of known repositories to search.
URI[] reposToSearch =
   manager.getKnownRepositories(IRepositoryManager.REPOSITORIES_ALL);
// Grab the planner.
IPlanner planner = (IPlanner) ServiceHelper.getService(
   Activator.bundleContext,IPlanner.class.getName());
for (int i=0; i<reposToSearch.length; i++)
   try {
      if (loadMonitor.isCanceled())
         throw new InterruptedException();
      manager.loadRepository(reposToSearch[i],
         loadMonitor.newChild(100/reposToSearch.length));
   } catch (ProvisionException e) {
      // TODO Auto-generated catch block
      e.printStackTrace();
   }
}
```

21.3.3 Searching Repositories

Now that the repositories are loaded, we need to create a ProvisioningContext
to search the loaded repositories for updates using a Collector. The process
involves going through all the available installable units, checking whether there
is a more recent installable unit available, and recording it. In p2 terminology, an
installable unit describes things that can be installed, updated, or uninstalled. The
concept of an installable unit maps to features quite well. In the end, when you
see installable units in the p2 API, think of features and plug-ins. However, note
that it's an abstraction and can describe anything that can be installed, updated,
or uninstalled.

```
org.eclipsercp.hyperbola/P2Util.java
Collector collector = profile.query(InstallableUnitQuery.ANY,
   New Collector(), null);
ProvisioningContext pc = new ProvisioningContext(reposToSearch);
SubMonitor updateSearchMonitor = sub.newChild(100,
SubMonitor.SUPPRESS_ALL_LABELS);
while (iter.hasNext()) {
   if (updateSearchMonitor.isCanceled())
      throw new InterruptedException();
   IInstallableUnit iu = (IInstallableUnit) iter.next();
   IInstallableUnit[] replacements = planner.updatesFor(iu,pc,
      updateSearchMonitor.newChild(100/collector.size()));
   if (replacements.length > 0) {
      iusWithUpdates.add(iu);
      if (replacements.length == 1)
         replacementIUs.add(replacements[0]);
      else {
         IInstallableUnit repl = replacements[0];
```

```
        for (int i = 1; i < replacements.length; i++) {
          if (replacements[i].getVersion().compareTo(
            repl.getVersion()) > 0) {
              repl = replacements[i];
              replacementIUs.add(repl);
          }
        }
      }
    }
}
```

21.3.4 Executing a Provisioning Plan

The final step in the update process is to build a profile change request and obtain
a provisioning plan to execute against the engine. To begin, we create a Profile-
ChangeRequest with the proper installable units obtained when querying the available
repositories. Next, we obtain the IEngine service and create a ProvisioningPlan
with the change request to pass to the engine.

org.eclipsercp.hyperbola/P2Util.java
```
ProfileChangeRequest changeRequest = new ProfileChangeRequest(profile);
changeRequest.removeInstallableUnits(
   (IInstallableUnit[]) iusWithUpdates.toArray(
     new IInstallableUnit[iusWithUpdates.size()]));
changeRequest.addInstallableUnits(
   (IInstallableUnit[]) replacementIUs.toArray(
     new IInstallableUnit[replacementIUs.size()]));
ProvisioningPlan plan =
   planner.getProvisioningPlan(changeRequest,
     pc, sub.newChild(100, SubMonitor.SUPPRESS_ALL_LABELS));
IEngine engine = (IEngine) ServiceHelper.getService(
   Activator.bundleContext, IEngine.class.getName());
IArtifactRepositoryManager artifactMgr =
   (IArtifactRepositoryManager) ServiceHelper.getService(
     Activator.bundleContext,
     IArtifactRepositoryManager.class.getName());
// Perform the provisioning plan.
pc.setArtifactRepositories(artifactMgr.getKnownRepositories(
   IRepositoryManager.REPOSITORIES_ALL));
IStatus status = engine.perform(profile,
   new DefaultPhaseSet(), plan.getOperands(),
   pc, sub.newChild(100, SubMonitor.SUPPRESS_ALL_LABELS));
```

Now that we have a better grasp of how to use p2 to query and install
updates, it's possible to build any type of user interface using these facilities.

NOTE

As of Eclipse 3.5, the p2 API is provisional and will likely change in the future. In the
next release of Eclipse (3.6), the p2 API is expected to be solidified and simplified.

21.4 Metadata Management

As described before, p2 provides facilities for software dependency management and for performing all of the necessary steps to get an application physically installed and configured into an end user's system. The information that describes the dependencies between application components and the steps required to properly configure a running system is called the *p2 metadata*. In many cases this metadata can be computed directly from the information in your plug-in and feature manifests, and an extra step is simply required to *publish* this data into a format suitable for consumption by p2. In other cases plug-in or application developers may need to author or customize the p2 metadata for their software.

21.4.1 Publishing Metadata

There are three different ways p2 repositories can be created: using the PDE **Export** wizards, using PDE Build, or using the publisher. Under the covers, PDE uses the publisher to generate the proper p2 metadata. The *publisher* is the means by which deployable entities like features or products get added to repositories. For example, the publisher can be used to create p2 metadata from a plug-in or a feature. The publisher consists of an extensible set of publishing actions, applications, and Ant tasks that allow users to generate p2 repositories from a number of different sources. Inside the `org.eclipse.equinox.p2.publisher` and `org.eclipse.equinox.p2.updatesite` plug-ins, there are four command-line applications you can use to generate p2 metadata:

- `org.eclipse.equinox.p2.publisher.FeaturesAndBundlesPublisher`
- `org.eclipse.equinox.p2.publisher.ProductPublisher`
- `org.eclipse.equinox.p2.publisher.UpdateSitePublisher`
- `org.eclipse.equinox.p2.publisher.CategoryPublisher`

For example, the `org.eclipse.equinox.p2.publisher.ProductPublisher` application can be used to generate metadata from an Eclipse product definition file as shown here:

```
eclipse -application org.eclipse.equinox.p2.publisher.ProductPublisher
    -metadataRepository file:/<some location>/repository
    -artifactRepository file:/<some location>/repository
    -productFile /<location>/hyperbola.product
    -append
    -executables /<deltapack>/<executables feature location>
    -flavor tooling
    -configs gtk.linux.x86
```

See the p2 publisher documentation on the Eclipse wiki for more information: *http://wiki.eclipse.org/Equinox/p2/Publisher.*

21.4.2 Customizing Metadata

On occasion the metadata that is automatically generated by p2 for bundles, features, and products does not provide everything required to successfully provision an IU. Since Eclipse 3.5, p2 supports the use of a publishing advice file (a `p2.inf` file) that can be used to augment the metadata for an installable unit. The advice file allows an author to customize capabilities, properties, and instructions. The advice file is a properties file and can be placed within

- Plug-ins (`META-INF/p2.inf`): The instructions are added to the IU for the plug-in.
- Features (a `p2.inf` file colocated with the `feature.xml`): The instructions are added to the IU for the feature group.
- Products (a `p2.inf` file colocated with the `.product` file): The instructions are added to the root IU for that product.

Version substitution is a common practice, and two special version parameters are supported:

- `$version$`—returns the string form of the containing IU's version
- `$qualifier$`—returns just the string form of the qualifier of the containing IU's version

The syntax of a touchpoint advice file is listed here:

```
instructions.{phase} = {raw actions}
instructions.{phase}.import =

  {qualified action name} [,{qualified action name}]*
```

where {phase} is a p2 installation phase (`collect`, `configure`, `install`, `uninstall`, `unconfigure`).

The qualified action names for the IU's touchpoint type are implicitly imported. All other actions need to be imported. For example, to use the `instructions.install` advice, we would have to import it as shown here:

```
instructions.install.import=\
  org.eclipse.equinox.p2.touchpoint.natives.ln,\
  org.eclipse.equinox.p2.touchpoint.natives.chmod
```

21.4.3 Touchpoint Instructions

An IU is installed using the facilities provided by a touchpoint. The IU metadata consists of a reference to the touchpoint and describes instructions to execute in various p2 engine phases. Each instruction (e.g., install) describes a sequence of actions to execute for the referenced touchpoint. Examples of common actions are creating and removing directories, changing permissions or linking a delivered artifact, adding repository metadata, and installing and removing bundles. For a concrete example, look at the next sample, which uses a touchpoint instruction to symbolically link Linux libraries within a bundle:

```
instructions.install=\
    ln(targetDir:@artifact,linkTarget:foo/lib.1.so,linkName:lib.so);\
    chmod(targetDir:@artifact,targetFile:lib/lib.so,permissions:755);
instructions.install.import=\
    org.eclipse.equinox.p2.touchpoint.natives.ln,\
    org.eclipse.equinox.p2.touchpoint.natives.chmod
```

As of Eclipse 3.5, two touchpoints have been implemented (native and eclipse). In Table 21-1 we list the various native touchpoint instructions you can use in your application, from unzipping to copying files.

Table 21-1   Native Touchpoint Actions

Touchpoint Action	Parameters	Description
cleanupzip	source, target	Removes unzipped files and directories that were unzipped from source into target; i.e., an "undo operation" of an unzip instruction.
unzip	source, target	Unzips the source into the target directory. The source can be the special @artifact source path, which denotes the download cache location for the first artifact key in the IU.
mkdir	path	Creates the directory specified by the parameter path.
rmdir	path	Removes the directory specified by the parameter path. Action has no effect if the referenced directory contains files.
link	targetDir, linkTarget, linkName, force	Performs the system action ln -s (if the operating system supports it) with the parameters linkTarget being the source file, targetDir the directory where the symbolic link will be created, and linkName the name of the resulting link in the targetDir. The force parameter is a Boolean in string form (i.e., true/false) and indicates if an existing link with the same name should be removed before the new link is created.

(continues)

Table 21–1   Native Touchpoint Actions (*Continued*)

Touchpoint Action	Parameters	Description
chmod	targetDir, targetFile, permissions, options	Changes permission on a file using the system chmod command. The targetDir parameter is either a path or the special @artifact which is a reference to the directory where the first artifact included in the installable unit is located. The parameter targetFile is the name of a file, and permissions is written as for the chmod system command.
remove	path	Removes a file or a directory (and all files under this directory) as referenced by the parameter path.
copy	source, target, overwrite	Copies a file or a directory (and all of its contents) denoted by the source path to the target path.
cleanupcopy	source, target	Cleans up what was installed earlier with a copy from source to target.

In Table 21-2 we list some of the Eclipse-related touchpoint actions you can use within your application, from installing features to adding repositories. See the p2 documentation for the full list of Eclipse touchpoint actions.

Table 21–2   Eclipse Touchpoint Actions

Touchpoint Action	Parameters	Description
installBundle	bundle	Installs a bundle artifact specified by the parameter bundle.
uninstallBundle	bundle	Uninstalls a bundle artifact via the parameter bundle.
installFeature	feature, featureId, version	Installs the feature referenced by the parameter feature (matched against artifacts in the IU). The feature is installed with the ID specified by the parameter featureId or, if this parameter has the value default, with the ID specified in the artifact referenced by feature. The feature is installed with the version specified in version or with the version specified in the artifact referenced by the feature parameter if the version parameter has the value default.
uninstallFeature	feature, featureId, version	Uninstalls a feature.
setStartLevel	startLevel	Sets the start level to the value specified in the parameter startValue.

(continues)

Table 21–2 Eclipse Touchpoint Actions (*Continued*)

Touchpoint Action	Parameters	Description
markStarted	started	Marks the bundle referenced by the first artifact key in the IU as started or not via the Boolean parameter (true/false) started.
setProgramProperty	propName, propValue	Sets the program property named propName to the value specified in propValue. Program properties are used by the executable program to, among other things, locate the JARs needed to start Eclipse.
addRepository	location, type, enabled	Adds the repository at location of type type to the list of known repositories. The repository will then be available when the profile is installed or updated in the future. The enabled parameter takes a Boolean value (true/false) indicating whether the add repository should be enabled. The value of the location parameter must be a well-formed URI. The type parameter value must be the value of one of the IRepository.TYPE_* constants. Specifically, type 0 indicates a metadata repository, and type 1 indicates an artifact repository.

21.5 Repository Management

Repositories are at the heart of p2, and there are many techniques for interacting with them. For example, a common use case is for users to be able to mirror external repositories within a repository of their own because of company policies or to provide developers faster access to artifacts.

21.5.1 Mirroring Repositories

p2 provides two applications that support copying (mirroring) the content of remote repositories to a local repository. The artifact mirroring application supports duplicating a complete artifact repository into a target repository. To perform this operation you simply need an Eclipse installation that contains the org.eclipse.equinox.p2.artifact.repository bundle. The following command will copy the complete contents of a source repository into the destination repository:

```
<eclipseInstall>\eclipse.exe
   -application
       org.eclipse.equinox.p2.artifact.repository.mirrorApplication
   -source http://download.eclipse.org/releases/galileo
   -destination file:d:/artifactLocalRepository/
```

If the destination repository does not already exist, the mirroring application will create a new repository with the same properties as the source repository.

21.5.2 Composite Repositories

As repositories continually grow in size, they become harder to manage. The goal of composite repositories is to make this task easier by allowing site maintainers to have a parent repository that refers to multiple child repositories. Users are then able to reference the parent repository, and the content of all the child repositories will be transparently available to them. In order to automate composite repository actions in release engineering builds, Ant tasks (e.g., `p2.composite.repository`) have been provided that can be called to create and modify composite repositories. The tasks are defined in the `org.eclipse.equinox.p2.repository.tools` plug-in.

21.5.3 Content Categorization

By default, the p2 user interface groups all the IUs by category. If an IU is not categorized, it will not be displayed in the user interface. There are currently two supported methods for categorizing content: a category definition file, as we discussed in Section 14.7, "Defining Categories," and a touchpoint advice file, as discussed in Section 21.3.

21.6 Installation Management

The easiest way to install plug-ins and features is via the Software Updates dialog we encountered while working with Hyperbola. However, there are use cases where installation has to happen programmatically or via the command line, such as in build and scripted environments. In p2 this is achieved using a tool called the p2 *director* that can perform installation operations in a headless fashion. The director application, `org.eclipse.equinox.p2.director`, is a command-line tool for installing additional software or uninstalling software from an Eclipse-based product. This application is capable of provisioning a complete installation from scratch or simply extending your application. Depending on your needs, it can be executed both inside and outside the target product being provisioned. For example, the next command will install the C/C++ Development Tools (CDT) into Eclipse:

```
<eclipseInstall>\eclipsec.exe
   -application org.eclipse.equinox.p2.director
   -repository http://download.eclipse.org/releases/galileo
   -installIU org.eclipse.cdt.feature.group/<version>
```

You can also use the director to perform installations outside the host Eclipse installation. In this case the provisioning operation happens *outside* the targeted product. The targeted product is not started. This allows you to both modify an existing installation and create a complete installation from scratch, given proper metadata. This also has the advantage that since the targeted product does not need to be started, the provisioning operation can be performed on any platform for any other platform (e.g., on a Linux machine, you can add plug-ins to a windows-based target application).

For example, the command listed here will install the CDT into an existing Eclipse SDK.

```
<eclipseInstall>\eclipsec.exe
   -application org.eclipse.equinox.p2.director
   -repository http://download.eclipse.org/releases/galileo
   -destination c:/someOtherEclipse/
   -profile SDKProfile
   -installIU org.eclipse.cdt.feature.group/<version>
```

In summary, if you need to install anything using p2, use the Software Updates dialog; if you're running headless, the p2 director application can be useful.

21.7 Summary

After reading this chapter, you should have a grasp of p2 terminology and how the major parts of p2 work together. Although with Hyperbola we only scratch the surface of what we can do with p2, we encourage you to explore p2 further and see how you can take advantage of it in your applications. Key to the p2 design is that it is a provisioning platform. It supports a number of common workflows and scenarios out of the box and leaves open the option for you to customize and extend to suit your requirements.

21.8 Pointers

○ The p2 wiki (*http://wiki.eclipse.org/Equinox_p2*) should be your first stop when looking for more information about p2.

○ **Platform Developer Guide > Reference > Provisioning platform, p2.**

○ The OSGi and Equinox book contains more information about p2: McAffer, Jeff, Paul VanderLei, and Simon Archer. *OSGi and Equinox: Creating Highly Modular Java Systems* (Addison-Wesley, 2010), ISBN 0321585712.

CHAPTER 22

Dynamic Plug-ins

Applications are often dynamic. New functions are added, old functions are removed, but the system keeps running. Equinox and Eclipse enable this kind of behavior and the RCP base plug-ins tolerate it, but the ability does not come free—you must follow certain practices to make the most of these scenarios.

This chapter discusses the unique challenges presented to plug-in writers as they attempt to handle the comings and goings of plug-ins in the environment. In particular, the following topics are covered:

- ❍ The notions of dynamic awareness and dynamic enablement
- ❍ Hyperbola as an example of an application requiring dynamic facilities
- ❍ Common dynamic plug-in scenarios
- ❍ Coding practices, mechanisms, and design approaches for handling these scenarios

22.1 Making Hyperbola Dynamic

The main goal here is to make Hyperbola react correctly when plug-ins are added or removed. The first step is to understand how the Hyperbola plug-ins are connected to each other and to plug-ins in upper layers. For example, imagine a scenario where Hyperbola had XMPP MUC capabilities provisioned on the fly or some other scenario like videoconferencing, file transfer, or any other XMPP extension.

Beyond the details of installing the function there are the issues related to getting Hyperbola to notice the arrival of new functions and the management of interconnections when plug-ins are removed from the system—these are the topics addressed in this chapter.

Figure 22-1 gives a rough outline of the Hyperbola plug-ins involved in MUC support and shows how they would relate to each other.

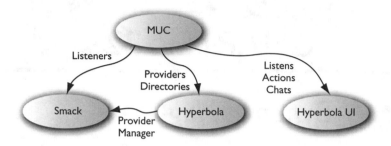

Figure 22–1   Hyperbola plug-in structure

First, let's look at the comings and goings of content handler plug-ins. The MUC support brings along the following elements that need to be linked into Hyperbola:

Providers—These are the packet handlers that might be plugged into Hyperbola via an extension point. They are in turn supplied to Smack using Hyperbola's provider manager.

Listeners—The MUC infrastructure needs to register various listeners, both at the UI level for selection events and such and at the Smack level to monitor message traffic, participant presence, and so on.

UI parts—The MUC UI needs to be displayed and driven by the user. This requires action sets, views, and editors contributed via extension points.

In this scenario the MUC plug-ins register various listeners, and Eclipse or Hyperbola instantiates the various contributed extensions. MUC also explicitly registers GroupChat objects with Hyperbola's SessionManager.

The MUC support has the following requirements:

○ MUC must register and unregister packet handlers as the MUC support is installed or uninstalled.

○ MUC must clean up installed listeners on removal.

○ Hyperbola and Smack must react to the arrival and departure of packet handlers.

○ The Hyperbola UI must react to the coming and going of action contributions.

○ Hyperbola must react to the invalidation of GroupChat objects.

The rest of this chapter looks at how to handle each of these requirements in the context of Hyperbola, the MUC example, and more general scenarios so that you can apply them to your domain.

22.2 Dynamic Challenges

Being dynamic is all about managing the links between types, their instances, and plug-ins. There are two main challenges of trying to operate in a dynamic world: being *dynamic-aware* and being *dynamic-enabled*. Being enabled is relatively straightforward to achieve because it's a self-centered concern—all you have to do is to clean up after yourself. Dynamic awareness is an outward involvement, ensuring that the links you have to others are updated as plug-ins are added to and removed from the system. Because awareness is tricky to get right, most of the remaining text in this chapter outlines techniques and helpers for making your plug-ins dynamic-aware.

22.3 Dynamic Awareness

Dynamic awareness has to do with updating your plug-ins' data structures in response to changes in the set of installed plug-ins; that is, a dynamic-aware plug-in is one that can handle *other* plug-ins coming and going. Dynamic awareness needs to be considered wherever a plug-in has a data structure that is based on types, objects, or contributions from other plug-ins. In the Hyperbola case, extensions such as MUC contribute packet handlers, menu entries, and chat objects. This means Hyperbola definitely has to be dynamic-aware.

Dynamic awareness comes in two flavors: *addition* and *removal*. We say that a plug-in is *dynamic-aware for addition* if it is set up to handle the dynamic addition of plug-ins to the system. Similarly, we say that a plug-in is *dynamic-aware for removal* if it can handle the dynamic removal of plug-ins from the system.

Addition is generally easier to deal with as there is less cleanup. Structures can simply be augmented, caches flushed, or new capabilities discovered on the fly. Handling the removal of relationships may be as easy as flushing some caches, or it may be as complicated as tracking contributed or constructed objects, deleting them as required, and cleaning up afterward.

22.3.1 Dynamic Extension Scenarios

The most common dynamic-awareness challenge is for plug-ins that host extension points. The extensions for a plug-in are woven into the extension registry when the contributing plug-in is *resolved*—when all of its dependencies are met. Similarly, if the plug-in subsequently becomes unresolved, say, when a prerequisite plug-in is removed, its extensions are removed from the registry. Section 27.6, "Bundle Lifecycle," gives more detail on the lifecycle of plug-ins.

Both *executable extensions*—extensions that provide code—and *descriptive extensions*—extensions that provide just information—are problematic for dynamic awareness. The problems arise as a result of caching information from others in your plug-in. Whether it is caching of the extension itself or of any objects created via executable extensions, the cache's coherence must be maintained.

In Hyperbola the core messaging model exposes two extension points that accept providers:

- ❍ `org.eclipsercp.hyperbola.extensionProviders`

- ❍ `org.eclipsercp.hyperbola.iqProviders`

Contributed extensions list the packet types in which they are interested and identify a class to handle such packets. When a matching packet is encountered, the contributed class is instantiated, as well as the instance used to handle the packet. The MUC plug-ins contribute executable extensions to both of these to handle MUC message flow.

If Hyperbola were not dynamic-aware for addition, it might miss the addition of these providers and thus be unable to handle MUC messages. If it were not dynamic-aware for removal, it would miss the removal of the extensions and continue trying to use the MUC handlers even though a function might have been removed. Furthermore, an uninstalled plug-in is not garbage-collected until all instances of its types are collected and all references to its types are dropped; that is, it continues occupying memory until its types and objects can all be collected. Technically, you can continue using existing types and objects even after the plug-in is uninstalled, but the state of the plug-in is not guaranteed—yet another reason why dynamic awareness is important.

The next three sections enumerate dynamic extension scenarios and how to handle them. In general, they revolve around whether or not the supplied extension is descriptive or executable and whether or not you cache values discovered in the registry or consult the registry each time you need something.

22.3.1.1 Scenario 1: No Caching

If your plug-in consults the extension registry each time a value is needed, the burden of being dynamic-aware is substantially reduced. All data lives in the extension registry and is maintained for you. The downside of this approach is that accessing the extension registry is likely slower than consulting an optimized, special-purpose data structure or cache in your plug-in. If the extensions are accessed infrequently, however, this trade-off is reasonable.

For example, Hyperbola can use this approach for the providers, but since there is no caching, the extension registry would be consulted for every data packet that does not have a built-in handler. This is fine for simple chatting, but it is likely not satisfactory if more intensive operations such as file transfer or video-conferencing use the same mechanism.

22.3.1.2 Scenario 2: Extension Caching

The performance of extension lookup can be improved by caching the structure of the extensions. For example, Hyperbola might keep an explicit, in-memory table keyed by packet type where the value is the contributing extension. This table needs to be updated accordingly when a plug-in contributing a handler is added to the system. Similarly, if an existing plug-in is removed, its contributed handlers must be removed. Updating the cache is quite trivial—the changed key/value pair is simply added or removed.

This approach improves the time to access the extensions and find the correct handler class for a given packet, but it suffers on two counts: First, it essentially duplicates the extension structure and data; and second, it requires additional infrastructure to implement dynamic awareness.

In some cases there may be no choice. For example, the Resources plug-in's *markers* extension point takes marker extensions and builds a multiple inheritance hierarchy of marker types. This structure must be computed rather than read directly from the extension registry, so it inherently requires some level of caching. As such, the Resources plug-in must implement some dynamic-awareness support to clean up the cache when the set of resolved plug-ins changes. The cache cleanup is more complicated as the cached markers' data structure is inherently interconnected.

To support this need, the extension registry broadcasts *registry change events* (IRegistryChangeEvent) to registered *registry change listeners* (IRegistryChange-Listener) whenever registry contributions are added or removed. The listeners can then query an *extension delta* (IExtensionDelta) to find out what changed and how. This information is in turn used to update the cached data structures.

Updating the cache need not be a heavyweight operation. For example, if the cache is not critical and rebuilding is not overly expensive, flushing the entire cache on change is reasonable. This approach is sketched in the following code snippet:

```
public class ExtensionManager implements IRegistryChangeListener {
    private Map cache = null;
    public void registryChanged(IRegistryChangeEvent event) {
        cache = null;
    }
```

```
    private Map getCache() {
      Map result = cache;
      if (result == null)
        return initializeCache();
      return result;
    }
    public Object getExtension(String id) {
      return getCache().get(id);
    }
}
```

Registry change listeners are notified serially, but you still have to be concerned about threads accessing the cache while listeners are clearing it. The code in getCache() gets a reference to the cache and uses that reference. The cache may be flushed at any point after that and the *old* value used. That's acceptable because there were no guarantees about ordering here anyway. Notice that this coding pattern closes the window between getting and testing the cache state, and returning the cache as the result.

Of course, another situation may not be that easy. If cache entries are expensive to rebuild, it is better to add and remove entries incrementally. The following snippet shows how to handle change events and traverse the deltas:

```
public void registryChanged(IRegistryChangeEvent event) {
  // Get the changes for one of my extension points
  // and walk through processing the changes.
  IExtensionDelta delta[] = event.getExtensionDeltas(
      "org.eclipsercp.hyperbola", "iqProviders");
  for (int i = 0; i < delta.length; i++)
    switch (delta[i].getKind()) {
      case IExtensionDelta.ADDED :
        // Add an extension in some application-specific way.
        cache.add(delta[i].getExtension());
        break;
      case IExtensionDelta.REMOVED :
        // Remove an extension in some application-specific way.
        cache.remove(delta[i].getExtension());
        break;
    }
}
```

Here the listener queries the delta from the change event for any changes to the org.eclipsercp.hyperbola.iqProviders extension point. For extension additions, you can choose to aggressively populate the cache with the new extensions or just ignore the additions and look for them later when you have a cache miss. For removals, you need to tear down any data structures and remove the extension from the cache.

22.3.1.3 Scenario 3: Object Caching

The packet handler lookup mechanism is still not as good as it could be. Even with extension caching, Hyperbola still has to look up the required class and instantiate a handler for each packet. Assuming the handlers are context-free, one of each type could be cached and used to handle packets as required.

Even if Hyperbola does not cache the extensions themselves—so Scenario 2 is not applicable—Hyperbola may hold on to either the handler class or some created handler instances. This prevents the contributing plug-ins from being properly garbage-collected. Furthermore, the created handlers cannot be left active when the contributor is removed—the handler is likely to be invalid because its plug-in has been shut down and removed.

NOTE

It is instructive to note that the Eclipse UI plug-ins have various extension points that cover each of these scenarios. Before the dynamic-awareness requirements were placed on the UI, it cached most extension information and created objects. In some cases this resulted in duplicate information and inefficiencies. It also inhibited the registry's ability to flush its caches and adapt its space requirements to the current usage patterns. And, of course, it meant that the UI plug-ins would have to do considerably more work to be dynamic-aware. In the end, the approach was to remove the various levels of caching whenever appropriate and rely on direct access to the extension registry or configuration elements.

If Hyperbola is to be dynamic-aware, the handlers it instantiates must be tracked so they can be cleaned up if their contributor is removed. To make it just a little more complicated, it turns out that Smack wants to cache the handler instances for efficiency purposes.

One thing to watch in this scenario is that the cached objects often play a deeper role in the rest of your system; that is, they may be woven tightly into the fabric of the application. The challenge is to understand the interconnections and ultimately reduce them so there is less to clean up.

To update the object structure, you can use the same sort of listener as the one described in Scenario 2. This time, however, the cache contains contributor-supplied objects (i.e., handlers) rather than Hyperbola's internal data structures. In the case of Hyperbola and Smack, it turns out that there is only one reference to any given handler. The registry change listener simply tells Smack to remove all providers contributed by the deleted extension. The following code snippet shows this in action:

```
public void registryChanged(IRegistryChangeEvent event) {
  IExtensionDelta delta[] = event.getExtensionDeltas(
      "org.eclipsercp.hyperbola", "iqProviders");
  for (int i = 0; i < delta.length; i++)
    if (delta[i].getKind() == IExtensionDelta.REMOVED) {
      IExtension extension = delta[i].getExtension();
      IConfigurationElement[] elements =
          extension.getConfigurationElements();
      for (int j = 0; j < elements.length; j++) {
        IConfigurationElement element = elements[j];
        String elementName = element.getAttribute("elementName");
        String namespace = element.getAttribute("namespace");
        ProviderManager.getDefault().removeIQProvider(elementName,
            namespace);
      }
    }
}
```

Notice that each extension may contribute several handlers and the provider list cache has entries for each provider. Note also that the cache is primed lazily so there is no need to handle extension additions as they happen.

To handle more complex situations, the registry supplies utility classes that help with tracking and disposing object references. In the code snippet below, the HyperbolaProviderManager implements IExtensionChangeHandler and registers itself with an IExtensionTracker to get notification of changes in select extensions.

Extension trackers track objects created for an extension. These objects might be the result of using IConfigurationElement.createExecutableExtension() or an object created manually. Either way, the objects share the common trait that they should be cleaned up when the related extension disappears.

org.eclipsercp.hyperbola/HyperbolaProviderManager.java
```
public class HyperbolaProviderManager
    implements IExtensionChangeHandler {
  private IExtensionTracker tracker;

  public void start() {
    initializeTracker();
  }

  private void initializeTracker() {
    tracker = new ExtensionTracker();
    IFilter filter =
        ExtensionTracker.createNamespaceFilter(HyperbolaPlugin.ID);
    tracker.registerHandler(this, filter);
  }

  public void stop() {
    tracker.close();
  }
```

```
public void addExtension(IExtensionTracker tracker,
    IExtension extension) {
  // New extensions are accessed on demand.
}

public void removeExtension(IExtension extension, Object[] objects) {
  for (int i = 0; i < objects.length; i++)
    removeProvider(objects[i]);
}

public Object getProvider (String elementName, String namespace,
    String type) {
  String point = type.equals(IQ) ?
"org.eclipsercp.hyperbola.iqProviders"
    : "org.eclipsercp.hyperbola.extensionProviders";
  IConfigurationElement[] decls = Platform.getExtensionRegistry()
      .getConfigurationElementsFor(point);
  for (int i = 0; i < decls.length; i++) {
    IConfigurationElement element = decls[i];
    if (elementName.equals(element.getAttribute("elementName"))
        && namespace.equals(element.getAttribute("namespace"))) {
      try {
        Object provider = element
          .createExecutableExtension("className");
        tracker.registerObject(element.getDeclaringExtension(),
            provider, IExtensionTracker.REF_WEAK);
        return addProvider(elementName, namespace, type, provider);
      } catch (CoreException e) {
        e.printStackTrace();
      }
    }
  }
  return null;
}
}
```

Looking through the code from the top down, we see that `initializeTracker()`
creates an `ExtensionTracker` and adds the provider manager as a handler. Notice
that the filter used means that the provider manager is notified of changes only
to extension points in the Hyperbola plug-in's namespace. You can narrow this
to individual extension points, but this is good enough here.

The provider manager is notified of changes through `addExtension()` and
`removeExtension()`. Since provider extensions are accessed on demand, we do
not need to do anything for addition.

On removal, however, we do need to ensure that any registered providers are
removed. The `removeExtension()` method receives a list of objects that the
tracker is tracking relative to the given extension. This list is populated by the
provider manager whenever it creates a provider, as shown in `getProvider()`.
Ignoring the detail of how the provider is discovered, at some point a class supplied

by an extension is instantiated. The resultant object is then registered with the tracker using `registerObject()`. The provider is then added to the provider manager's internal data structure. It is this data structure that needs to be updated if the extension is removed. You saw that code in the method `removeExtension()`.

Notice also that the tracker uses weak references (`REF_WEAK`) to track the providers. This ensures that provider objects do not stay live in the system just because they are being tracked.

The use of extension trackers is somewhat overkill in this case, but the example gives you an idea of the mechanism's power. You can use one tracker to track many different extension points and many different objects. You can also use it as your primary data structure by calling `getObjects(IExtension)` to access all tracked objects for the given extension.

22.3.2 Object Handling

Hyperbola is fundamentally listener-based. Clients can listen for packets, connections, authentication messages, and so on. Every time a client adds a listener, it creates a link between itself and Hyperbola. If the client disappears, the link needs to be cleaned up.

NOTE

Here we talk about "listeners," but we really mean "any object given to, and held on by, another plug-in." It could be an actual listener or some other callback handler, a factory, or the implementation of an algorithm. If you register a reference, you should unregister it.

In a perfect world, all clients would be dynamic-enabled and would clean up after themselves. Failure to clean up listeners prevents the uninstalled client from being garbage-collected—this is effectively a leak. Here are a few strategies you can use to handle contributed objects:

Ignore—Assume that everyone is a good citizen and code your notifier robustly to handle any errors that might occur when notifying a stale listener. This tolerates the removal of the contributing plug-in but leaves dangling listeners and has the potential to leak memory.

Validity testing—Include a validity test in your listener API. Before notifying any listener, the notifier tests its validity. Invalid listeners are removed from the listener list. The registering client then invalidates all its listeners when it is stopped. This lazily removes the listeners but still has the potential to leak if the notifier never tries to broadcast to, and thus test the validity of, an invalid listener.

Weak listener list—Using a weak data structure such as WeakReferences or SoftReferences to maintain the listener list allows defunct listeners to simply disappear. Since clients typically have to maintain strong references to their listeners to support unregistering, there is little danger of the listeners being prematurely garbage-collected.

Co-register the source—Rather than just registering the listener, have clients register both themselves and the listener. You then listen for bundle events (see the next section) and proactively remove listeners contributed by bundles being removed.

Introspection—Every object has a class. The plug-in that loaded the class can be found using PackageAdmin.getBundle(listener.getClass()). With this information you can tweak the co-registration approach to use introspection and cleanup. This approach is transparent but can be a bit costly and does not catch cases where one plug-in adds a listener that is an instance of a class from a different plug-in.

In the end, there are no right answers. The different strategies have different characteristics. The point is that you must be aware of the inter-plug-in linkages and make explicit decisions about how they are managed. You should choose the coding patterns that best suit your requirements (speed, space, complexity) and apply them consistently and thoroughly.

NOTE

In all of these cases, there are windows of opportunity for Hyperbola to accidentally attempt to notify a stale listener. As with any notification mechanism, it is important that the notification code be robust enough to handle any errors that might occur. You should consider using Platform.run(ISafeRunnable) to help manage such errors.

22.3.3 Bundle Listeners

BundleListeners are a powerful OSGi mechanism for handling change in a running system. Whenever a bundle changes state in the system, all registered BundleListeners are notified. Listeners typically do the same sort of cache management described earlier and as shown in this snippet:

```
public class Activator implements BundleActivator {
  private BundleListener listener;
  private Object cache = null;

  public void start(BundleContext context) throws Exception {
    listener = new CacheManager();
    context.addBundleListener(listener);
  }

  public void stop(BundleContext context) throws Exception {
    context.removeBundleListener(listener);
  }

  public class CacheManager implements BundleListener {
    public void bundleChanged(BundleEvent event) {
      if (cache == null)
        return;
      synchronized (cache) {
        if (event.getType() == BundleEvent.UNINSTALLED
            || event.getType() == BundleEvent.UNRESOLVED)
          cache.remove(event.getBundle());
      }
    }
  }
}
```

In this case the listener is registered as soon as the bundle is started. It listens for UNINSTALLED and UNRESOLVED bundle events and removes the affected bundle from the cache it is managing. Notice that this code is a good citizen as it removes its listener when the bundle is stopped.

22.4 Dynamic Enablement

Dynamic enablement means being a good plug-in citizen; that is, a dynamic-enabled plug-in is written to correctly handle its own dynamic addition and removal. If you don't clean up, you become a leak. Leaks bloat the system and eventually cause it to run out of memory or become intolerably slow. In the case of MUC support, this means correctly unregistering listeners and other objects that are hooked into the base Hyperbola facilities.

Depending on the implementation of the MUC support, being dynamic-enabled may also mean disposing OS resources. The OS does not know when a bundle is stopped. To the OS, the JVM is still running, so it has to maintain all resources allocated to the JVM process. These include

○ Open files

○ Graphical objects such as images, colors, and fonts

○ Sockets

For MUC support to be dynamic-enabled, it must clean up any such resources as they are removed or stopped.

22.4.1 Cleaning Up after Yourself

Developers often assume that when their plug-in's stop() method is called, Eclipse is exiting. Thus, they do only mild cleanup, if any at all. These plug-ins are not dynamic-enabled. A dynamic-enabled plug-in is one that

- Ensures all objects it registers are unregistered when no longer needed
- Implements a rigorous stop() method as a backstop

Plug-ins that register listeners, handlers, and UI contributions via code or allocate shared resources must take care to unregister or dispose of such objects when they are obsolete. This is just good programming practice. If you call an add() method, ensure that you call the matching remove() when appropriate. Similarly, this should be done for alloc() and free(), create() and dispose(), and so on.

To implement a backstop, your bundle activator needs to know which objects to dispose. This can be hard-coded if the set is rather limited and known ahead of time. For example, if your plug-in holds a socket open, ensure it is closed in the stop() method.

More generally, you can track the objects needing disposal. The code blocks below sketch how this works. The activator maintains a weak set of objects that need disposal. Throughout the life of the plug-in, various disposable objects are added to and removed from the set. When the plug-in is finally stopped, all remaining disposable objects are disposed. The set is weak to avoid leaks in situations where an object is added but not removed, even though it is no longer live.

```
public interface IDisposable {
  public void dispose();
}

public class Activator implements BundleActivator {
  private Map disposables = new WeakHashMap(11);
  private static Activator instance = null;

  public Activator getInstance() {
    return instance;
  }

  public Activator() {
    super();
    instance = this;
  }
```

```java
    public void addDisposable(IDisposable object) {
      disposables.put(object, null);
    }

    public void removeDisposable(IDisposable object) {
      disposables.remove(object);
    }

    public void stop(BundleContext context) throws Exception {
      for (Iterator i = disposables.keySet().iterator(); i.hasNext();)
        ((IDisposable) i.next()).dispose();
      disposables = null;
    }
  }

public class Listener implements IDisposable, IRegistryChangeListener
{
    public Listener() {
      super();
      Activator.getInstance().addDisposable(this);
    }

    public void registryChanged(IRegistryChangeEvent event) {
      // Do some processing here.
    }

    public void dispose() {
      Platform.getExtensionRegistry().removeRegistryChangeListener(this);
    }
  }
```

At the end of the last snippet there is an example of a registry change listener that lists itself as a disposable on creation. You can register the disposable at any point as long as it is added before the plug-in stops. When the plug-in stops, the listener is guaranteed to be removed from the event source—the extension registry in this case. If the listener is removed from the source and not the disposal list, either it becomes garbage and is removed transparently or it is unregistered from the source when the plug-in is stopped. Unregistering a listener that is not registered is a no-op.

NOTE

For clarity and simplicity, we have omitted the synchronization code and error checking needed to make this pattern robust.

22.5 Summary

Dynamic update and addition of functions to running applications is an important part of the total user experience—Hyperbola would be significantly diminished without it. Even with the Runtime mechanisms that support dynamic plugins, being dynamic is not free. It is somewhat akin to concurrent programming. You need to revisit and isolate your assumptions—likely a good thing to do anyway! In many cases the outcome is well worth the effort.

22.6 Pointers

○ The OSGi and Equinox book contains more in-depth information about creating dynamic applications: McAffer, Jeff, Paul VanderLei, and Simon Archer. *OSGi and Equinox: Creating Highly Modular Java Systems* (Addison-Wesley, 2010), ISBN 0321585712.

CHAPTER 23

RCP Everywhere

Up to now, Hyperbola has been contained within a single plug-in and has been designed to run as a stand-alone desktop application. In this chapter we look at restructuring Hyperbola to run in many different environments: on PDAs, in kiosks, or plugged into the Eclipse IDE. In addition, we talk about how to set up your development process to simplify supporting multiple product configurations from one code base. In this chapter we

- ○ Explain why multiple product configurations are interesting in the real world
- ○ Detail the factoring of Hyperbola into multiple product configurations
- ○ Examine how Hyperbola's code is layered to be reusable across multiple configurations
- ○ Provide rules to help refactor your own products
- ○ Outline tips and tricks for designing platforms from your products
- ○ Detail how to identify RCP-friendly plug-ins

23.1 Sample Code

The sample code for this chapter is different from the other samples in this book. Whereas the other samples are either part of the Part II tutorial or derived from it, the code for this chapter is a completely refactored Hyperbola that includes many more features that were not added in the tutorial chapters. The other versions of Hyperbola were pedagogical in nature and left out many details needed to make a real product, such as exception handling and nifty features. This Hyperbola contains it all—it's dynamic-enabled and -aware, has more UI features, and, more important, is split into several plug-ins to support making it run *everywhere*.

23.2 The Scenario

Imagine a scenario where Hyperbola has been deployed in a hospital. Before Hyperbola, staff used e-mail to communicate with units when trying to admit a patient and secure a bed. The hospital has 425 beds and things are pretty hectic. From time to time, registration personnel lost track of requests and patients were forgotten. With Hyperbola installed, front-desk staff can use instant messaging to contact the admitting and bed control departments. Messages appear on all desktops so anyone from the admitting team can respond immediately and confirm the allocation.

During the first few months, Hyperbola became immensely popular and provided a real alternative to e-mail. It was a success and other departments quickly started to see the value of the technology in their own workflows. It was so popular, in fact, that the hospital expanded its requirements—it wanted Hyperbola to run everywhere.

Doctors wanted to use PDAs to contact other doctors, nurses, and lab technicians as they made their rounds. Patients would be able to chat with family and other patients from their in-room touch screen kiosks or from kiosks in the ER and waiting rooms. The research centers and labs wanted to be hooked in. And, of course, the IT department wanted to have Hyperbola extend its developers' Eclipse IDE.

23.2.1 About the Scenario

The scenario painted here is not real but was inspired by a news article about St. Rita's Medical Center (*http://stritas.org*), describing its use of instant messaging in much the way we initially set out this scenario.

Hospitals are diverse environments employing medical professionals, IT staff (i.e., developers and technicians), administrators, and management personnel. Quite by chance we have heard of imaging technicians using Eclipse as an IDE, medical researchers using Eclipse to conduct and manage trials, and administrators using it to track patients. The initial scenario was extended to include these use cases. That having been said, all the Hyperbola configurations described here are very real and run on the 3.5.1 version of Eclipse.

The instant messaging scenarios and Eclipse RCP are even more compelling when you realize that XMPP (the basis of Hyperbola messaging) is extremely extensible and Hyperbola, via Eclipse, exposes this. Hyperbola becomes a platform for collaboration among everyone in the enterprise—videoconferencing, records exchange, lab collaboration—there is no limit.

Even if you are not interested in such a diverse set of runtime environments and functionality, your product may have evaluation, "lite," and enterprise configurations. It may need to stand alone as well as extend other products. The design philosophies for setting up and managing these configurations are similar.

23.3 Product Configurations

There are two types of Eclipse product configurations: stand-alone and extension. The hospital scenario requires both. Stand-alone products are "traditional" RCP applications and have been the focus of this book. Hyperbola's typical configuration is as a stand-alone application. It has its own entry point (i.e., an IApplication and an application extension point), a WorkbenchAdvisor, a product extension, and other product-level branding such as a splash screen and a customized launcher. This type of product is used at the nursing station, on administrator desktops and kiosks, and in PDAs.

By contrast, an extension product is one intended to extend an existing stand-alone product. As such, extension products do not have an application entry point or the same degree of customization typically associated with a stand-alone product—extension products do not have their own WorkbenchAdvisors. This configuration is used for the hospital's developers and other tool-based workers who are already using another Eclipse-based product such as the Eclipse IDE.

One of the selling points of Hyperbola in this scenario is that Hyperbola can simply be integrated with other Eclipse-based applications as the hospital's needs expand.

Figure 23-1 shows how common groups of plug-ins, called *framework plug-ins*, are used in combination with product-specific plug-ins to build both extension and stand-alone product configurations. The various configurations share a common set of framework plug-ins and optionally add their own customization plug-ins to the mix. Most of the functionality of the product lives in the framework plug-ins and is reused in all product configurations. The trick is deciding what to include in the framework plug-ins and what to put in the product configurations.

Supporting a wide range of product configurations is a very powerful advantage—it gives your product more exposure and provides users with access to your product when and where they need it. This sounds great on paper, but in reality, creating a fully configurable product suite is easiest if you make it an explicit design objective. As in any software system, if reuse is not a concern, the code will not be reusable.

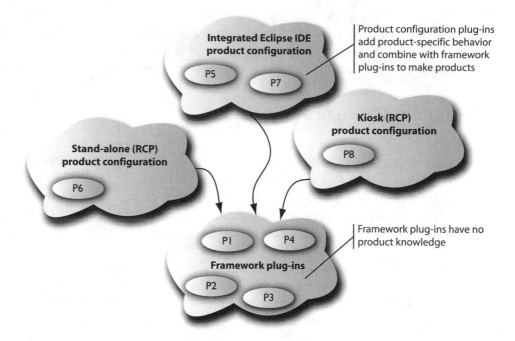

Figure 23-1   A product with several product configurations

The essence of promoting reuse is the ability to split Hyperbola into several configurations that run in different environments but share as much code as possible. This section looks at restructuring Hyperbola as several plug-ins. We detail what goes in each plug-in, plug-in naming conventions, and implications for building and packaging. The rest of the chapter then builds on this refactoring and describes and compares Hyperbola configurations for the different execution environments.

23.3.1 Restructuring Hyperbola

The best way to understand the restructuring of Hyperbola is to contrast the prototype structure built in Part II with the multiconfiguration structure developed here. Figure 23-2 shows the Hyperbola plug-in structure in the prototype. The product information is embedded in the monolithic Hyperbola plug-in that includes the advisors, the product description, and the basic messaging infrastructure. This is a natural organization that is easy to understand—perfect for a prototype.

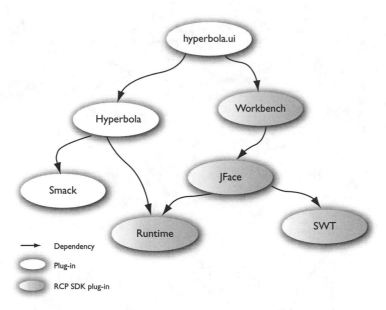

Dependency

Plug-in

RCP SDK plug-in

Figure 23–2 Hyperbola that supports one product configuration

Figure 23-3 shows Hyperbola after being restructured to support multiple configurations. The figure shows framework plug-ins and product configurations. The framework plug-ins contain the Hyperbola application logic, Contacts view, and chat editor, with all product-specific files and code removed.

Product configurations pull together the product-specific and common parts of Hyperbola to run in a particular environment. They typically include some number of product plug-ins that coordinate and position the various elements defined in the framework. The configurations also include features that capture the complete set of required plug-ins.

The key point here is that the UI components and actions are implemented *once* and then reused in different product configurations. The benefits cannot be overestimated. As the rest of this chapter highlights, this approach clarifies the structure of the system and enables the use of your function in vastly different scenarios. The amount of code specific to individual configurations is kept to a minimum and sometimes is completely eliminated.

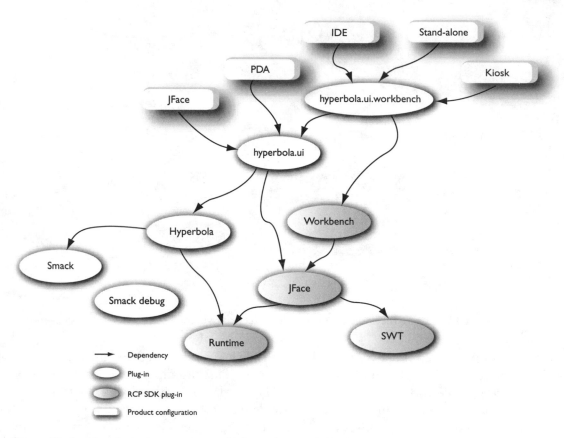

Figure 23–3 Hyperbola that supports multiple product configurations

23.3.2 Hyperbola Projects

There are three basic configurations of Hyperbola at the root of the four execution environments in the hospital scenario:

Workbench—a stand-alone product that includes the UI Workbench

JFace—a stand-alone product that relies only on JFace

IDE—an extension product that plugs into an existing Eclipse IDE

These configurations can be tweaked and parameterized to fit all the use cases outlined previously. For example, both the desktop and kiosk requirements can be met using the Workbench configuration. Before digging into that, let's look at the basic configurations. Figure 23-4 shows the Hyperbola feature and plug-in projects needed to support all of the hospital's requirements.

```
⊞  🗁  org.eclipsercp.hyperbola
⊞  🗁  org.eclipsercp.hyperbola.discovery.update
⊞  🗁  org.eclipsercp.hyperbola.feature.base
⊞  🗁  org.eclipsercp.hyperbola.feature.debug
⊞  🗁  org.eclipsercp.hyperbola.feature.ide
⊞  🗁  org.eclipsercp.hyperbola.feature.jface
⊞  🗁  org.eclipsercp.hyperbola.feature.muc
⊞  🗁  org.eclipsercp.hyperbola.feature.pocketpc
⊞  🗁  org.eclipsercp.hyperbola.feature.workbench
⊞  🗁  org.eclipsercp.hyperbola.kiosk.adaptor
⊞  🗁  org.eclipsercp.hyperbola.muc
⊞  🗁  org.eclipsercp.hyperbola.product.ide
⊞  🗁  org.eclipsercp.hyperbola.product.jface
⊞  🗁  org.eclipsercp.hyperbola.product.pocketpc
⊞  🗁  org.eclipsercp.hyperbola.product.workbench
⊞  🗁  org.eclipsercp.hyperbola.splash
⊞  🗁  org.eclipsercp.hyperbola.ui
⊞  🗁  org.eclipsercp.hyperbola.ui.workbench
⊞  🗁  org.eclipsercp.hyperbola.update
⊞  🗁  org.eclipsercp.kiosk
⊞  🗁  org.eclipsercp.kiosk.win32
⊞  🗁  org.jivesoftware.smack
⊞  🗁  org.jivesoftware.smack.debuggers
```

Figure 23–4 Hyperbola projects with support for multiple product configurations

23.3.3 Project Naming

This list looks daunting at first but makes sense once you understand the naming convention. The word *product* is used in a name to identify plug-ins that adapt infrastructure pieces to product configurations (e.g., the org.eclipsercp.hyperbola **.product**.workbench plug-in contributes the actions and views for Hyperbola as a regular RCP stand-alone application).

As we mentioned in Section 14.3, "Defining Features," and Chapter 21, "Installing and Updating with p2," the word *feature* is used to distinguish feature projects from all others. Again, the challenge here is that the feature and plug-in namespaces are separate, so technically you can have plug-ins and features with the same name. This, of course, would be very confusing, not to mention the difficulty of managing plug-in project names in the workspace.

Finally, the framework or infrastructure plug-in names have unqualified names that reflect their functional content (e.g., org.eclipsercp.hyperbola.ui contains a generic UI function for Hyperbola).

This naming convention may not suit your environment, but it has been useful in the development of Hyperbola and in helping explain the structures in this book.

23.3.4 Why So Many Projects?

You may still be asking why there are so many projects. The short answer is that each exists because either there is a need for reuse of that function or there is a corresponding product configuration defined by that project. This leads to our first rule:

Rule 1: Top-level feature—Have a top-level feature and plug-in for every product configuration.

Following this rule allows you to describe the complete set of plug-ins required for each product configuration in a form that is clear, complete, and understood by various parts of the Eclipse tooling. There are several other benefits to this approach:

❍ Simply exporting the feature is one way to package the configuration.

❍ The feature or root plug-in also serves as an anchor point for creating product definitions (`.product` files).

❍ Features are required if you plan to use the Eclipse Update Manager in your deployments.

❍ Features are also required if you want to use PDE's automated build mechanisms.

❍ A top-level plug-in serves as the home for the feature branding content.

Underneath these top-level structures, Hyperbola's feature set is factored into as many reusable features as needed. Don't go overboard or there will be one feature for every plug-in. Remember, features are lists of plug-ins to build or deploy together—they are an abstraction to help you structure and manage your world. If you have 100 plug-ins that always go together, one feature should suffice. On the other hand, if you want to manage only handfuls of plug-ins at a time, use more features.

Go back now and look at the list of projects in Figure 23-4 and compare it to the structure shown in Figure 23-3—there is a project in the list for every element in the structure diagram. This is a simple and straightforward approach.

23.4 Hyperbola Product Configurations

Now that we have covered some of the organizational strategies that help with the management of product configurations, let's take a more detailed look at the configurations needed for Hyperbola in the hospital scenario. The configurations shown in Figure 23-3 are reviewed in subsequent sections.

Just to recap, the product as a whole is defined by a product configuration that contains the following elements:

○ One or more product definitions (assuming a stand-alone scenario).

○ UI contributions such as action placement. These may be done in code or declaratively in the `plugin.xml`, depending on the situation.

○ A list of plug-ins to include in the configuration. This is optionally specified using one or more features. Using features as outlined in Chapter 14, "Adding Software Management," is highly recommended.

○ Product-level branding, such as launcher icons, window images, and splash screens.

○ A product configuration definition (`.product`) file that serves as an anchor point for all of the above.

Each product configuration should have a clear definition of where these elements are coming from and what they contain. Given that you have a top-level feature for every product configuration, it is reasonable to put your product definition files in the corresponding feature. In fact, if you do that, the product definition will identify exactly one feature in its list of contents—its containing feature. This is a convenient correspondence that helps keep things simple.

23.4.1 The JFace Configuration

As the name implies, the UI of this configuration is based solely on JFace. It does not include the UI Workbench. The primary motivator for this configuration is footprint—a smaller footprint decreases both download speed and space on disk. Remember that "on disk" means "in memory" on many PDA devices.

This Hyperbola configuration nets out to about 3MB total (excluding the JRE). This is clearly a reasonable size for a download as well as for a footprint on a PDA or desktop. Since the Eclipse RCP plug-ins require only the CDC Foundation class libraries, a JRE capable of running this is only about 6MB. So Hyperbola, complete and ready to run, is under 10MB—still quite a reasonable download. It gets even better when you consider that most of the bulk is reusable components such as the VM, SWT, JFace, and OSGi, which may already be on the machine or device.

Figure 23-5 shows the content of the `org.eclipsercp.hyperbola.product.jface` plug-in. Its `plugin.xml` contributes both product and application extensions. The product defines some branding for Windows, Linux, and so on, while the application simply opens a Hyperbola window.

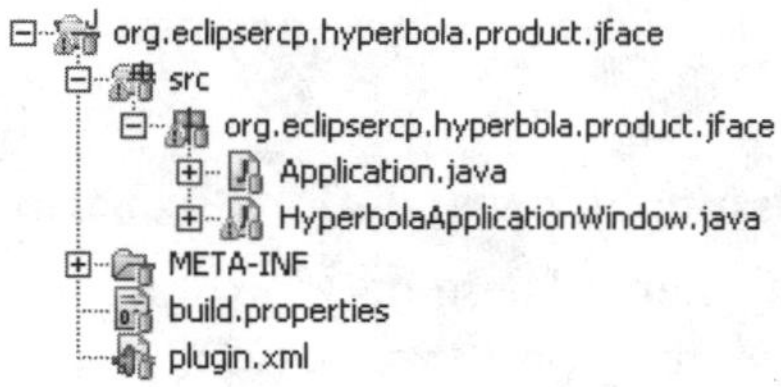

```
org.eclipsercp.hyperbola.product.jface
  src
    org.eclipsercp.hyperbola.product.jface
      Application.java
      HyperbolaApplicationWindow.java
  META-INF
  build.properties
  plugin.xml
```

Figure 23–5   JFace product plug-in contents

The Hyperbola window defines its own layout that contains just a ContactsViewer and populates the menu bar and context menus with actions. Both the ContactsViewer and the needed actions are the same ones used in the other configurations. They are defined in the org.eclipsercp.hyperbola.ui framework plug-in and are simply composed here.

The other component of the configuration is the feature that gathers the relevant plug-ins. The feature is shown here. Notice that it *includes* the Hyperbola base feature (all the bits of Hyperbola that are common) and picks and chooses only those plug-ins from the Eclipse RCP base feature that are needed for this scenario. Notice that the splash screen is in a separate plug-in as some configurations such as the PDA do not need one.

org.eclipsercp.hyperbola.feature.jface/feature.xml
```
<feature
    id="org.eclipsercp.hyperbola.feature.jface"
    label="JFace Hyperbola Chat Client"
    version="1.0.0">

  <includes id="org.eclipsercp.hyperbola.feature.base"/>
  <plugin id="org.eclipsercp.hyperbola.product.jface"/>
  <plugin id="org.eclipsercp.hyperbola.splash"/>
  <plugin id="org.eclipse.core.commands"/>
  <plugin id="org.eclipse.core.runtime"/>
  <plugin id="org.eclipse.jface"/>
  <plugin id="org.eclipse.osgi"/>
  <plugin id="org.eclipse.swt"/>
  <plugin id="org.eclipse.swt.win32.win32.x86"/>
  <plugin id="org.eclipse.swt.linux.gtk.x86"/>
  <plugin id="org.eclipse.swt.macosx.carbon.ppc"/>
  ...
</feature>
```

This feature also contains a product configuration file that captures all the relevant information from launcher name and icons to product feature set and splash screen.

23.4.2 The PDA Configuration

PDAs are characterized by their reduced footprint and screen real-estate requirements. The obvious choice here is to deploy the JFace configuration discussed previously to the handheld device. It is a reasonable size and runs well on the reduced SWT drops available for Pocket PCs. The main changes needed are to update the JFace configuration feature to include the new SWT fragment and supply a new application that sets up the JFace window screen dimensions appropriately.

Of course, there is also work to be done in adapting Hyperbola's UI to the metaphors and practices native to the device. In some cases this may mean reducing functionality or changing the use of wizards or dialogs. The code samples supplied provide some of the initial structure needed but do not fully integrate Hyperbola into the Pocket PC world.

23.4.3 The Extension Configuration (IDE)

Integrating Hyperbola into an existing product such as the Eclipse IDE turns out to be relatively simple. Figure 23-6 shows that the IDE configuration consists entirely of static markup—no code is required. Everything needed is already defined, according to the rules set out in this chapter, in the base Hyperbola UI-related plug-ins.

Figure 23–6 IDE product plug-in contents

The `plugin.xml` contributes and positions numerous actions and various views, perspectives, preference pages, and wizards, all using extensions. The plug-in does not contribute an application or product definition as it is destined to extend an existing IDE-based product.

NOTE

The extension contributions used here are specific to the IDE product. For example, the `menubarPath` value used for action contributions may differ from product to product. This is what makes this example so interesting. The integration is done entirely in static markup that places actions and other contributions in the context of the base product. Adapting to a different product may mean defining some additional markup.

The feature definition for this configuration simply lists the Hyperbola base feature of the relevant Hyperbola plug-ins. The standard Eclipse plug-ins are required but are assumed to be there as part of the RCP feature in the base product.

```
org.eclipsercp.hyperbola.feature.ide/feature.xml
<feature
    id="org.eclipsercp.hyperbola.feature.ide"
    label="IDE Hyperbola Chat Client"
    version="1.0.0">

  <requires>
    <import feature="org.eclipse.rcp" version="3.1.0"/>
  </requires>
  <includes id="org.eclipsercp.hyperbola.feature.base"/>
  <plugin id="org.eclipsercp.hyperbola.ui.workbench"/>
  <plugin id="org.eclipsercp.hyperbola.product.ide"/>
</feature>
```

Since this configuration is an extension product, it does not need a product configuration file—the branding and launcher information contained in the configuration file is not relevant here. The feature itself is sufficient to enable exporting or building the product configuration. Notice also that the feature *requires* the RCP base feature rather than *including* it; that is, the RCP feature is assumed to be present.

23.4.4 The Workbench Configuration

The stand-alone Workbench configuration is the most complex of the three configurations. It gathers together a more diverse set of plug-ins and more attention is paid to branding. It's very close to the Hyperbola you developed in Part II—it has all the telltale signs of a typical RCP application such as Workbench advisors, its own application, and branding.

Figure 23-7 shows the content of the product plug-in. Notice that the bulk of the classes are advisors that define the product's look and feel, action placement, and such. Like the other configurations, any required UI elements such as actions and views are defined in the generic, product-independent framework plug-ins and merely identified and positioned here. This version of Hyperbola also supports nonrectangular windows, so there is a set of advisors for that.

Since this is a stand-alone configuration, the plug-in contributes product and application extensions and defines an application class as the main entry point. The plug-in also contributes Intro extensions and content (e.g., introContent.xml and the css folder) to help first-time users.

The top-level feature shown below includes the org.eclipse.rcp feature—the base set of plug-ins that constitute the base Eclipse RCP—and the

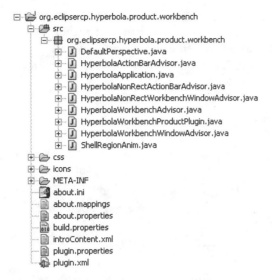

Figure 23–7 Hyperbola Workbench product plug-in

`org.eclipsercp.hyperbola.feature.base` feature. It also identifies several additional plug-ins, including the splash screen and MUC support.

`org.eclipsercp.hyperbola.feature.workbench/feature.xml`

```
<feature
        id="org.eclipsercp.hyperbola.feature.workbench"
        label="Hyperbola Workbench Chat Client"
        version="1.0.0">

    <includes id="org.eclipse.rcp"/>
    <includes id="org.eclipsercp.hyperbola.feature.base"/>
    <plugin id="org.eclipsercp.hyperbola.ui.workbench"/>
    <plugin id="org.eclipsercp.hyperbola.muc"/>
    <plugin id="org.eclipsercp.hyperbola.splash"/>
    <plugin id="org.eclipsercp.hyperbola.product.workbench"/>
</feature>
```

The feature project contains a product configuration file that captures the relevant product information, including the launcher name and icons, product feature set, and splash screen. This product configuration is largely the same as that of the JFace configuration but with different product/application settings.

23.4.5 A Hyperbola Kiosk

Using Eclipse as a base for kiosk systems is attractive. It is modular, updatable, and highly customizable. The sample code for the chapter contains a generic kiosk mechanism for Eclipse. This mechanism is not specific to Hyperbola; that is, the hospital scenario does not call for a chat kiosk but rather a kiosk that has chat capabilities. The actual patient or emergency room kiosk may well have many more facilities, from specifying food preferences and ordering movies to checking waiting times.

NOTE

Kiosk or "restricted desktop" mode is not part of Eclipse. We have developed the simple structure outlined but leave the code for locking down the desktop and restricting users to product developers. Different OSs and window systems have varying levels of support for locked-down modes, and this is beyond the scope of our work here.

Hyperbola in the kiosk scenario is interesting because it is not stand-alone; the kiosk infrastructure is the base product. Yet we still want Hyperbola's window branding to show through—Hyperbola must still supply the various advisors. To get this effect, the stand-alone Workbench configuration is wrapped in an adapter that supplies its unique window and action bar advisors.

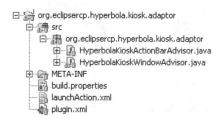

Figure 23–8   Kiosk adapter plug-in

Figure 23-8 shows the content of the Hyperbola kiosk adapter plug-in. As per the kiosk mode setup, the adapter contributes the Hyperbola perspective to the kiosk desktop and identifies the window advisor to use for Hyperbola windows. This way, whenever the user runs Hyperbola from the kiosk desktop, he or she is just opening a Hyperbola perspective, which in turn is branded using the supplied advisors. This is an important point. The different products installed on the kiosk desktop can all be branded differently.

The advisors supplied here are subclasses of the originals found in the Workbench product configuration, but they have been tweaked to present a slightly different look and set of actions. Of course, some care must be taken with the actions made available. For example, the regular Hyperbola ExitAction exits the Workbench, and thus Eclipse, and thus the entire kiosk mechanism. Such dangerous actions are simply trimmed out of the Hyperbola menus by the HyperbolaKiosk-ActionBarAdvisor.

23.5 Code Structure

Now that you have seen the general structure of Hyperbola, let's look at how classes, images, views, editors, viewers, and extension points are split among plug-ins. The ability to build multiple configurations of Hyperbola hinges on the plug-in dependencies being crafted to allow reuse across the different product configurations. You do not want to write actions or dialogs twice!

Dependency management is perhaps one of the biggest challenges when designing componentized systems. Developing Hyperbola as one monolithic tower of functionality was initially practical, but the approach does not scale well—deployment options are limited and code reuse is inhibited. On the other hand, Hyperbola as a set of loosely coupled and smaller plug-ins is much more flexible.

Factoring Hyperbola into a set of interdependent plug-ins is a step in the right direction but is really only the beginning of the journey. Exercising good API hygiene and rigorous dependency management improves coding efficiency by minimizing ripple effects and increases the ability to reuse plug-ins in different application configurations. This leads to the most important rule to remember:

Rule 2: Manage dependencies—Minimize and layer plug-in dependencies.

Developers need to be conscious of the interdependencies they are establishing. Dragging 20MB of code into your system just to get one small bit of functionality does not make sense—but it happens.

23.5.1 Hyperbola Layering

Let's start with a quick overview of the functionality included in each of the refactored Hyperbola framework plug-ins. The significant difference between this structure and the Hyperbola in the rest of the book is the refactoring of Hyperbola into core and UI plug-ins. The UI plug-ins are further factored into JFace- and Workbench-related plug-ins. Otherwise, the remainder of the refactoring involves moving all the contributions into the product configurations.

`org.eclipsercp.hyperbola`—This plug-in contains the data model and XMPP protocol operations that do not require UIs. This is the core messaging infrastructure that enables the use of Hyperbola messaging in a wide range of environments, all the way down to being embedded in medical instruments.

`org.eclipsercp.hyperbola.ui`—This plug-in contains all the base UI features that do not require the Workbench. This includes the actions, `ContactsViewer`, `ChatViewer`, preference pages, images, and wizards. This plug-in contains most of the interesting code needed to implement a Hyperbola UI and is based on JFace. In the Part II Hyperbola, the `ContactsView` and `ChatEditor` contained both the container and viewer logic. This made it hard to show a chat in a window or view. In this version of Hyperbola, we split the basic UI constructs from their placement in the UI. This provides more flexibility in placing different UI elements (e.g., in dialogs, windows, views, or editors).

`org.eclipsercp.hyperbola.ui.workbench`—This plug-in wraps the basic UI pieces from the Hyperbola UI plug-in. This includes a `ContactsView` wrapper for the `ContactsViewer` and a `ChatEditor` wrapper for the `ChatViewer`. Both of these are contributed via the Workbench extension points. This plug-in defines these UI elements but *does not* place them in the Workbench—that is left to a product plug-in. This plug-in does, however, contribute a set of command definitions for the actions that are defined by the base UI plug-in. This enables Workbench key bindings. The only extensions defined in this plug-in are to declare the views, editors, and commands.

The remainder of this section explains some guidelines that were used to arrive at this structure that you can use in your own products.

23.5.2 Workbench Contributions

When you contribute to various Workbench extensions, such as action sets, preference pages, perspective extensions, views, and editor actions, they must be contributed to a specific product. In general, you cannot write a plug-in that integrates tightly with the IDE and then expect to integrate it unchanged with a random RCP-based application.

The issue is not mechanical but rather practical—the UI context for the plug-in is different. Menu bar paths may be different, the integration points may disappear, and your plug-in needs to adapt. Figure 23-9 illustrates this situation. The plug-in on the left may physically load and run if dropped into the product's `plugins` directory, but it is pure luck if its menus, toolbars, and views appear correctly.

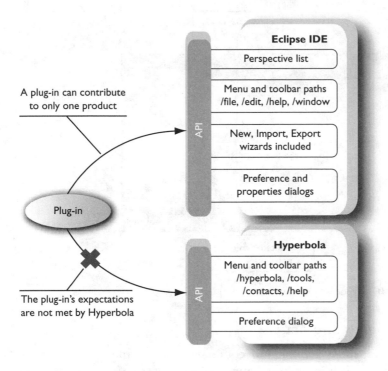

Figure 23-9   Plug-ins need to know their integration partners

To develop UI plug-ins that can be used in different applications, you must separate the implementation of UI elements from their contributions.

Rule 3: Framework plug-ins—Minimize Workbench contributions in framework plug-ins.

The goal is to define as much as possible, in generic terms, without committing to the details of how the UI component is placed or contributed. Leave that to the product plug-ins.

What happens when you don't follow this rule? Figure 23-10 shows what happens when you add the `org.eclipse.ui.editors` and `org.eclipse.ui.externaltools` plug-ins to the Hyperbola Workbench product configuration. Of course, if you are adding the plug-ins, you likely want to use their functionality, but you may want to present it differently. For example, these plug-ins are designed to be used in Eclipse IDE-based products and they place their actions accordingly. This is not a bug in the plug-ins but rather a choice that was made by the plug-in designers.

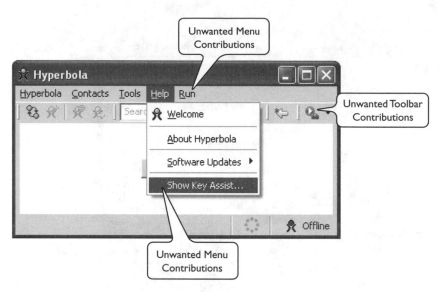

Figure 23–10   Hyperbola running with a non-framework plug-in

23.5.3 Commands and Actions

In Hyperbola, most actions and commands are defined in the `org.eclipsercp`
`.hyperbola.ui` plug-in and implement `IAction`. `IAction` is used because it is part
of JFace—the action definitions do not needlessly drag the Workbench into product
configurations. This supports the desire to run Hyperbola on PDAs and smaller
environments. Another common layering technique is to define *operations*—
essentially non-UI actions that perform work on your data model. You can then
wrap one or more operations into appropriate actions that appear in the UI. This
has the bonus of further decoupling behavior from how it is modeled in the UI.
Another strategy is simply to use commands as discussed in Chapter 18 if you
have no desire to use actions. Commands already provide the necessary decoupling required to work in a variety of environments. Command definitions can
exist in the `org.eclipsercp.hyperbola.core` plug-in, and the UI-specific definitions like key bindings can exist in the `org.eclipsercp.hyperbola.ui` plug-in.

23.5.4 Key Bindings

Because of differences in the key binding support in SWT and the Workbench,
key bindings are left to the product configuration using the actions. In the case of
a configuration running without the Workbench, accelerators are set on the
action itself using SWT accelerators.

```
addContactAction = new AddContactAction(shell, session);
addContactAction.setAccelerator(SWT.CTRL | 'N');
```

When running with the Workbench, commands are created for each action and then used to add key bindings, as shown in the following snippet. Notice that the same Action class is used, but instead of being initialized with an accelerator, the action's ID is registered with the Workbench, as discussed in Chapter 12, "Adding Key Bindings."

```
addContactAction = new AddContactAction(shell, session);
register(addContactAction);
```

When designing for multiple products, you often have to define multiple sets of key bindings, one for each product. For example, with Hyperbola, the stand-alone configuration defines its own key configuration, but when Hyperbola is used to extend the IDE, it has to define key bindings in the context of the IDE to increase integration and avoid key binding collisions.

23.5.5 Views and Editors

As we have seen, to enable maximum flexibility in building applications without the Workbench, most of the UI elements are created using only JFace primitives. At first this is a bit shocking—people often think, "I'm implementing a view" or "I'm implementing an editor." Rather, we have focused on implementing the basic UI elements that match the domain problems, and then we have looked at views and editors as containers for these elements. Once again, there is a separation between the UI elements and how or where they are presented—you design the UI components separately from the containers and then plug them together as needed.

Put another way, you should build the core UI elements based on your application's data models and user interactions and then use a decoupling pattern, such as Inversion of Control (IoC),[1] to enable the use of these elements in different scenarios.

Rule 4: UI decoupling—Decouple UI components from their container.

In Hyperbola, the ContactsViewer and ChatViewer UI components are built on a few base concepts, such as XMPP sessions and SWT composites. In Work-

---

1. IoC is a design pattern that helps teams avoid the dependency hell that results when an application grows into a large pseudo platform without taking care to adequately decouple logic. One well-known synonym for IoC is DIP—Dependency Inversion Principle *(http://en.wikipedia.org/wiki/Dependency_injection)*.

bench-based configurations these base UI components are used to build views and editors, whereas in JFace-based configurations they are simply added to the top-level shells as appropriate.

23.5.6 Wizards, Preferences, and Property Pages

Hyperbola's wizards, preference pages, and property pages follow the same pattern as actions—they are defined using only JFace and then contributed by the product configurations. When these pages are used in Workbench configurations, they are adapted to implement the appropriate Workbench interface (e.g., `IWorkbenchWizard`, `IWorkbenchPreferencePage`, and `IWorkbenchPropertyPage`). Adapting a JFace component to be compatible with a Workbench extension is extremely easy. You just wrap the JFace component with the appropriate Workbench interface and implement the one or two Workbench-specific operations.

In JFace configurations these pages are simply placed in the relevant wizard or preference page dialogs. Note that property pages are really just preference pages shown for a specific object. This allows you to arrange the pages differently in different product configurations, for example, keeping all preference pages flat in one, not organized in another, or grouped into a main category in another.

23.5.7 Optional Dependencies

Instead of layering dependencies by splitting plug-ins, you can layer dependencies within the same plug-in using optional dependencies.

> **Rule 5: Optional dependencies—Use optional dependencies for intra-plug-in layering.**

This capability was outlined in Chapter 21. Hyperbola does not use optional features, but the EMF core plug-in contains a good example of how this works and where to use it. In the EMF core plug-in, all the code related to the Eclipse Resources plug-in is collected into one package. The EMF core model is designed around an abstract data model that accommodates both `java.io.File` and `org.eclipse.core.resources.IResource` data objects. The dependency on the plug-in `org.eclipse.core.resources` is then marked as optional, as shown below. Since the bulk of the EMF code is isolated from the Resources API, EMF continues to run even if the Resources plug-in is not installed—EMF clients are never able to pass in or expect back Resources objects.

```
org.eclipse.emf.ecore/plugin.xml
Require-Bundle:
  org.eclipse.core.runtime,
  org.eclipse.core.resources;resolution:=optional
```

This approach allows the same EMF plug-in to be used in both stand-alone RCP configurations and Eclipse IDE-based configurations. It also helps prevent a combinatorial explosion of plug-ins in each layer of your system. The disadvantage of layering within a plug-in is that unused code may be shipped with an application. In this case EMF's Resources support is not separable and must be shipped with all EMF systems.

23.5.8 Icons and Images

When we first started breaking up Hyperbola, we found that images were being duplicated in several places. In addition to being a waste of disk space, this approach is very hard to manage—we were always forgetting to update images here or there and were still finding old images months after the refactoring.

The alternative is to treat images like code and share them. In the refactored world, all Hyperbola images are in `org.eclipsercp.hyperbola.ui` and are simply used by other plug-ins. Image sharing in code is done by exposing an `ImageRegistry` on a common plug-in and using it from clients. For example, the pattern shown here occurs in several places in Eclipse itself:

```
Hyperbola.getDefault().getSharedImages().getImage(IMG_ONLINE);
```

URLs can be used to share images in declarative files and extension definitions. For example, the following URL indicates that the image at `icons/pub/chat.gif` in the `org.eclipsercp.hyperbola.ui` plug-in should be used as the icon for the editor:

```
org.eclipsercp.hyperbola.ui/plugin.xml
<extension point="org.eclipse.ui.editors">
  <editor
    class="org.eclipsercp.hyperbola.internal.ui.ChatEditor"
    icon=
      "platform:/plugin/org.eclipsercp.hyperbola.ui/icons/pub/chat.gif"
    default="false"
    name="Chat"
    id="org.eclipsercp.hyperbola.chateditor"/>
</extension>
```

TIP

Just like sharing code, sharing images should be done only though API; that is, if a plug-in exposes its images as API, you can use them. If not, you should not. Uncontrolled reaching into other plug-ins and using images (or any file, for that matter) exposes you to more change than you might like.

23.6 Designing a Platform

Not only has Hyperbola been refactored to run in many configurations, it has also turned into a *platform* for messaging clients. The progression from a simple product to a platform involves pushing functionality down into framework plug-ins. The focus shifts from shipping one specific product to understanding what functionality is generic and how other products can be built around that functionality. That is the nature of the platform.

To build a platform, you should first consider the rules outlined in this chapter. Your plug-ins need to be framework plug-ins to have a platform. Given a set of framework plug-ins, you should look for ways to add extensibility.

One way is to use standard coding techniques and APIs. Section 27.5, "Services," introduces the OSGi notion of *services* as a further means of making a system extensible. Throughout this book you have been using Eclipse's extension registry mechanism, as discussed in Section 2.5.3, "Extension Registry."

This section covers the use of extension points to allow other plug-ins to customize or extend your framework plug-ins. To recap, the advantages of extensions and extension points are the following:

- ❍ They are declarative. Declarative extensions can be filtered, checked, and composed. This improves UI scalability and enables various approaches for presenting, scoping, and filtering contributions.

- ❍ They promote lazy loading of code. Plug-ins contributing extensions can have a presence in the system without requiring their code to be loaded.

- ❍ They can be added and removed at runtime. As you saw in Chapter 22, "Dynamic Plug-ins," this means that plug-ins can be added and removed after the application has started.

- ❍ The mechanism can be used to contribute code and/or data.

23.6.1 Extension Points

By now you are familiar with contributing extensions to the extension points defined by the Eclipse platform, but you have not actually written one of your own. Adding an extension point involves first declaring the extension point in a plug-in and describing it to other plug-ins. The plug-in is then coded to use contributed extensions as set out in the description.

Creating an extension point declaration is done using the **Add...** button on the **Extension Points** page of the relevant plug-in editor. Figure 23-11 shows an example of declaring the `iqProviders` extension point in the `org.eclipsercp`
`.hyperbola` plug-in. The **Extension Point Schema** file location field is filled in

automatically. Schemas are used to describe the expected structure of extensions contributed to an extension point. They describe everything from the set of tags and attributes to the kinds of values placed in the attributes. See **Platform Plug-in Development Guide > Tasks > Creating an extension point schema** in the online Help for details on schemas and using the schema editor.

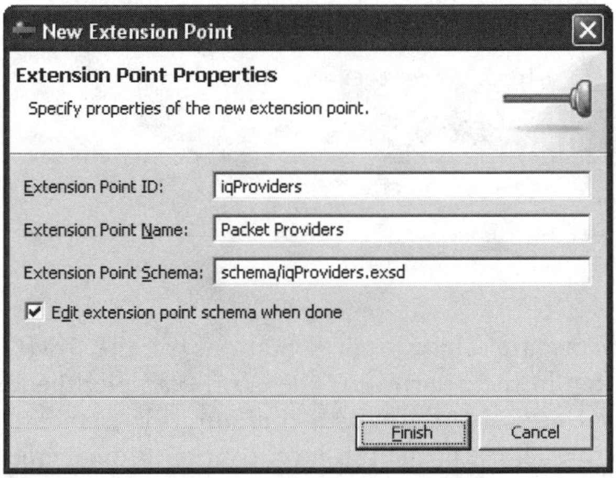

Figure 23–11   New extension point declaration

Once the extension point has been defined, various plug-ins can contribute extensions that conform to the schema. The snippet below shows the XML markup for an iqProviders extension. Typically, developers use the facilities on the plug-in editor's **Extensions** page to define and manage their extensions.

```
org.eclipsercp.hyperbola.muc/plugin.xml
<extension
     name="MUC IQ Providers"
     point="org.eclipsercp.hyperbola.iqProviders">
  <provider
     elementName="x"
     namespace="jabber:x:conference"
     className="org.jivesoftware.smackx.GroupChatInvitation$Provider"
  />
```

As you saw earlier, the Eclipse Runtime maintains a registry that connects extensions and extension points. The org.eclipsercp.hyperbola plug-in can access extensions contributed to its iqProviders extension point by accessing this extension registry, as shown in the snippet below. The extension point's fully qualified ID is used to get a set of *configuration elements*.

```
org.eclipsercp.hyperbola/HyperbolaProviderManager
public IQProvider getProvider (String elementName, String namespace) {
  String point = "org.eclipsercp.hyperbola.iqProviders";
  IConfigurationElement[] decls = Platform.getExtensionRegistry()
      .getConfigurationElementsFor(point);
  for (int i = 0; i < decls.length; i++) {
    IConfigurationElement element = decls[i];
    if (elementName.equals(element.getAttribute("elementName"))
        && namespace.equals(element.getAttribute("namespace"))) {
      try {
        return
            (IQProvider) element.createExecutableExtension(
              "className");
      } catch (CoreException e) {
        e.printStackTrace();
      }
    }
  }
  return null;
}
```

Configuration elements are object representations of the XML elements under the <extension> tag in the plugin.xml files; for example, the <provider> markup in the preceding example surfaces as a configuration element. Accessing the registry as shown returns a list of the top-level configuration elements across all extensions in the given extension point. This is convenient where the identity of the extensions and the number of configuration elements per extension are not important.

The iqProviders extension point requires extensions to identify a class that implements an IQProvider interface. The details are not particularly important. The key point is that the Hyperbola plug-in is allowing other plug-ins to contribute code that is used to extend the capabilities of Hyperbola—in this case, to handle different messaging protocols.

The preceding snippet scans the set of configuration elements and when it finds an applicable one, it instantiates the class identified in the extension by calling createExecutableExtension(String). The result object is then used according to the contract of IQProvider.

23.6.2 Extension Factories

In the previous example the class to instantiate was given as a fully qualified class in the className attribute of the extension. This requires the identified class to implement a public zero-argument constructor and restricts the initialization that can be done on the resultant object. Another approach is to use an *extension factory* to create or discover the desired object. Factories are useful as they allow more complex discovery and initialization. For example, executable extensions can be discovered using OSGi service lookup or Web service discovery. Factories hide these implementation details from the extension point.

If the class identified in an extension implements `IExecutableExtensionFactory`, the factory class is instantiated and the instance is given the information in the related configuration element. It then uses this information to determine what kind of object to return. For example, the snippet below from Section 17.3, "Standard Workbench Actions," shows the UI's `ExtensionFactory` being used to create a progress view. Note that the UI's extension factory is free to decide how it creates the requested progress view. The Javadoc for `IExecutableExtension` and the individual factories details the acceptable syntax of the data following the factory name in the markup.

org.eclipsercp.hyperbola/plugin.xml
```
<extension point="org.eclipse.ui.views">
   <view
       class="org.eclipse.ui.ExtensionFactory:progressView"
       ...
```

23.6.3 Named and Anonymous Extensions

Extension IDs are, in some cases, optional. For example, the `provider` extension discussed previously did not have an `id` attribute. Extensions to the Runtime's `applications` extension point, however, do require IDs, as shown in the snippet below. Both anonymous and named extensions are prevalent in Eclipse.

org.eclipsercp.hyperbola/plugin.xml
```
<extension
    id="application"
    point="org.eclipse.core.runtime.applications">
  <application>
    <run class="org.eclipsercp.hyperbola.Application"/>
  </application>
</extension>
```

The choice of whether or not to have named extensions is completely up to the plug-in defining the extension point. In the case of the Runtime's `applications` extension point, the ID is required because the Runtime is given an application ID to run by the user or the product. It needs to find the extension that matches that ID, instantiate the associated class, and run it. Having a system-managed ID is convenient.

In the case of most UI extension points and those in Hyperbola, extensions are treated anonymously. Anonymous extensions allow many contributions, each in its own configuration element, in one extension. This is sometimes simpler and clearer for developers.

The benefit of having IDs on extensions is that you can call the optimized `IExtensionRegistry` method, `getExtension(String, String)`, to fetch a specific extension as opposed to having to traverse or remember the extensions yourself. For example, the `HyperbolaProviderManager` code snippet in the previous section repeatedly iterates over all contributed configuration elements to find the appropriate provider, whereas the Runtime can simply access the registry and directly look up the required application extension.

23.7 RCP-Friendly Plug-ins

A common question is how to tell if a plug-in is *RCP-friendly*. We use the term *friendly* as a synonym of what we've also been calling *framework* plug-ins. These are plug-ins that are designed to work in *any* product. Most people ask this question when they are building an RCP product and want to use someone else's plug-ins. The simple answer is that if a plug-in manages its dependencies and uses optional dependencies appropriately, it is a framework plug-in and is RCP-friendly.

Unfortunately, Eclipse does not include markup to quickly identify plug-ins that have these characteristics. The easiest way for you to tell if a plug-in follows Rule 2 (Manage dependencies) and Rule 3 (UI decoupling) is to look for the following:

○ Open the `plugin.xml` for the plug-in you are examining and look at the set of plug-ins it requires. If it requires a product, for example, the Eclipse IDE, it is not a framework plug-in.

○ Next, look at its extensions for specific references to toolbar or menu paths, preference pages, or other contributions that place elements in the UI. In general, views and editors are acceptable since they do not appear in the UI unless they are explicitly placed. See Section 23.5.3.

A common misconception is that depending on plug-ins from outside the RCP base, for example, the Resources plug-in, means you are not RCP-friendly. This is not necessarily true. If the prerequisite plug-in's dependencies follow the rules, it is RCP-friendly. The `org.eclipse.core.resources` plug-in *is* in fact RCP-friendly.

23.8 Summary

After reading this chapter, you should have a solid base on which to build your own set of product configurations. Even though Hyperbola is a relatively small example, the hospital scenario shows how it can be expanded to have a real impact across enterprises.

By following our rules, we ended up with something that is extremely flexible. These rules can be applied to any size product:

Rule 1: Top-level feature—Have a top-level feature for every product configuration.

Rule 2: Manage dependencies—Minimize and layer plug-in dependencies.

Rule 3: Framework plug-ins—Minimize Workbench contributions in framework plug-ins.

Rule 4: UI decoupling—Decouple UI components from their containers.

Rule 5: Optional dependencies—Use optional dependencies for intra-plug-in layering.

Emboldened readers are now able to build and deploy applications in a vast array of scenarios, from integration into existing products (e.g., IDEs) to field-force PDAs and customer kiosks.

23.9 Pointers

○ The OSGi and Equinox book contains more in-depth information about OSGi and using Eclipse in a variety of environments: McAffer, Jeff, Paul VanderLei, and Simon Archer. *OSGi and Equinox: Creating Highly Modular Java Systems* (Addison-Wesley, 2010), ISBN 0321585712.

CHAPTER 24

Building Hyperbola

Up to this point you have been using the PDE **Export Product** wizard to create end-user-deliverable versions of Hyperbola. As the Hyperbola product grows and has more configurations, and there are more developers working on it, there's a pressing need for automated, reproducible, and accessible builds.

Building Eclipse systems by hand is somewhat challenging and tedious. The compile-time classpath for any given plug-in includes the code from all its prerequisites. Just computing the classpath and build order is hard. Mix in variations such as different source locations (e.g., projects in the workspace, checked out from CVS in the file system, or both) and the myriad of output packaging options and you need help.

So far, PDE's **Export** wizards have insulated you from most of these details. Unfortunately, those wizards are hard to automate, as you have to click around in a UI to launch a build. It is also hard to make repeatable as it depends on the contents of the user's workspace. Product teams and communities need *release engineering* builds that are automated and more rigorous.

Fortunately, the same underlying infrastructure used for exporting plug-ins, features, and products from the workspace can be used to perform release engineering builds of Eclipse-based products. This mechanism is called *PDE Build*. PDE Build compiles and packages a set of features and plug-ins according to the dependency information in their manifests and a set of control parameters. The output is an archive or directory structure that can be deployed either directly, via an update site, or even using Java Network Launch Protocol (JNLP). In short, PDE Build helps you create regular and reproducible builds.

This chapter dives into PDE Build and guides you through setting up an automated build for Hyperbola. We cover

○ Configuring and running a product build

○ Running feature-based builds

○ The different `build.properties` files associated with building

○ Customizing the build scripts

○ Automatic version number qualification

24.1 What Is PDE Build?

At its heart, PDE Build is an Ant script generator. It takes in a collection of plug-ins and features, as well as their manifests and `build.properties` files, and generates a set of Ant build scripts. These scripts are run to produce a build. The export operations you have been doing throughout this book use PDE Build under the covers.

PDE Build is quite flexible. It can consume hybrid mixes of plug-ins and features that are prebuilt and those that remain to be built. Some may be included in the final output, and others may not. The output of a build can also vary from plug-ins in directories to update sites and ZIP archives of JAR'd and signed plug-ins and features.

The build mechanism builds plug-ins and features, or cascades of the transitively included features and plug-ins starting at a root feature. Cross-platform building is also supported.

The main benefit of PDE Build is that it brings all this together into one relatively simple process. Developers express their normal runtime dependencies in manifest files and a mapping from development-time structure to runtime structure in the feature and plug-in `build.properties` files. PDE Build does the rest.

Key to this process is the automatic generation of the build scripts. Using the input manifests and `build.properties`, PDE generates Ant scripts that copy identified files and compile identified code using a classpath derived by effectively flattening the plug-in dependency graph. The runtime classpath for a plug-in is defined as a complex graph of plug-in dependencies as described in its manifest file. The classes referenced at runtime are also needed at compile time, so the compile-time classpath is similarly complex. PDE Build uses the Runtime's plug-in resolution and wiring mechanisms to derive the classpath for each plug-in being built.

As we mentioned before, you have already been using PDE Build if you followed along with the feature- or product-exporting examples. When you use these actions, you are, under the covers, running PDE Build. The rest of this chapter explores the use of PDE Build in a release engineering setting, where reproducibility and automation are key concerns.

24.2 Plug-in `build.properties`

Before we get too far into PDE Build itself, let's recap what you have used as a build process so far in the book. Since the PDE wizards have been doing most of the work, you have seen the `build.properties` file for the Hyperbola plug-ins and features. This file is exposed on the **Build** page of the plug-in and feature editors.

The role of the `build.properties` file is to map development-time structures in a plug-in's project onto the structures described in the plug-in's manifest and needed at runtime. For example, by adding elements to the **Binary Build** section, you are stating that the deployable version of the plug-in must include those elements.

The various PDE editors and wizards take care of managing binary build entries for most of the common cases. When you add images or other runtime resources to a plug-in, you have to update the binary build information in the `build.properties` to ensure that they are included in the build result.

`build.properties` HELP

The various `build.properties` file options are documented in **Help > PDE Guide > Reference > Build Configuration > Feature and Plug-in Build Configuration**.

24.2.1 Control Properties

The plug-in editor's **Build** page helps set up common build-related properties. To add more advanced properties, you have to edit the `build.properties` file directly using the plug-in editor's **build.properties** page. When you set up automated builds, these advanced build properties become more relevant. Here we provide an example properties file and Table 24-1 for reference. See the PDE Help for a full list of build properties.

```
build.properties
bin.includes=plugin.xml, META-INF/, ., icons/, html/
bin.excludes=html/private*.html
source..=src/
extra..=library.jar
```

Table 24–1   Plug-in Build Properties

Property	Description
bin.includes	A comma-separated list of development-time resources that are copied into the plug-in when it is built. This list must include the plug-in metadata files MANIFEST.MF and plugin.xml, if present, as well as any code. Use "." when you want a JAR'd plug-in or plug-in-relative paths to get directory-based plug-ins. Be sure to list additional files such as icons, message catalogs, and licensing files.
	Entries in the list are expressed using Ant pattern syntax. The most common patterns include * (e.g., *.html) and a trailing "/" (e.g., html/) to indicate that a directory structure is to be included.
	The bin.includes line in the example declares that plugin.xml and the contents of the META-INF, icons, and html directories should be included in the binary version of the plug-in.
bin.excludes	A comma-separated list of development-time resources that should not be included in the binary version of this plug-in. The entries in this list override those in the bin.includes list. Excludes list entries are also expressed as Ant patterns.
	The bin.excludes line in the example declares that all "private" HTML files should not be included in the deployable runtime version of the plug-in.
source.\<library>	The set of development-time resources to compile to create the Java executable element identified by \<library>. Here, \<library> is typically "." to indicate the plug-in itself. Alternatively, it is the name of a JAR file. The value is a comma-separated list of Ant patterns that identifies files passed to the Java compiler during the build.
	The source.. line in the example declares that the files in the src directory are compiled and the output is placed in the root of the plug-in as indicated by the second "." in source...
extra.\<library>	A comma-separated list of elements to add to the compile-time classpath when compiling the source as defined in a corresponding source.\<library> property. This is commonly needed when you have JARs you compile against but do not ship and do not include in any of the plug-ins this plug-in requires.

PDE uses this information, in combination with the plug-in manifests, to generate a build.xml script for each plug-in that is then run during the build process.

24.2.2 Using Custom Build Scripts

You can opt out of build script generation by supplying your own build.xml and selecting **Custom Build** on the **Build** page of the plug-in editor, as shown in Figure 24-1.

If you opt for a custom build.xml, you take complete responsibility for implementing the build script that has all the right targets and that does all the

Build Configuration

☑ Custom Build

Figure 24–1   **Custom Build** selection

right things. A better solution is to use custom callbacks, as described in Section 24.5.1, "Customizing the Build Scripts."

24.3 Setting Up a Builder

To see how this works in practice, let's set up a managed build process for Hyperbola. The code for this build is based on Chapter 14, "Adding Software Management." The client consists of the product definition, several Hyperbola-related features and plug-ins, and various prebuilt plug-ins from the target platform.

- ❍ Start by creating a simple project for the build scripts using **File > New... > Project > General > Project**. Call it `hyperbola.builder`.
- ❍ In the file system, navigate to your Eclipse IDE install and go to the `org.eclipse.pde.build` plug-in. For example, look in `c:\ide\eclipse\plugins\org.eclipse.pde.build_3.5.1` if your IDE is installed in `c:\ide`.
- ❍ Copy both `templates\headless-build build.properties` and `scripts\productBuild productBuild.xml` to the `hyperbola.builder` project. These are templates for the files used to control builds. In the subsequent sections the templates are filled in and used to build the product.

The builder's `build.properties` file is quite different from the other `build.properties` files you have seen so far. It contains key/value pairs that define the input parameters to the build itself. The `productBuild.xml` is an Ant build file that controls the building of products. Having both files here allows you to override or add behavior to the build.

24.3.1 Tweaking the Target for PDE Build

In addition to setting up the builder project, you must also ensure that the required binary dependencies are available. In particular, you need the right executable launcher for the platform you are building—PDE Build cannot assume it's already present or know where it is.

The executables for all supported platforms are available in the *executables feature*. This feature is not intended to be installed; rather it contains native executables for a wide range of platforms. The easiest way to get the executables feature is to get the Eclipse *delta pack*. We saw the delta pack in Section 3.5, "Target Platform Setup." Ensure that your target has the delta pack.

With the target set up, we have everything needed to run PDE Build. Unfortunately, as of this writing, PDE Build does not directly support the use of target definition files in its execution. This means that you must manually manage your binary prerequisites. To help with this we have included a simple tool, the **Target Export** wizard, that collects all of the plug-ins and features from the current target and places them in a single directory. You can then use the output of this tool in PDE Build. Run it now as follows:

○ Select **File > Export > Plug-in Development > Target definition** to export the plug-ins and features that constitute the current target.

○ Choose a directory for the Hyperbola binary dependencies, for example, c:\hyperbola_prereqs, and click **Finish**.

24.3.2 build.properties

Now that the build structure is in place, it needs to be customized to build our plug-ins. Following is a summary of the changes needed to the template build.properties that was copied to the builder project. Some of the properties shown are needed later but are listed here to show the big picture. If a property is not listed here, it does not need to be changed. Of course, you should replace the file system locations appropriately.

```
hyperbola.builder/build.properties
# Product and packaging control
product=/hyperbola.products/hyperbola.product
runPackager=true
archivePrefix=hyperbola

# Build naming and location
buildDirectory=${user.home}/eclipse.build
buildType=I
buildId=TestBuild
buildLabel=${buildType}.${buildId}

# base identification and location
skipBase=true
base=C:/hyperbola_prereqs
baseLocation=${base}
baseos=win32
basews=win32
basearch=x86
pluginPath=

# cross-platform building
configs=win32, win32, x86 & linux, gtk, x86
```

```
# CVS access control
skipMaps=true
mapsRepo=:pserver:anonymous@example.com</path/to/repo>
mapsRoot=<path/to/maps>
mapsCheckoutTag=HEAD
skipFetch=true

# Publish the build to a p2 repository.
p2.gathering = true
p2.metadata.repo = file://${buildDirectory}/repository/hyperbola
p2.artifact.repo = file://${buildDirectory}/repository/hyperbola
p2.compress = true

# Java class libraries and compile controls
#bootclasspath=${java.home}/lib/rt.jar
compilerArg=
```

Let's look at each of these values and see how they affect the build. There are, of course, many more properties, but understanding these should give you an idea of how the build goes together and the level of control you have. The main information in `build.properties` covers roughly seven areas of concern in the build process. Each of these is detailed in one of the following sections. They are presented roughly in decreasing order of interest; that is, you have to set up the values in the first section but may not have to change things in the last section.

24.3.2.1 Product and Packaging Control

These properties describe what you are building, the branding you want, and the shape of the output:

product—The location of the product file that describes what is being built. The value takes the form /<id>/path/to/.product, where <id> is the ID of the feature or plug-in that contains the .product file.

archivePrefix—The specified prefix is added to the beginning of all paths in the output archive. This gives you control over the shape of your product when it is extracted on the user's machine.

24.3.2.2 Build Naming and Locating

These properties allow you to control the working directories and names for the build output:

buildDirectory—The absolute file system path where the build is executed. All build input is downloaded to this location, and all compilation and composition are done under this directory. You should keep this path reasonably short to avoid exceeding file system length limits. This is the only directory to which the builder needs write permissions.

buildType—An arbitrary string used to name the build output and identify the type of build. For example, organizations often have nightly (N) builds, maintenance (M) builds, integration (I) builds, and so on. There is no need to limit this value to a single character.

buildId—The buildId is used in composing the name of the output archives. Typically, the ID conveys some semantics, such as TestBuild or CustomerX, or a full date stamp, such as 20090109.

buildLabel— This is used in the naming of the output directories. The buildLabel is typically a composition of buildType and buildId.

24.3.2.3 Base Identification and Location

Most of the time you are building a set of plug-ins that sits on top of some base. Think of the base as the target for your workspace—it is all the plug-ins and features that you are *not* developing yourself. This may be the Eclipse SDK, or it may be a whole product suite if you are a value-add developer. The properties here allow you to set where the base is, what's inside, and how to get it if it is not present:

base—The location of the product on which the build is based. This is used to determine if the base needs to be installed. If the directory exists, its contents are assumed to be complete. If it does not exist, the build system fetches the base and installs it at this location. In the example, we set the base to be the target platform that was exported using the **Target Definition Export** wizard.

baseLocation—The location of the actual base install against which the plug-ins being built are to be compiled. This is the logical equivalent of the target used during development—all the plug-ins and features come from elsewhere. Note that this can be a full Eclipse install using link directories. This is specified separately from base because different products have different internal structures. For example, the standard Eclipse downloads include an eclipse directory in their structure. In these cases the baseLocation is just ${base}/eclipse. In our case we exported our target to c:/hyperbola_prereqs so we can use that directly as both the base and the baseLocation.

baseos, basews, basearch—The os, ws, and arch values for the base set of Eclipse components in the install. Eclipse installations may support many platform configurations, so these settings are used to clarify the set of base plug-ins, fragments, and features to use. If there are several configurations in your base, pick one and assign the properties accordingly.

skipBase—A marker property that, if set, indicates that fetching the base should be skipped.

pluginPath—A list of locations where additional plug-ins and features can be found. Entries in this list are separated with the platform-specific separator.

24.3.2.4 Cross-Platform Building

This property helps control cross-platform building:

configs—An ampersand-separated list of target machine configurations for which you want to build. Each configuration consists of an os, ws, arch triple, such as win32, win32, x86. The build process creates a separate output for each configuration. If the configuration is not set or is set to *, *, *, the build is assumed to be platform-independent. In this example we are building Hyperbola for Linux GTK and Windows.

24.3.2.5 Software Configuration Management (SCM) Access Control

The build process can automatically check out the source for the build from an SCM system. The location of the source is dictated by *map* files, which can themselves be checked out from an SCM system. The following properties let you bootstrap that process by setting basic locations and SCM tags to use:

mapsRepo—The SCM repository that contains the map files needed for the build.

mapsRoot—The path in the SCM mapsRepo to the map files for the build.

mapsCheckoutTag—The SCM tag used to check out the map files. The map files, in turn, control the SCM tags used for checking out the plug-in and feature projects.

skipMaps—A marker property that, if set, indicates that the map files are local and should not be checked out.

fetchTag—A property used to override the SCM tags defined in the map files. For example, setting it to HEAD is useful for doing nightly builds with CVS.

skipFetch—A marker property that, if set, indicates that the source for the build is local and should not be checked out.

24.3.2.6 Publishing a Product Build to a p2 Repository

Depending on the way you wish to deploy your software, a p2 repository may be more convenient than platform-specific ZIP files. The following properties control the creation of a p2 repository containing the results of the build. The repositories can be used by others to provision Hyperbola and can also be used by PDE Build to build plug-ins intended to run on top of this product.

p2.gathering—A marker property that, if set, indicates that all the build artifacts should be gathered into a p2 repository. During a product build, the p2 repositories are created in a temporary directory and the repository must be explicitly mirrored to the final output directory.

p2.metadata.repo—The location where the metadata repository is written if p2.gathering is on.

p2.artifact.repo—The location where the artifact repository is written if p2.gathering is on.

p2.compress— A marker property that, if set, indicates that the repositories should be compressed if p2.gathering is on.

The artifact and metadata repository properties should identify repository locations under a shared parent. Later in Section 24.5.2, "Repositories and Additional Dependencies," we may need to use the location of the parent as the repoBaseLocation.

24.3.2.7 Java Class Libraries and Compiler Control

Of course, the build is primarily concerned with compiling Java code. The properties here allow you to define the compilation classpath as well as various arguments passed to the Java compiler:

bootclasspath—The default boot classpath to use when compiling code. This should point to all the classes that are expected to be on the boot classpath when the product being built is run. The value is a semicolon-separated list of file system locations.

compilerArg—A list of arguments to pass to the compiler.

Managing Ant Properties

PDE Build makes heavy use of Ant constructs and in particular Ant properties. The properties listed here are treated as normal Ant properties, so ${variable} substitution is supported. Also, values such as the bootclasspath are passed directly to the associated Ant task.

The so-called *marker* properties are ones that are simply set or not set. The value is irrelevant and not checked. For simplicity, we tend to show the value as true, but setting the value to false does *not* unset the property.

It is often convenient to use build.properties to set up defaults and then override these values for a particular build. This is done by setting properties from the command line using the -D<prop>=<value> VM argument syntax.

For more advanced settings, see the Ant documentation at *http://ant.apache.org*.

24.4 Running the Builder

Now that the builder is defined, you are ready to build Hyperbola. For most of this chapter we assume that you are working locally and already have the Hyperbola code in your workspace. For simplicity, we also assume that you exported your target to `c:/hyperbola_prereqs`. With these assumptions, the builder does not need to access a server. To set this up, make sure that `build.properties` has the following settings:

hyperbola.builder/build.properties
```
skipBase=true
base=c:/hyperbola_prereqs
baseLocation=${base}
skipMaps=true
skipFetch=true
```

Because the plug-ins and features are not being checked out from CVS, you need to create the build directory by hand. In the following steps replace `${buildDirectory}` with the value from the `build.properties`, for example, `${user.home}/eclipse.build`.

- Create `${buildDirectory}`.
- Create `${buildDirectory}/plugins`.
- Create `${buildDirectory}/features`.
- Copy the required feature projects to the `features` directory and the plug-in projects to the `plugins` directory. Figure 24-2 indicates which projects are needed and what the layout should look like in the end.

COPY FILES EVERY TIME

Since the builder is not checking files out of CVS every time, the projects must be copied every time their content changes.

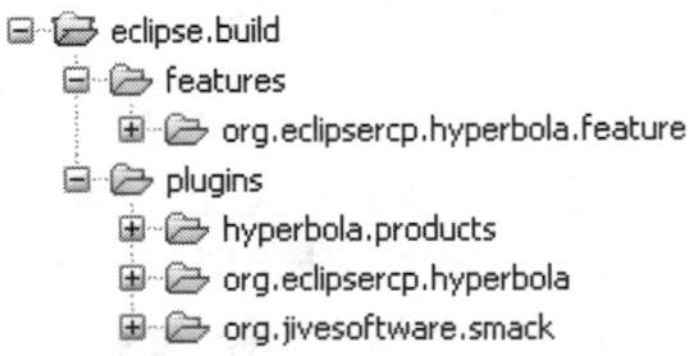

```
eclipse.build
  features
    org.eclipsercp.hyperbola.feature
  plugins
    hyperbola.products
    org.eclipsercp.hyperbola
    org.jivesoftware.smack
```

Figure 24–2   Build layout

Now run the builder. The easiest way is to use a command prompt and change your working directory to the location of your builder. For example, if you have been following along, the builder files `build.properties` and `productBuild.xml` are in the `hyperbola.builder` project in the workspace. Once there, run Eclipse's AntRunner application using the command line shown below. The `-buildfile` argument specifies the build file to run. Here we use `productBuild.xml`. The `-consoleLog` argument ensures that you can see the output messages as the build progresses.

```
cd <workspace location>\hyperbola.builder
c:\ide\eclipse\eclipse.exe
   -application org.eclipse.ant.core.antRunner
   -buildfile productBuild.xml -consoleLog
```

CHOOSE THE HEADLESS ANTRUNNER

Make sure you choose `org.eclipse.ant.core.antRunner` and not `org.eclipse.ant.ui.antRunner` when launching the build.

The build produces the structure shown in Figure 24-3 in the `${buildDirectory}/${buildLabel}` directory. In our example the output goes in `${user.home}/eclipse.build/I.TestBuild`. This directory contains one archive per configuration that was built and a p2 repository. Each archive is a complete, ready-to-run Hyperbola client.

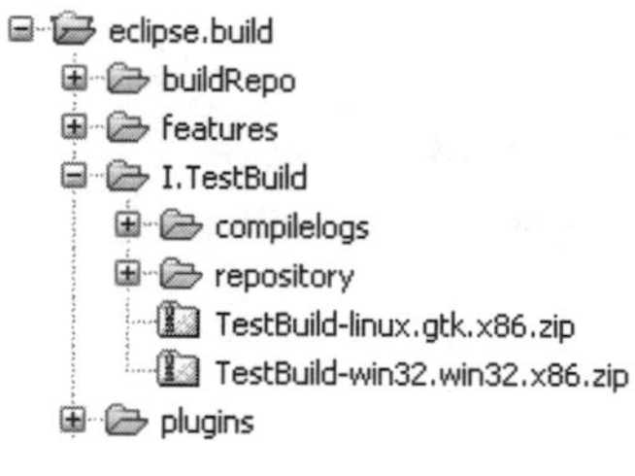

```
⊟ 🗁 eclipse.build
   ⊞ 🗁 buildRepo
   ⊞ 🗁 features
   ⊟ 🗁 I.TestBuild
      ⊞ 🗁 compilelogs
      ⊞ 🗁 repository
          🗋 TestBuild-linux.gtk.x86.zip
          🗋 TestBuild-win32.win32.x86.zip
   ⊞ 🗁 plugins
```

Figure 24–3   Build output

The `compilelogs` directory contains the build logs for each plug-in that was built. The various assembly and packaging scripts in the build directory are left over from the build and can be deleted. They are automatically deleted and regenerated each time the builder is run.

The `repository` directory contains the p2 repository from which Hyperbola can be installed.

Debugging the Build

Builds are notoriously hard to get right. Spelling mistakes, commented lines, and typos all contribute to builders that just do not work. The Eclipse IDE includes comprehensive support both for authoring Ant files and for debugging Ant scripts. There are a few quirks to setting this up for PDE Build, so the steps are detailed here.

You must have the root build script in your workspace. If you have been following along, you should have the product build script in your workspace. If not, you can import it:

○ Use the **Import > Plug-ins and Fragments** wizard to import the
   org.eclipse.pde.build plug-in.

○ In the wizard, set the **Plug-in Location** to your IDE location (e.g.,
   c:\ide\eclipse) and choose **Import As > Binary projects**.

○ Click **Next**, select the org.eclipse.pde.build plug-in, and **Add** it to the list.

○ Click **Finish**.

Now you have to set up a launch configuration to run PDE Build's build.xml, the root of the build mechanism:

○ Navigate to org.eclipse.pde.build/scripts/productBuild/
   productBuild.xml and use the context menu's **Debug As > Ant Build...**
   to open the Ant launch configuration dialog.

○ On the **JRE** page, select **Run in the same JRE as the workspace**.

○ On the **Properties** page, uncheck **Use global properties...** and use **Add
   Property...** to add a property called builder, as shown in Figure 24-4.

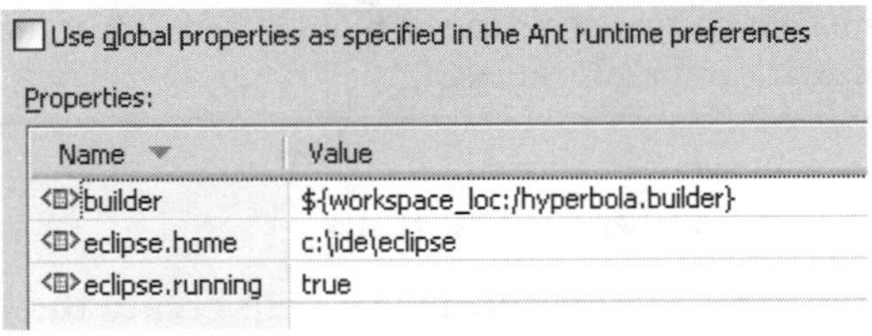

Name ▼	Value
builder	${workspace_loc:/hyperbola.builder}
eclipse.home	c:\ide\eclipse
eclipse.running	true

☐ Use global properties as specified in the Ant runtime preferences

Properties:

Figure 24–4 Ant builder properties

○ Click **Debug** and run the build.

Everything should work as before. Now you can open PDE's Ant scripts, such as productBuild.xml, and add breakpoints by double-clicking in the left margin or using the **Toggle Breakpoint** context menu. Debug the build again. When the breakpoint is hit, you can inspect Ant properties and step over and into Ant statements.

24.5 Tweaking the Build

Now that you've seen the basics of how to build a system, here are some of the more common and useful customizations. These are not mandatory but are generally useful.

24.5.1 Customizing the Build Scripts

The `templates` directory in the `org.eclipse.pde.build` plug-in has many useful script templates. These should be copied into your builder and customized as needed. Table 24-2 presents an overview of the most relevant templates. For more information on customizing a build, see the Eclipse online Help documentation at *http://help.eclipse.org* and navigate to **Plug-in Development Environment Guide > Tasks > PDE Build**.

Table 24–2   PDE Build Templates

Script	Description
`headless-build/customTargets`	This script provides Ant targets that are called between the major phases of the build. There are pre- and post-targets for events such as fetching the source, generating build scripts, packaging, etc.
`customAssembly`	This script provides customization points that will be called during the assembly and packaging phases of the build.
`features/customBuildCallbacks`	The build callbacks template enables features to provide their own custom steps to the build. The feature custom build callback supports only the `gather.bin.parts` target.
`plugins/customBuildCallbacks`	The custom build callbacks template enables plug-ins to provide their own custom steps to the build. There are a number of targets that can be customized.

24.5.2 Repositories and Additional Dependencies

For Hyperbola, we used the **Target Export** wizard to help create the base against which everything was compiled. However, this approach may not be ideal when configuring a build server. You may have various headless scripts and other facilities to get all the parts you need. If the dependencies end up in different directories, the `pluginPath` and `repoBaseLocation` properties can be used.

The `pluginPath` property points to a separated list of additional locations in which PDE Build can look for prebuilt dependencies.

The repoBaseLocation points to a single directory that may contain one or more p2 repositories either in zipped or extracted form. When this property is used, you must also specify the transformedRepoLocation property and point it to a writable location on disk. PDE Build copies the contents of the base repositories and transforms them into a runnable form. All the plug-ins and features in the transformedRepoLocation are then added to the pluginPath.

RUNNABLE REPOSITORIES REQUIRED

Repositories generally come with all their content as JARs. Features, and some plug-ins, however, need to be expanded on disk to be useful at build time; that is, they need to be in *runnable form*. PDE Build ensures that the given base repositories are transformed appropriately.

24.5.3 *Fetching from an SCM System*

PDE Build can also be configured to check out the source for the plug-ins and features being built from an SCM system, such as CVS or SVN. It uses the notion of *map files* to map feature and plug-in IDs onto SCM repository locations and tags. This allows you to identify the top-level product or feature and let PDE Build figure out that you really mean "check out a particular location in a particular repository using a particular SCM tag." A map file contains a series of lines, each of which takes the following form:

```
feature|fragment|plugin@elementId=\
    cvs tag,:method:user@host/path/to/repo \
    [,cvs password][,path/in/repository]
```

CVS IS AN EXAMPLE

In this discussion we use CVS as the example SCM system. The syntax and concepts are equivalent if you are using SVN or some other SCM system.

If the path in the repository, the last element, is not specified, PDE Build assumes that the element to fetch is at the root of the repository and has the same name as the element. If your artifacts are in a different location in the repository, you must specify the complete path from the root of the repository to the directory containing the contents of the element, that is, the full path of the parent directory of the feature.xml or plugin.xml. Note that this path must *not* start with a "/".

In your ${buildDirectory} create a maps directory, and in that directory create a hyperbola.map file that contains the following entries. Be sure to replace the repository information and the tag. You can use HEAD for the tag if you only ever want to build from HEAD.

```
hyperbola.map
plugin@org.eclipsercp.hyperbola=tag,:method:user@host/ repo
feature@org.eclipsercp.hyperbola.feature=tag,:method:user@host/ repo
```

To save space, we have included only one feature and one plug-in in this map file. In practice, you must add an entry for each plug-in and feature that needs to be built. All other elements are assumed to be in the base and do not need to be fetched or built.

Enable fetching by commenting out the skipFetch property in build.properties. Leave skipMaps=true for now. Delete the plugins and features directories from the ${buildDirectory} and run the build. Notice that the source listed in the map is checked out and built.

Fetching the Product File

In the case of a product build there is a bit of a catch-22 situation. The .product file drives the list of features and plug-ins to be built. This file is typically in a plug-in or feature project in the SCM, but the map file mechanism does not have a way of indicating which project or where it is. Since the .product file drives the fetch phase of the build and the fetch phase cannot fetch it, it must be checked out explicitly.

This can be accomplished using a custom build step early on in the build, for example, by adding the following Ant instructions to the postSetup target in custom-Targets.xml:

```
customTargets.xml
  <target name="postSetup">
    <antcall target="getBaseComponents" />
    <ant antfile="${genericTargets}" target="fetchElement">
      <property name="type" value="feature | plug-in"/>
      <property name="id" value="id of feature or plug-in project" />
    </ant>
  </target>
```

See Section 24.5.1, "Customizing the Build Scripts," for more information on the customTargets.xml file.

Integrating with SCM Systems

Source code repositories and SCM systems figure heavily in the overall release engineering process. PDE Build supports several tools such as CVS and SVN. CVS is supported out of the box, whereas SVN requires the installation of some additional plug-ins. In both cases standard command-line SCM tools are used to fetch content—PDE Build does not assume the existence of an Eclipse workspace, so the normal Eclipse SCM clients cannot be used.

If you are on a UNIX machine, chances are you have CVS and SVN already installed—type cvs or svn at the command line to check. If not, consult your OS installer instructions.

On Windows you have to manually download and install the clients. You can get CVS from *http://cvsnt.org* and SVN from *http://tigris.org* or *http://polarion.com*.

SVN users need to augment the standard PDE Build infrastructure with the ability to read SVN-oriented map file entries and use SVN for fetching. See the instructions on the PDE wiki at *http://wiki.eclipse.org/PDEBuild*.

24.5.4 Fetching the Maps

Sharing the map files in the SCM repository is the next logical step. There may be many map files, for example, each controlled by different teams. The simplest structure is to have a directory in the repository that holds the map files. Different teams then update their map files, and the build automatically picks up their changes.

During the build process, the getMapFiles target in customTargets.xml is called to download all the map files. The behavior of getMapFiles is controlled by setting various properties in build.properties, as shown here:

```
hyperbola.builder/build.properties
# skipMaps=true
mapsRepo=:pserver:anonymous@example.com/path/to/repo
mapsRoot=path/to/maps
mapsCheckoutTag=HEAD
```

If skipMaps is commented out, getMapFiles checks out the contents of ${mapsRoot} from ${mapsRepo} using ${mapsCheckoutTag} and puts it into a maps area in ${buildDirectory}.

Set this up in the build.properties, check your map files into a repository, and delete the entire contents of ${buildDirectory}. Now run the builder and watch that first the maps are checked out, then the features and plug-ins. Then the build should continue as normal.

24.5.5 Auto-substitution of Version Numbers

Deployed features are full of version numbers—included plug-ins and features are all identified by precise versions. Listing and managing these specific version numbers at development time is challenging, to say the least. If the version of a plug-in changes, all referencing features have to be updated. This is cumbersome and error-prone.

To simplify the process, PDE Build includes support for automatically substituting version numbers during the build. You saw this in Chapter 9, "Packaging Hyperbola," where included plug-ins and features were identified as version 0.0.0. The use of 0.0.0 tells PDE Build to substitute the version number of the plug-in or feature used in the build. This eliminates the need to change the containing feature definition during development and ensures that the deployed version numbers are always correct. This is the default behavior of PDE Build.

You can lock in version numbers by setting them explicitly in the feature editor. For example, on the **Plug-ins** page of the feature editor, select **Versions...** in the **Plug-ins and Fragments** section. There you can select various policies for managing the version numbers. The options specified in the dialog apply to all plug-ins and fragments. If you want to lock down some plug-in version numbers but leave some to be assigned at build time, you have to use the **feature.xml** page and edit the file directly.

24.5.6 Qualifying Version Numbers

It is often handy to have output version numbers qualified by a build timestamp or other information. PDE Build supports a mechanism for optionally *qualifying* select plug-in and feature version numbers during the build process.

Open the `org.eclipsercp.hyperbola` plug-in's editor, and on the **Overview** page set the plug-in **Version** field to `1.0.0.qualifier`. Do the same for the `org.eclipsercp.hyperbola.feature`. During the build process, the `qualifier` segment of the version is replaced with a user-selected value. This should be done for all plug-ins and features.

By default, the qualifier is derived from the context of the build. For example, if the build is based on checking out particular CVS tags using the map files described earlier, the qualifier for each plug-in or feature is the CVS tag used to check out the source for the plug-in. This way, the plug-in's full version number is based on its source.

If the build is not based on SCM tags or is using some sort of default tag—for example, the CVS HEAD tag used in continuous integration builds—the qualifier for the version is the millisecond clock time at which the plug-in or feature was built.

You can force the value of the qualifier to be uniform across the build by setting the `forceContextQualifier` property in the builder's `build.properties`, as shown below. You should take care to use qualifier strings that are valid for file and folder names as the qualifier shows up in the build output disk content. You should also take care to ensure that qualifiers are monotonically increasing so that successive builds have *larger* version numbers.

hyperbola.builder/build.properties
```
forceContextQualifier=someQualifierString
```

It is also possible to control the qualification of plug-ins and features on an individual basis by setting the `qualifier` property in the relevant `build.properties`, as shown here:

org.eclipsercp.hyperbola/build.properties
```
qualifier=<arbitrary string value here>
```

24.5.7 Identifying and Placing Root Files

In product scenarios it is often required that various files be included in the root of the product distribution. This commonly includes various licenses and legal files and perhaps even a JRE. The PDE Build *root files* mechanism allows you to do this.

The root files mechanism is actually part of the feature build structure. Like plug-ins, features have their own `build.properties` file that maps the development-time structure onto the runtime structure. This is where you describe the set of files to copy to the root of the final build output. The snippet below shows a typical feature `build.properties` file. The `bin.includes` property behaves exactly as described for plug-ins. The remainder of this section details the setup for root files. See the PDE Help for a full list of feature build properties.

*.feature/build.properties
```
bin.includes=feature.xml, about.html, feature.properties,\
   license.html, root=rootfiles
```

The program launcher and related configuration files—for example, `hyperbola.exe`, `hyperbolà.ini`, and `config.ini`—do appear at the root of an install but are not technically root files if you are building products. Products inherently identify and include the executable and these various configuration files, so they should not be specified again in a feature root file list.

The **Product Definition** and **Export** wizards do not give you full control, however. For example, arbitrary root files such as licenses and legal files cannot be directly identified. These files must be enumerated in the `build.properties` for a feature included in the product. The properties relevant to defining the root files are listed here:

root—Files listed here are always copied to the root of the output. If a directory is listed, all files in that directory are copied to the root of the output.

root.<os.ws.arch>—There should be one of these lines for each OS, window system, and processor architecture combination that has unique root files. For example, if you need to include compiled libraries or executables, you should identify them on the root lines for the appropriate configurations.

Each property value is a comma-separated list of files to copy to the root of the output. The files are identified using one of the following techniques:

○ The contents of a directory structure are included by listing the parent directory itself. For example, `root=rootfiles` copies the entire contents of the `rootfiles` directory in the feature to the root of the build output. This is the most common setup seen in features.

○ Individual files must be identified by prefixing their location with `file:`. For example, the line `root.linux.gtk.x86=file:linux/special_executable` copies just the `special_executable` file to the root. Note that the given path is relative to the feature and the containing directory structure is not copied.

○ Absolute paths can be specified by prefixing the location with `absolute:`.

ROOT FILE PRECEDENCE

Many features can contribute to the root files for a build. The feature root files in parent features overwrite those of their children.

Executable files and libraries often need to have special permissions set when they are placed in the final archive so that when end users unpack the archives, the product is ready to run. You can control the permissions of the root files by defining a property of the form

`root[.os.ws.arch].permissions.<perm_pattern>=<files>`

The `os.ws.arch` configuration identification is optional. The `<perm_pattern>` is a UNIX file permissions triple, such as 755, which should be familiar to `chmod` users. The value of the property is a comma-separated list of files to which the permissions should be applied. Ant patterns are supported for identifying files. Since permissions are applied once the files have been copied to their position in the root directory, all paths to permission files should be relative to the output root. Nonexistent files are silently skipped, and folders must be indicated with a trailing "/".

24.6 Building Add-on Features

So far this chapter has focused on building stand-alone RCP applications using Eclipse product definitions. The true utility of a pluggable architecture, however, is the ability to extend a system with additional plug-ins. Here we show how to build and package some additional plug-ins, such as multiuser chat support, that can optionally be installed into Hyperbola.

In Chapter 21, "Installing and Updating with p2," we showed you how to export features independently. Here we do basically the same thing but this time using PDE Build in a release engineering context.

24.6.1 Setting Up a Feature Builder

To try this out, let's set up a managed build process for the Hyperbola MUC feature. Overall the process is very much like the product builds done previously. As in Section 24.3, "Setting Up a Builder," set up a build project primed with files from PDE itself:

○ Start by creating a simple project called `feature.builder` using **File > New... > Project > General > Project** and prime it with template build scripts from your IDE.

○ In the file system, navigate to the install location of your Eclipse IDE and go to `org.eclipse.pde.build`. For example, look in `c:\ide\eclipse\plugins\ org.eclipse.pde.build_3.5.1` if your IDE is installed in `c:\ide`.

○ From there copy `build.properties` and `build.xml` from the `templates\ headless-build` directory into your new builder project.

24.6.2 `build.properties`

The `build.properties` file used to control the building of a top-level feature is similar to the one used to build a product. The most significant properties are highlighted in the next code snippet, and we describe the differences between the product `build.properties` and the file we need here.

```
feature.builder/build.properties
# feature identification
topLevelElementType = feature
topLevelElementId = org.eclipsercp.hyperbola.feature.muc
runPackager=true
archivePrefix=muc_feature

# build naming and location
buildDirectory=${user.home}/muc_feature.build
```

```
# base identification and location
skipBase=true
baseLocation=C:/hyperbola_prereqs
repoBaseLocation=${buildDirectory}/repository
transformedRepoLocation=${buildDirectory}/transformedRepo
baseos=win32
basews=win32
basearch=x86

# SCM access control
skipMaps=true
skipFetch=true

# Publish the build to a p2 repository.
p2.gathering = true

# cross-platform building
configs = *, *, *
```

Let's look at each of these properties and how they affect the build. In particular, we focus on how these properties differ from those specified in a product build.

> **topLevelElementType**—This property indicates the type of the top-level element being built—feature or plugin. It is not used when building products.
>
> **topLevelElementID**— This indicates the ID of the feature or plug-in to build.
>
> **repoBaseLocation**—This is the parent folder of the repository locations specified when building the client. The contents are used to compile and assemble the result.
>
> **transformedRepoLocation**—The contents of the repositories used may need to be converted into a runnable form. Runnable components are put in this location. Notice that baseLocation contents may still be needed if the feature being built brings in functionality that is not yet part of Hyperbola.
>
> **p2.gathering**—Features that are built should be published to a repository from which clients can install the MUC feature. In a feature build, unlike product builds, specifying the repository location in p2.metadata.repo and p2.artifact.repo is optional. If not specified, the repository is in the build output location.
>
> **configs**—Since there is no platform-specific code in the MUC feature, we can simply state that we are building for all platforms by setting the configs property to *, *, *.

24.6.3 Running the Feature Build

Feature builds are invoked in the same way as the product build in Section 24.4, "Running the Builder"; that is, you must

- ○ Create ${buildDirectory}

- ○ Create ${buildDirectory}/plugins

- ○ Create ${buildDirectory}/features

- ○ Copy the required plug-ins and features to the plugins/ and features/ directories as shown in Figure 24.5

- ○ Invoke org.eclipse.ant.core.antRunner as shown here:

```
cd <workspace location>/feature.builder
c:\ide\eclipse\eclipse.exe
    -application org.eclipse.ant.core.antRunner
    -buildfile build.xml -consoleLog
```

```
muc_feature.build
    features
        org.eclipsercp.hyperbola.feature.muc
    plugins
        org.eclipsercp.hyperbola.muc
```

Figure 24–5 Feature build layout

---

build.xml NOT productBuild.xml

When invoking a feature build, the -buildfile argument is build.xml as opposed to productBuild.xml.

The build produces a structure as shown in Figure 24-6. The content goes in the ${buildDirectory}/${buildLabel} directory or, in our example, in ${user.home}/ muc _feature.build/I.TestBuild. This directory contains an archive that consists of a fully built multiuser chat feature. Because the p2.gathering property was specified, the archive is also a p2 repository.

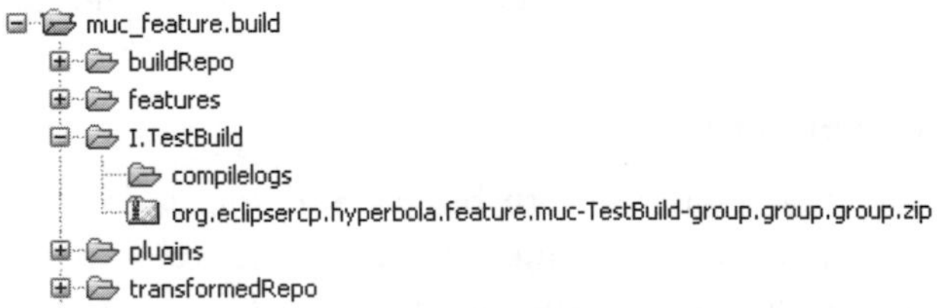

```
muc_feature.build
    buildRepo
    features
    I.TestBuild
        compilelogs
        org.eclipsercp.hyperbola.feature.muc-TestBuild-group.group.group.zip
    plugins
    transformedRepo
```

Figure 24–6 Feature build output

To install the multiuser chat support into your Hyperbola client, simply launch Hyperbola, select **Help > Install New Software ... > Add ... > Archive ...**, and select the archive file produced from the build. You can then select **Hyperbola MultiUserChat Support**. **Note:** If you don't see any software listed when you select the repository, ensure that you deselect **Group items by category**.

24.7 Assembling Multiple Configurations

Up to now you have seen how to build a single product or feature; however, in practice you may want to assemble multiple configurations from the same build. You may assemble a basic and a professional version of the product, or configure some versions to ship with source code. If these different configurations are constructed by running a series of product builds in succession, you will build the same artifacts multiple times with possibly different plug-in qualifiers.

This section demonstrates how to build a single repository and use that repository to assemble two different configurations. One configuration will be identical to the Hyperbola product built in Section 24.4, and the other one will be a Hyperbola SDK—a Hyperbola product with source code and developer documentation.

24.7.1 What Is an SDK?

When working on a large project in a team environment, it is often undesirable (or not practical) for each developer to check out the entire project from source control. Many developers work in unrelated areas of the system and simply need to "use" or extend the existing functionality with no intention of changing it. While you can easily make use of a binary plug-in bundle, often having the source code available makes development much easier. To support this, you can create and deploy SDK features, that is, features that contain both the binary bundles and the source code. By shipping an SDK feature you are assured that the source code you ship is synchronized with the binary artifacts your clients are building against.

24.7.2 Building an SDK Feature

To build an SDK feature that includes both binary and source bundles, create a new feature project (**File > New... > Project > Plug-in Development > Feature Project**). Call it `org.eclipsercp.hyperbola.sdk.feature`. Under the **Included Features** tab add the `org.eclipsercp.hyperbola.feature`, and under the **feature.xml** tab manually add `org.eclipsercp.hyperbola.feature.source` as an included feature. Your `feature.xml` should contain the following lines:

```
<includes id=" org.eclipsercp.hyperbola.feature " version="0.0.0"/>
<includes id=" org.eclipsercp.hyperbola.feature.source"
  version="0.0.0"/>
```

Eclipse will likely report a warning that the org.eclipsercp.hyperbola
.feature.source reference cannot be found. This warning can be safely ignored
since the source feature will be generated at build time. The source feature will
contain the source bundles for the Hyperbola feature.

To instruct the build system to generate this feature, open the build.properties
file for the Hyperbola SDK feature and add the following:

```
generate.feature@org.eclipsercp.hyperbola.feature.source=\
  org.eclipsercp.hyperbola.feature
```

From here you can follow the same steps as you did in Section 24.6, "Building Add-on Features," to build the SDK feature.

BUILDING INDIVIDUAL SOURCE BUNDLES

It is highly recommended that you build a single source plug-in for each binary
plug-in. By default, PDE Build will create a single plug-in containing all the source.
To instruct PDE Build to create a single source plug-in for each binary plug-in, set
individualSourceBundles=true in your top-level build.properties file.

24.7.3 Simultaneously Assembling Multiple Configurations

To build and assemble multiple configurations simultaneously, you first build a
top-level feature that contains all possible features. This master build is then
sliced into a variety of different configurations through subsequent product
builds. However, instead of pointing to an SCM system (or unbuilt plug-ins on
disk), you simply point to the results of the master build. Since the master build
contains all your binary features and plug-ins, PDE Build will use these in the
final packaging step.

To set this up for Hyperbola, first create a top-level feature (called
org.eclipsercp.hyperbola.toplevel.feature) that contains all the Hyperbola
features in your workspace. At a minimum, this top-level feature should contain
both org.eclipsercp.hyperbola.feature and org.eclipsercp.hyperbola.sdk
.feature. If you have created other add-on features, feel free to include them
here, too.

Once you have created the top-level feature, following the steps from Section
24.6, "Building Add-on Features," create and run a feature build. Ensure that

your `topLevelFeature` is `org.eclipsercp.hyperbola.toplevel.feature` and set `p2.gathering=true`. This will instruct PDE Build to publish the results of this build to a p2 repository which can then be used to assemble a variety of configurations.

In order to assemble different configurations, simply craft `.product` files composed of the top-level features you wish to build. To build the Hyperbola product, for example, change the following lines in the `build.properties` file from Section 24.3.2, "`build.properties`":

hyperbola.builder/build.properties
```
# product and packaging control
product=/hyperbola.products/sdk.product
runPackager=true

# base identification and location
skipBase=true
base=C:/hyperbola_prereqs
baseLocation=${base}

# cross-platform building
configs=win32, win32, x86 & linux, gtk, x86

# CVS access control
skipMaps=true
skipFetch=true
repoBaseLocation=/location/of/the/p2/repository
transformedRepoLocation=${buildDirectory}/transformed_repo
```

Ensure that `skipMaps` and `skipFetch` are both set to `true`, and remove all the plug-ins and features in your build directory. Finally, copy the `hyperbola.products` project to your plug-in directory and run a product build as outlined in Section 24.4, "Running the Builder." This will produce a series of Hyperbola SDK products for each platform specified in your `build.properties` file. To assemble other configurations, simply change the included features in the product and rerun the build.

24.8 Summary

Here we covered the basics and got you started using PDE Build to compile and assemble the plug-ins, features, and products related to Hyperbola. Regular and repeatable automated builds are a critical part of the development process. Without these, teams cannot integrate and have no idea if the system works.

PDE Build offers comprehensive tooling for building RCP and Eclipse-related artifacts. It is highly sophisticated and extensible. It is also very specialized. It is not a general-purpose build system. Since it is based on Ant, however, it can be integrated with one of the many build choreographing systems such as Hudson or CruiseControl. We strongly recommend setting up such a build process as early as possible in the life of your project.

CHAPTER 25

Testing

Despite the best efforts of software engineers, bugs occur in even the most carefully crafted applications. And so an entire subset of the software industry has arisen from the need for testing.

Hyperbola needs testing, too. Until now in the development of Hyperbola, we have not paid much attention to testing given that we have written no test cases. Many software developers embrace the notion of writing test cases first (or at least early). While we count ourselves among them, it's worth noting that we have chosen to take a tutorial-based approach to building Hyperbola as opposed to a test-driven approach. This is because while taking a test-driven approach is a good development practice, it is not necessarily the best way to learn or teach. Now that you have a basic understanding of creating RCP applications, we can learn to test Hyperbola. In particular, we will go over

- ❍ General issues around testing Hyperbola that can be applied to any RCP application
- ❍ How to run tests using Eclipse
- ❍ Implementing a unit test for one piece of Hyperbola using JUnit
- ❍ Implementing a user interface unit test for Hyperbola using SWTBot

25.1 Making Hyperbola Testable

Before we launch into implementing automated tests for Hyperbola, let's discuss some of the practices that enable the creation of clean test cases. These points relate to all kinds of software development.

POJOs—The most important practice to make sure your code is testable is to write your domain logic as pure POJOs. Allowing specific dependencies to leak into your domain logic makes writing and running simple JUnit tests significantly more difficult.

Dependency injection—Decoupling and allowing elements to be reused enable alternative implementations. This allows for mock objects to be used with ease and follows the programming mantra of "Don't call us, we'll call you."

There are other practices out there that can make your code more testable, but we'll leave that for you as a topic of exploration. From our experiences, the principles we outlined go a long way to ensure that your code can be tested, regardless of the framework you use.

25.2 Unit Testing Hyperbola

25.2.1 Test Strategy

Let's start by writing a simple test for the `ConnectionDetails` in the Hyperbola model. We want to verify that we are able to construct the object and that it has valid values. Our testing will use JUnit, which conveniently resides in the target platform. We'll show only enough JUnit as necessary to get the tests running.

25.2.2 Writing the Test Case

It makes sense to put the test code in a separate project from the Hyperbola model code that it tests. Notice that the `ConnectionDetails` class itself is not visible to other projects since it isn't exported by the `org.eclipsercp.hyperbola` plug-in. To accomplish this, we will create a fragment project.

Fragments

Fragments allow optional functionality to be added to another plug-in, known as the *host*. At runtime a fragment is merged with its host and has full visibility of all the packages in its host, so it is ideal for containing unit tests.

Follow these steps to create the fragment project that will contain the new test:

○ Select **File > New > Project > Plug-in Development > Fragment Project** to create a fragment project called `org.eclipsercp.hyperbola.tests`.

○ On the last page of the wizard select `org.eclipsercp.hyperbola` as the host.

○ Open the manifest editor on the fragment bundle and turn to the **Dependencies** tab. Add the following plug-ins to the **Required Plug-ins** section: `org.junit`.

○ Create a `ContactGroupTestCase` class in a package called `org.eclipsercp.hyperbola.tests` with `junit.framework.TestCase` as its superclass. Use the following snippet to complete the class:

```
org.eclipsercp.hyperbola.tests/ConnectionDetailsTestCase
        public class ConnectionDetailsTestCase extends TestCase {
        public void testConnectionDetails() throws Exception {
            ConnectionDetails details = new ConnectionDetails("user",
                "localhost", "password");
            assertEquals(details.getUserId(), "user");
            assertEquals(details.getServer(), "localhost");
            assertEquals(details.getPassword(), "password");
            }
    }
```

25.2.3 Running the Test Case

Once the `ConnectionDetailsTestCase` is written, it's easy to run: From the context menu on the test case class, select **Run As > JUnit Test**, and the results will be shown in the JUnit view. The view should show a solid green bar, as seen in Figure 25-1, indicating that the test case passed.

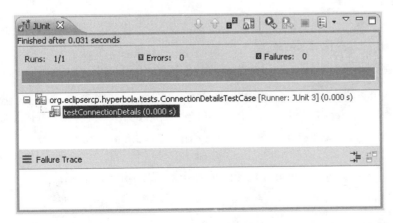

Figure 25–1   Successful run in the JUnit test view

25.3 User Interface Testing Hyperbola

Testing user interfaces can be a daunting task for any application, especially without a framework. For RCP applications you have a few commercial and open-source options when it comes to testing user interfaces. For the purposes of simplicity and accessibility, we will use the SWTBot framework (which is freely available at eclipse.org) to test the user interface of Hyperbola.

25.3.1 SWTBot

SWTBot is an open-source user interface and functional testing tool for SWT and Eclipse-based applications. SWTBot provides APIs that are simple to exercise and hide the complexities involved with SWT and Eclipse. To take advantage of SWTBot, we have to install it into our IDE and target platform. SWTBot is available from its update site: *http://download.eclipse.org/technology/swtbot/galileo/dev-build/update-site*.

25.3.2 Test Strategy

To get an idea of how SWTBot works, let's start by writing a user interface test case that opens up the Preferences dialog, selects the automatic login preference, and verifies that the preference is actually enabled. We'll show only enough of SWTBot to get the tests running. SWTBot is very extensive when it comes to user interface testing, and we encourage you to explore the SWTBot documentation to learn more.

25.3.3 Writing the Test Case

Follow these steps to create the fragment project that will contain the new test:

- ○ Select **File > New > Project > Plug-in Development > Plug-in Project** to create a plug-in project called `org.eclipsercp.hyperbola.tests.ui`. Click **Finish**.
- ○ Open the manifest editor on the fragment bundle and turn to the **Dependencies** tab.
- ○ Add the following bundles to the **Required Plug-ins** section:

```
org.eclipse.swtbot.eclipse.finder
org.eclipse.swtbot.finder
org.eclipse.swtbot.junit4_x
org.hamcrest
org.apache.commons.collections
org.junit4
org.eclipse.ui
```

○ Create a `HyperbolaPreferenceDialogTestCase` class in a package called `org.eclipsercp.hyperbola.tests.ui` with `junit.framework.TestCase` as its superclass. Use the following snippet to complete the class:

org.eclipsercp.hyperbola.tests.ui/HyperbolaPreferenceDialogTestCase

```
@RunWith(SWTBotJunit4ClassRunner.class)
public class HyperbolaPreferenceDialogTestCase extends TestCase {
        private static SWTWorkbenchBot bot;

        @BeforeClass
        public static void beforeClass() throws Exception {
                bot = new SWTWorkbenchBot();
        }

        @Test
        public void testLoginAutomaticallyPreference() throws Exception {
                IPreferenceStore preferences =
                        new ScopedPreferenceStore(new ConfigurationScope(),
                                "org.eclipsercp.hyperbola");
                assertFalse(preferences.getBoolean("prefs_auto_login"));

                bot.menu("Hyperbola").menu("Preferences").click();
                SWTBotShell shell = bot.shell("Preferences");
                shell.activate();
                bot.tree().select("General");
                bot.checkBox("Login automatically at startup").click();
                bot.button("OK").click();

                assertTrue(preferences.getBoolean("prefs_auto_login"));
        }
}
```

The test creates an SWTWorkbenchBot object that allows for convenient inspection of SWT widgets. The first three lines of the testLoginAutomaticallyPreference method verify that the automatic login preference is disabled by accessing the preference store for the org.eclipsercp.hyperbola plug-in. The next four lines use the SWTWorkbenchBot to open the Preferences dialog in Hyperbola and select the **General** preference page. The next two lines click the **automatically login** check box to apply the preference and close the Preferences dialog. Finally, we verify that the preference was set via the Hyperbola preference store.

Notice that the amount of code we had to write for testing the user interface was fairly trivial because of the SWTWorkbenchBot class. The only complicated code had to deal with verifying that the preference was properly set. For all intents and purposes, user interface tests can be written quickly.

25.3.4 Running the Test Case

Once the HyperbolaPreferenceDialogTestCase is written, it's easy to run: From the Workbench select **Run > Run Configurations...** and create a new **SWTBot**

Test launch configuration as seen in Figure 25-2. Ensure that the product being executed is the `org.eclipsercp.hyperbola.product` and not the `org.eclipse.sdk.ide` product.

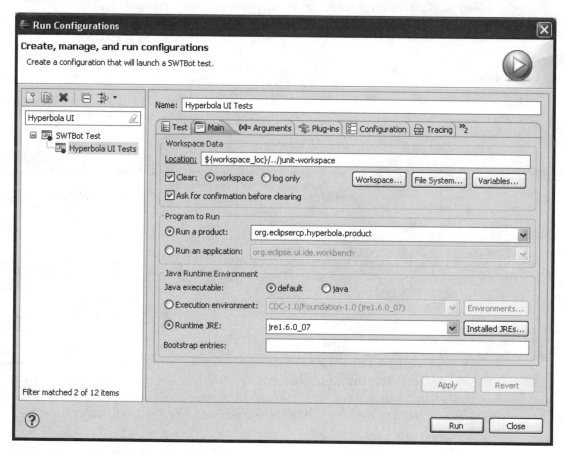

Figure 25–2 SWTBot launch configuration

The results will be shown in the JUnit view. The view should show a solid green bar, as seen in Figure 25-3, indicating that the user interface test passed.

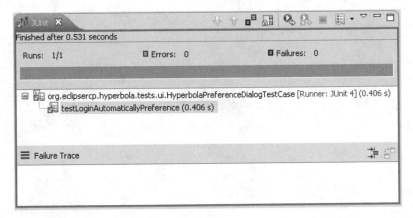

Figure 25–3   Successful SWTBot test run in the JUnit test view

25.4 Summary

In this chapter we finally got around to writing some tests for Hyperbola. We presented two mechanisms for testing: unit testing and user interface testing. Both are vitally important to the quality of the overall application. The tests in this chapter are certainly far from comprehensive and should be used as a learning exercise when you start writing tests for your own applications.

25.5 Pointers

- ❍ The SWTBot wiki (*http://wiki.eclipse.org/SWTBot*) should be your first stop when user interface testing Eclipse-based applications.
- ❍ For mock object frameworks, we highly recommend EasyMock (*http://easymock.org*) or Mockito (*http://mockito.org*).

CHAPTER 26

The Last Mile

We are now down to what telephone companies call "the last mile"—actually delivering the product to the end users. There are, of course, many different ways that you can deliver Hyperbola and other Eclipse-based products to end users. Here we cover some of these options and detail other issues related to installing and configuring Eclipse-based products on the user's machine. In particular, we cover

- Delivery techniques such as archives, p2 installers, native installers, repositories, and JNLP
- Initializing an install before first use
- Setting up shared installs

26.1 Archives

The simplest and most widely supported delivery mechanism is using standard ZIP and TAR archive files. As you have seen, the Eclipse tooling directly supports the creation of these archives, from the workspace using either **File > Export... > Eclipse product** or **File > Export... > Deployable plug-ins and fragments,** or by using the automated build setup detailed in Chapter 24, "Building Hyperbola." To these archives you can add the JRE and any additional files needed for the product.

NOTE

Including the JRE in your product distribution is a mixed blessing. On the one hand, it simplifies the install and reduces the chances of problems on the user's machine. On the other hand, it greatly increases the size of the distribution and its footprint on disk.

You should weigh the installation scenarios and potential legal requirements carefully and determine what is best for your product. Of course, if you code your application to be independent of the JRE, you have more options.

The archives can be delivered over the Internet or on direct-read media. End users unpack the archive in some location on disk and run the provided executable. This is suitable for simple systems and reasonably knowledgeable users but has the following drawbacks:

○ Not all OSs have the required archive-reading software installed by default.

○ The OS cannot manage the install since it is just a set of files unpacked on disk. This makes uninstallation a manual process.

○ There are no scripting capabilities, so setting up or querying for system settings and configuring the product during the install is cumbersome.

26.2 Native Installers

A common approach to installing end-user applications is through a *native installer* such as InstallShield, NSIS, RPM, and such. The great thing about Eclipse is that it is just a set of files written to a location on the target machine—no special registry keys or other hooks are required. As such, you can use any of these installers to deliver your Eclipse-based applications.

All of the installers function by delivering a set of files to the user's machine. They vary in how the files are delivered and their mechanisms, if any, for querying the user as to what he or she wants installed and configuring the installed files by running scripts.

Native installers let users install applications so that they are tightly integrated with the underlying OS. So, if your Windows version needs to create registry keys or hook system menus, a native installer can help. Similarly, on Linux installs, RPMs can be registered in the RPM database.

Because of the wide variation in setup and capabilities, a native installer tutorial is beyond the scope of this book—you should choose the technologies that best suit your environment and meet the needs of your users.

26.3 p2 Installer

There is also a small, separate installer you can use to install Eclipse or your application, the p2 installer. The p2 installer is basically the director application we saw in Section 21.6, "Installation Management," with a bit of infrastructure for feeding the command line in various ways. As a result, the installer can do anything that p2 can do. Users download and run the installer via JNLP, manually or via some other custom means.

Using the Equinox p2 installer to download and install your application offers several benefits over doing so manually:

○ It supports multithreading and mirroring, allowing for fast downloads.

○ It uses Pack200 compression, cutting required bandwidth in half.

○ It automatically picks the best possible mirror and can dynamically switch mirrors in case of failure.

○ It supports code signature validation to ensure that the download is from a trusted source.

You can get the Equinox installer from the **Provisioning** section of the Equinox download page; see *http://download.eclipse.org/equinox*. Note that the p2 installer is purposely simple. It was designed specifically to ask only the absolute minimum of questions. The code for the installer is very simple and can be easily adapted to your specific needs.

26.4 Java Web Start (JNLP)

Java Web Start, also known as JNLP, is a mechanism whereby applications are stored on a Web server and exposed to users as links on a Web page. When the user clicks on a link, the browser uses its JNLP content type handler to read the JNLP manifest and download, install, and launch the described Java resources.

26.4.1 How Java Web Start Works

Without turning this into a Java Web Start tutorial, the following is a brief introduction to the technology and its use with Eclipse.

A Web Start application is described by one or more `.jnlp` files. These are XML manifests that describe the application itself (e.g., its name, location, description) and the set of JARs that make up the application. JNLP manifest files can also include, or be extended by, other JNLP manifest files. The following is the top-level Hyperbola JNLP manifest file with the interesting parts highlighted:

```
hyperbola.jnlp.feature/rootfiles/hyperbola.jnlp
<?xml version="1.0" encoding="UTF-8"?>
<jnlp
    spec="1.0+"
    codebase="http://eclipsercp.org/hyperbola"
    href="hyperbola.jnlp">
  <information>
    <title>Hyperbola Chat Client</title>
    <vendor>eclipsercp.org</vendor>
    <homepage href="http://eclipsercp.org" />
    <description>Hyperbola Chat Client</description>
    <icon kind="splash" href="splash.gif"/>
    <offline-allowed/>
  </information>
  <security>
    <all-permissions/>
  </security>
  <application-desc main-class="org.eclipse.core.launcher.WebStartMain">
    <argument>-nosplash</argument>
  </application-desc>
  <resources>
    <j2se version="1.4+" />
    <jar href="org.eclipse.equinox.launcher_00.v20090128-1500.jar"/>
    <extension
        name="Hyperbola Chat Feature"
        href="features/org.eclipsercp.hyperbola.feature_1.0.0.jnlp"/>
    <property
        name="osgi.instance.area"
        value="@user.home/Application Data/hyperbola"/>
    <property
        name="osgi.configuration.area"
        value="@user.home/Application Data/hyperbola"/>
    <property
        name="eclipse.product"
        value="org.eclipsercp.hyperbola.product "/>
  </resources>
</jnlp>
```

This file and the referenced resources are placed on a Web server, and the manifest file is linked to from any number of Web pages. When the user clicks the link, the browser sees that it is a JNLP manifest file and invokes the Java Web Start infrastructure to handle the content. This is much like the way browsers handle Flash or PDF content. Depending on the browser configuration, the Web Start support and JRE may be dynamically downloaded and installed into the browser on first use.

After downloading and caching the JARs and extensions described in the JNLP manifest file, the Web Start handler starts Java and the requested application. While this process is kicked off via your browser, the resultant application is not run *in* the browser. Once a Java Web Start application is installed, the JARs and manifests need not be downloaded again. The second time the link is selected, the cached files are used. In some scenarios the application can be configured to run directly from the user's desktop.

An additional point of interest is the Equinox launcher JAR included in the manifest. Notice that the `<application-desc>` tag identifies the `WebStartMain` rather than the standard Eclipse `Main` class as the entry point.

Top-level JNLP manifest files essentially play the role of `hyperbola.exe`, `hyperbola.ini`, and the `config.ini` in standard Eclipse deployments. They define command-line arguments, some VM arguments, and the splash screen and set various system properties.

26.4.2 Hyperbola and Java Web Start

To illustrate how Web Start works in practice, let's set up Hyperbola to run via Web Start. Look back at the JNLP manifest and notice the `<extension>` tag. The JNLP manifest file listed there *extends* the current file. The snippet below shows the key elements of the extension file. Notice that it lists some plug-in JARs and it, too, has an extension—the structure is recursive.

```
org.eclipsercp.hyperbola.feature_1.0.0.jnlp
<?xml version="1.0" encoding="UTF-8"?>
<jnlp spec="1.0+" codebase="http://eclipsercp.org/hyperbola">
  <information>
    <title>Hyperbola</title>
    <vendor>eclipsercp.org</vendor>
  </information>
  <resources>
    <extension name="RCP"
      href="features/org.eclipse.rcp_3.5.0.jnlp" />
    <jar href="plugins/org.eclipsercp.hyperbola_1.0.0.jar"/>
    ...
</jnlp>
```

This structure looks remarkably like Eclipse features—some amount of identification and location information followed by a list of included plug-ins and nested lists. In general, the structure of JNLP manifest files is completely under your control. Eclipse maps features to JNLP manifest files as a matter of convenience and to enable tooling reuse.

For example, PDE takes advantage of this correlation and allows you to augment software sites with JNLP information as the features are built. This is convenient since software sites are already on the Web and already have the plug-ins needed. This approach has the added benefit that you do not have to change mind-sets or build two parallel configurations. The tooling does not, however, generate the top-level JNLP manifest file described previously—you have to do that.

To build the JNLP-enabled update site, first create a feature to describe the Web Start version of Hyperbola. This time, name the feature `hyperbola.jnlp .feature`. Once that is created, add `org.eclipsercp.hyperbola.feature` to the **Included Features** list, and on the **build.properties** page remove the `bin.includes` line altogether. Add in a root declaration, as shown below. It should be the only line in the file.

```
root=rootfiles
```

In the case of building an update site, declared root files get copied to the root of the site. In the Web Start case, we want the Equinox launcher JAR and the top-level JNLP manifest file to be at the root.

Create a `rootfiles` directory at the root of the `hyperbola.jnlp.feature` project and copy in the Equinox launcher JAR from your target. Use **File > New > File** to create a text file called `hyperbola.jnlp` in the `rootfiles` directory. This is the top-level JNLP manifest file. Fill it in with the content shown earlier. For simplicity, set the `codebase` attribute to `file:/c:/site`—you can change that later when you deploy to a real site.

When you are done, the `hyperbola.jnlp.feature` project should look like Figure 26-1. As usual, you can get a preconfigured setup from the sample code for this chapter.

Figure 26–1   Hyperbola JNLP feature

26.4.3 JAR Signing

Eclipse must run with `all-permissions` since it creates class loaders, reads and writes files, and performs other protected operations. To run a Java Web Start application with `all-permissions`, all JARs must be signed. Signing makes the JARs a bit bigger but otherwise does not affect their normal use. The PDE **Export** wizard allows you to sign JARs as they are exported or added to a build output.

Before you can sign a JAR, you must have a *keystore* set up. To do this for production scenarios, you should acquire the appropriate certificates from a trusted certificate authority. If you use your own self-signed key, your users will get warnings that the JAR signatures cannot be authenticated.

For testing, you can set up a simple keystore using the `keytool` program included with typical JDKs, as shown below. For more options, see the `keytool` documentation.

```
keytool -genkey -alias <alias> -keypass <password>
```

NOTE

Eclipse uses the `jarsigner` application typically found in the `bin` directory of a JDK. As such, you must be running with a JDK or have `jarsigner` on the system's program path to sign JARs.

Once you've set up the keystore, sign the Equinox launcher JAR you added to the `hyperbola.jnlp.feature` project using the command below. The `<alias>` is an arbitrary string of your choosing.

```
jarsigner.exe <location of equinox launcher.jar> <alias>
```

26.4.4 Exporting for Java Web Start

Now you are ready to export Hyperbola for Web Start. Open the **File > Export... > Deployable features** wizard and select the `hyperbola.jnlp.feature`. Ensure that the **Package as individual JAR archives** check box is checked, and for this example set the export location to `c:\site`. Select the **JAR Signing** tab shown in Figure 26-2.

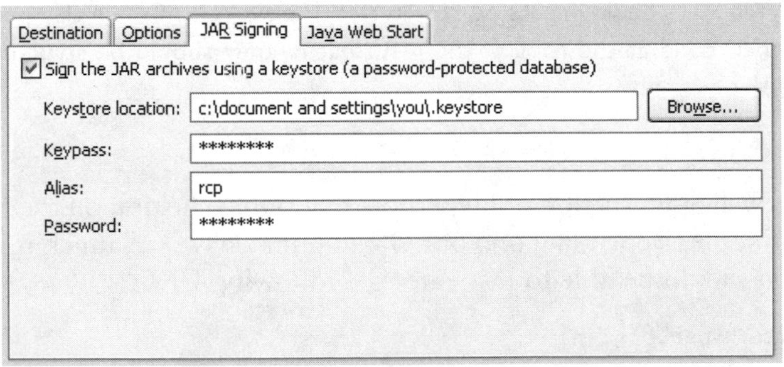

Figure 26-2 Hyperbola JAR signing options

Fill in your JAR signing information and then switch to the **Java Web Start** tab as shown in Figure 26-3.

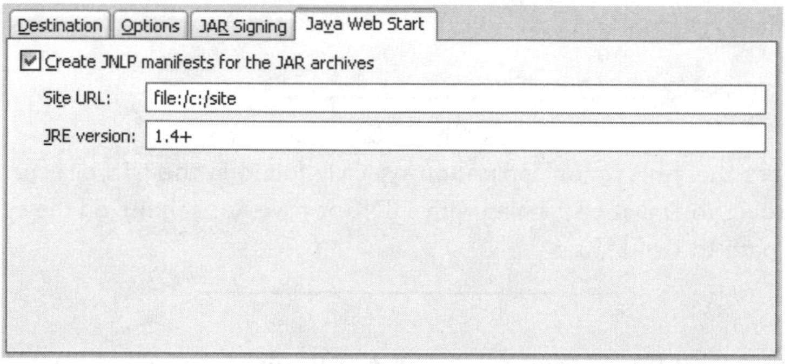

Figure 26–3   Hyperbola Java Web Start options

Ensure that the **Site URL** is the same as you put in your top-level `hyperbola .jnlp` manifest file. Note that by default, `keytool` creates the keystore in your home directory in a file called `.keystore`.

Click **Finish**, and PDE builds and signs the features and plug-ins included in Hyperbola. Note that signing JARs is costly, so expect your exports to take a little longer.

TIP

Web Start mechanisms only handle JARs. It is recommended that all plug-ins being used in Web Start deployments be structured to have "." on their classpath and have all their code at the root of the JAR; that is, they should be structured as normal JAR'd plug-ins.

Test the Web Start version of Hyperbola by double-clicking on the `hyperbola .jnlp` manifest file. Depending on your OS, you may have to launch it via a Web browser. You should be able to just enter the following URL:

```
file:/c:/site/hyperbola.jnlp
```

or, if that doesn't work, create the simple HTML file shown next and click on the link:

```
<html>
  <a href="file:/c:/site/hyperbola.jnlp">Start Hyperbola</a>
</html>
```

26.4.5 Building JNLP Manifests

The PDE Build automated build infrastructure can also be configured to generate JNLP manifest files. Go back to the setup you had in Chapter 24, add the following to the builder's `build.properties`, and build the `hyperbola.jnlp.feature`. You might want to set the output format to be `-folder` to build the required software site directly.

```
hyperbola.builder/build.properties
jnlp.codebase=file:/c:/site
jnlp.j2se=1.4+
sign.alias=<alias>
sign.keystore=<keystore location>
sign.keypass=<key password>
sign.storepass=<password>
```

NOTE

If you do not want to code your password in the `properties` file, it can be supplied on the command line using a `-D` VM argument (e.g., `-Dsign.storepass=<password>`).

26.4.6 Java Web Start and p2

Each time the user starts a Web Start application, the Web Start infrastructure checks to see if the application has been changed. If it notices updated manifests or JARs, it replaces the local copies with the newer versions—Web Start manages the install. As such, there is no particular need to use the p2 technology in Web Start configurations. `webStartMain` automatically discovers and installs downloaded plug-ins based on the classpath used to start the Java Web Start JVM.

It is possible, however, to use the Equinox p2 mechanism in concert with Web Start. Once the Web Start–based application is running (and assuming it includes the p2 infrastructure), users can use p2 to add functions, as outlined in Chapter 14. Newly acquired features and plug-ins are downloaded to a local site of their choosing and installed into Eclipse. These features and plug-ins are managed on the client by p2—Web Start does not install new versions for you even if they are added to the Web Start download site.

26.5 Initializing the Install

Eclipse manages a number of caches to improve performance. Typically, these are written to the configuration area of the application. The caches are simply read during subsequent sessions—they are rewritten only if something in the install changes; that is, on its second invocation, Eclipse generally does not write anything to disk. This is a great performance optimization for subsequent invocations, but it requires both some writable storage and somewhat more time for the first run.

To alleviate this, you can initialize an install after laying down all of its files on disk. Initializing tells Eclipse to build any structures and caches that it needs and results in the user's first run of the product being faster. The standard initialization process starts Eclipse normally, but just before running product code, it exits. To initialize Hyperbola, run with the -initialize option as follows:

```
hyperbola -initialize
```

To reinitialize Hyperbola, execute the line below. This discards any previously computed caches and then initializes the install as normal.

```
hyperbola -clean -initialize
```

26.6 Preinitialized Configurations

Initializing an install is also useful when setting up Hyperbola to run off a read-only medium such as a CD. In this scenario you want to do the first run of Hyperbola before burning the CD and include all the preinitialized caches on the CD. Depending on the application, this can eliminate the need for writable media altogether.

The trick here is to initialize everything needed to run Hyperbola. The built-in initialization you get with -initialize treats only the internal Eclipse caches. To initialize Hyperbola, you can easily write a special application that initializes the Hyperbola state and then run the application when Hyperbola is installed, as shown here:

```
hyperbola -application org.eclipsercp.hyperbola.initializer
```

Data required by other plug-ins is more difficult. The most common problem is files that need to be extracted from plug-in JARs before they can be used. For example, native libraries, HTML files, and the like all need to be extracted from their containing plug-in JARs before being used.

The infrastructure around these files does the extraction on demand at runtime. For example, when a library is opened, the class loader triggers the extraction of the library and then opens the extracted copy. Similarly, the About information is extracted before being viewed with a Web browser. To fully preinitialize Hyperbola, then, you have to touch all of these files and ensure that they are extracted and cached so that you can burn them onto the CD.

Fortunately, all you have to do is call `FileLocator.resolve(URL)` for each file or directory that needs to be extracted. The hard part then is identifying all of these files. Eclipse does not have direct support for this, but the Eclipse Platform Core team does supply an `initializer` application on their home page. See the **Core** page on *http://eclipse.org/platform*. See also Eclipse Bug 90535 for more details.

26.7 Multiuser Install Scenarios

In UNIX and enterprise environments, it is often useful to *share* one install of Hyperbola among many users. Rather than having a copy of Hyperbola on each end-user machine, Hyperbola is installed on a central server and simply instantiated by each user.

Some of the advantages of this approach are

○ Reduced management cost since there is only one install to manage
○ Increased control over what plug-ins people are running since the configuration can be protected by file system permissions
○ Better integration into the native environment; for example, shared application installs are the norm in the UNIX world

Some issues to consider are

○ How to update shared configurations while users are using them
○ How to manage data stored by an instance in the configuration area
○ Additional complexity in the initial setup

NOTE

This section manipulates the location of the Eclipse configuration and instance areas to get various sharing and separation effects. Please refer to Chapter 27, "OSGi," for details on how to use and control these areas.

By default, Eclipse expects to have or create a configuration area inside the install directory (e.g., `/Hyperbola/configuration`), as shown in Figure 26-4.

Hyperbola does not need a workspace in the classic Eclipse sense, but it does use an *instance area* to store information such as the window layout. The instance location should be set in the relevant `config.ini`. Section 27.9, "Data Areas,"

Figure 26–4 Independent installs

discusses this in detail, but in this example the `config.ini` might contain the following:

```
osgi.instance.area=@user.home/hyperbola
```

26.7.1 Shared Installs

The independent install approach works well for stand-alone installs on individual machines where users have global privileges. In shared scenarios, however, you typically want to protect the install by marking it read-only.

When Eclipse runs in a read-only install, it notices that the default configuration location (i.e., the install area) is not writable and looks for an alternative. Unless you use -configuration, the configuration area is placed under the user's home directory, as shown in Figure 26-5.

NOTE

If you change the location of the configuration folder using the –configuration flag, be warned that the parent folder must also be writable as Eclipse writes some configuration information there, too. For example, running Hyperbola with –configuration ~me/hyperbola/configuration will add a number of files to the ~me/hyperbola directory.

Here, Hyperbola is installed on the server and locked. Various clients access the installed files and run. Since the server does not have a configuration, each client does its own initialization and builds its own configuration. Notice that this essentially splits the setup on the right of Figure 26-5. The server install is the same as the Hyperbola directory and the clients are the same as the ~me directory. The configurations on the clients are distinct and must be updated independently. In effect, the installed files are being shared, but not the configurations.

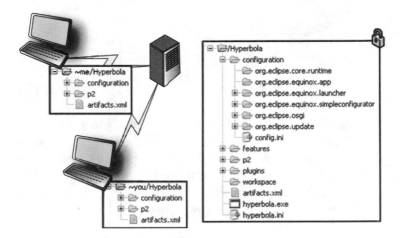

Figure 26–5 Shared install

The location of the configuration area in this scenario is controlled by the shared config.ini on the server. It includes the following line to set the configuration location, as shown in the figures:

```
osgi.configuration.area=@user.home/hyperbola/configuration
```

26.7.2 Bundle Pooling

Sharing plug-ins among multiple RCP applications can save both disk space and download time since each plug-in has to be retrieved and installed only once. Sharing plug-ins in a central location is known as *bundle pooling*. A bundle-pooled scenario is shown in Figure 26-6. Here the server contains some plug-in install sites (e.g., /common/plugins) and a p2 agent. The p2 agent is responsible for managing the different installs that use the plug-ins in this bundle pool. The figure shows a variety of clients using the same set of plug-ins.

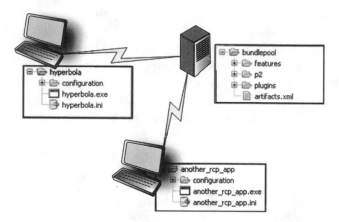

Figure 26–6   Multiple (shared) configurations

Setting up a bundle pool cannot be done by simply "unzipping" an RCP app. Instead, the RCP app must be "installed" using the director application. The director application specifies the install, the bundle pool, and the agent location. The following snippet shows how to install Hyperbola with a bundle pool from a p2 repository. Refer to Chapter 24, "Building Hyperbola," for a description of how to build Hyperbola and create a p2 repository.

```
./eclipse -application org.eclipse.equinox.p2.director \
  -metadataRepository http://metadata/repository
  -artifactRepository http://artifact/repository
  -installIU org.eclipsercp.hyperbola.product
  -profile Hyperbola
  -bundlePool c:/bundlepool
  -destination c:/hyperbola
  -p2.os win32
  -p2.ws win32
  -p2.arch x86
  -vmargs
  -Declipse.p2.data.area=c:/bundlepool/p2
```

If you install other configurations of Hyperbola, or any RCP app for that matter, you can use the same bundle pool location. If a plug-in already exists in the bundle pool, it will be reused.

NOTE

When reusing a bundle pool, you must use the same `eclipse.p2.data` area. This is because p2 manages all the plug-ins in the bundle pool and removes them when they are no longer used.

26.8 Summary

Deployment is a critical step in the overall process of making and delivering an RCP application to your users. Eclipse installs are relatively simple structures of files, and they can be delivered using a wide variety of mechanisms from simple archives to native installers or network-based installs such as Java Web Start. Enterprise users can set up shared installs that offer varying amounts of sharing and flexibility. So Eclipse not only helps you build your RCP products, but it helps you deliver them, too.

Each of the approaches described has benefits and drawbacks. These mostly revolve around the issues of separating users and ease of managing configurations. As an RCP application writer, you should allow for these installation scenarios and thus give your users the option of how to install your product.

26.9 Pointers

The reference section of the standard Eclipse plug-in developer Help (**Help > Platform Plug-in Developer Guide > Reference > Other reference information**) contains details of the system properties, file formats, and other structures discussed in this chapter.

PART V

Reference

There are several pieces of the RCP that do not fit neatly into a greater topic or compelling use cases and scenarios. These pieces nonetheless are vital to a full understanding and use of the Eclipse RCP. This last part of the book includes reference chapters covering the Eclipse implementation and use of the OSGi framework specification, the Eclipse databinding framework, and information about useful RCP plug-ins found in the Eclipse Platform.

CHAPTER 27

OSGi

In Chapter 2, "Eclipse RCP Concepts," we outlined the basic OSGi and Eclipse concepts of plug-ins/bundles, applications, products, and the extension registry. Further chapters provided additional detail in the context of particular problems or scenarios related to Hyperbola, our omnipresent chat client example. This chapter digs into the OSGi concepts and constructs that underlie Equinox and Eclipse.

You should think of this chapter as reference material and use it as needed. We cover many advanced topics and explain exactly what your application does from start to finish—the kind of information you need when you have problems and are up late at night troubleshooting. Of course, you are free to read through the chapter and pick up background information and various helpful tips and tricks that can be applied every day.

The material here is by no means a complete treatment of OSGi and its use in Eclipse; that is the subject of an entire separate volume, *OSGi and Eclipse* (Addison-Wesley, 2010); see *http://equinoxosgi.org*. This chapter is, however, useful for people who are

○ Curious about how plug-ins relate to OSGi constructs such as bundles

○ Troubleshooting their application, for example, tracking down a ClassNotFoundException

○ Designing a set of plug-ins and fragments

○ Looking to understand more about how Eclipse starts, runs, and stops

It is worth pointing out here that the OSGi framework specification is just that, a specification for a framework. The framework is intended to be implemented and run on a wide range of platforms and environments. As such, it does not say anything about, for example, how bundles are installed, how they are started, how they are laid out on disk, or even if they are laid out on disk. It is up to implementations to define these characteristics.

The bulk of this chapter is devoted to mapping the OSGi specification onto the Eclipse use case. Readers are encouraged to read the OSGi Framework Specification Release 4 from *http://osgi.org* and treat this chapter as a guide to the Eclipse implementation and use of that specification.

27.1 OSGi and the Eclipse Runtime

Eclipse is based on an implementation of the OSGi framework specification via the Equinox project. The Eclipse Runtime is a very thin veneer over the OSGi APIs that serves as a compatibility layer both for existing code and coding practices and for existing terminology and documentation.

The most important aspect of this layering is in the area of plug-ins. Eclipse users, its documentation and many books, and UIs all refer to *plug-ins* as the components that make up Eclipse applications, but now, under the covers, everything is implemented in terms of OSGi *bundles*. This is not as dramatic as it sounds because **the OSGi notion of a bundle is synonymous with the Eclipse notion of a plug-in.** A statement from Chapter 2 bears repeating here:

> There are **no fundamental or functional differences between plug-ins and bundles** in Eclipse. Both are mechanisms for grouping, delivering, and managing code. In fact, the traditional Eclipse Plugin API class is just a thin, optional layer of convenience functioning on top of OSGi bundles. To Eclipse, everything is a bundle. As such, we use the terms interchangeably and walk around chanting, "A plug-in is a bundle. A bundle is a plug-in. They are the same thing."

At the conceptual and structural levels, this mapping certainly holds, but what about at the code level? The org.eclipse.core.runtime.Plugin class seems pivotal to the Eclipse model. Let's look at this more closely by decomposing the roles of a traditional Eclipse Plugin class and see how it fits with the OSGi structures:

Identity to others—Plug-ins are passed around and their function accessed via the Plugin object.

Identity to the system—The system creates and manages Plugin objects that hold or represent state for the system.

Lifecycle handler—Plugin objects implement start(BundleContext) and stop(BundleContext) methods to do initialization and cleanup.

Handy access point—`Plugin` classes often have handy methods that give internal and external access to plug-in behavior. For example, the `ResourcesPlugin` `.getWorkspace()` returns the current workspace managed by the Resources plug-in.

By contrast, OSGi separates these roles into different objects, as described below. The methods on `Plugin` and methods that take `Plugin` arguments are then implemented in terms of these objects.

`Bundle` = Identity to others—Other bundles can ask the system for a Bundle object, query its state (e.g., started or stopped), look up files using `getEntries()`, and control it using `start()` and `stop()`. Developers do not implement bundles—the OSGi framework supplies and manages `Bundle` objects for you.

Do not confuse the `Bundle` object with any `Plugin` object you may choose to define. `Plugin` classes are purely optional, and the system-supplied `Plugin` class is there as a helper only. The `Bundle` object, on the other hand, is mandatory and completely defined and managed for you.

You can access the complete set of installed `Bundle` objects using various methods on `Platform` and `BundleContext`.

`BundleContext` = Identity to the system—At various points in time, bundles need to ask the system to do something for them, for example, install another bundle or register a service. Typically, the system needs to know the identity of the requesting bundle, for example, to confirm permissions or attribute services. The `BundleContext` fills this role.

A `BundleContext` is created and managed by the system as an opaque token. You simply pass it back or ask it questions when needed. This is much like `ServletContext` and other container architectures.

`BundleContexts` are given to bundles when they are started, that is, when the `BundleActivator` method `start(BundleContext)` is called. This is the sole means of discovering the context. If the bundle code needs the context, its activator must cache the value.

`BundleActivator` = Lifecycle handler—Some bundles need to initialize data structures or register listeners when they are started. Similarly, they need to clean up when they are stopped. Implementing a `BundleActivator` allows you to hook these start and stop events and do the required work.

The traditional `Plugin` class is in fact an implementation of the `BundleActivator` interface. `BundleActivators` define `start(BundleContext)` and `stop(Bundle-Context)` methods as replacements for the now deprecated `Plugin` methods `startup()` and `shutdown()`.

NOTE

OSGi does not have explicit support for the role of "handy access point" as outlined above. This role can be filled by any class.

Identity Theft

Of the three OSGi objects outlined here, only your Bundle object is meant for others to reference. That, in fact, is its role. Since your BundleContext is your identity to the system, you do not really want to hand it out to others and allow them to pretend to be you. Hold your context near and dear and be careful not to share it via convenience methods or exposed fields.

Similarly, your BundleActivator controls your initialization state. Normally it is invoked solely by the system. If you give others access to your activator, they can call start(BundleContext) and stop(BundleContext) directly and circumvent any checks and management that the system does. If you extend Plugin and make the class available to others, you should consider having a separate BundleActivator.

27.2 The Shape of Plug-ins

On disk, a bundle is a JAR containing a set of Java-related files. Figure 27-1 shows an example.

Figure 27–1   Standard JAR'd bundle layout

Figure 27-2, on the other hand, shows the bundle as a directory. Notice that everything is the same, except the code is in junit.jar rather than in the various org.* directories.

Figure 27–2 Directory bundle layout

These two forms of plug-ins are equivalent—Equinox and the tooling (e.g., PDE, p2, etc.) manage both forms equally well. Here are some useful tips to help you decide which format is better for your plug-ins:

Use directories

❍ If the plug-in contains many files that must be directly on the native file system. Examples of such files are shared libraries (e.g., DLLs), program executables, and JARs. Most Eclipse facilities (e.g., class loaders, Intro, Help, About, etc.) transparently extract the required files on demand, so the main concern here is efficiency. Extracting doubles the disk footprint and incurs a one-time cost. If the plug-in has many such files or they are large, consider packaging the plug-in as a directory.

Use JARs

❍ If the plug-in contains many small files that would otherwise fragment the disk

❍ If the plug-in contains highly compressible files

❍ If you want to sign the plug-ins and have that signature maintained after installation to support install verification and running with security (e.g., for Web Start)

The Eclipse SDK is about 95 percent JAR'd plug-ins. Of those that are not JAR'd, more than half are documentation, source, and other plug-ins that include large volumes of nested archives. The rest are left as directories for various reasons, as mentioned previously. So it's recommended that you deploy your plug-ins as JARs.

While this is transparent to both the user and the developers coding to the API of the plug-in, there are a few considerations for the developers of JAR'd plug-ins to note:

❍ JAR'd plug-ins should always have a classpath of "." or no classpath specification (this implies "."). A "." signifies that the JAR itself is the classpath entry since the JAR directly contains the code.

○ It is technically possible to run a JAR'd plug-in that has nested JARs on the classpath. Such nested JARs are automatically extracted and cached by the OSGi framework. As noted earlier, this effectively duplicates the amount of disk space required for the plug-in. More significantly, however, the tooling (both PDE and JDT) is unable to manage classpaths that include nested JARs. The net result is that while your plug-in runs, it takes more space and others cannot compile against it.

○ Similarly, Equinox understands JAR'd plug-ins with code in packages that do not start at the root of the JAR (e.g., `/bin/org/eclipse/…`). Again, the tooling is not set up for that structure. In particular, all standard Java compilers recognize only package structures directly at the root of a JAR. Developers are unable to code against JARs structured in this way.

○ The PDE export operations automatically JAR plug-ins that have "." on the classpath and create directory structures for those that do not.

27.3 Fragments

Sometimes it is not possible to package a plug-in as one unit. There are two common scenarios where this occurs:

Platform-specific content—Some plug-ins need different implementations on different OSs or window systems. You could package the code for all platforms in the plug-in, but this is bulky and cumbersome to manage when you want to add another platform. Splitting the plug-in into one for common code and others for platform-specific code is another possibility. This is problematic since implementation objects often need to access one another's package-visible members. This is not possible across plug-in boundaries.

Locale-specific content—Plug-ins often need locale-specific text messages, icons, and other resources. Again, it is possible to package the required resources for all locales together in the plug-in, but this is similarly cumbersome and wasteful. It would be better to package locale content separately and deploy only what is needed.

Eclipse supports these use cases using *fragments*. Fragments are just like regular plug-ins except their content is seamlessly merged at runtime with a *host* plug-in rather than being stand-alone. A fragment's classpath elements are appended to its host's classpath, and its registry contributions are made under the host's ID. You cannot express dependencies on fragments, just their hosts.

Figure 27-3 shows examples of both platform- and locale-specific fragments. Both fragments have a manifest file that identifies the fragment, its version, and

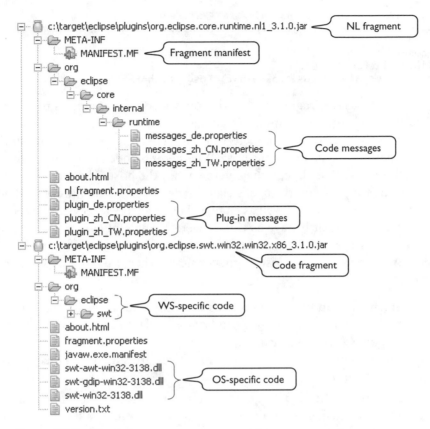

Figure 27–3 Plug-in fragments

its host ID and version range. The following is an example of the markup found in the Runtime's National Language (NL) fragment:

```
org.eclipse.core.runtime.nl1/MANIFEST.MF
Bundle-SymbolicName: org.eclipse.core.runtime.nl1
Bundle-Version: 3.1.0
Fragment-Host: org.eclipse.core.runtime;bundle-version="[3.1.0,4.0.0)"
Bundle-ClassPath: .
```

The next snippet is from the Windows SWT fragment's manifest file. Notice the highlighted platform filter line. This is an Eclipse-specific header that identifies the set of environmental conditions that must be met for this bundle to be resolved. In this case the osgi.os, osgi.ws, and osgi.arch system properties must match the given values. The syntax of the filter is that of standard Lightweight Directory Access Protocol (LDAP) filters and is detailed in the OSGi specification.

```
org.eclipse.swt.win32.win32.x86/MANIFEST.MF
Bundle-SymbolicName: org.eclipse.swt.win32.win32.x86; singleton:=true
Bundle-Version: 3.1.0
Fragment-Host: org.eclipse.swt; bundle-version="[3.0.0,4.0.0)"
Eclipse-PlatformFilter:
 (& (osgi.ws=win32) (osgi.os=win32) (osgi.arch=x86))
```

In both cases the fragments directly contain code or resources to be appended to the host's classpath. Adding a fragment's classpath entries, or the fragment itself, to the host is a vital characteristic of fragments. Fragments generally contain implementation detail for the host. Whether it is code or messages, the contents need to be accessed as though they were part of the host. The only way to do this is to put the fragment on the host's class loader. This gives bidirectional access to the classes and resources as well as enables Java package-level visibility. At runtime the host and fragment behave as if they were a single plug-in.

Fragments are a powerful mechanism, but they are not for every use case. There are several characteristics to consider when you are looking at using fragments:

Fragments are additive—Fragments can only add to their host; they cannot override content found in the host. For example, their classpath contributions are *appended* to those of the host, so if the host has a class or resource, all others are ignored. Their files and resources are similarly added to those of the host plug-in.

Fragments cannot be prerequisites—Since they represent implementation detail, their existence should be transparent to other plug-ins. As such, plug-ins cannot depend on fragments.

Fragments are not intended to add API—Since you cannot depend on fragments, they ought not expose additional API since plug-in writers are not able to express a dependency on that API.

Fragments can add exports—Normally, fragments are used to supply internal implementation detail. In certain instances such as testing and monitoring fragments, however, they may need to extend the set of packages exported by the host. They do this using normal Export-Package syntax. To support development-time visibility, the host plug-in should be marked with the header Eclipse-ExtensibleAPI: true. This tells PDE to expose the additional fragment exports to plug-ins that depend on the host.

Figure 27-4 shows the OSGi console of a running Eclipse application after typing the short status (ss) command. Notice that the org.eclipse.resources.win32 fragment (12) is shown as installed (and resolved) and bound to the Resources host plug-in (13). Notice also that the report for the Resources plug-in also lists

Figure 27–4 Fragment resolution status

plug-in 88 as an attached fragment. It is not shown here, but it is actually the Core Tools Resource Spy fragment. This illustrates that you can have multiple fragments attached to the same host.

The OSGi Console

It is quite curious that in this day and age of GUIs, a simple command-line UI such as the OSGi console should cause such a stir. When people first see that there is a console under the covers, the geek in them comes out and they succumb to the need to manually install, start, stop, and uninstall bundles.

This is good fun, but the console is actually quite powerful and useful for both controlling and introspecting a running system. In addition to controlling bundles, you can investigate specific bundles, diagnose problems with bundles not being resolved, find various contributed services, and so on.

The console is not started by default. To get a console, start Eclipse using the -console command-line argument and look for the console's osgi> prompt in either the shell you used to launch Eclipse or the new shell created if you launched Eclipse from a desktop icon. Type help to get a complete list of available commands.

27.4 Version Numbering

The pair of a plug-in ID and its version should uniquely identify the plug-in's content. Since the plug-in ID never changes, the version number must change whenever the content of the plug-in changes. Plug-in version numbers are made up of four parts: major.minor.service.qualifier:

> **Major**—Differences in the major part indicate significant differences such that backward compatibility is not guaranteed.

Minor—Changes in the minor part indicate that the newer version of the plug-in is backward-compatible with the older version, but it includes additional functionality and/or API.

Service—The service part indicates the presence of bug fixes and minor implementation (i.e., hidden) changes over previous versions.

Qualifier—The qualifier is not interpreted by OSGi. Qualifiers are compared using standard string comparison.

Following these numbering semantics is important. As plug-ins come to depend on one another, they need to know about changes in the compatibility contract as well as update their requirements. For example, the following plug-in declaration claims that the Hyperbola plug-in works with *any* version of the Runtime plug-in. This is likely incorrect.

org.eclipsercp.hyperbola/MANIFEST.MF
```
Bundle-SymbolicName: org.eclipsercp.hyperbola
Bundle-Version: 1.0.0
Require-Bundle: org.eclipse.core.runtime
```

A more likely scenario is that Hyperbola is buying into the Runtime API at a specific minimum level. For example:

org.eclipsercp.hyperbola/MANIFEST.MF
```
Bundle-SymbolicName: org.eclipsercp.hyperbola
Bundle-Version: 1.0.0
Require-Bundle: org.eclipse.core.runtime;bundle-version="[3.1.0,4.0.0)"
```

In this case Hyperbola is happy with any Runtime plug-in from 3.1 to 4.0 (not including 4.0). This is the traditional Eclipse match="compatible" scenario—the default behavior. Here the Hyperbola plug-in is saying that it needs 3.1-level functionality.

On the other hand, the specification below is the same as the traditional Eclipse match="perfect" and is too strict—it prevents the Hyperbola plug-in from running on any version of the Runtime other than 3.1.0. Unfortunately, that means that if users update the Runtime to version 3.1.1 to fix a bug, Hyperbola no longer resolves and no longer works.

org.eclipsercp.hyperbola/MANIFEST.MF
```
Bundle-SymbolicName: org.eclipsercp.hyperbola
Bundle-Version: 1.0.0
Require-Bundle: org.eclipse.core.runtime;bundle-version="[3.1.0,3.1.0]"
```

So the challenge here is to specify the version dependencies loosely enough that the plug-ins work in various settings, but tightly enough that the required API contracts are guaranteed. Of course, this mechanism works only if plug-in producers update their plug-in's version number according to the version semantics and thus give their consumers a chance to get it right.

27.5 Services

Services are a key element of the OSGi architecture. In short, the service mechanism is a way for one bundle to register a service provider (i.e., an implementation of some Java type) and have others discover and use that service. The services model is powerful and flexible.

On the surface, the functionality supplied by OSGi services and that of the Eclipse extension mechanism appear to overlap somewhat. Indeed, both are mechanisms for facilitating and managing interactions between components, but they are more complementary than overlapping.

The service mechanism has a component that implements some interface and then registers its implementation as publicly available. Interested components acquire and use implementations as needed. The mechanism is quite effective for decoupling dynamic components and implementation from specification.

By contrast, the extension mechanism is a means for some implementation to expose extensibility. It results in a private contract between the extension point definer and the extension contributor. For example, the UI renders views and allows components to contribute views for it to render. View contributors contribute directly to the UI plug-in and do not expect to find their view being used by others.

Furthermore, extensions are declarative and can carry more than just code. View extensions, for example, include the name of the view and the icons to use in addition to the name of the class that implements the view. Similarly, documentation extensions carry no code at all—just documentation archives—so there is no service implementation to register.

Services are not covered extensively in this book because Eclipse RCP makes relatively little use of them. This is not a statement against services, but rather a pragmatic realization that historically services were not part of Eclipse, and restructuring large bodies of code to use services is just not an effective use of the Eclipse team's time.

Over time, we expect to see services used more and more as appropriate. In fact, with the advent of e4, the service style of programming, and actual OSGi services, is seeing more use. You are encouraged to look at the *OSGi and Equinox* book (Addison-Wesley, 2010) (see *http://equinoxosgi.org*) and the OSGi framework specification from *http://osgi.org* to see if services make sense in your architecture. See also the `BundleContext.getService*()` methods and the `ServiceTracker` utility class.

In general, Eclipse is able to concurrently run multiple versions of the same plug-in; that is, `org.eclipsercp.hyperbola` versions 1.0 and 2.0 can be both installed and running at the same time. This is part of the power of the OSGi's component model. Dependent plug-ins are bound to particular versions of their prerequisites and see only the classes supplied by them.

There are cases, however, where there really should be only one version of a given plug-in in the system. For example, SWT makes certain assumptions about its control over the display and main thread. SWT cannot cohabitate with other SWTs. More generally, this occurs wherever one plug-in expects to have exclusive access to a global resource, whether it be a thread, an OS resource, a Transmission Control Protocol (TCP) port, or the extension registry namespace.

To address this, OSGi allows a bundle to be declared as a *singleton*. The bundle in the example below is marked as a singleton. This tells OSGi to resolve at most one version of the bundle. All other version constraints in the system are then matched against the chosen singleton version.

```
org.eclipse.core.runtime/MANIFEST.MF
Bundle-SymbolicName: org.eclipse.core.runtime;singleton:=true
Bundle-Version: 3.5.0
```

The most common reason to mark a plug-in as a singleton is that it declares extensions or extension points. The extension registry namespace is a shared resource that is populated by bundle IDs. If we allowed multiple versions of the same bundle to contribute to the registry, interconnections would be ambiguous.

By default, bundles that declare extensions or extension points but do not have a MANIFEST.MF are marked as singletons. If you have a MANIFEST.MF, you should annotate it accordingly.

27.6 Bundle Lifecycle

Bundles go through a number of states in their lives. Understanding these helps you understand when and why various things happen to your bundle and what you can do about it. Section 22.3.3, "Bundle Listeners," details how to monitor any events arising from bundles changing state.

Deployed—When a bundle is deployed, it is laid down on disk (e.g., extracted from an archive) and is physically available. Note that bundles may be deployed to a server and may never actually be present on the executing machine. This state is not formally represented in the system, but the term *deployed* is used to talk about a bundle that could become installed.

Installed—An installed bundle is one that has been deployed and presented to the OSGi framework as a candidate for execution. Installed bundles do not yet have a class loader, and if the Equinox Extension Registry is running, their registry contributions are not yet added to the extension registry.

Resolved—Resolved bundles have been installed and all of their prerequisites have been satisfied by other bundles, which are also resolved. If the Equinox Extension Registry bundle is active, the contributions of resolved bundles are added to the extension registry. Resolved bundles may have a class loader and may be fully operational. As shown in Figure 27-5, there are some bundles that can stay in the resolved state and never become started.

Starting—A resolved bundle that is transitioning to the active state passes through the starting state. Bundles remain in the starting state while their activator's start(BundleContext) method is executing.

Active—A started bundle is one that has been resolved and whose start() method has been successfully run. Active bundles have a class loader and are fully operational.

Stopping—An active bundle that is transitioning back to the resolved state passes through the stopping state. Bundles remain in the stopping state while their activator's stop(BundleContext) method is executing.

Uninstalled—An uninstalled bundle is a bundle that was previously in the installed state but has since been uninstalled. Such bundles are still present in the system but may behave in unexpected ways.

Figure 27–5 Example console output showing bundle state

Figure 27-6 shows the details of the state transitions for bundles. Notice that the deployed state is not shown as it is outside the scope of Equinox and OSGi. Being deployed simply means that the bundle is available to be installed.

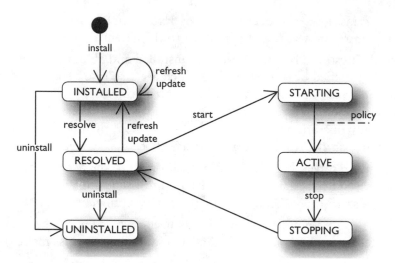

Figure 27–6   Bundle state transitions

27.6.1 BundleActivator

In support of the starting and stopping lifecycle transitions, a bundle can supply an *activator* class. As we mentioned earlier, the standard Plugin class implements the OSGi-defined BundleActivator interface. Activators are instantiated by the OSGi framework, and their start(BundleContext) and stop(BundleContext) methods are called when a bundle is started or stopped. Extending Plugin is the traditional Eclipse coding pattern, but you are free to implement the BundleActivator interface directly. Eclipse's Plugin class is essentially a helper that supplies some useful methods for logging, preference accessing, and so on. Use whichever technique suits your needs.

TIP

The BundleActivator methods are called on whatever thread happens to be executing at the time the bundle changes state. Your start(BundleContext) and stop(BundleContext) methods should be coded accordingly.

Either way, if you define an activator class, you need to tell the framework about it. Use the **Activator** field in the **General Information** section on the plug-in editor's **Overview** page, as shown in Figure 27-7.

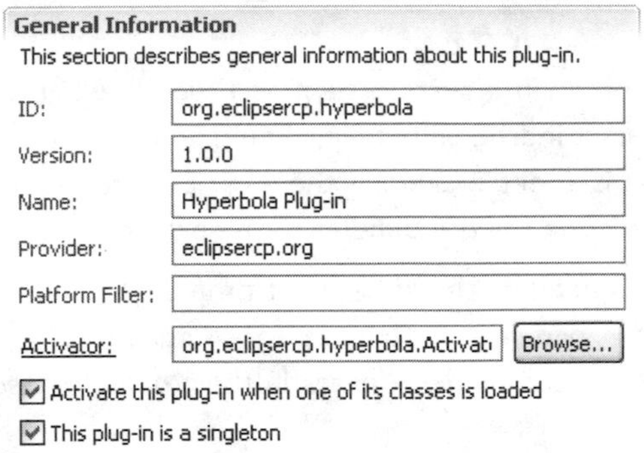

Figure 27–7   Specifying the bundle activator class

27.6.2 The Downside of Activators

Having given details and examples of how to write and identify your activator or `Plugin` class, we caution you against using them. Running code on activation is an overused capability. One of the basic tenets of Eclipse is that laziness is good— **"Run no code before its time."** In our experience, the `start(BundleContext)` and `stop(BundleContext)` methods rarely need to be implemented.

Bundles can be activated for many different reasons in many different contexts. We commonly see bundles that load and initialize models, open and verify caches, and do all manner of other heavyweight operations in their `start(BundleContext)` methods. The cost of this is added to the startup time and footprint of your application and is not always justified.

We once found a bundle that was loading 11MB of *code* as a side effect of being activated. First of all, that's a lot of code. More critically, however, there were several cases where activation occurred as a result of some trivial processing of resource navigator decorators.

Decorators are those little annotations you see on base resource icons that indicate the resource has a marker, is part of a repository, and so on. The bundle in question supplied a very small class to determine if a given project needed domain-specific decoration. The loading of this one class triggered the activation of the bundle. The authors assumed that if the bundle was started, the entire complex model it maintained would be needed. Of course, the decorator processing was trivial; it did not require the model at all and often determined that no decoration was required—all that work and space were completely wasted.

This is just one example of activator abuse. A better approach is to initialize your caches and data structures as required with more precision.

NOTE

Startup time is a bit of a misnomer in a system such as Eclipse. What is really important is the time taken to start individual bundles. Equinox itself starts in milliseconds. The rest of the time is spent executing the `start(BundleContext)` methods and other initialization code for the bundles in the system.

Since bundles are started only as needed, the initial start time of your application may be fast, but as the user progressively touches more functionality, more bundles are activated—lengthy activations delay users in their quest to use your application.

27.6.3 Uses for Activators

So if activators are bad, why do they exist? Well, they are actually valuable in certain scenarios:

Registering services or listeners—As the code snippet below illustrates, `start(BundleContext)` adds a listener and `stop(BundleContext)` removes it. This is well formed, small, and quick.

```
public class Activator implements BundleActivator {
  private BundleListener listener = null;

  public void start(BundleContext context) {
    listener = new BundleListener() { ... };
    context.addBundleListener(listener);
  }
  public void stop(BundleContext context) {
    if (listener != null)
      context.removeBundleListener(listener);
    listener = null;
  }
}
```

Starting shared mechanisms—The canonical example here is a Web container bundle. When this bundle is started, it opens a socket and starts listening on a port. When it is stopped, it closes all sockets and releases all resources. Even here, however, care should be taken to do as little work as possible until it is needed—the server may never need to service a request!

Cleaning up—When a bundle is stopped, it should release the shared resources it has allocated. Sometimes this allocation occurs in the activator's `start(BundleContext)` method as above, but it may also occur lazily as shown below. Cleanup should be done proactively and immediately; that is, do not return from `stop(BundleContext)` until all cleanup for your bundle is complete. Here the `ImageRegistry` is created lazily. Note that there is no startup overhead in this activator.

```java
public class Activator implements BundleActivator {
  private ImageRegistry registry = null;

  public void stop(BundleContext context) {
    if (registry != null) {
      registry.dispose();
      registry = null;
    }
  }
  public ImageRegistry getRegistry() {
    ImageRegistry result = registry;
    if (result != null)
      return result;
    synchronized(this) {
      registry = new ImageRegistry();
      ... populate registry ...
      return registry;
    }
  }
}
```

27.7 Early Activation

By this time you should have gotten the idea that doing work when your bundle starts is a bad thing. It may cause unnecessary work and delay others from getting the function they want. Even worse is forcing your bundle to be started when Eclipse starts. This makes the end user wait for the system to come up.

There are, however, some scenarios where both evils are necessary. The example of a Web container highlights this. Consider an application that inherently supplies external access via a Web browser. The implementation includes a bundle that supplies a Web container. The container's operation is dependent on it, opening a TCP port and servicing HTTP requests received from clients. Since this is an inherent part of the application, it should happen automatically and not depend on some user action to start the server.

There are two ways of doing this in Eclipse: the early activation extension point and the `osgi.bundles` list. Both are detailed in the following sections.

27.7.1 Early Activation Extensions

The Eclipse UI plug-in defines the `org.eclipse.ui.startup` extension point. Contributed extensions must supply a class that implements `IStartup`. You must use the UI's default Workbench to manage the UI to use this mechanism. Once the

Workbench is initialized and running, the startup extensions are run. For each extension, the given class is loaded and instantiated and earlyStartup() is called on the resultant object.

NOTE

It is tempting to make your Plugin or BundleActivator implement IStartup. Don't. Both Plugin and BundleActivator are managed objects and should not be instantiated by you or supplied as executable extensions. Failure to follow this rule confuses Equinox and leads to unpredictable behavior.

Extensions are run in random order and you cannot make any assumptions about the thread used to run the extensions. In practice, they are run on a worker thread spawned specifically for this purpose.

The UI also manages preferences to track which registered extensions to invoke. In the IDE these are visible on the **General > Startup and Shutdown** preferences page.

27.7.2 osgi.bundles

The osgi.bundles list is a comma-separated list of bundles that are automatically installed and optionally started when Eclipse is run. It is maintained as a system property and typically defined in the config.ini file of a configuration. The default entry for the Eclipse IDE is shown here:

```
$ECLIPSE_HOME/configuration/config.ini
osgi.bundles=\
  org.eclipse.core.runtime@2:start,\
  org.eclipse.update.configurator@3:start
```

Each entry is of the following form:

```
<URL | simple bundle location>[@ [<startlevel>] [":start"]]
```

Simple bundle locations are interpreted as relative to the OSGi framework's parent directory. URLs must be of the form platform:/base/ or file:. In general, the URLs may include a version number (e.g., .../location_1.2.3). If a version is not specified, the system binds to the location that matches exactly or to the versioned location with the latest version number. If a version number is given, only exact matches are considered.

27.7.3 Start Levels

In the example osgi.bundles property in the previous section, the start level value indicates the OSGi *start level* at which the bundle should run. OSGi start levels are much like UNIX start levels. As the system starts, the start level is increased and all bundles marked as started at a particular level are started before those of the next level. So, for example, by the time bundles at level 4 are started, all those needing to be started at level 3 have been started. If a level is not specified, the framework uses the default start level determined by the value of the osgi.bundles .defaultStartLevel system property (currently 4 in Eclipse). If the start tag is added, the bundle is marked as started after being installed.

You can inject your bundle into the startup sequence by controlling its start level. This allows you to, for example, add login prompters before the application is run, control the bundles that are installed, or do last-minute cleanup as the system shuts down.

WARNING

This mechanism is for advanced use only. You really have to understand how the system works before looking to manage start levels manually. Note also that the current start level values are not API and are subject to change in future releases.

27.8 Lazy Activation

A bundle can be manually activated and deactivated by calling the Bundle methods start() or stop(), respectively. These methods are public OSGi API, but you should never need to call them yourself. Lazy activation works by having Equinox detect the first time a bundle is asked to supply a class. Normally, a resolved bundle does not have a class loader; it is simply present in the system and all its prerequisites are satisfied. When a resolved bundle is asked to supply a class, Equinox ensures that the bundle is activated.

When the class loader is created, the bundle's start() method is called. This, in turn, causes the bundle's activator to be loaded and its start(BundleContext) method to be called. This is all done *before* attempting to load the requested class. After a successful start() call, the requested class is loaded and returned as normal.

The net effect is that you can always be sure that your bundle has been activated by the time its code is running (except, of course, the code involved in evaluating the activator's start(BundleContext)). This frees you from continually having to check. It also means that the system as a whole can be lazier. There is no need for a central management agent or complicated policy to determine when bundles should be started—they are simply started as needed.

It's worth highlighting some of the typical scenarios that do (and do not) cause activation:

- Using `IConfigurationElement.createExecutableExtension()` **does** cause the bundle supplying the specified class to be activated. Note the subtlety here. It is not the bundle defining the extension, but rather the one defining the class specified in the extension. Typically these are the same, but not always.

- Calling `Bundle.loadClass(String)` **does** cause activation of the bundle that eventually supplies the requested class. Again, note the subtlety. If, for example, bundle A asks bundle B and B asks bundle C and C eventually loads and returns the class, bundle B is not activated. B was simply a step along the way.

- Loading a class from bundle A that *depends on* a class from bundle B **does** activate B. Here the notion of *depends on* is derived from the JVM specification. If loading and verifying the class from A requires a class from B, B's class is loaded and B is activated. This can occur if A's class extends B's or references B's in a method signature.

- Accessing, traversing, or otherwise using a bundle's extensions **does not** cause activation.

- Bundle activation is not transitive; that is, activating a bundle A that depends on another bundle B **does not** in and of itself cause B to be activated. Of course, if classes are loaded from B while activating A, B is activated.

OSGi and Bundle Lazy Activation

In a conventional OSGi framework, bundles must be explicitly started and activated by calling their `Bundle.start()` method. The OSGi framework specification is silent on how or when `start()` is called—typically this is done by a central management agent or simply by having the framework always start all bundles.

In Eclipse, the only viable point of management is the OSGi framework, Equinox, itself. You can enable this mechanism by adding the following line to the `MANIFEST.MF` of your plug-in:

```
Bundle-ActivationPolicy: lazy
```

This can be done from the manifest editor by selecting the **Activate this plug-in when one of its classes is loaded** box in the **General** section of the **Overview** tab.

27.9 Data Areas

Applications often need to read or store data. Depending on the use case, this data may be stored in one of many locations. Consider preferences as an example.

Typical products use at least some preferences. The preferences themselves may or may not be defined in the product's plug-ins. For example, if you are reusing plug-ins from different products, it is more convenient to manage the preferences outside the plug-in.

In addition, applications often allow users to change preference values or use preferences to store recently opened files, recent chat partners, and so on. These values might be stored uniquely for each user or shared among users. In scenarios where applications operate on distinct data sets, some of the preferences may even relate to the particular data and should be stored or associated with that data.

Preferences are just one example, but they illustrate the various scopes and lifecycles that applications have for the data they read and write. Eclipse defines four *data areas* that capture these characteristics and allow application writers to properly control the scope of their data:

Install—The install area is where Eclipse itself is installed. The install area is generally read-only. The data in the install area is available to all instances of all configurations of Eclipse running on the install. See also `Platform.getInstallLocation()` and `osgi.install.area`.

Configuration—The configuration area is where the running configuration of Eclipse is defined. Configuration areas are generally writable. The data in a configuration area is available to all instances of the configuration. Chapter 26, "The Last Mile," contains additional detail on the configuration area. See also `Platform.getConfigurationLocation()` and `osgi.configuration.area`.

Instance—The instance area is the default location for user-defined data (e.g., a workspace). The instance area is typically writable. Applications may allow multiple sessions to have concurrent access to the instance area but must take care to prevent things like lost updates. See also `Platform.getInstanceLocation()` and `osgi.instance.area`.

NOTE

The Eclipse IDE's *workspace* is an **example** of the use of instance locations. The Resources plug-in implementers chose to make the default location for projects be in the instance area defined by Equinox. Eclipse IDE users commonly think they are setting the Resource's workspace location, but actually they are setting Equinox's instance location.

User—The user area is where Eclipse manages data specific to a user, but independent of the configuration or instance. The user area is typically based on the Java `user.home` system property and the initial value of the `osgi.user.area` system property. See also `Platform.getUserLocation()` and `osgi.user.area`.

In addition to these Eclipse-wide areas, Equinox defines two locations specifically for each installed plug-in:

State location—This is a location within the instance area's metadata. See `Plugin.getStateLocation()`.

Data location—This is a location within the configuration's metadata. See `Bundle.getDataFile()`.

Each of these locations is controlled by setting the system properties described before Eclipse starts (e.g., in the `config.ini`). Locations are URLs. For simplicity, file paths are also accepted and automatically converted to `file:` URLs. For better control and convenience, there are also a number of predefined symbolic locations that can be used. Note that not all combinations of location type and symbolic value are valid. Table 27-1 details which combinations are possible.

@none—Indicates that the corresponding location should never be set either explicitly or to its default value. For example, an RCP-style application that has no instance data may use `osgi.instance.area=@none` to prevent extraneous files being written to disk. @none must not be followed by any path segments.

@noDefault—Forces a location to be undefined or explicitly defined (i.e., Eclipse does not automatically compute a default value). This is useful when you want to allow for data in the corresponding location, but the Eclipse default value is not appropriate. @noDefault must not be followed by any path segments.

@user.home—Directs Eclipse to compute a location value relative to the user's home directory. @user.home can be followed by path segments. In all cases, the string @user.home is replaced with the value of the Java `user.home` system property. For example, setting

`osgi.instance.area=@user.home/myWorkspace`

results in a value of

`file:/users/fred/myWorkspace`

@user.dir—Directs Eclipse to compute a location value relative to the current working directory. @user.dir can be followed by path segments. In all cases, the string @user.dir is replaced with the value of the Java user.dir system property. For example, setting

```
osgi.instance.area=@user.dir/myWorkspace
```

results in a value of

```
file:/usr/local/eclipse/myWorkspace
```

Since the default case is for all locations to be set, valid, and writable, some plug-ins may fail in other setups, even if they are listed as possible. For example, it is unreasonable to expect a plug-in focused on instance data, such as the Resources plug-in, to do much if the instance area is not defined. It is up to plug-in developers to choose the setups they support and design their functions accordingly.

Table 27–1   Location Compatibilities

Location/Value	Supports Default?	File/URL	@none	@noDefault	@user.home	@user.dir
Install	No	Yes	No	No	Yes	Yes
Configuration	Yes	Yes	Yes*	Yes*	Yes	Yes
Instance	Yes	Yes	Yes	Yes	Yes	Yes (default)
User	Yes	Yes	Yes	Yes	Yes	Yes

* Indicates that this setup is technically possible but pragmatically quite difficult to manage. In particular, without a configuration location, Equinox may get only as far as starting the OSGi framework.

Note that each of the locations can be statically marked as read-only by setting the corresponding property osgi.AAA.area.readonly=true, where AAA is one of the area names.

27.10 Summary

The strength of Eclipse lies in its use of modularity via its robust plug-in model. This, in turn, maps directly onto the OSGi framework specification and its bundle model. Plug-ins bring advantages of scale, composition, serviceability, and flexibility. The costs of this power are the rigor and attention to detail required when defining plug-ins—poorly defined plug-ins are hard to compose and reuse in the same way as poorly defined objects.

This chapter exposes the essential details of the OSGi component model and the Eclipse implementation of the OSGi specification. We touched on some of the framework's configuration options and provided a number of guidelines for building your plug-ins.

With this information you will design and implement better components that run more efficiently and have more class loading and composition options.

27.11 Pointers

- ○ The OSGi Web site (*http://osgi.org*) has a good set of resources to get you started with OSGi outside the Eclipse world.

- ○ The Equinox Web site (*http://eclipse.org/equinox*) contains resources related to Eclipse's implementation of OSGi.

- ○ The EclipseRT Web site (*http://eclipse.org/eclipsert*) has a list of frameworks and tools you can use in your OSGi-based applications.

- ○ The OSGi and Equinox book contains more in-depth information about OSGi: McAffer, Jeff, Paul VanderLei, and Simon Archer. *OSGi and Equinox: Creating Highly Modular Java Systems* (Addison-Wesley, 2010), ISBN 0321585712.

CHAPTER 28

Eclipse Databinding

As we have seen, there's an impressive stack of technologies available to you while building RCP applications. One of these technologies that we have avoided using in Hyperbola is called Eclipse databinding. At the highest level, Eclipse databinding is a set of abstractions that allow for synchronization between objects. The most relevant use case for RCP developers is simplifying user interface programming by using Eclipse databinding to bind user interface components to model objects.

In this book we've been careful to keep Hyperbola code as simple as possible while demonstrating the power of RCP. We avoided using Eclipse databinding in Hyperbola because of the initial complexity of learning any new framework. This chapter presents a dive into the design, capabilities, and usage of databinding. In particular, we

- Learn how to get started with databinding in RCP applications such as Hyperbola
- Introduce the architecture and terminology behind databinding
- Identify common coding patterns for working with databinding

28.1 Getting Started

To take advantage of Eclipse databinding, you need to add the main Eclipse databinding plug-in, `org.eclipse.jface.databinding`, to your application. Generally this is an easy task since Eclipse databinding ships with the `org.eclipse.rcp` feature. The main plug-in of interest is `org.eclipse.jface.databinding` which has very few dependencies, as shown in Figure 28-1.

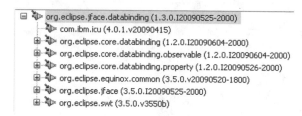

Figure 28–1   Eclipse databinding dependencies

It's important to note that Eclipse databinding was designed to be user-interface-agnostic. There is default support provided for SWT and JFace via the `org.eclipse.jface.databinding` plug-in. There is nothing preventing you from using Eclipse databinding in a headless fashion or with other user interface toolkits. As an example, Eclipse databinding support is available for the Eclipse Modeling Framework (EMF) and even the Google Web Toolkit (GWT).

28.2 Why Databinding?

While developing user interfaces, it's common to have a domain model and some widgets that map to that domain model. For example, if you have a user address book application, you have a domain model that represents contact information, and you have a set of user interface controls that manipulate the domain model. So while you're typing in the name of a contact, under the covers there's some synchronization going on between the user interface control and the model to make sure the model is up to date. Or, if you look at it the other way around, if you invoke a change to the model, the user interface control must be aware of that change and update itself to show the latest model content.

Fortunately, many widgets have models that make this synchronization process easier, but the problem still remains that your domain model isn't in the form of the widget model. This results in a lot of error-prone boilerplate synchronization code.

Databinding helps solve this synchronization problem by allowing you to bind data between two items, updating one side of the relationship when the other side changes.

28.3 Architecture

The general principle behind Eclipse databinding is the synchronization of values between objects. Synchronization is often carried out in both directions and includes steps like validation and conversion. In a typical example, the synchronization happens between model objects and user interface objects such as SWT. In Eclipse databinding, the value objects you're interested in *observing* changes to are called *observables*. The object that represents the value synchronization of two or more observables is called a *binding*. The flow of data between observables and a binding is shown in Figure 28-2.

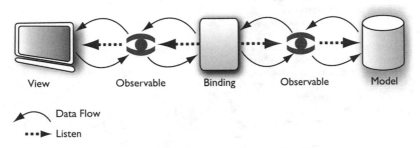

Figure 28–2 Eclipse databinding architecture

28.4 Observables

Observables represent an abstraction for setting values, getting values, and observing changes in objects. If you're familiar with design patterns, an observable is simply an abstraction of the *Observer pattern* that is codified into two interfaces: IObservable and IObservableValue. The IObservable interface defines a way to listen for state changes. The IObservableValue interface extends IObservable to add the concept of a specific value, along with methods for getting and setting that value. To take advantage of databinding, you have to create observables for your model or view objects. Thankfully, Eclipse databinding comes with different types of observable factories to help you create observables.

28.4.1 PojoObservables

The PojoObservables factory is responsible for creating observables for Plain Old Java Objects (POJOs), as shown in Figure 28-3.

To create observables, you must call the respective method on the PojoObservables factory. For example, if we had a Person POJO that had a name field, the coding pattern to create an observable would be as outlined in the following snippet:

```
Person person = new Person();
person.setName("Chris Aniszczyk");
// Fill in other person details.
IObservableValue nameObservable =
    PojoObservables.observeValue(person, "name");
```

```
 S  observeDetailList(Realm, IObservableValue, String, Class) : IObservableList
 S  observeDetailList(IObservableValue, String, Class) : IObservableList
 S  observeDetailMap(Realm, IObservableValue, String) : IObservableMap
 S  observeDetailMap(IObservableValue, String) : IObservableMap
 S  observeDetailSet(Realm, IObservableValue, String, Class) : IObservableSet
 S  observeDetailSet(IObservableValue, String, Class) : IObservableSet
 S  observeDetailValue(Realm, IObservableValue, String, Class) : IObservableValue
 S  observeDetailValue(IObservableValue, String, Class) : IObservableValue
 S  observeList(Object, String) : IObservableList
 S  observeList(Object, String, Class) : IObservableList
 S  observeList(Realm, Object, String) : IObservableList
 S  observeList(Realm, Object, String, Class) : IObservableList
 S  observeMap(Object, String) : IObservableMap
 S  observeMap(Object, String, Class, Class) : IObservableMap
 S  observeMap(Realm, Object, String) : IObservableMap
 S  observeMap(Realm, Object, String, Class, Class) : IObservableMap
 S  observeMap(IObservableSet, Class, String) : IObservableMap
 S  observeMap(IObservableSet, String) : IObservableMap
 S  observeMaps(IObservableSet, Class, String[]) : IObservableMap[]
 S  observeMaps(IObservableSet, String[]) : IObservableMap[]
 S  observeSet(Object, String) : IObservableSet
 S  observeSet(Object, String, Class) : IObservableSet
 S  observeSet(Realm, Object, String) : IObservableSet
 S  observeSet(Realm, Object, String, Class) : IObservableSet
 S  observeValue(Object, String) : IObservableValue
 S  observeValue(Realm, Object, String) : IObservableValue
```

Figure 28–3 PojoObservables factory methods

NOTE

The downside of using PojoObservables is that your observables don't support synchronization back to whatever you're bound to. For example, if you're using PojoObservables in combination with SWTObservables, your user interface won't react to any changes that happen to your POJOs behind the scenes as there is no effective way to listen to changes in POJOs. However, changes that happen in your user interface will be propagated to your POJOs. It's important to note this if your use cases require synchronization to happen both ways using Eclipse databinding.

28.4.2 `BeansObservables`

The `BeansObservables` factory is responsible for creating observables that adhere to the JavaBeans specification, as shown in Figure 28-4. The `BeansObservables` factory is identical to the `PojoObservables` factory except for the fact that it allows for property change events, which enables synchronization to happen both ways.

```
observeDetailList(Realm, IObservableValue, String, Class) : IObservableList
observeDetailList(IObservableValue, String, Class) : IObservableList
observeDetailMap(Realm, IObservableValue, String) : IObservableMap
observeDetailMap(IObservableValue, String) : IObservableMap
observeDetailSet(Realm, IObservableValue, String, Class) : IObservableSet
observeDetailSet(IObservableValue, String, Class) : IObservableSet
observeDetailValue(Realm, IObservableValue, Class, String, Class) : IObservableValue
observeDetailValue(Realm, IObservableValue, String, Class) : IObservableValue
observeDetailValue(IObservableValue, Class, String, Class) : IObservableValue
observeDetailValue(IObservableValue, String, Class) : IObservableValue
observeList(Object, String) : IObservableList
observeList(Object, String, Class) : IObservableList
observeList(Realm, Object, String) : IObservableList
observeList(Realm, Object, String, Class) : IObservableList
observeMap(Object, String) : IObservableMap
observeMap(Object, String, Class, Class) : IObservableMap
observeMap(Realm, Object, String) : IObservableMap
observeMap(Realm, Object, String, Class, Class) : IObservableMap
observeMap(IObservableSet, Class, String) : IObservableMap
observeMap(IObservableSet, String) : IObservableMap
observeMaps(IObservableSet, Class, String[]) : IObservableMap[]
observeMaps(IObservableSet, String[]) : IObservableMap[]
observeSet(Object, String) : IObservableSet
observeSet(Object, String, Class) : IObservableSet
observeSet(Realm, Object, String) : IObservableSet
observeSet(Realm, Object, String, Class) : IObservableSet
observeValue(Object, String) : IObservableValue
observeValue(Realm, Object, String) : IObservableValue
```

Figure 28–4   `BeansObservables` factory methods

To create observables, you must call the respective method on the `Beans-Observables` factory. For example, if we had updated our `Person` object to be a JavaBean, the coding pattern to create an observable would be as outlined in this snippet:

```
Person person = new Person();
person.setName("Chris Aniszczyk");
// Fill in other person details.
IObservableValue nameObservable =
    BeansObservables.observeValue(person, "name");
```

TIP

Advanced users of Eclipse RCP may use EMF in their projects to help develop their model-related code. If you're using EMF, there's Eclipse databinding support via EMFObservables via the org.eclipse.emf.databinding plug-in.

28.4.3 SWTObservables

The SWTObservables factory is responsible for creating observables for a variety of SWT widgets, as shown in Figure 28-5.

```
● ˢ observeBackground(Control) : ISWTObservableValue
● ˢ observeBounds(Control) : ISWTObservableValue
● ˢ observeDelayedValue(int, ISWTObservableValue) : ISWTObservableValue
● ˢ observeEditable(Control) : ISWTObservableValue
● ˢ observeEnabled(Control) : ISWTObservableValue
● ˢ observeFocus(Control) : ISWTObservableValue
● ˢ observeFont(Control) : ISWTObservableValue
● ˢ observeForeground(Control) : ISWTObservableValue
● ˢ observeImage(Widget) : ISWTObservableValue
● ˢ observeItems(Control) : IObservableList
● ˢ observeLocation(Control) : ISWTObservableValue
● ˢ observeMax(Control) : ISWTObservableValue
● ˢ observeMessage(Widget) : ISWTObservableValue
● ˢ observeMin(Control) : ISWTObservableValue
● ˢ observeSelection(Control) : ISWTObservableValue
● ˢ observeSingleSelectionIndex(Control) : ISWTObservableValue
● ˢ observeSize(Control) : ISWTObservableValue
● ˢ observeText(Control) : ISWTObservableValue
● ˢ observeText(Control, int) : ISWTObservableValue
● ˢ observeText(Control, int[]) : ISWTObservableValue
● ˢ observeText(Widget) : ISWTObservableValue
● ˢ observeTooltipText(Control) : ISWTObservableValue
● ˢ observeTooltipText(Widget) : ISWTObservableValue
● ˢ observeVisible(Control) : ISWTObservableValue
```

Figure 28–5 SWTObservables factory methods

To create observables, you must call the respective method on the SWTObservables factory. For example, if we wanted to observe an SWT Text field that would eventually bind to the Person object's name field, the coding pattern to create the observable would look like the following snippet:

```
Person person = new Person();
// Create and fill in person details.
Text nameText = new Text(shell, SWT.BORDER);
IObservableValue textObservable =
    SWTObservables.observeText(nameText, SWT.Modify);
```

```
IObservableValue nameObservable =
    BeansObservables.observeValue(person, "name");
```

TIP

By default, if you observe a text value, you get updates per keystroke (SWT.Modify). This may not be the optimal strategy if any validation you do is expensive. To help with this problem, you can take advantage of SWTObservables.observe-DelayedValue(500, observable) to delay notification of a value change by a certain number of milliseconds.

28.4.4 ViewersObservables

The ViewersObservables factory is responsible for creating observables for JFace viewers, as shown in Figure 28-6.

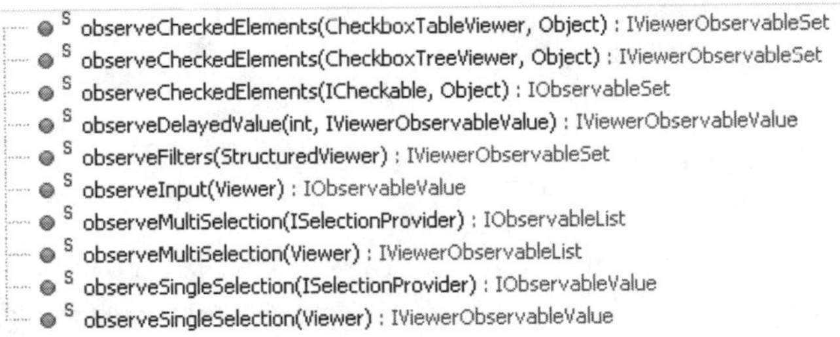

```
⊚ S observeCheckedElements(CheckboxTableViewer, Object) : IViewerObservableSet
⊚ S observeCheckedElements(CheckboxTreeViewer, Object) : IViewerObservableSet
⊚ S observeCheckedElements(ICheckable, Object) : IObservableSet
⊚ S observeDelayedValue(int, IViewerObservableValue) : IViewerObservableValue
⊚ S observeFilters(StructuredViewer) : IViewerObservableSet
⊚ S observeInput(Viewer) : IObservableValue
⊚ S observeMultiSelection(ISelectionProvider) : IObservableList
⊚ S observeMultiSelection(Viewer) : IViewerObservableList
⊚ S observeSingleSelection(ISelectionProvider) : IObservableValue
⊚ S observeSingleSelection(Viewer) : IViewerObservableValue
```

Figure 28–6   ViewersObservables factory methods

28.4.5 MasterDetailObservables

The MasterDetailObservables factory, as shown in Figure 28-7, allows for the observation of an attribute, the *detail*, of an observable representing selection or another transient instance, the *master*.

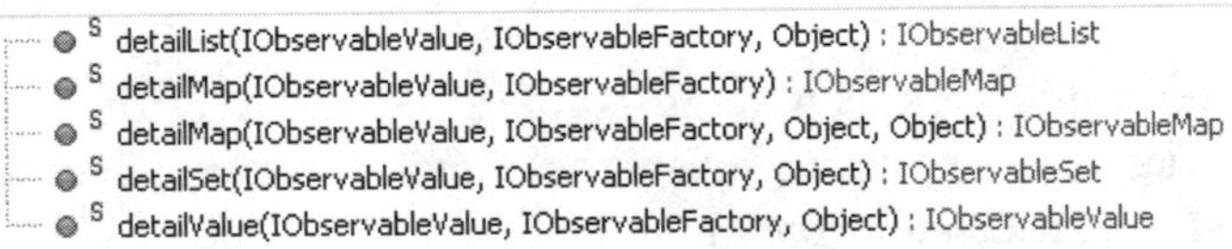

```
⊚ S detailList(IObservableValue, IObservableFactory, Object) : IObservableList
⊚ S detailMap(IObservableValue, IObservableFactory) : IObservableMap
⊚ S detailMap(IObservableValue, IObservableFactory, Object, Object) : IObservableMap
⊚ S detailSet(IObservableValue, IObservableFactory, Object) : IObservableSet
⊚ S detailValue(IObservableValue, IObservableFactory, Object) : IObservableValue
```

Figure 28–7   MasterDetailObservables factory methods

28.4.6 WorkbenchObservables

The WorkbenchObservables factory is responsible for creating observables for Workbench-related objects, as shown in Figure 28-8.

● ^S observeAdaptedSingleSelection(IServiceLocator, Class) : IObservableValue
● ^S observeDetailAdaptedValue(IObservableValue, Class) : IObservableValue

Figure 28–8   WorkbenchObservables factory methods

28.4.7 Realms

A realm can be thought of as a special thread or a lock that serializes access to a set of observables in that realm. Each observable belongs to a realm. It can be accessed only from that realm, and it will always fire change events on that realm. One example of a realm is the SWT UI thread. As for the SWT UI thread, you can execute code within a realm by using Realm.asyncExec(); in fact, the SWT realm implementation just delegates to Display.asyncExec(). This means that while the databinding framework can be used in a multithreaded environment, each observable is essentially single-threaded.

28.5 Properties

The properties framework is an improved set of observable factories and was created as an alternative to the existing set of observable factories we discussed in the previous section. The benefits that the properties framework provides over the existing set of observable factories are listed here:

Portability—It's possible to pass around property values as a generic property factory in a type-safe fashion.

Immutability—This reinforces the portability benefit so users don't have to worry about memory leaks.

Chainable—It's possible to chain properties and observe deeply nested properties.

The properties framework as it stands should be used over the existing set of observable factories that we discussed in the previous section because of these benefits. For example, use BeanProperties instead of BeansObservables to create observables, WidgetProperties instead of SWTObservables, and so on.

28.5.1 PojoProperties

The PojoProperties factory is responsible for creating observables for POJOs, as shown in Figure 28-9.

- ⊙ ˢ list(Class, String) : IBeanListProperty
- ⊙ ˢ list(Class, String, Class) : IBeanListProperty
- ⊙ ˢ list(String) : IBeanListProperty
- ⊙ ˢ list(String, Class) : IBeanListProperty
- ⊙ ˢ map(Class, String) : IBeanMapProperty
- ⊙ ˢ map(Class, String, Class, Class) : IBeanMapProperty
- ⊙ ˢ map(String) : IBeanMapProperty
- ⊙ ˢ map(String, Class, Class) : IBeanMapProperty
- ⊙ ˢ set(Class, String) : IBeanSetProperty
- ⊙ ˢ set(Class, String, Class) : IBeanSetProperty
- ⊙ ˢ set(String) : IBeanSetProperty
- ⊙ ˢ set(String, Class) : IBeanSetProperty
- ⊙ ˢ value(Class, String) : IBeanValueProperty
- ⊙ ˢ value(Class, String, Class) : IBeanValueProperty
- ⊙ ˢ value(String) : IBeanValueProperty
- ⊙ ˢ value(String, Class) : IBeanValueProperty
- ⊙ ˢ values(Class, String[]) : IBeanValueProperty[]
- ⊙ ˢ values(String[]) : IBeanValueProperty[]

Figure 28–9 PojoProperties factory methods

To create observables, you must call the respective method on the Pojo-Properties factory. For example, if we had a Person POJO that had a name field, the coding pattern to create an observable would look like this:

```
Person person = new Person();
// Fill in person details.
IObservableValue nameObservable =
    PojoProperties.value("name").observe(person);
```

28.5.2 BeanProperties

The BeanProperties factory is identical to the PojoProperties API and is responsible for creating observables for JavaBeans (see Figure 28-9).

To create observables, you must call the respective method on the Bean-Properties factory as outlined in this snippet:

```
Person person = new Person();
// Fill in person details.
IObservableValue nameObservable =
    BeanProperties.value("name").observe(person);
```

28.5.3 WidgetProperties

The WidgetProperties factory is responsible for creating observables for SWT widgets, as shown in Figure 28-10.

```
S background() : IWidgetValueProperty
S bounds() : IWidgetValueProperty
S editable() : IWidgetValueProperty
S enabled() : IWidgetValueProperty
S focused() : IWidgetValueProperty
S font() : IWidgetValueProperty
S foreground() : IWidgetValueProperty
S image() : IWidgetValueProperty
S items() : IWidgetListProperty
S location() : IWidgetValueProperty
S maximum() : IWidgetValueProperty
S message() : IWidgetValueProperty
S minimum() : IWidgetValueProperty
S selection() : IWidgetValueProperty
S singleSelectionIndex() : IWidgetValueProperty
S size() : IWidgetValueProperty
S text() : IWidgetValueProperty
S text(int) : IWidgetValueProperty
S text(int[]) : IWidgetValueProperty
S tooltipText() : IWidgetValueProperty
S visible() : IWidgetValueProperty
```

Figure 28–10   WidgetProperties factory methods

To create observables, you must call the respective method on the Widget-Properties factory as outlined here:

```
Person person = new Person();
// Fill in person details.
Text nameText = new Text(shell, SWT.BORDER);
IObservableValue textObservable =
    WidgetProperties.text(SWT.Modify).observe(nameText);
IObservableValue nameObservable =
    BeanProperties.value("name").observe(person);
```

28.5.4 WorkbenchProperties

The WorkbenchProperties factory is responsible for creating observables for Workbench objects, as shown in Figure 28-11.

```
S adaptedValue(Class) : IValueProperty
S multipleSelection() : IListProperty
S multipleSelection(String, boolean) : IListProperty
S singleSelection() : IValueProperty
S singleSelection(String, boolean) : IValueProperty
```

Figure 28–11   WorkbenchProperties factory methods

To create observables, you must call the respective method on the `Workbench-Properties` factory as outlined in the following snippet:

```
// Observe a single selection via the Workbench selection service.
ISelectionService s =
        (ISelectionService)getSite().getService((ISelectionService.class));
IObservableValue selectionObservable =
    WorkbenchProperties.singleSelection().observe(s);
```

28.6 Bindings

In Eclipse databinding, bindings synchronize the value of two observables, in particular two `IObservableValue` instances. To bind two observables, we need a `DataBindingContext`, which is the point of contact for the creation and management of bindings. In the following snippet, we expand upon our person example and use a `DataBindingContext` to bind an SWT `Text` field with a value representing a phone number in our `Person` object:

```
Person person = new Person();
// Fill in person details.
DataBindingContext context = new DataBindingContext();
IObservableValue textObservable =
    WidgetProperties.text(SWT.Modify).observe(numberText);
IObservableValue nameObservable =
    BeanProperties.value("phoneNumber").observe(person);
context.bindValue(textObservable, nameObservable);
```

The synchronization process is composed of validation and conversion phases, as shown in Figure 28-12. The specific phases are dependent on the type of binding, whether it's a value or list binding. In our example we are using a value-based binding.

A binding has an associated update strategy which dictates how the synchronization between observables takes place. This update strategy is embodied in the `UpdateValueStrategy` class and includes the process of conversion and validation. To control the policy of how an update strategy is performed, there are four constants you can specify in its creation:

UpdateValueStrategy.POLICY_NEVER—This policy denotes that the source observable's state should not be tracked and that the destination observable's value should never be updated. This effectively makes bindings one-way and is used in cases like `ComputedValue` where one observable is unmodifiable.

UpdateValueStrategy.POLICY_CONVERT—This policy denotes that the source observable's state should be tracked, including validating changes except before the set value phase. Furthermore, the destination observable's value should be updated only on request.

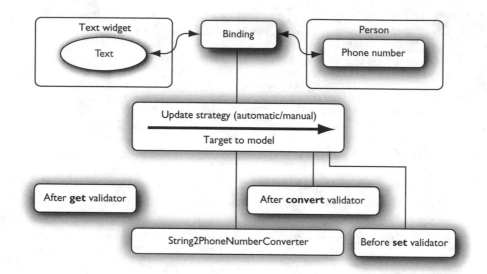

Figure 28–12   A typical Eclipse databinding flow

UpdateValueStrategy.POLICY_ON_REQUEST—This policy denotes that the source observable's state should not be tracked but the validation, conversion, and updating of the destination observable's value should be performed explicitly when requested.

UpdateValueStrategy.POLICY_UPDATE—This policy denotes that the source observable's state should be tracked and that validation, conversion, and updating of the destination observable's value should be performed automatically on every change of the source observable's value.

28.6.1 Conversion

The conversion process will convert the value from the type of the source observable into that of the destination observable. For example, in Figure 28-13 we are converting a string to a value of whatever object represents a phone number in the person object. One can imagine a phone number object that has separate fields representing international and area codes along with a field for the rest of the phone number. The conversion process is controlled with an IConverter object that is registered as part of an UpdateValueStrategy via the setConverter (IConverter converter) method. To simplify working with Eclipse databinding, the UpdateValueStrategy class comes with default converters, shown in Figure 28-13, for common scenarios.

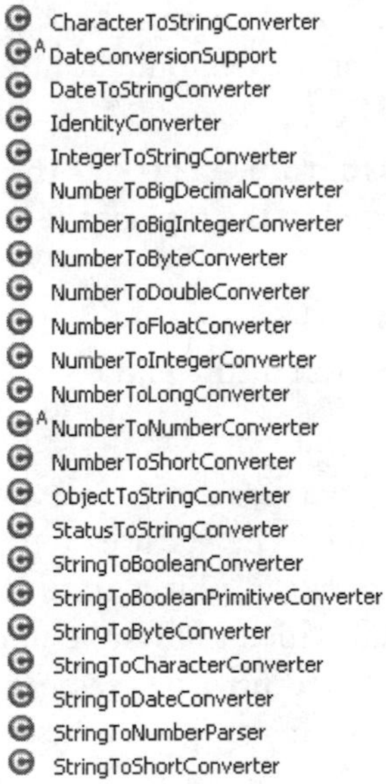

- CharacterToStringConverter
- A DateConversionSupport
- DateToStringConverter
- IdentityConverter
- IntegerToStringConverter
- NumberToBigDecimalConverter
- NumberToBigIntegerConverter
- NumberToByteConverter
- NumberToDoubleConverter
- NumberToFloatConverter
- NumberToIntegerConverter
- NumberToLongConverter
- A NumberToNumberConverter
- NumberToShortConverter
- ObjectToStringConverter
- StatusToStringConverter
- StringToBooleanConverter
- StringToBooleanPrimitiveConverter
- StringToByteConverter
- StringToCharacterConverter
- StringToDateConverter
- StringToNumberParser
- StringToShortConverter

Figure 28–13 Default converters included in Eclipse databinding

To write your own converter, it's useful to look at how some of the default converters are written. For example, in the next snippet, StatusToStringConverter extends the Converter utility class that implements IConverter and does the processing required to convert an IStatus object to a string:

```
org.eclipse.core.databinding/StatusToStringConverter
public class StatusToStringConverter extends Converter {
      public StatusToStringConverter() {
            super(IStatus.class, String.class);
      }
      public Object convert(Object fromObject) {
            if (fromObject == null) {
                  throw new IllegalArgumentException
                  ("Parameter was null.");
            }
            IStatus status = (IStatus) fromObject;
            return status.getMessage();
      }
}
```

28.6.2 Validation

In Eclipse databinding there's an opportunity to validate values in three unique phases, as shown in Figure 28-13:

setAfterGetValidator(IValidator validator)—This sets the validator to be invoked after the source value is retrieved at the beginning of the synchronization process.

setAfterConvertValidator(IValidator validator)—This sets the validator to be invoked after the source value is converted to the type of the destination observable.

validateBeforeSet(IValidator validator)—This sets the validator to be invoked before the value is set on the destination at the end of the synchronization process.

The validation process is controlled with IValidator objects which are responsible for determining if a given value is valid. The statuses returned from the validation phases are aggregated in a MultiStatus object until a status of IStatus.ERROR or IStatus.CANCEL is encountered, which aborts the update strategy process. In the following snippet it's easy to see how to create a validator using the ValidationStatus utility class to create the proper statuses and then binding two observables with the update strategy:

```
UpdateValueStrategy s =

    new UpdateValueStrategy().setBeforeSetValidator(new IValidator() {
        public IStatus validate(Object value) {
                String s = (String) value;
                if (s.contains(" ")) {
                        return ValidationStatus.error("no spaces please");
                }
                return ValidationStatus.ok();
        }
DataBindingContext context = new DataBindingContext();
IObservableValue textObservable =
    WidgetProperties.text(SWT.Modify).observe(numberText);
IObservableValue nameObservable =
    BeanProperties.value("phoneNumber").observe(person);
context.bindValue(textObservable, nameObservable, s, null);
```

TIP

Validation in the context of bindings can look at only one value at a time. To enable cross-field validation involving more than one value in databinding, see the MultiValidator helper class. Furthermore, MultiValidator prevents data from being copied to the model while there is a validation error.

28.6.3 Support Classes

To simplify the usage of databinding in the context of common Eclipse user interface facilities such as dialogs, viewers, and wizard pages, Eclipse databinding provides a set of support classes:

WizardPageSupport—connects the validation result from the given databinding context to the given wizard page, updating the wizard page's completion state and message accordingly

TitleAreaDialogSupport—connects the validation result from the given databinding context to the given TitleAreaDialog, updating the dialog's error message accordingly

DialogPageSupport—connects the validation result from the given databinding context to the given dialog page, updating the page's error message accordingly

PreferencePageSupport—connects the validation result from the given databinding context to the given preference page, updating the page's valid state and error message accordingly

ViewerSupport—helper methods for binding observables to StructuredViewer or an AbstractTableViewer

28.7 Summary

After reading this chapter, you should have a grasp of the fundamentals of Eclipse databinding and how to use it in RCP applications. Eclipse databinding avoids repetitive, error-prone code and has the power to simplify the process of building user interfaces for RCP applications.

28.8 Pointers

○ The databinding wiki contains useful tips, snippets, and tutorials: *http:// wiki.eclipse.org/JFace_Data_Binding*.

CHAPTER 29

Eclipse Ecosystem

The success of a platform can be measured by the size of its community and ultimately by the number of applications built with it. As the size of a community increases, so does the collection of components that are produced and made available—either commercially or for free. By these metrics, the Eclipse ecosystem is a huge success. The community is vibrant, the number of projects doing interesting and widely relevant work is impressive, and the majority of the world's major software companies are members of the Eclipse Foundation. This translates into a huge number of useful, quality plug-ins that can save you time and money.

You have probably noticed that the RCP SDK includes only a few plug-ins. In Part II you learned how to add Eclipse Platform plug-ins such as Help and Update to Hyperbola. The Eclipse SDK includes more then 100 plug-ins, many of which are useful in RCP applications. Add that to the others available at eclipse.org and the hundreds available on Web sites such as sourceforge.net and marketplace.eclipse.org and it is clear that a key part of developing an RCP application is deciding which existing plug-ins to use and how they help solve the problems of your application domain.

A complete survey of the existing plug-ins is beyond the scope of this book and would likely be obsolete before it even reached your hands. Instead, this chapter contains an overview of the plug-ins in the Eclipse SDK that can be used in RCP applications.

29.1 Where to Find Plug-ins

There are two main reasons to look for additional plug-ins: Either you are looking to augment your Eclipse IDE with more tooling (e.g., Web tooling, C tools, etc.) or you need more functionality for your RCP application. You can find both in the following places.

Before going on a treasure hunt for plug-ins, read Section 23.6, "Designing a Platform," to learn how to identify plug-ins that are meant to be reused in RCP applications. Some plug-ins are written for a particular product and are not what we call *RCP-friendly*.

Eclipse SDK (*www.eclipse.org/downloads*)—The SDK includes more than 85 plug-ins, including Java tooling (JDT), plug-in tooling (PDE), Help, Update, and various other bits and pieces. Chances are you are using the SDK to develop your plug-ins, but you might also want to include some of these in your target application.

Eclipse Tools (*www.eclipse.org/tools*)—The Eclipse Tools project includes many interesting and useful tooling extensions for the Eclipse IDE. These include the GEF, a visual editor (VE), Mylyn, and so on. Several of these projects (e.g., GEF) contain runtime elements that you add to your application.

Eclipse Modeling (*www.eclipse.org/modeling*)—The Eclipse Modeling project includes a plethora of modeling frameworks and tools that can help you build RCP applications, including the EMF and related projects.

Eclipse Technology (eclipse.org/technology)—The Eclipse Technology project includes all manner of experimental and not-so-experimental work on tooling and runtime technologies. There are subprojects for memory analysis, collaborative development, Linux tooling, and much more. Again, some of these projects include additional tooling for your development environment, some include runtime elements for your target, and some include both.

Other Eclipse projects—Eclipse.org hosts a number of other top-level projects such as Web tooling (WTP), test and performance (TPTP), and modeling and reporting (BIRT). Again, some are strictly tooling to help you build or implement your application, and some include or generate application runtime facilities.

Links to community resources—The Eclipse community is very active and includes many sites that either host or point to collections of plug-ins. The community resources page at *http://eclipse.org/community/sources.html#links* includes links to the major plug-in repositories and directories.

Search the Web—There are many other sources for Eclipse plug-ins. For example, *http://marketplace.eclipse.org* and *http://sourceforge.net* host hundreds of Eclipse plug-ins.

29.2 Eclipse Platform Plug-ins

The Eclipse Platform is dedicated to providing a robust, full-featured, and commercial-quality platform for the development of highly integrated tools. The Eclipse Platform is thus an excellent source of product-quality plug-ins that can be used in your applications.

In an effort to keep the RCP download small, only a small set of the platform plug-ins is included in the RCP SDK. However, as you saw in Chapter 13, "Adding Help," and Chapter 14, "Adding Software Management," you can add plug-ins from the Eclipse SDK to your application.

There is one caveat, however. As mentioned in Chapter 23, "RCP Everywhere," and in particular as explained in Section 23.3, "Product Configurations," plug-ins are designed to work either with a specific product or alternatively with any product. The Eclipse Platform contains both types. The plug-ins that depend on the existence of the IDE product, for example, having a dependency on the `org.eclipse.ui.ide` plug-in, are not meant to be used by RCP applications. If you aren't sure, review the checklist in Section 23.7 for how to determine if a plug-in can be used in an RCP application.

In this chapter we review the Eclipse SDK plug-ins that can be used by RCP applications. We do not have enough pages to provide an exhaustive reference to each, but we provide enough detail for you to understand how they work and where to find more information.

29.3 Product Introduction

Plug-ins	`org.eclipse.ui.intro`
Dependencies	`org.eclipse.core.runtime`, `org.eclipse.help`, `org.eclipse.ui`, `org.eclipse.ui.forms`

When users start an application for the first time, they often do not know how or where to begin. This leads them to either dismiss the application because they don't understand its features or waste precious time trying to figure out how to get started.

Intro support solves these problems by giving users an introduction to the features of the product the first time it is started. This is your opportunity to direct users to important starting points, highlight interesting capabilities, and ultimately help users understand what your product is and how to use it.

The Workbench provides an extension point named `org.eclipse.ui.intro` and an interface to describe Intro pages named `IIntroPart`. The Workbench does not, however, provide any reusable pieces that make it easy to create an Intro page. Applications can either provide their own IIntroPart implementation or use the org.eclipse.ui.intro plug-in and its helpers to build a nicer Intro page.

By default, the Intro page is shown the first time a product is started. The showing of the Intro pages is controlled by the preference IWorkbenchPreferences .SHOW_INTRO. The actual creation and triggering are done in WorkbenchWindow-Advisor.openIntro(). The default implementation opens the contributed Intro content, but you can override this to do whatever you like.

The lifecycle of the Intro part is as follows:

○ The Intro part is created on Workbench startup. As with editor and view areas, this area is managed by an Intro site (implementing org.eclipse.ui.intro .IIntroSite).

○ The ID of the current product (Platform.getProduct()) is used to choose the Intro part to show.

○ The Intro part class (implementing org.eclipse.ui.intro.IIntroPart) is created and initialized with the Intro site.

○ While the Intro part is being shown to the user, it can transition back and forth between full and standby modes (either programmatically or explicitly by the user).

○ Eventually the Intro part is closed (either programmatically or explicitly by the user) and the current perspective takes over the entire Workbench window area.

A good way to understand how to build Intro pages is to look at the Intro template. Create a new RCP plug-in project, and from the list of templates select **RCP application with intro**. The sample code for Chapter 25 includes Intro support for Hyperbola, and the Workbench itself includes a standard action to open the Intro page called org.eclipse.ui.actions.ActionFactory.INTRO.

29.4 Resources

Plug-ins	org.eclipse.core.resources
Dependencies	org.eclipse.core.runtime

The Resources plug-in offers a layer above java.io.File that adds support for markers, builders, change notifications, local history, and persistent and session properties. It introduces a workspace in which projects, files, and folders are created and manipulated. Projects are root folders in the workspace and contain files and folders. This plug-in is the basis for all IDE tooling in Eclipse.

It is a common misconception that the Resources plug-in is only for tools. In fact, Resources is all about file manipulation. If your application does a lot of sophisticated file manipulation, either explicitly or under the covers, you might be interested in Resources. Of course, you can always use `java.io.File` and related classes to manage files directly.

29.4.1 Overview of Resources Key Features

From the very beginning of Eclipse, it was clear that there was a need for a plug-in that provides base-level resource support on which to build programming language tooling such as compilers, debuggers, versioning, and search. When you look at the services provided by the Resources plug-in, it is obvious that they were added specifically to satisfy these requirements. Following is a small overview of the features provided by this plug-in:

Change notifications—When resources are changed, there is always someone that cares (e.g., UI viewers, builders). The plug-in provides efficient deltas that describe the changes made to a set of resources. This is useful since file notifications are not part of the standard Java class libraries.

Incremental builders—Incremental project builders transform or manipulate resources to produce additional resources. For example, the Java development tools define an incremental project builder that compiles a Java source file into a class file any time a file is added or modified in a Java project. It also keeps track of dependent files and recompiles them when necessary.

Markers—During the course of editing or building a resource, a plug-in may need to tag resources to communicate problems or other information to the user. The resource marker mechanism is used to manage this kind of information. A marker is like a yellow sticky note stuck to a resource. On the marker you can record information about a problem (e.g., location, severity) or a task to be done. Markers can also be used to simply record a location as a bookmark.

Properties—Resources have properties that can be used to store meta-information about a resource. Your plug-in can use these properties to hold application-specific information about a resource. Resource properties are declared, accessed, and maintained by various plug-ins and are not interpreted by the Platform. When a resource is deleted from the workspace, its properties are also deleted.

Derived resources—Many resources get created in the course of translating, compiling, copying, or otherwise processing files that the user creates and edits. Derived resources are resources that are not original data and can be re-created from their source files. It is common for derived files to be excluded from certain kinds of processing. For example, derived resources are typically not kept in a team repository since they clutter the repository, change regularly, and can be re-created from their source files.

The eclipse.org Web site has many examples and articles that explain how to use these features. If you do not need any of these features, just go ahead and use `java.io.File` instead. Otherwise, the next sections provide a basic introduction to the plug-in.

29.4.2 Getting Started with Resources

The Resources plug-in provides access to resources via a *workspace*. Imagine the workspace as the container for all resources through which you must pass to access any resource. The snippet below shows how to access the workspace and create a project and file. Projects are the top-level elements in the workspace.

```
IWorkspace workspace = ResourcesPlugin.getWorkspace();
IProject project = workspace.getRoot().getProject("New Project");
if (!project.exists())
  project.create(new NullProgressMonitor());
if (!project.isOpen())
  project.open(new NullProgressMonitor());
IFile myFile = project.getFile("perfs.txt");
myFile.create(
    new ByteArrayInputStream("contents".getBytes()),
    true, new NullProgressMonitor());
```

`IResources` (e.g., `IFile`, `IFolder`) objects are handles to state maintained by the workspace. This allows you to access a resource before it exists and at the same time hold on to a resource that has been deleted.

29.4.3 Resources in the Workbench

Prior to Eclipse 3.0, resources were at the heart of the Workbench, and building an application that did not include resources was not possible. When the RCP was created, these dependencies were moved to `org.eclipse.ui.ide` or the IDE product. The IDE uses the workspace resource model as its underlying data model. The IDE plug-in, and the extensions defined within it, are *not designed to be reused* in other RCP applications; that is, although it is technically possible to either subclass or reference IDE classes, it is not particularly supported by the generic UI Workbench. So, if you are developing an IDE-style product, you should consider extending the existing IDE application rather than developing your own RCP application.

29.5 Text Editing

Plug-ins	`org.eclipse.text, org.eclipse.jface.text, org.eclipse.ui` `.workbench.texteditor, org.eclipse.swt`
Dependencies	`org.eclipse.core.runtime, org.eclipse.jface, org.eclipse.ui`

If you need to show or edit text in your application, you need the text editing framework. Programming languages have evolved, but the fact remains that developers spend most of their time writing code in a text editor of some sort. Given Eclipse's origin as an IDE, the text infrastructure included in the platform is very advanced and includes state-of-the-art text editing features.

The breadth of support provided by the text editing framework comes at a price—it's complex. Basic text editing capabilities are fairly easy to implement, but as soon as you start adding advanced features such as syntax highlighting, content assist, and annotations, you have to invest some time to understand the framework. This section shows you how to add basic text editing to an RCP application.

29.5.1 Text Plug-ins

The text framework is split across several plug-ins to modularize and encapsulate functionality. For example, this allows reuse of the text model without implying a dependency on text presentation. Figure 29-1 shows how these plug-ins are layered and what functionality is included in each plug-in.

Support for `IResource` text editing is provided by the `org.eclipse.ui.editors` plug-in and is tightly coupled to the Eclipse IDE product. As such, it is not part of the RCP. There are, however, many pieces of the text infrastructure that are available for use in RCP applications. The remainder of this section demonstrates how to integrate text editing support into an RCP application.

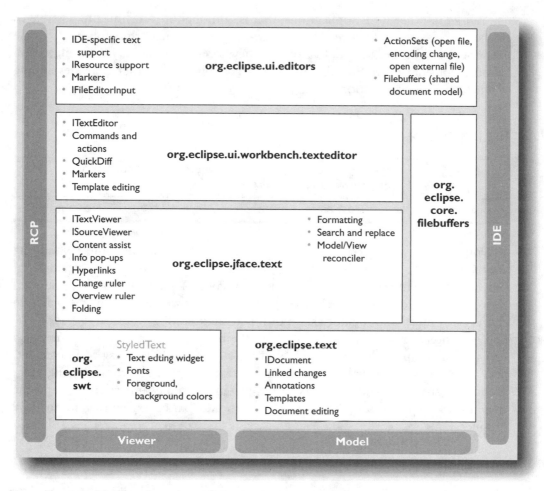

Figure 29–1   Overview of text-related plug-ins

29.5.2 *Editing versus Editor*

The text framework can be used to implement a full-featured programming language editor and can also be used to allow editing of text in a dialog or show output for a console.

Given its architecture, you can use `org.eclipse.text` to manipulate text without a presentation. The `org.eclipse.jface.text` plug-in provides the link between the model (`IDocument`) and the view (`StyledText`) via the `TextViewer`. The coupling to the Workbench, in particular to editors, is provided by the `org.eclipse.ui.workbench.texteditor` plug-in with the addition of an `AbstractTextEditor`.

As a developer of an RCP application, you can pick and choose the text features you need from the framework.

29.5.3 Text *and* StyledText

The simplest way to either show or allow editing of text is to use the SWT Text control. This is a native control that is good enough for many simple editing requirements. The SWT custom control called StyledText is a step up from the Text control. It is a subclass of Canvas and allows editing of text, changing the font and colors of text regions, and changing the cursor. Because it is a Canvas, clients can draw directly on the widget and extend the presentation of the text. For example, a common pattern is to add a line styler to StyledText to show syntax highlighting.

```
text = new StyledText (shell,
    SWT.BORDER | SWT.MULTI | SWT.V_SCROLL | SWT.H_SCROLL);
text.addLineStyleListener(new ChatLineStyler());
text.setEditable(false);
Color bg = Display.getDefault().getSystemColor(SWT.COLOR_GRAY);
text.setBackground(bg);
text.setText(chatContents);
```

If all you require is a rich edit control, using StyledText is good enough. You can embed the control in dialogs or views—and bingo! You have rich edit capabilities. If you want more bells and whistles such as content assist, hyperlinks, overview, and outline rulers, the Text plug-ins are what you need.

EXAMPLES

The examples that come with the Eclipse IDE contain a good sample of both a Java editor implemented directly above StyledText and a Java editor implemented using the Text plug-ins. You can install the examples into the Eclipse IDE by showing the Welcome page from **Help > Welcome** and following the **Samples** link.

29.5.4 IDocument

Manipulating text is error-prone and difficult; you have to manage lines, indexes, wrapping, and many other details to keep the text correct. IDocument is a text model designed to help with manipulating text and, in some cases, with storing text so it can be presented. For example, documents can be partitioned into disjointed parts by using token- and rule-based filters. Partitions are useful for syntax highlighting and are stored with a document to avoid having to maintain additional data structures. Think of an `IDocument` as a `java.util.StringBuffer` on steroids.

29.5.5 `TextViewers` and `TextEditors`

The next step up from using SWT controls to display text is using the `TextViewer` classes in `org.eclipse.jface.text`. A `TextViewer` connects a `StyledText` control with an `IDocument` model, and a `TextEditor` provides support for displaying a `TextViewer` in an editor. This sounds simple, but many details are being taken care of for you by the viewer and editor.

Below is a quick example of how to provide a simple text editor. Here we create a concrete implementation of `AbstractTextEditor` and a concrete `IDocumentProvider`. The document provider connects the document to the editor and allows sharing of documents between editors. Figure 29-2 shows how this works in more general terms.

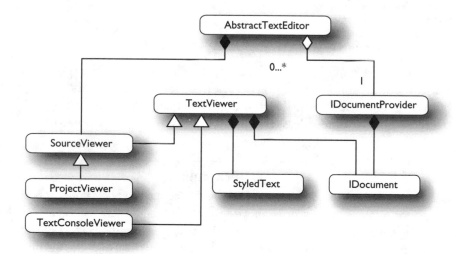

Figure 29–2   Relationships among key text classes

```
public class SimpleEditor extends AbstractTextEditor {
   public SimpleEditor() {
      super();
      configureInsertMode(SMART_INSERT, false);
      this.enableOverwriteMode(true);
      setDocumentProvider(new SimpleDocumentProvider());
   }
}
```

AbstractTextEditor provides most of the features you need from a basic editor. As a result, our simple text editor implementation only needs to hook the document provider to the editor.

The SimpleDocumentProvider handles reading and saving the file. When the editor is opened, it is provided with an IEditorInput that describes the file to be opened. The editor delegates the task of manipulating the bytes in the file to the document provider. Your main coding job is to provide implementations of the following methods for the document provider:

createDocument()—loads the file from disk and creates the IDocument with the contents of the file

doSaveDocument()—saves the file to disk

isModifiable()—decides if the user can edit the file

isReadOnly()—decides if the document is going to be able to be saved

29.5.6 What Is Missing?

Because org.eclipse.ui.editors is not part of RCP, there are some features that are not available to RCP applications. For example, the most feature-filled editor is AbstractDecoratedTextEditor. It supports line numbers, change ruler, overview ruler, print margins, and current line highlighting.

In addition, the UI Editors plug-in contains IResource editing support. As a result, there is no easy way of editing an IFile without creating your own specific document provider. Have a look at FileDocumentProvider for hints if you need to implement IResource-aware editors.

The sample code for this chapter includes an example text editor. You can see it in action by opening an XML file or text file using **Hyperbola > Open File....**

29.6 Consoles

Plug-ins	org.eclipse.ui.console
Dependencies	org.eclipse.core.runtime, org.eclipse.jface.text, org.eclipse.ui, org.eclipse.core.expressions, org.eclipse.ui.workbench.texteditor

Consoles are traditionally used to display raw output from a running program and also accept keyboard commands. They are also very common in IDEs. Instead of having each plug-in define its own Console views, the Console plug-in provides a single view into which other plug-ins can contribute their consoles.

This makes it much easier for users to find consoles—all they have to do is open one view, and from there they can easily toggle between the available consoles.

The Console plug-in also provides many helpful classes for creating consoles. For example, in Chapter 16, "Perspectives, Views, and Editors," we showed how simple it is to add an XMPP messaging console to Hyperbola. The plug-in also provides many features useful in writing text consoles, for example, hyperlinking and text coloring. To find out more about the console, see the example in Chapter 16 and look at `org.eclipse.ui.console.TextConsole` and the extension points provided by the Console plug-in.

29.7 Variables

Plug-ins	`org.eclipse.core.variables`
Dependencies	`org.eclipse.core.runtime`

This plug-in provides classes and interfaces to support the definition and contribution of variables for the purpose of string substitution. It supports the recursive replacement of variables referenced by name in arbitrary strings with the value of the variable. Two types of variables are provided: value variables (`IValueVariable`) and dynamic variables (`IDynamicVariable`).

A value variable has a simple setter and getter for its value. A dynamic variable has an associated resolver that provides a variable's value each time it is referenced (replaced) in a string substitution. A dynamic variable may also provide an argument in its reference, which can be used by its resolver to determine its substitution value.

A variable manager (`IStringVariableManager`) is provided to manage the set of defined variables. Value variables may be created via API on the variable manager or contributed via the `valuevariables` extension point. Dynamic variables must be contributed via the `dynamicvariables` extension point.

The variable manager provides change notification for value variables and an API for performing string substitution. Substitution simply takes a string containing variable patterns and returns that string with all the variables replaced by their associated variable values.

Variables are referenced in strings by enclosing them in braces, preceded by a dollar sign. For example, `abc${foo}ghi` is composed of the strings abc and ghi sandwiching the variable foo. If the value of foo is def, string substitution gives abcdefghi.

In the case of dynamic variables, an optional argument is supplied by appending a colon and argument value after the variable name, for example, `${foo:bar}`.

In this case the resolver associated with foo is given the referenced argument, bar, when asked to resolve a value for the variable foo.

29.8 Outline and Property Views

Plug-ins	org.eclipse.ui.views
Dependencies	org.eclipse.core.runtime, org.eclipse.ui, org.eclipse.help

The Outline and Property views are not included in the RCP, but you can easily include them in your application by adding the org.eclipse.ui.views plug-in to your target.

To use the Property or Outline view, add the views to a perspective using the usual IPageLayout.addView() or IPageLayout.addStandaloneView() methods, or open them programmatically using IWorkbenchPage.showView(). The view IDs for both are found on IPageLayout, even though the views are not part of the Workbench. This is historical. Before RCP, they were part of the IDE Workbench. For backward-compatibility reasons, they were left there.

Both views are interesting because they work by supporting the active editor and switch their content as the editor is changed. They do this by listening to part changes, and they query the active part to see if they have anything to contribute to the outline or property views.

29.9 Forms

Plug-ins	org.eclipse.ui.forms
Dependencies	org.eclipse.core.runtime, org.eclipse.ui

If you've opened a plugin.xml file using the plug-in manifest editor, you've seen the Forms plug-in in action. The Forms plug-in provides Web-like UIs by modestly extending SWT to manipulate style bits, colors, fonts, and other properties to get the desired look and feel. It's actually become a standard to use forms in editors that display and allow editing of structured data.

The Eclipse Forms classes handle many of the SWT details needed to write nice-looking and well-behaved editors. For example, the FormToolkit widget factory is responsible for creating form-friendly SWT controls for use in custom form layouts that handle wrapping and scrolling for you.

29.10 Browser

Plug-ins	`org.eclipse.ui.browser`
Dependencies	`org.eclipse.core.runtime, org.eclipse.ui`

The Browser plug-in and the Workbench's browser APIs and extension point provide all you need to open a URL in either an internal or an external Web browser. Although the Workbench provides the generic APIs, such as `IWorkbenchBrowser.createBrowser(String)`, the Browser plug-in provides the implementation for this by extending the `org.eclipse.ui.browserSupport` extension point.

To use the Browser plug-in, simply add it to your target and then access the Workbench's browser support via `IWorkbench.getBrowserSupport()`. From the returned `IWorkbenchBrowser` you can call `createBrowser(String)` to get the default browser `IWebBrowser` reference. You can then call `IWebBrowser.openURL(URL)` to open a Web page. The Browser plug-in contributes a preference page that allows the user to configure the browser to use to show Web pages.

29.11 The Common Navigator Framework

Plug-ins	`org.eclipse.ui.navigator`
Dependencies	`org.eclipse.core.runtime, org.eclipse.ui`

A typical JFace viewer like the Hyperbola group viewer provides the user with a view of objects using a single content provider, label provider, sorter, and filter. The Common Navigator Framework (CNF) extends this idea by allowing a single view to dynamically use multiple and unrelated sets of content providers, label providers, sorters, and filters. These can be activated in the view depending on declarative expressions or using API calls.

The CNF uses the idea of Navigator Content Extensions (NCE) which can refer to a content provider, label provider, sorter, or drag adapter (note that filters are configured separately). An NCE has associated expressions that tell it when it is active. NCEs are also presented to users in the view context menu so that they can turn them on or off in order to show the view in different ways. Examples of NCEs are a resource content extension that controls how resources are presented and a Java content extension that shows Java projects. In the IDE's Project Explorer, you can turn off the Java content extension to get a pure resource view of the workspace.

Check out the **Platform Plug-in Developer's Guide > Programmer's Guide > Common Navigator Framework** for more detailed information on how to use the CNF in your application.

29.12 Declarative Services

Plug-ins	`org.eclipse.equinox.ds`
Dependencies	`org.eclipse.osgi, org.eclipse.equinox.util`

In Chapter 14 we needed to access some OSGi services like the `IProfileRegistry` in order to work with the p2 API and add software management support to Hyperbola. To access these services, we used the `BundleContext` API and some relatively boilerplate code. The `org.eclipse.equinox.ds` plug-in contains an implementation of the Declarative Services (DS) specification that's part of the standard OSGi compendium services.

DS allows you to declaratively wire OSGi services together across plug-ins. Using DS, you can specify what services your plug-in provides and what services are required. This is all specified using XML, and the `org.eclipse.equinox.ds` plug-in is responsible for wiring everything together. We highly recommend using DS if interacting with OSGi services.

29.13 Summary

Here we have seen just a taste of the wide range of plug-ins available from eclipse.org for use in writing RCP applications. There are plug-ins for text manipulation, user assistance, resource management, and so on. Beyond the Eclipse Platform and eclipse.org, the list becomes almost boundless.

The net result is that before writing your function, you should look around for existing plug-ins that you can reuse. When browsing plug-ins, always ensure that the plug-in was designed to be used in other applications. To do this, refer to the rules and guidelines from Section 23.7 for how to determine if a plug-in is RCP-friendly. The corollary to this is that you may also want to contribute some of your plug-ins back to the community for others to use.

Index

A Hands-On Guide to Equinox and the OSGi Framework

Jeff McAffer, Paul VanderLei, Simon Archer

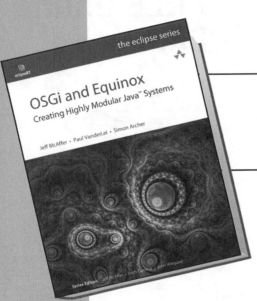

In *OSGI and Equinox: Creating Highly Modular Java™ Systems*, three leading experts show developers—for the first time—exactly how to make the most of these breakthrough technologies for building highly modular dynamic systems.

For every Eclipse developer, regardless of previous experience, this book

- Combines a complete hands-on tutorial, online sample code at every step, and deep technical dives for working developers

- Covers the OSGi programming model, component development, OSGi services, Eclipse bundle tooling, server-side Equinox, and much more

- Offers knowledge, guidance, and best practices for overcoming the complexities of building modular systems

- Addresses practical issues ranging from integrating third-party code libraries to server-side programming

- Includes a comprehensive case study that goes beyond prototyping to deliver a fully refined and refactored production system

Whatever your application, industry, or problem domain, if you want to build state-of-the-art software systems with OSGi and Equinox, you will find this book to be an essential resource.

For more information and sample material visit
informit.com/title/9780321585714

FREE Online Edition

Your purchase of *Eclipse Rich Client Platform, Second Edition* includes access to a free online edition for 45 days through the Safari Books Online subscription service. Nearly every Addison-Wesley Professional book is available online through Safari Books Online, along with more than 5,000 other technical books and videos from publishers such as Cisco Press, Exam Cram, IBM Press, O'Reilly, Prentice Hall, Que, and Sams.

SAFARI BOOKS ONLINE allows you to search for a specific answer, cut and paste code, download chapters, and stay current with emerging technologies.

Activate your FREE Online Edition at
www.informit.com/safarifree

> **STEP 1:** Enter the coupon code: YWAIQVH.

> **STEP 2:** New Safari users, complete the brief registration form.
> Safari subscribers, just log in.

If you have difficulty registering on Safari or accessing the online edition, please e-mail customer-service@safaribooksonline.com